DATE DUE

DEMCO 128-5046

SOMETHING ABOUT THE AUTHOR

ISSN 0276-816X

SOMETHING ABOUT THE AUTHOR

Facts and Pictures about Authors
and Illustrators of Books for Young People

EDITED BY
ANNE COMMIRE

VOLUME 38

GALE RESEARCH COMPANY
BOOK TOWER
DETROIT, MICHIGAN
48226

Editor: Anne Commire

Associate Editors: Agnes Garrett, Helga P. McCue

Assistant Editors: Dianne H. Anderson, Lori J. Bell, Joyce Nakamura,
Linda Shedd, Cynthia J. Walker

Sketchwriters: Rachel Koenig, Eunice L. Petrini

Researcher: Kathleen Betsko

Editorial Assistants: Lisa Bryon, Carolyn Kline, Marilyn O'Connell,
Susan Pfanner, Elisa Ann Sawchuk

Production Director: Carol Blanchard

External Senior Production Associate: Mary Beth Trimper

External Production Associate: Dorothy Kalleberg

Internal Senior Production Assistant: Louise Gagné

Internal Production Assistants: Sandy Rock, Lord T. Seyon

Text Layout: Vivian Tannenbaum

Art Director: Arthur Chartow

Special acknowledgement is due to the members of the *Contemporary Authors* staff
who assisted in the preparation of this volume.

Publisher: Frederick G. Ruffner

Executive Vice-President/Editorial: James M. Ethridge

Editorial Director: Dedria Bryfonski

Director, Literature Division: Christine Nasso

Senior Editor, Something about the Author: Adele Sarkissian

Contents

A

B

C

Contents

Introduction

As the only ongoing reference series that deals with the lives and works of authors and illustrators of children's books, *Something about the Author (SATA)* is a unique source of information. The *SATA* series includes not only well-known authors and illustrators whose books are most widely read, but also those less prominent people whose works are just coming to be recognized. *SATA* is often the only readily available information source for less well-known writers or artists. You'll find *SATA* informative and entertaining whether you are:

—a student in junior high school (or perhaps one to two grades higher or lower) who needs information for a book report or some other assignment for an English class;

—a children's librarian who is searching for the answer to yet another question from a young reader or collecting background material to use for a story hour;

—an English teacher who is drawing up an assignment for your students or gathering information for a book talk;

—a student in a college of education or library science who is studying children's literature and reference sources in the field;

—a parent who is looking for a new way to interest your child in reading something more than the school curriculum prescribes;

—an adult who enjoys children's literature for its own sake, knowing that a good children's book has no age limits.

Scope

In *SATA* you will find detailed information about authors and illustrators who span the full time range of children's literature, from early figures like John Newbery and L. Frank Baum to contemporary figures like Judy Blume and Richard Peck. Authors in the series represent primarily English-speaking countries, particularly the United States, Canada, and the United Kingdom. Also included, however, are authors from around the world whose works are available in English translation, for example: from France, Jean and Laurent De Brunhoff; from Italy, Emanuele Luzzati; from the Netherlands, Jaap ter Haar; from Germany, James Krüss; from Norway, Babbis Friis-Baastad; from Japan, Toshiko Kanzawa; from the Soviet Union, Kornei Chukovsky; from Switzerland, Alois Carigiet, to name only a few. Also appearing in *SATA* are Newbery medalists from Hendrik Van Loon (1922) to Beverly Cleary (1984). The writings represented in *SATA* include those created intentionally for children and young adults as well as those written for a general audience and known to interest younger readers. These writings cover the spectrum from picture books, humor, folk and fairy tales, animal stories, mystery and adventure, science fiction and fantasy, historical fiction, poetry and nonsense verse, to drama, biography, and nonfiction.

Information Features

In *SATA* you will find full-length entries for people who are appearing in the series for the first time. This volume, for example, marks the first appearance of Ray Broekel, C.B. Falls, Eric Fraser, Evert Hartman, Jacob Landau, Janet McCaffery, and Ron Wilson, among others. Since Volume 25, each *SATA* volume also includes newly revised and updated biographies for a selection of early *SATA* listees who remain of interest to today's readers and who have been active enough to require extensive revision of their earlier entries. The entry for a given biographee may be revised as often as there is substantial new information to provide. In Volume 38 you'll find revised entries for Mitsumasa Anno, Phyllis Krasilovsky, Astrid Lindgren, Beni Montresor, and Ellen Raskin.

Brief Entries, first introduced in Volume 27, are another regular feature of *SATA*. Brief Entries present essentially the same types of information found in a full entry but do so in a capsule form and without illustration. These entries are intended to give you useful and timely information while the more time-consuming process of compiling a full-length biography is in progress. In this volume you'll find Brief Entries for Nate Aaseng, David and Ronda Armitage, Sandra Boynton, Dik Browne, Michael Hardcastle, Dick King-Smith, Margaret Lane, and Marilyn Singer, among others.

Obituaries have been included in *SATA* since Volume 20. An Obituary is intended not only as a death notice but also as a concise view of a person's life and work. Obituaries may appear for persons who have entries in earlier *SATA* volumes, as well as for people who have not yet appeared in the series. In this volume Obituaries mark the recent deaths of Sheila Burnford, Bob Clampett, Norma Farber, James B. Garfield, Elizabeth Goudge, Eleanor Graham, and others.

Each *SATA* volume provides a cumulative index in two parts: first, the Illustrations Index, arranged by the name of the illustrator, gives the number of the volume and page where the illustrator's work appears in the current volume as well as all preceding volumes in the series; second, the Author Index gives the number of the volume in which a person's biographical sketch, Brief Entry, or Obituary appears in the current volume as well as all preceding volumes in the series. These indexes also include references to authors and illustrators who appear in *Yesterday's Authors of Books for Children*. Beginning with Volume 36, the *SATA* Author Index provides cross-references to authors who are included in *Children's Literature Review*.

Illustrations

While the textual information in *SATA* is its primary reason for existing, photographs and illustrations not only enliven the text but are an integral part of the information that *SATA* provides. Illustrations and text are wedded in such a special way in children's literature that artists and their works naturally occupy a prominent place among *SATA*'s listees. The illustrators that you'll find in the series include such past masters of children's book illustration as Randolph Caldecott, Kate Greenaway, Walter Crane, Arthur Rackham, and Ernest L. Shepard, as well as such noted contemporary artists as Maurice Sendak, Edward Gorey, Tomie de Paola, and Margot Zemach. There are Caldecott medalists from Dorothy Lathrop (the first recipient in 1938) to Alice and Martin Provensen (the latest winners in 1984); cartoonists like Charles Schulz, ("Peanuts"), Walt Kelly ("Pogo"), Hank Ketcham ("Dennis the Menace"), and Georges Rémi ("Tintin"); photographers like Jill Krementz, Tana Hoban, Bruce McMillan, and Bruce Curtis; and filmmakers like Walt Disney, Alfred Hitchcock, and Steven Spielberg.

In a dozen years of recording the metamorphosis of children's literature from the printed page to other media, *SATA* has become something of a repository of photographs that are unique in themselves and exist nowhere else as a group, particularly many of the classics of motion picture and stage history and photographs that have been specially loaned to us from private collections.

What a *SATA* Entry Provides

Whether you're already familiar with the *SATA* series or just getting acquainted, you will want to be aware of the kind of information that an entry provides. In every *SATA* entry the editors attempt to give as complete a picture of the person's life and work as possible. In some cases that full range of information may simply be unavailable, or a biographee may choose not to reveal complete personal details. The information that the editors attempt to provide in every entry is arranged in the following categories:

1. The "head" of the entry gives

—the most complete form of the name,
—any part of the name not commonly used, included in parentheses,
—birth and death dates, if known; a (?) indicates a discrepancy in published sources,
—pseudonyms or name variants under which the person has had books published or is publicly known, in parentheses in the second line.

2. "Personal" section gives

—date and place of birth and death,
—parents' names and occupations,

—name of spouse, date of marriage, and names of children,
—educational institutions attended, degrees received, and dates,
—religious and political affiliations,
—agent's name and address,
—home and/or office address.

3. "Career" section gives

—name of employer, position, and dates for each career post,
—military service,
—memberships,
—awards and honors.

4. "Writings" section gives

—title, first publisher and date of publication, and illustration information for each book written; revised editions and other significant editions for books with particularly long publishing histories; genre, when known.

5. "Adaptations" section gives

—title, major performers, producer, and date of all known reworkings of an author's material in another medium, like movies, filmstrips, television, recordings, plays, etc.

6. "Sidelights" section gives

—commentary on the life or work of the biographee either directly from the person (and often written specifically for the *SATA* entry), or gathered from biographies, diaries, letters, interviews, or other published sources.

7. "For More Information See" section gives

—books, feature articles, films, plays, and reviews in which the biographee's life or work has been treated.

How a *SATA* Entry Is Compiled

A *SATA* entry progresses through a series of steps. If the biographee is living, the *SATA* editors try to secure information directly from him or her through a questionnaire. From the information that the biographee supplies, the editors prepare an entry, filling in any essential missing details with research. The author or illustrator is then sent a copy of the entry to check for accuracy and completeness.

If the biographee is deceased or cannot be reached by questionnaire, the *SATA* editors examine a wide variety of published sources to gather information for an entry. Biographical sources are searched with the aid of Gale's *Biography and Genealogy Master Index*. Bibliographic sources like the *National Union Catalog*, the *Cumulative Book Index*, *American Book Publishing Record*, and the *British Museum Catalogue* are consulted, as are book reviews, feature articles, published interviews, and material sometimes obtained from the biographee's family, publishers, agent, or other associates.

For each entry presented in *SATA*, the editors also attempt to locate a photograph of the biographee as well as representative illustrations from his or her books. After surveying the available books which the biographee has written and/or illustrated, and then making a selection of appropriate photographs and illustrations, the editors request permission of the current copyright holders to reprint the material. In the case of older books for which the copyright may have passed through several hands, even locating the current copyright holder is often a long and involved process.

We invite you to examine the entire *SATA* series, starting with this volume. Described below are some of the people in Volume 38 that you may find particularly interesting.

Highlights of This Volume

JACQUES-YVES COUSTEAU......world renowned undersea explorer who was responsible for the development of the aqualung, only one of many innovative devices he has designed to aid in man's exploration of the sea. Cousteau's expeditions aboard his ship *Calypso* have resulted in Oscar-winning movies and over fifty television films. In books like the *Silent World, The Living Sea,* and *World without Sun,* he shares with young adult readers the intricate structure and beauty of his undersea world—and the need for its preservation. "Man exists," Cousteau observes, "only because his home-planet, Earth, is the one celestial body we know of where life is at all possible. And life is possible on earth because earth is a 'water planet'. . . . The ocean is life."

CLARA INGRAM JUDSON......historian and biographer, who regarded America as "a beautiful tapestry made up of threads of many kinds and colors...beautiful because the threads were varied and different." In biographies like her Newbery Award honor books *Abraham Lincoln, Friend of the People, Theodore Roosevelt, Fighting Patriot,* and *Mr. Justice Holmes,* Judson created a panoramic view of the people and events that shaped the development of the New World. Since 1961 the Clara Ingram Judson Award has been given annually to the most outstanding Midwestern author of children's books, a testimony to the dedication and devotion Judson put into over seventy-nine books for children.

PHYLLIS KRASILOVSKY......who, at the age of nineteen, marched into the offices of Doubleday with manuscripts for two books and demanded that they be read. Luckily, the editor had a good sense of humor and was impressed with Krasilovsky's spunkiness. Both books were accepted on the spot. Through the years Krasilovsky has juggled careers as wife, mother, and writer. She lives and works in a nineteenth-century house once inhabited by Thomas Wolfe's editor. Writing, she admits, can be a lonely profession but it is unique in its rewards as well. "Sometimes I feel like a madman," she muses, "sitting all by myself, making things happen sentence by sentence. It gives me such a sense of power...as if I were a miniature God." Krasilovsky wields her power in books for children like *The Cow Who Fell in the Canal, The Very Tall Little Girl,* and *The Shy Little Girl.*

ASTRID LINDGREN......who read so voraciously as a child in Sweden that all her teachers and schoolmates firmly predicted she would become a writer. In the face of their certainty, Lindgren made a vow—she would *never* write a book. That promise was broken, but not until she was nearly forty years old. It was then that Lindgren created her most enduring character—the carrot-haired, pig-tailed Pippi Longstocking. Stories of the brash little Swedish girl have been adapted for stage, motion pictures, and television. A Hans Christian Andersen Award winner, Lindgren reveals her secret for writing children's books: "You have to relive your own childhood and *remember* with your very soul what the world looked like, and how it felt to the touch; what you laughed at, and what you cried over. . . ." Part of Lindgren's childhood goes into each of her books like *The Tomten, The Brothers Lionheart,* and *Ronia, The Robber's Daughter.*

ELLEN RASKIN......author and illustrator, who filled her books with characters based on childhood memories, both imaginary and real. Raskin best remembered her Grandpa Hersh, "a short and pudgy man, who wore garters on his arms to hike up his too-long shirt sleeves." Grandpa Hersh became Uncle Florence in *Figgs and Phantoms* and his spirit was always present in her works, "adding his goodness to my humor. . . . [and] . . . rounding my characters with love." Raskin often sat down to write without a plot in mind, relying on her characters to develop the storyline. Her Newbery Award winner *The Westing Game* began "with no wish of an idea, just the urge to write another children's book." This somewhat unorthodox approach to writing produced award-winning books like *Nothing Ever Happens on My Block, The Mysterious Disappearance of Leon (I Mean Noel),* and *Who, Said Sue, Said Whoo?.*

HELEN SEWELL......noted illustrator of over seventy books, among them the first editions of Laura Ingalls Wilder's "Little House" series. The daughter of a U.S. Navy commander, Sewell had traveled around the world by the time she was seven. At twelve she became the youngest part-time art student at Pratt Institute, enrolling full time at the age of sixteen. Sewell's talent as an artist was appreciated by many, including editor Louis Untermeyer who called her illustrations "amazing creations...translations of one art in terms of another." In addition to the Wilder books, Sewell's drawings accompanied the texts of writers like Elizabeth Coatsworth, Alice Dalgliesh, and Eleanor Farjeon.

These are only a few of the authors and illustrators that you'll find in this volume. We hope you find all the entries in *SATA* both interesting and useful. Please write and tell us if we can make *SATA* even more helpful to you.

Forthcoming Authors

A Partial List of Authors and Illustrators Who Will Appear
in Forthcoming Volumes of *Something about the Author*

Abels, Harriette S.
Allard, Harry
Allen, Agnes B. 1898-1959
Allen, Jeffrey 1948-
Anders, Rebecca
Andrist, Ralph K. 1914-
Ardley, Neil (Richard) 1937-
Ashley, Bernard 1935-
Austin, R. G.
Axeman, Lois
Ayme, Marcel 1902-1967
Bains, Rae
Baker, Olaf
Balderson, Margaret 1935-
Barkin, Carol
Bartlett, Margaret F. 1896-
Batherman, Muriel 1926(?)-
Bauer, Caroline Feller 1935-
Bauer, John Albert 1882-1918
Beckman, Delores
Beim, Jerrold 1910-1957
Beim, Lorraine 1909-1951
Bernheim, Evelyne 1935-
Bernheim, Marc 1924-
Birnbaum, Abe 1899-
Boegehold, Betty 1913-
Boning, Richard A.
Bonners, Susan
Bourke, Linda
Bowen, Gary
Bracken, Carolyn
Brewton, Sara W.
Bridgman, Elizabeth P. 1921-
Bromley, Dudley 1948-
Bronin, Andrew 1947-
Bronson, Wilfrid 1894-
Brooks, Ron(ald George) 1948-
Brown, Roy Frederick 1921-
Brownmiller, Susan 1935-
Buchanan, William 1930-
Buchenholz, Bruce
Budney, Blossom 1921-
Burchard, Marshall
Burke, David 1927-
Burstein, Chaya M.
Butler, Dorothy 1925-
Butler, Hal 1913-
Calvert, Patricia
Camps, Luis 1928-
Carey, M. V. 1925-
Carley, Wayne
Carlson, Nancy L.
Carrie, Christopher
Carroll, Ruth R. 1899-

Cauley, Lorinda B. 1951-
Chang, Florence C.
Charles, Carole
Charles, Donald 1929-
Chartier, Normand
Chase, Catherine
Chessare, Michele
Cline, Linda 1941-
Cohen, Joel H.
Cole, Brock
Cooper, Elizabeth Keyser 1910-
Cooper, Paulette 1944-
Cosgrove, Margaret 1926-
Coutant, Helen
Dabcovich, Lydia
D'Aulnoy, Marie-Catherine
  1650(?)-1705
David, Jay 1929-
Davies, Peter 1937-
Dawson, Diane
Dean, Leigh
Degens, T.
DeGoscinny, Rene
Deguine, Jean-Claude 1943-
Demarest, Chris L. 1951-
Deweese, Gene 1934-
Dillon, Barbara
Ditmars, Raymond 1876-1942
Duggan, Maurice (Noel) 1922-1975
Dumas, Philippe 1940-
East, Ben
Edelson, Edward 1932-
Edwards, Linda S.
Eisenberg, Lisa
Elder, Lauren
Elgin, Kathleen 1923-
Elwood, Roger 1943-
Endres, Helen
Eriksson, Eva
Erwin, Betty K.
Etter, Les 1904-
Everett-Green, Evelyn 1856-1932
Falkner, John Meade 1858-1932
Farmer, Penelope 1939-
Fender, Kay
Filson, Brent
Fischer, Hans Erich 1909-1958
Flanagan, Geraldine Lux
Flint, Russ
Folch-Ribas, Jacques 1928-
Fox, Thomas C.
Freschet, Berniece 1927-
Frevert, Patricia D(endtler) 1943-
Funai, Mamoru R. 1932-

Gans, Roma 1894-
Garcia Sanchez, J(ose) L(uis)
Gardner, John Champlin, Jr. 1933-1982
Garrison, Christian 1942-
Gathje, Curtis
Gelman, Rita G. 1937-
Gemme, Leila Boyle 1942-
Gerber, Dan 1940-
Gobbato, Imero 1923-
Goldstein, Nathan 1927-
Goode, Stephen 1943-
Gordon, Shirley
Gould, Chester 1900-
Grabianski, Janusz 1929(?)-1976
Graeber, Charlotte Towner
Gutman, Bill
Harris, Marilyn 1931-
Hayman, LeRoy 1916-
Healey, Larry 1927-
Heine, Helme 1941-
Heller, Linda 1944-
Henty, George Alfred 1832-1902
Herzig, Alison Cragin
Hicks, Clifford B. 1920-
Higashi, Sandra
Hill, Douglas Arthur 1935-
Hockerman, Dennis
Hollander, Zander 1923-
Hood, Thomas 1779-1845
Howell, Troy
Hull, Jessie Redding
Hunt, Clara Whitehill 1871-1958
Hunt, Robert
Inderieden, Nancy
Irvine, Georgeanne
Jackson, Anita
Jackson, Kathryn 1907-
Jackson, Robert 1941-
Jacobs, Francine 1935-
James, Elizabeth
Jameson, Cynthia
Janssen, Pierre
Jaspersohn, William
Jewell, Nancy 1940-
Johnson, Harper
Johnson, Sylvia A.
Kahn, Joan 1914-
Kalan, Robert
Kantrowitz, Mildred
Kasuya, Masahiro 1937-
Keith, Eros 1942-
Kelley, True Adelaide 1946-
Kirn, Ann (Minette) 1910-
Koenig, Marion

Kohl, Herbert 1937-
Kohl, Judith
Kramer, Anthony
Kredenser, Gail 1936-
Krensky, Stephen 1953-
Kurland, Michael 1938-
Laure, Jason 1940-
Lawson, Annetta
Leach, Christopher 1925-
Lebrun, Claude
Leckie, Robert 1920-
Leder, Dora
Le-Tan, Pierre 1950-
Lewis, Naomi
Lindblom, Steve 1946-
Lindman, Maj (Jan)
Lines, Kathleen
Livermore, Elaine
Lye, Keith
MacKinstry, Elizabeth (?)-1956
Mali, Jane Lawrence
Manes, Stephen 1949-
Marryat, Frederick 1792-1848
Marxhausen, Joanne G. 1935-
May, Dorothy
Mayakovsky, Vladimir 1894-1930
McCannon, Dindga
McKim, Audrey Margaret 1909-
McLenighan, Valjean 1947-
McLoughlin, John C. 1949-
McNaughton, Colin 1951-
Melcher, Frederic G. 1879-1963
Mendoza, George 1934-
Michel, Anna 1943-
Miller, J(ohn) P. 1919-
Molesworth, Mary L. 1839(?)-1921
Molly, Anne S. 1907-
Moore, Lilian
Moore, Patrick 1923-
Moskowitz, Stewart
Muntean, Michaela
Murdocca, Sal
Newsom, Carol
Nickl, Peter
Obligado, Lillian Isabel 1931-
Odor, Ruth S. 1926-
Oppenheim, Shulamith (Levey) 1930-
Orr, Frank 1936-

Orton, Helen Fuller 1872-1955
Overbeck, Cynthia
Owens, Gail 1939-
Packard, Edward 1931-
Parenteau, Shirley L. 1935-
Parker, Robert Andrew 1927-
Paterson, A(ndrew) B(arton) 1864-1941
Patterson, Sarah 1959-
Pavey, Peter
Pelgrom, Els
Peretz, Isaac Loeb 1851-1915
Perkins, Lucy Fitch 1865-1937
Peterson, Jeanne Whitehouse 1939-
Phillips, Betty Lou
Plowden, David 1932-
Plume, Ilse
Poignant, Axel
Pollock, Bruce 1945-
Polushkin, Maria
Porter, Eleanor Hodgman 1868-1920
Poulsson, Emilie 1853-1939
Powers, Richard M. 1921-
Prager, Arthur
Prather, Ray
Preston, Edna Mitchell
Pursell, Margaret S.
Pursell, Thomas F.
Pyle, Katharine 1863-1938
Rabinowitz, Solomon 1859-1916
Rappoport, Ken 1935-
Reich, Hanns
Reid, Alistair 1926-
Reidel, Marlene
Reiff, Tana
Reiss, Elayne
Reynolds, Marjorie 1903-
Rockwood, Joyce 1947-
Rohmer, Harriet
Rosier, Lydia
Ross, Pat
Ross, Wilda 1915-
Roy, Cal
Rudstrom, Lennart
Sargent, Sarah 1937-
Schneider, Leo 1916-
Sebestyen, Ouida 1924-
Seidler, Rosalie
Shea, George 1940-

Shreve, Susan 1939-
Silbert, Linda P.
Slepian, Jan(ice B.)
Smith, Alison
Smith, Catriona (Mary) 1948-
Smith, Ray(mond Kenneth) 1949-
Smollin, Michael J.
Steiner, Charlotte
Stevens, Leonard A. 1920-
Stine, R. Conrad 1937-
Stubbs, Joanna 1940-
Sullivan, Mary Beth
Suteev, Vladimir Grigor'evich
Sutherland, Robert D. 1937-
Sweet, Ozzie
Tafuri, Nancy
Thaler, Mike
Thomas, Ianthe
Timmermans, Gommaar 1930-
Todd, Ruthven 1914-
Tourneur, Dina K. 1934-
Treadgold, Mary 1910-
Velthuijs, Max 1923-
Villiard, Paul 1910-1974
Waber, Bernard 1924-
Wagner, Jenny
Walker, Charles W.
Walsh, Anne Batterberry
Watts, Franklin 1904-1978
Wayne, Bennett
Werner, Herma 1926-
Westman, Paul 1956-
Weston, Martha
Whelen, Gloria 1923-
White, Wallace 1930-
Wild, Jocelyn
Wild, Robin
Winter, Paula 1929-
Winterfeld, Henry 1901-
Wolde, Gunilla 1939-
Wong, Herbert H.
Woolfolk, Dorothy
Wormser, Richard 1908-
Wright, Betty R.
Yagawa, Sumiko
Youldon, Gillian
Zistel, Era
Zwerger, Lisbeth

In the interest of making *Something about the Author* as responsive as possible to the needs of its readers, the editor welcomes your suggestions for additional authors and illustrators to be included in the series.

Acknowledgments

Grateful acknowledgment is made to the following publishers, authors, and artists for their kind permission to reproduce copyrighted material.

ADDISON-WESLEY PUBLISHING CO., INC. Illustration from *The Flying Orchestra* by Ulf Löfgren. Adapted by Ray Broekel. Copyright © 1969 by Ulf Löfgren and Almquist & Wiksell Forlag AB (Stockholm). Reprinted by permission of Addison-Wesley Publishing Co., Inc.

ANGUS & ROBERTSON LTD. Sidelight excerpts from *The Ocean World of Jacques Cousteau*, Volume I: *Oasis in Space* by Jacques Cousteau./ Sidelight excerpts from *The Ocean World of Jacques Cousteau*, Volume IV: *Window in the Sea* by Jacques Cousteau. Both reprinted by permission of Angus & Robertson Ltd.

ATHENEUM PUBLISHERS, INC. Illustration by Frances Gruse Scott from *I Pinch of Sunshine, ½ Cup of Rain* by Ruth Cavin. Text copyright © 1973 by Ruth Cavin. Illustrations copyright © 1973 by Frances Gruse Scott./ Illustration by Trina Schart Hyman from *South Star* by Betsy Gould Hearne. Copyright © 1977 by Betsy Gould Hearne./ Jacket painting by Yoshi Miyake from *Soul-Singer of Turnos* by Ardath Mayhar. Text copyright © 1981 by Ardath Mayhar. Jacket painting copyright © 1981 by Yoshi Miyake./ Illustration by Beni Montresor from "The Selfish Giant" in *The Birthday of the Infanta and Other Tales* by Oscar Wilde. Abridged text and pictures copyright © 1982 by Beni Montresor./ Illustration by Beni Montresor from *Willy O'Dwyer Jumped in the Fire* by Beatrice Schenk deRegniers. Text copyright © 1968 by Beatrice Schenk deRegniers. Pictures copyright © 1968 by Beni Montresor./ Illustration by Beni Montresor from *May I Bring a Friend?* by Beatrice Schenk deRegniers. Text copyright © 1964 by Beatrice Schenk deRegniers. Pictures copyright © 1964 by Beni Montresor./ Illustration by Ellen Raskin from *Nothing Ever Happens on My Block* by Ellen Raskin. Copyright © 1966 by Ellen Raskin./ Illustration by Ellen Raskin from *Spectacles* by Ellen Raskin. Copyright © 1968 by Ellen Raskin./ Illustration by Ellen Raskin from *The World's Greatest Freak Show* by Ellen Raskin. Copyright © 1971 by Ellen Raskin./ Illustration by Ellen Raskin from *Who, Said Sue, Said Whoo?* by Ellen Raskin. Copyright © 1973 by Ellen Raskin./ Illustration by Ellen Raskin from *Twenty-two, Twenty-three* by Ellen Raskin. Copyright © 1976 by Ellen Raskin. All reprinted by permission of Atheneum Publishers, Inc.

AVON BOOKS. Illustration by Teje Etchemendy from *Stranger from the Stars* by Nancy Etchemendy. Text copyright © 1983 by Nancy Etchemendy. Illustrations copyright © 1983 by Avon Books./ Illustration by Ellen Raskin from *The Mysterious Disappearance of Leon (I Mean Noel)* by Ellen Raskin. Copyright © 1971 by Ellen Raskin. Both reprinted by permission of Avon Books.

BANTAM BOOKS, INC. Illustration by Leslie Morrill from *The Bytes Brothers Input an Investigation* by Lois and Floyd McCoy, Jr. Text copyright © 1983 by Lois Rich McCoy and Floyd McCoy, Jr. Illustrations copyright © 1983 by Bantam Books, Inc. Cover art copyright © 1984 by Bantam Books, Inc. Reprinted by permission of Bantam Books, Inc.

BEHRMAN HOUSE, INC. Illustration by Jim Hellmuth from *Meet Our Sages* by Jacob Neusner. Copyright © 1980 by Jacob Neusner. Reprinted by permission of Behrman House, Inc.

THE BODLEY HEAD LTD. Sidelight excerpts from *Anno's Journey* by Mitsumasa Anno. Copyright © 1977 by Fukuinkan Shoten Publishers./ Sidelight excerpts from *Anno's Italy* by Mitsumasa Anno. Copyright © 1978 by Fukuinkan Shoten Publishers./ Sidelight excerpts from "Postscript," in *The Unique World of Mitsumasa Anno: Selected Works (1968-1977)* by Mitsumasa Anno. Copyright © 1980 by Kodansha Ltd. All reprinted by permission of The Bodley Head Ltd.

WILLIAM COLLINS SONS & CO. LTD. Illustration by Mitsumasa Anno from *Anno's Italy* by Mitsumasa Anno. Copyright © 1978 by Fukuinkan Shoten Publishers. Reprinted by permission of William Collins Sons & Co. Ltd.

COWARD, McCANN & GEOGHEGAN, INC. Illustration by Harald Wiberg from *The*

FOUR WINDS PRESS. Illustration by Ellen Raskin from *Moose, Goose and Little Nobody* by Ellen Raskin. Copyright © 1974 by Ellen Raskin. Reprinted by permission of Four Winds Press.

FUKUINKAN SHOTEN PUBLISHERS. Sidelight excerpts from *Anno's Journey* by Mitsumasa Anno. Copyright © 1977 by Fukuinkan Shoten Publishers./ Sidelight excerpts from *Anno's Italy* by Mitsumasa Anno. Copyright © 1978 by Fukuinkan Shoten Publishers. Both reprinted by permission of Fukuinkan Shoten Publishers.

GARRARD PUBLISHING CO. Illustration by Paul Frame from *Sutter's Fort* by Willard and Celia Luce. Copyright © 1969 by Willard and Celia Luce. Reprinted by permission of Garrard Publishing Co.

GROSSET & DUNLAP, INC. Illustration by Charles L. Wrenn from *Mary Jane in England* by Clara Ingram Judson. Copyright 1928 by Barse & Co. Reprinted by permission of Grosset & Dunlap, Inc.

LIBRAIRIE HACHETTE. Photographs from *Jacques-Yves Cousteau's World without Sun*, edited by James Dugan. Copyright © 1964 by Cdt. Jacques-Yves Cousteau and Jaspard, Polus & Cie (Monaco). English translation copyright © 1965 by William Heinemann Ltd. Reprinted by permission of Librairie Hachette.

HAMISH HAMILTON LTD. Illustration by Joe Lasker from *The Boy Who Loved Music* by David Lasker. Text copyright © 1979 by David Lasker. Illustrations copyright © 1979 by Joe Lasker./ Sidelight excerpts from *The Silent World* by Capt. J. Y. Cousteau and Frederic Dumas. Both reprinted by permission of Hamish Hamilton Ltd.

HARPER & ROW, PUBLISHERS INC. Sidelight excerpts from *The Silent World* by Capt. J.Y. Cousteau and Frederic Dumas./ Sidelight excerpts from *The Living Sea* by Jacques Cousteau and James Dugan./ Jacket illustration by Ronald Himler from *The Earth Witch* by Louise Lawrence. Copyright © 1981 by Louise Lawrence./ Illustration by Beni Montresor from *Belling the Tiger* by Mary Stolz. Text copyright © 1961 by Mary Stolz. Pictures copyright © 1961 by Beni Montresor./ Illustration by Beni Montresor from *Bedtime!* by Beni Montresor. Copyright © 1978 by Beni Montresor./ Illustration by C. Walter Hodges from *The Flight and Adventures of Charles II* by Charles Norman. Copyright © 1958 by Charles Norman./ Illustration by Helen Sewell from *Farmer Boy* by Laura Ingalls Wilder. Copyright 1933 by Harper & Brothers./ Illustration by Dirk Zimmer from *The Star Rocker* by Joseph Slate. Text copyright © 1982 by Joseph Slate. Illustrations copyright © 1982 by Dirk Zimmer. All reprinted by permission of Harper & Row, Publishers Inc.

HASTINGS HOUSE, PUBLISHERS INC. Illustration by Victor Ambrus from "Prince Mirko" in *The Book of Magical Horses* by Margaret Mayo. Copyright © 1976 by Margaret Mayo. Reprinted by permission of Hastings House, Publishers Inc.

HERALD PRESS. Illustration by James Converse from *Strawberry Mountain* by Birdie L. Etchison. Copyright © 1982 by Herald Press./ Illustration by Ivan Moon from *Walk Safe through the Jungle* by Katharine E. Matchette. Copyright © 1974 by Herald Press./ Illustration by Allan Eitzen from *Wilderness Journey* by Ruth Nulton Moore. Copyright © 1979 by Herald Press. All reprinted by permission of Herald Press.

HOLT, RINEHART & WINSTON. Illustration by Richard Egielski from *Mary's Mirror* by Jim Aylesworth. Text copyright © 1982 by Jim Aylesworth. Illustrations copyright © 1982 by Richard Egielski./ Illustration by Peter Farmer from *Elizabeth* by Eileen Dunlop. Copyright © 1975 by Eileen Dunlop. Both reprinted by permission of Holt, Rinehart & Winston.

THE HORN BOOK, INC. Sidelight excerpts from an article "A Conversation with Mitsumasa Anno," by Hisako Aoki, April, 1983 in *Horn Book*. Copyright © 1983 by The Horn Book, Inc./ Sidelight excerpts from an article "Acceptance," by Clara Ingram Judson, October, 1960 in *Horn Book*. Copyright © 1960 by The Horn Book, Inc./ Sidelight excerpts from an article "Helen Sewell, 1896-1956: The Development of a Great Illustrator," by Louise Seaman Bechtel, October, 1957 in *Horn Book*. Copyright © 1957 by The Horn Book, Inc./ Sidelight excerpts from an article "Illustrator Meets the Comics," by Helen Sewell, March, 1948 in *Horn Book*. Copyright 1948 by The Horn Book, Inc./ Sidelight excerpts from *Newbery and Caldecott Medal Books: 1956-1965*, edited by Lee Kingman. Copyright © 1965 by The Horn Book, Inc./ Sidelight excerpts from *Illustrators of Children's Books: 1957-1966*, compiled by Lee Kingman. Copyright © 1968 by The Horn Book, Inc. All reprinted by permission of The Horn Book, Inc.

HOUGHTON MIFFLIN CO. Illustration by Eileen Christelow from *Henry and the Red Stripes* by Eileen Christelow. Copyright © 1982 by Eileen Christelow./ Illustration by Annie Gusman from *The Ugly Book* by Arthur Crowley. Text copyright © 1982 by Arthur Crowley. Illustrations copyright © 1982 by Annie Gusman./ Jacket illustration by Donna Diamond from

Love in a Different Key by Marjorie Franco. Text copyright © 1983 by Marjorie Franco. Jacket illustration copyright © 1983 by Donna Diamond./ Illustration by Trina Schart Hyman from *The Shy Little Girl* by Phyllis Krasilovsky. Text copyright © 1970 by Phyllis Krasilovsky. Illustrations copyright © 1970 by Trina Schart Hyman./ Illustration by Richard Cuffari from *The Perilous Gard* by Elizabeth Marie Pope. Copyright © 1974 by Elizabeth Marie Pope./ Illustration by Joseph Duffy from *Elizabeth Catches a Fish* by Jane Resh Thomas. Text copyright © 1977 by Jane Resh Thomas. Illustrations copyright © 1977 by Joseph Duffy. All reprinted by permission of Houghton Mifflin Co.

HUMAN SCIENCES PRESS, INC. Illustration by Mark Hannon from *The Goodbye Painting* by Linda Berman./ Illustration by Gretchen Mayo from *Change* by Laura Greene. Copyright © 1981 by Laura Greene. Both reprinted by permission of Human Sciences Press, Inc.

ALFRED A. KNOPF, INC. Illustration by Raymond Lufkin from *Story of the Negro* by Arna Bontemps. Copyright 1948, 1955, © 1969 by Arna Bontemps./ Illustration by Beni Montresor from *A for Angel* by Beni Montresor. Copyright © 1969 by Beni Montresor./ Illustration by Beni Montresor from *I Saw a Ship A-Sailing* by Beni Montresor. Copyright © 1967 by Beni Montresor./ Illustration by Beni Montresor from *Cinderella*, adapted from the opera "La Cenerentola" by Gioacchino Rossini. Copyright © 1965 by Beni Montresor. All reprinted by permission of Alfred A. Knopf, Inc.

KODANSHA LTD. Sidelight excerpts from "Postscript," in *The Unique World of Mitsumasa Anno: Selected Works (1968-1977)* by Mitsumasa Anno. Copyright © 1980 by Kodansha Ltd. Reprinted by permission of Kodansha Ltd.

J. B. LIPPINCOTT CO. Illustration by Ellen Raskin from *Lady Ellen Grae* by Vera and Bill Cleaver. Copyright © 1968 by Vera and William J. Cleaver./ Illustration by Velma Ilsley from *Mystery at the Shoals* by Duane Bradley. Copyright © 1962 by Duane Bradley. Both reprinted by permission of J. B. Lippincott Co.

LOTHROP, LEE & SHEPARD BOOKS. Illustration by Consuelo Joerns from *Blizzard at the Zoo* by Robert Bahr. Text copyright © 1982 by Robert Bahr. Illustrations copyright © 1982 by Consuelo Joerns./ Illustration by Judith Allan from *It's Easy to Have a Snail Visit You*, edited by Caroline O'Hagan. Text copyright © 1980 by Culford Books Ltd. Illustrations copyright © 1980 by Judith Allan./ Jacket illustration by Tom Huffman from *Invite a Bird to Dinner* by Beverly Courtney Crook. Text copyright © 1978 by Beverly Courtney Crook. Illustrations copyright © 1978 by Tom Huffman. All reprinted by permission of Lothrop, Lee & Shepard Books.

MBI, INC. Illustration by Helen Sewell from *Pride and Prejudice* by Jane Austen. Copyright 1940 by The Limited Editions Club for the George Macy Companies, Inc./ Illustration by Edward A. Wilson from *The Man without a Country* by Edward Everett Hale./ Illustration by Edward A. Wilson from *Westward Ho!* by Charles Kingsley./ Illustration by Edward A. Wilson from *The Rime of the Ancient Mariner* by Samuel Taylor Coleridge./ Illustration by Edward A. Wilson from *Treasure Island* by Robert Louis Stevenson. All reprinted by permission of MBI, Inc.

MACMILLAN, INC. Illustration by Ninon from *Scaredy Cat* by Phyllis Krasilovsky. Copyright © 1959 by Macmillan Publishing Co., Inc./ Illustration by Ilon Wikland from *Lotta on Troublemaker Street* by Astrid Lindgren. Copyright © 1962 by Astrid Lindgren. Copyright © 1963 by The Macmillan Co./ Illustration by Helen Sewell from *Away Goes Sally* by Elizabeth Coatsworth. Copyright 1934 by Macmillan Publishing Co., Inc. All reprinted by permission of Macmillan, Inc.

JULIAN MESSNER. Cover illustration by Sanford Hoffman from *The Boys Who Saved the Children* by Margaret Baldwin. Text copyright © 1981 by Margaret Baldwin. Cover design copyright © 1981 by Lisa Hollander. Reprinted by permission of Julian Messner.

WILLIAM MORROW & CO., INC. Illustration by Joan Sandin from *Grandpa's Maria* by Hans-Eric Hellberg. Text copyright © 1969 by Hans-Eric Hellberg. English translation copyright © 1974 by Methuen Children's Books Ltd. Illustrations copyright © 1974 by Joan Sandin./ Illustration by Janet McCaffery from *The Witch of Hissing Hill* by Mary Calhoun. Copyright © 1964 by Mary Calhoun./ Jacket illustration by Ted Bernstein from *On the Ropes* by Otto R. Salassi. Copyright © 1981 by Otto R. Salassi. All reprinted by permission of William Morrow & Co., Inc.

OXFORD UNIVERSITY PRESS, INC. Jacket illustration by Mike Heslop from *A Whisper of Lace* by Gillian Cross. Copyright © 1982 by Gillian Cross./ Illustration by Eric Fraser from "Hassan the Brave" in *Egyptian and Sudanese Folk-Tales*, retold by Helen Mitchnik. Copyright © 1978 by Helen Mitchnik./ Illustration by Helen Sewell from *Azor and the Haddock* by Maude

Crowley. Copyright 1949 by Oxford University Press, Inc. All reprinted by permission of Oxford University Press, Inc.

PARENTS MAGAZINE PRESS. Illustration by Mamoru Funai from *The Man Who Cooked for Himself* by Phyllis Krasilovsky. Text copyright © 1981 by Phyllis Krasilovsky. Illustrations copyright © 1981 by Mamoru Funai. Reprinted by permission of Parents Magazine Press.

PHILOMEL BOOKS. Sidelight excerpts and illustration by Mitsumasa Anno from *Anno's Journey* by Mitsumasa Anno. Copyright © 1977 by Fukuinkan Shoten Publishers./ Sidelight excerpts from *Anno's Italy* by Mitsumasa Anno. Copyright © 1978 by Fukuinkan Shoten Publishers./ Sidelight excerpts from "Postscript," in *The Unique World of Mitsumasa Anno: Selected Works (1968-1977)* by Mitsumasa Anno. Copyright © 1980 by Kodansha Ltd./ Illustration by Mitsumasa Anno from *Anno's Britain* by Mitsumasa Anno. Copyright © 1981 by Kuso-kobo./ Illustration by Mitsumasa Anno from *Anno's U.S.A.* by Mitsumasa Anno. Copyright © 1983 by Fukuinkan Shoten Publishers./ Illustration by Mitsumasa Anno from *Anno's Medieval World* by Mitsumasa Anno. Copyright © 1979 by Fukuinkan Shoten Publishers./ Illustration by Sheila Sancha from *Knight after Knight* by Sheila Sancha. Copyright © 1974 by Sheila Sancha. All reprinted by permission of Philomel Books.

CLARKSON N. POTTER, INC. Illustration by Bruce Cayard from *A Children's Almanac of Words at Play* by Willard R. Espy. Copyright © 1982 by Willard R. Espy. Reprinted by permission of Clarkson N. Potter, Inc.

G. P. PUTNAM'S SONS. Jacket illustration by George Loh from *Basketball's Greatest Teams* by Al Hirshberg. Copyright © 1965 by Al Hirshberg. Reprinted by permission of G. P. Putnam's Sons.

RAINTREE PUBLISHERS, INC. Illustration from *Trains and Railroads* by Howard W. Kanetzke. Copyright © 1978 by Raintree Publishers, Inc./ Illustration by Charles Shaw from *Caught on a Cliff Face* by Roger Schachtel. Copyright © 1980 by Raintree Publishers, Inc. Both reprinted by permission of Raintree Publishers, Inc.

RAND McNALLY & CO. Photograph by Maureen Fennelli from *Gymnastics and You* by Michael Resnick. Copyright © 1977 by Rand McNally & Co. Reprinted by permission of Rand McNally & Co.

CHARLES SCRIBNER'S SONS. Illustration by Robert Doremus from *Soldier Doctor* by Clara Ingram Judson. Copyright 1942 by Charles Scribner's Sons./ Illustration by Ugo Mochi from *A Natural History of Zebras* by Dorcas MacClintock. Text copyright © 1976 by Dorcas MacClintock. Illustrations copyright © 1976 by Ugo Mochi./ Illustration by Helen Sewell from *The Bears on Hemlock Mountain* by Alice Dalgliesh. Copyright 1952 by Alice Dalgliesh./ Jacket illustration by Andrew Rhodes from *Grandpa—and Me* by Stephanie S. Tolan. Copyright © 1978 by Stephanie S. Tolan. All reprinted by permission of Charles Scribner's Sons.

SCROLL PRESS, INC. Illustration by Horst Lemke from *Ride with Me through ABC* by Susan Bond. Copyright © 1965 by Sigbert Mohn Verlag. Reprinted by permission of Scroll Press, Inc.

THE SEABURY PRESS, INC. Photograph courtesy of NC News/Interpress Photos from *The Singing Pope* by Rinna Wolfe. Copyright © 1980 by The Seabury Press, Inc. Reprinted by permission of The Seabury Press, Inc.

SIMON & SCHUSTER, INC. Illustration by Whitney Darrow, Jr. from "The Captain's Shanty" in *The Fireside Book of Fun and Game Songs,* collected and edited by Marie Winn. Text copyright © 1974 by Marie Winn and Allan Miller. Illustrations copyright © 1974 by Whitney Darrow, Jr./ Illustration by Whitney Darrow, Jr. from *Shiver, Gobble and Snore* by Marie Winn. Text copyright © 1971 by Marie Winn. Illustrations copyright © 1971 by Whitney Darrow, Jr. Both reprinted by permission of Simon & Schuster, Inc.

STEMMER HOUSE PUBLISHERS, INC. Illustration by Lisa Atherton from *The Giggle and Cry Book* by Eileen Spinelli. Text copyright © 1981 by Eileen Spinelli. Illustrations copyright © 1981 by Lisa Atherton. Reprinted by permission of Stemmer House Publishers, Inc.

TEMPO BOOKS. Jacket illustration by Mort Engle from *S.W.A.K., Sealed with a Kiss* by Judith Enderle. Copyright © 1983 by Judith Enderle. Reprinted by permission of Tempo Books.

TROLL ASSOCIATES. Photograph from *Hunting the Killer Shark* by Otto Penzler. Copyright © 1976 by Troll Associates. Reprinted by permission of Troll Associates.

TROUBADOR PRESS, INC. Illustration by William R. Johnson from "King Kong" in

Famous Monsters Funbook by William R. Johnson. Copyright © 1981 by William R. Johnson. Reprinted by permission of Troubador Press, Inc.

VERLAG CARL UEBERREUTER. Illustration by Horst Lemke from *Kindergedichte* by Christian Morgenstern. Copyright © by Verlag Carl Ueberreuter. Reprinted by permission of Verlag Carl Ueberreuter.

THE VIKING PRESS. Illustration by C. B. Falls from *Red Sails to Capri* by Ann Weil. Copyright 1952 by Ann Weil./ Illustration by C. B. Falls from *Vast Horizons* by Mary Seymour Lucas. Copyright 1943 by Mary Seymour Lucas./ Illustration by C. B. Falls from *The First 3000 Years: Ancient Civilizations of the Tigris, Euphrates, and Nile River Valleys, and the Mediterranean Sea* by C. B. Falls. Copyright © 1960 by the Estate of C. B. Falls./ Illustration by Joe Lasker from *The Boy Who Loved Music* by David Lasker. Text copyright © 1979 by David Lasker. Illustrations copyright © 1979 by Joe Lasker./ Jacket illustration by Trina Schart Hyman from *Ronia, The Robber's Daughter* by Astrid Lindgren. Translated by Patricia Crampton. Copyright © 1981 by Astrid Lindgren. Translation copyright © 1983 by Viking Penguin, Inc./ Photograph by Bo-Erik Gyberg from *Pippi on the Run* by Astrid Lindgren. Text copyright © 1971 by Astrid Lindgren. Photographs copyright © 1971 by Semic International./ Illustration by Louis S. Glanzman from *Pippi in the South Seas* by Astrid Lindgren. Copyright © 1959 by Astrid Lindgren./ Illustration by Jan Pyk from *Karlsson-on-the-Roof* by Astrid Lindgren. Translated by Marianne Turner. Copyright 1955, © 1971 by Astrid Lindgren. Translation copyright © 1958 by Oxford University Press, Inc./ Illustration by Louis S. Glanzman from *Pippi Longstocking* by Astrid Lindgren. Copyright 1950, © 1978 by The Viking Press, Inc./ Illustration by Ilon Wikland from *Happy Times in Noisy Village* by Astrid Lindgren. Copyright © 1961 by Astrid Lindgren. Copyright © 1963 by The Viking Press, Inc./ Illustration by Eric Palmquist from *Rasmus and the Vagabond* by Astrid Lindgren. Copyright © 1960 by Astrid Lindgren./ Illustration by J. K. Lambert from *The Brothers Lionheart* by Astrid Lindgren. Translated by Joan Tate. Text copyright © 1973 by Astrid Lindgren. English text copyright © 1975 by Brockhampton Press Ltd. Illustrations copyright © 1975 by The Viking Press, Inc. All reprinted by permission of The Viking Press.

HENRY Z. WALCK, INC. Illustration by Helen Sewell from *Azor* by Maude Crowley. Copyright 1948 by Henry Z. Walck, Inc. Reprinted by permission of Henry Z. Walck, Inc.

FRANKLIN WATTS, INC. Photograph by Maureen McNicholas from *How to Get a Good Job* by Jane Claypool. Text copyright © 1982 by Jane Claypool. Photographs copyright © 1982 by Maureen McNicholas. Reprinted by permission of Franklin Watts, Inc.

JOHN WEATHERHILL, INC. Sidelight excerpts from "Author's Postscript" in *Topsy-Turvies: Pictures to Stretch the Imagination* by Mitsumasa Anno. Copyright © 1968, 1970 by Fukuinkan Shoten Publishers./ Illustration by Mitsumasa Anno from *Topsy-Turvies: Pictures to Stretch the Imagination* by Mitsumasa Anno. Copyright © 1968, 1970 by Fukuinkan Shoten Publishers./ Sidelight excerpts from *Upside-Downers: More Pictures to Stretch the Imagination* by Mitsumasa Anno. All reprinted by permission of John Weatherhill, Inc.

WORLD PUBLISHING CO. Illustration by C. B. Falls from *Kidnapped* by Robert Louis Stevenson. Copyright 1947 by The World Publishing Co./ Illustration by W. T. Mars from *Benny's Flag* by Phyllis Krasilovsky. Text copyright © 1960 by Phyllis Krasilovsky. Illustrations copyright © 1960 by W. T. Mars. Both reprinted by permission of World Publishing Co.

WORLD'S WORK LTD. Illustration by Ninon from *The Very Little Girl* by Phyllis Krasilovsky. Copyright 1953 by Phyllis Krasilovsky./ Illustration by Peter Spier from *The Cow Who Fell in the Canal* by Phyllis Krasilovsky. Text copyright 1953, © 1957 by Phyllis Krasilovsky. Illustrations copyright © 1957 by Peter Spier./ Illustration by Olivia H. H. Cole from *The Very Tall Little Girl* by Phyllis Krasilovsky. Text copyright © 1969 by Phyllis Krasilovsky. Illustrations copyright © 1969 by Olivia H. H. Cole./ Illustration by Janet McCaffery from *The Witch of Hissing Hill* by Mary Calhoun. Copyright © 1964 by Mary Calhoun. All reprinted by permission of World's Work Ltd.

Sidelight excerpts from an article "The Lively World," by Milton R. Bass, April 14, 1981 in *The Berkshire Eagle*. Reprinted by permission of *The Berkshire Eagle*./ Sidelight excerpts from an article "C. B. Falls, 1874-1960: A Career in Retrospect," by Norman Kent, February, 1960 in *American Artist*. Copyright © 1960 by Billboard Publications, Inc. Reprinted by permission of Billboard Publications, Inc./ Sidelight excerpts from an article "Never Violence," by Astrid Lindgren in *Bookbird*. Reprinted by permission of *Bookbird*./ Sidelight excerpts from an article "Meet Your Author: Hans-Eric Hellbert," June, 1976 in *Cricket* magazine. Copyright © 1976 by Open Court Publishing Co. Reprinted by permission of *Cricket* magazine./ Photograph courtesy of George Heinrich from the stage production of "Pippi Longstocking."

Presented during the 1982-83 season at The Children's Theatre Company and School. Reprinted by permission of George Heinrich./ Sidelight excerpts from an article "My Verona," by Beni Montresor in *Holiday*. Copyright © 1968 by *Holiday*. Reprinted by permission of *Holiday*./ Illustration by Jacob Landau from *Lion Hound* by Jim Kjelgaard. Copyright 1955 by Jim Kjelgaard. Reprinted by permission of Jim Kjelgaard./ Sidelight excerpts from an article "Writing for Juveniles Isn't All Fun," by Clara I. Judson, August, 1947 in *Library Journal*, Vol. 72, No. 14. Copyright 1947 by *Library Journal*. Reprinted by permission of *Library Journal*./ Sidelight excerpts from an article "Astrid Lindgren's Acceptance Speech at the Conferment of the Hans Christian Andersen Medal," by Astrid Lindgren, July, 1958 in *Bookbird*. Reprinted by permission of Astrid Lindgren.

Sidelight excerpts from an article "At Home in the Sea," by Jacques Cousteau, April, 1964 in *National Geographic Magazine*. Reprinted by permission of The National Geographic Society./ Sidelight excerpts from an article "Profiles: The Astonishment of Being," by Jonathan Cott, February 28, 1983 in *New Yorker*. Copyright © 1983 by Jonathan Cott. Reprinted by permission of New Yorker Magazine, Inc./ Sidelight excerpts from an article "Real-Life Fantasy," by John Gruen, December 11, 1976 in *Opera News*. Copyright © 1976 by *Opera News*. Reprinted by permission of *Opera News*./ Sidelight excerpts from an article "PW Interviews Marie Winn," by Sally A. Lodge, June 10, 1983 in *Publishers Weekly*. Reprinted by permission of *Publishers Weekly*./ Sidelight excerpts from an article "Newbery Award Acceptance Speech," by Ellen Raskin, August, 1979 in *Horn Book*. Reprinted by permission of Ellen Raskin./ Sidelight excerpts from an article "Characters and Other Clues," by Ellen Raskin, December, 1978 in *Horn Book*. Copyright © by Ellen Raskin. Reprinted by permission of Ellen Raskin./ Illustration from *The Flying Tigers* by John Toland. Copyright © 1963 by John Toland. Reprinted by permission of U.S. Air Force./ Sidelight excerpts from *The Washington Post*, August 15, 1983. Reprinted by permission of Washington Post Co.

PHOTOGRAPH CREDITS

Eileen Christelow: Ahren Ahrenholz; Jacques-Yves Cousteau: Les Requins Associés; Gillian Cross: S. N. Marshall Ltd.; Judith Enderle: Greg Moiseeff; Howard W. Kanetzke: Department of Photography, University of Wisconsin; Phyllis Krasilovsky: Carol Kitman; Astrid Lindgren: Copyright by Pressens Bild Ab; Janet McCaffery: Timothy Gaefas; Jacob Neusner: Brown News Bureau, Brown University; Evan Owen: B. J. Harris; Eileen Spinelli: Phil Sandmaier; Eleanora E. Tate: Bill Scroggins; John Toland: Arthur Shilstone; Ron Wilson: *Daventry Weekly Express;* Nancy Means Wright: Erik Borg; Marie Winn: Janet Malcolm.

SOMETHING ABOUT THE AUTHOR

AASENG, Nathan 1938-
(Nate Aaseng)

BRIEF ENTRY: Born July 7, 1953, in Park Rapids, Minn. Aaseng has concentrated his work primarily on biographies of famous sports personalities written for young readers. In what critics consider a clear and informative style, Aaseng reveals these sports figures through play-by-play scenes, personal glimpses, and discussions of their career achievements, allowing for a more intimate and individual look at the players. His first book, *Bruce Jenner: Decathlon Winner* (Lerner, 1979), is testimony to his competent and direct approach to sportswriting. In a story that relates Jenner's success in the 1976 Olympics, Aaseng also includes abundant information about the decathlon itself. *School Library Journal* observed, ''The story is told here simply and smoothly with a minimum of fictionalizing and a good feel for the tension and excitement of athletic competition.'' Among his writings about great athletes, Aaseng includes a book about a group of particularly special sports heroes. *Superstars Stopped Short* (Lerner, 1982) recounts the lives of eight athletes whose careers were tragically interrupted by personal injury or death, including Eddie Hart, Chi Cheng, and Lyman Bostock. *School Library Journal* noted that Aaseng ''handles these stories . . . with compassion.''

Aaseng has also written four books that involve reader participation. In the ''You are the Coach'' series, sports enthusiasts are asked to decide on strategic action and maneuvers for particular game situations described by Aaseng. ''Readers will watch their favorite sport more intelligently,'' *Booklist* commented, ''and certainly with more sympathy for the individuals who call the shots.'' Aaseng's most recent books, all published by Lerner, include *Baseball's Hottest Hitters* (1983), *Baseball's Playmakers* (1983), *Basketball's Sharpshooters* (1983), *Supersubs of Pro Sports* (1983), and *Football's Hardhitting Linebackers* (1983). *Home and office:* 2450 Cavell Ave. S., St. Louis Park, Minn. 55426. *For More Information See: Contemporary Authors*, Volume 106, Gale, 1982.

ACHEBE, Chinua 1930-

BRIEF ENTRY: Born November 16, 1930, in Ogidi, Nigeria. Achebe has worked for the Nigerian Broadcasting Company and is currently a professor at the University of Nigeria and a full-time writer. He is admittedly a political writer whose books focus on the impact of England's colonization of Africa. Many critics feel that as an African author, Achebe has learned to manipulate the English language as a tool to delineate symbolic differences between the Ibo and English cultures. Because of his adept handling of the English language and profound insight into human suffering and tragedy, Achebe is considered by most critics to be one of the most important contemporary African novelists. The majority of his works are for adults and deal with the evolution of the Ibo society. *Things Fall Apart* (McDowell Obelensky, 1959) and *No Longer At Ease* (Obelensky, 1961), two of his most famous novels, reveal the weaknesses of the Ibo culture through the protagonists' own personal weaknesses.

Achebe has also written four children's books, each filled with the same type of proverbs and folk tales he incorporates into his adult novels. *Chike and the River* (Cambridge University Press, 1966) is an adventure story of a young boy whose visit to another city teaches him many valuable lessons. *Twentieth-Century Children's Writers* observed, "This fast-moving adventure story emphasizes 'good' values which are both implicit in the action and explicitly stated in proverbs." In *The Drum* (Fourth Dimension, 1977), Achebe examines the tenuous balance between power and privilege in a story about a tortoise and the magic drum out of which he feeds other animals during a drought. Achebe has won numerous awards for his books, including the Margaret Wrong Memorial Prize, 1959, The Nigerian National Trophy, 1960, Jock Campbell-New Statesman Award, 1965, Commonwealth Poetry Prize, 1974, and the Lotus Award for Afro-Asian writers, 1975. Other children's books by Achebe include *How the Leopard Got His Claw* (Fourth Dimension, 1973), and *The Flute* (Fourth Dimension, 1977). *Home:* 305 Marguerite Cartwright Ave., Nsukka, Nigeria. *For More Information See: African Authors,* Black Orpheus Press, 1973; *Africa South of the Sahara,* Europa Publications Limited, 1978; *Contemporary Poets,* St. Martin's, 1980; *Contemporary Novelists,* St. Martin's, 1982; *Contemporary Authors, New Revision Series,* Volume 6, Gale, 1982; *Twentieth-Century Children's Writers,* St. Martin's, 2nd edition, 1983.

ALCOCK, Vivien   1924-

BRIEF ENTRY: Born September 23, 1924, in Worthing, England. Author of fantasy for children. After attending art school, Alcock decided to become a children's author, inspired by her daughter's love for original stories. Alcock says she enjoys telling stories, particularly those about ghosts and strange occurrences. Each of her books is written with a supernatural theme. In her first book, *The Haunting of Cassie Palmer* (Methuen, 1980), the seventh child of a seventh child is the focus for a story about a young girl's aversion to her power of second sight. Trouble begins on a dare, when Cassie successfully conjures up a ghost who immediately proclaims his friendship. In what *Bulletin for the Center of Children's Books* deemed "an impressive first novel, with a fusion of realism and fantasy . . . ," Alcock includes authentic characterization and concludes with a logical ending. *Twentieth-Century Children's Writers* observed that ". . . the book is a true original, maintaining throughout an elusive but highly distinctive tone. Lightness of touch, a sharply sardonic eye, an affection for children, and a cool accuracy for portraying them . . . are elements in a unique literary chemistry." *The Stonewalkers* (Methuen, 1981), Alcock's second novel, is the story of Poppy Brown, a compulsive liar, and her friend Belladonna, a stone statue. Poppy's come-uppance begins when the statue materializes into a human being and becomes an enemy instead of her trusted and faithful confidante. Described by *School Library Journal* as a "compelling fantasy," this book attests to Alcock's talent for writing believably in a difficult genre. "Vivien Alcock's second novel," *Times Literary Supplement* commented, "confirms her as a new writer who can command plot, character, nuance, and dialogue with a precision and sensitivity that sets her firmly among the elite of English fantasy authors for the young."

Alcock's expertise is seen once again in *The Sylvia Game* (Methuen, 1982). A strange painting and a mysterious drowning help create another book filled with suspense but dabbed with humor. *Times Literary Supplement* observed, "This book too opens with great vitality. It has gusto and humour to provide welcome relief from the sombre recurrent hints of the paranormal. Miss Alcock is unsentimental, but there is an unmistakable depth of feeling in her deft handling of her very human and imperfect characters." Alcock has also written *Travelers By Night* (Methuen, 1983), and *Ghostly Companions* (short stories; Methuen, 1984). *Home:* 59 Woodlane, London N.6, England. *For More Information See: Twentieth-Century Children's Writers,* 2nd edition, St. Martin's, 1983; *Contemporary Authors,* Volume 110, Gale, 1984.

ANNO, Mitsumasa   1926-

PERSONAL: Born March 20, 1926, in Tsuwano, Japan; son of Yojiro and Shikano Anno; married Midori Suetsugu, April 1, 1952; children: Masaichiro (son), Seiko (daughter). *Education:* Graduated from Yamaguchi Teacher Training College, 1948. *Home:* 4-5-5 Midoricho, Koganei Shi, Tokyo 184, Japan.

CAREER: Artist, educator, essayist, and author and illustrator of children's books. Taught at elementary schools in Tokyo

MITSUMASA ANNO

(From *Topsy-Turvies: Pictures to Stretch the Imagination* by Mitsumasa Anno. Illustrated by the author.)

for ten years. Has exhibited in major galleries and museums in Japan, Canada, the United States, and Great Britain. *Member:* Illustrators Council, Nikikai (artist's club). *Awards, honors: Topsy-Turvies: Pictures to Stretch the Imagination* was selected one of *New York Times* Best Illustrated Books of the Year and received *Chicago Tribune Book World's* Spring Book Festival Award, picture book honor, both 1970, was commended for the German Children's and Youth Book Award and received Brooklyn Art Books for Children citation, both 1973; Brooklyn Art Books for Children citation, 1973, for *Upside-Downers: More Pictures to Stretch the Imagination; Anno's Alphabet: An Adventure in Imagination* was chosen one of American Institute of Graphic Arts Fifty Books of the Year and commended for the Kate Greenaway Medal, both 1974, received *Boston Globe-Horn Book* award for illustration and selected one of *New York Times* Best Illustrated Books of the Year, both 1975, won Christopher Award and was included in Children's Book Showcase, both 1976, and received Brooklyn Art Books for Children citation, 1976, 1977, and 1978; Minister of Education prize, 1975; Golden Apple Award, Bratislava International Biennale, 1977; *Anno's Counting Book* selected *Boston Globe-Horn Book* Award honor book for illustration, 1977, and received honorable mention from New York Academy of Sciences outstanding science books for children, 1978; *Anno's Journey* selected *Boston Globe-Horn Book* Award honor book for illustration, 1978, and received Brooklyn Art Books for Children citation, 1979; *The Unique World of Mitsumasa Anno: Selected Works (1968-1977)* received Bologna Chil-

dren's Book Fair First Prize for Graphic Excellence in Books for Youth, 1978; Parent's Choice Award for illustration in children's books, 1980, for *Anno's Italy; Anno's Song Book* received Bologna Children's Book Fair First Prize for Graphic Excellence in Books for Children, 1980; *Anno's Britain* was selected one of *New York Times* Best Illustrated Books of the Year, 1982.

WRITINGS—All self-illustrated: *Fushigi na e,* Fukuinkan Shoten, 1968, published as *Topsy-Turvies: Pictures to Stretch the Imagination* (ALA Notable Book; *Horn Book* honor list), Walker/Weatherhill, 1970; *Sakasama,* Fukuinkan Shoten, 1969, published in America as *Upside-Downers: More Pictures to Stretch the Imagination,* translated by Meredith Weatherby and Suzanne Trumbull, Weatherhill, 1971; *Dr. Anno's Magical Midnight Circus,* translated by M. Weatherby, Weatherhill, 1972; *ABC no hon,* Fukuinkan Shoten, 1974, published in America as *Anno's Alphabet: An Adventure in Imagination* (ALA Notable Book), Crowell, 1975; *Kazoetemiyou,* Kodansha, 1975, published in America as *Anno's Counting Book* (*Horn Book* honor list), Crowell, 1977; *Tabi no Ehon,* Fukuinkan Shoten, 1977, published as *Anno's Journey* (*Horn Book* honor list; ALA Notable Book), Collins & World, 1978; *Ōkina Monono Sukina Ōsama.* Kodansha, 1976, published in America as *The King's Flower* (ALA Notable Book), Collins & World, 1979; *Mori no Ehon,* Fukuinkan Shoten, 1977, published in America as *Anno's Animals,* Collins & World, 1979; *Nippon no uta* (title means "Anno's Song Book"), Kodansha, 1979; *Tabi no Ehon*

(From *Anno's Journey* by Mitsumasa Anno. Illustrated by the author.)

II, Fukuinkan Shoten, 1978, published as *Anno's Italy* (originally published as *My Journey II*), Bodley Head, 1979, Collins & World, 1980; *Tendō setsu no hon*, Fukuinkan Shoten, 1979, published in America as *Anno's Medieval World*, adapted from the translation by Ursula Synge, Philomel Books, 1980.

Anno Mitsumasa no Gashū, Kodansha, 1980, translated and adapted by Samuel Crowell Morse, published as *The Unique World of Mitsumasa Anno: Selected Works (1968-1977)*, Philomel Books, 1980; *Mahōtsukai no ABC*, Kusó-kobó, 1980, published in America as *Anno's Magical ABC: An Anamorphic Alphabet*, (lettering by son, Masaichiro Anno), Philomel Books, 1981; *10-nin no yukai na hikkoshi*, Dowaya, 1981, published in America as *Anno's Counting House* (ALA Notable Book), Philomel, 1982; *Anno's Britain*, Philomel, 1982; (with M. Anno) *Anno's Mysterious Multiplying Jar*, Philomel, 1983; *Anno's USA*, Philomel, 1983. Also author of *Maze, First Book of Mathematics, Dr. Stone-Brain's Computer*, and *The Theory of Set*.

ADAPTATIONS: "Anno's Journey" (animated filmstrip), Weston Woods, 1983.

WORK IN PROGRESS: Several books in the field of mathematics for children and adults.

SIDELIGHTS: **March 20, 1926.** Born in Tsuwano, in western Japan. "Tsuwano is in a valley surrounded by mountains. As a child I always wondered what was on the other side of the mountain. A small airplane would come to our valley about once a year. With the sound of the airplane everybody would rush outside and wait until it came into sight. Then in a few seconds the airplane would disappear. Once it came while I was in the toilet. I remember how sad I was at having missed it.

"On the other side of the mountains were villages with rice fields, and beyond these rice fields was the ocean, which seemed to be very, very far away. When I reached the ocean for the first time in my life, I tasted it to see if it was really salty.

"Because my world was cut off from the outside world, first by the mountains and then by the ocean, the desire to go and see what lay on the other side grew stronger. I feel this is true, perhaps, of most Japanese people who travel far just to see how things are on the other side of the ocean." [Hisako Aoki, "A Conversation with Mitsumasa Anno," *Horn Book*, April, 1983.[1]]

During his childhood Anno was interested in drawing and mathematics, and earnestly desired to become an artist.

Left his hometown for further study after graduating from high school. ". . . What I remember most vividly is the homecoming: how I got off the train at the station, feeling happy and proud and a bit shy at the same time, thinking how much I had matured being away from Tsuwano but that the town would accept me as I was. Hermann Hesse expresses this very feeling as 'mein übermütiges Heimkehr-Gefühl' in his book *Schön ist die Jugend*. When I read how Hermann Hesse, as a student, went home to Calw, getting off the train at the end of the town, walking by the river, and crossing the bridge, my heart ached because everything was exactly the same with me. The only difference was the fact that there wasn't a storks' nest in Tsuwano. I could almost fit to his text my illustrations of the scenery of Tsuwano.

"Because Hesse's words so perfectly matched my own homecoming as a student, I felt that I had to go to Calw to see if it really looked the same. And when I went, it was completely different. I took a few photographs and drew some sketches and came back. I showed them to someone, together with the

(From *Anno's Britain* by Mitsumasa Anno. Illustrated by the author.)

(From *Anno's Italy* by Mitsumasa Anno. Illustrated by the author.)

sketches I had done of Tsuwano before, and said, 'They are different, aren't they?' He answered, 'No. They are surprisingly similar. They almost look alike.'

"Then it dawned on me that the sketches and photographs of Tsuwano and Calw represent the world as seen through my eyes, and they are my own compositions—which other people may see differently. I believe that this is one of the reasons for drawing, writing, photographing, or expressing oneself in any form. Through a creative work, people may experience something which they may not have experienced before."[1]

Anno graduated from Yamaguchi Teacher Training College and taught elementary school for sometime before engaging in an art career. ". . . As a teacher I tried to present material to pupils so that they could widen their scope of understanding and self-expression. At the same time I learned a lot from them.

"Children's way of seeing is actually different from that of adults; teachers and parents should understand this and not base everything on adult standards. For example, children's sense of perspective is different from ours, partly because their faces are smaller and their eyes are closer together. In addition, their experience is more restricted, so they have less to base their judgment on."[1]

1952. Married Midori Suetsugu. The couple has a son and a daughter.

1963. Made first trip to Europe, which later became a "journey book" entitled *Anno's Journey*. "I went to Europe and visited Scandinavia mainly, and then I traveled to England and south through Germany. I was not aware of it when I was working on the book, but having my traveler begin his journey by landing in a boat may be a reflection of the Japanese way of

thinking. A German artist possibly would not have started his journey that way. My purpose for traveling was not merely to see more of the world but to get lost in it. I did often get lost and faced many difficulties, but under such circumstances there were always unexpected discoveries and interesting experiences waiting for me."[1]

1970. First picture book was published in America as *Topsy-Turvies: Pictures to Stretch the Imagination*. "In Japan, where this book was first published, many people have seen many different things in these pictures. One professor of mathematics claims that in a single picture he has found twelve different 'impossibilities.' But is anything really impossible in the world of the imagination? A little boy wrote me saying? 'How can I go to the country where you drew your pictures?' Well, I told him, all you need to do is think yourself to that country, and there you'll be? Another young Japanese looked at this book and said to her mother: 'All those little men, they're really me.' How right she was!

"Impossible? No, that's a world used only by 'grownups.' Nothing is impossible to the young, not until we become caught in the problems of living and forget to make-believe. Perhaps these pictures of mine will keep all of us young a little longer, will stretch our imaginations enough to help keep us magically human. I hope so, I believe so—for nothing is impossible." [Mitsumasa Anno, "Author's Postscript," *Topsy-Turvies: Pictures to Stretch the Imagination*, Walker/Weatherhill, 1970.[2]]

1971. Second picture book was published in the United States as *Upside-Downers: More Pictures to Stretch the Imagination*. "This is a book without any rules. It's simply to be enjoyed and wondered over. . . . I still and always believe that one is never too young or too old, to begin learning how wide a little imagination can stretch the joy of living.

(From *Anno's Medieval World* by Mitsumasa Anno. Illustrated by the author.)

"We've also added a new dimension to the book by printing some of our wordplays upside-down—or should I say down-side-up? So a child can sit opposite his mother and they can both read the book to each other at the same time. Others may want to read the book for themselves, maybe by going through it one way and then turning it around and going back the other way. That's fine too. Because this is a book without any rules. It's simply to be enjoyed and perhaps wondered over a little. [Mitsumasa Anno, *Upside-Downers: More Pictures to Stretch the Imagination*, Weatherhill, 1971.³]

Three years later another picture book was well received in the United States. About this award-winning book, *Anno's Alphabet*, the illustrator-author commented: "As a Japanese I have never felt very close to the alphabet, and it is therefore possible for me to regard the letters of the alphabet quite objectively as materials with which to design freely. I think that Europeans have a deep cultural relationship with the alphabet, and as result find it difficult to achieve the sense of detachment from it that is so easy for me. . . ."

1975. Made another trip to Europe, exploring, observing, sketching, and painting as he went. ". . . I followed the path wherever it went, up and down hills, across rivers, through fields which spread out into great open spaces. There were forests and rivers wherever I travelled; in the forests there were deer and in the rivers there were trout. At the end of the road there were always houses gathered together to make a town, and in every town there were gates, leading from shops to squares and plazas, through graveyards and gardens to churches and cathedrals. One town had a castle in its midst; one castle was a town by itself. They gave me an image of the country, and each reflected the life of that town, that country.

"It is a world filled with variety, yet a simple place with a deep-rooted sense of culture, an appreciation of nature that preserves it from destruction and pollution. It is a beautiful world." [Mitsumasa Anno, *Anno's Journey*, Collins & World, 1978.⁴]

1980. Second journey book for children, *Anno's Italy*, was published in the United States. "'How is it that, although you are Japanese, you understand so well the history and cultural heritage of Europe?' This is a question I am often asked by Europeans, who look back with nostalgia in their eyes to the golden days when there were as yet no cars on the streets of their villages and cities. In answer, I like to tell about a wedding ceremony which I happened to see near Füssen in West Germany. As I stood at the back of the church, listening to the peaceful melody of the processional hymn, I saw the bridal party come into the church. Watching the ceremony, it was easy for me to pick out the bride and the bridegroom and their parents, as well as the bridesmaid and the best man and their friends. Among them I distinguished the mother of the bride at a glance, for she was wiping away her tears, again and again. It seems that, although languages, alphabets and customs are different in the various parts of the world, there are no differences at all in our hearts, especially when we are shedding tears at parting. What trifles the formal differences are, when you think of what our hearts have in common!

"The laws of physics and nature are universal, as are the principles of plant and animal life throughout the world. Among living creatures, more things are shared than are different. Seeing a sunset in Europe, I was impressed by the natural truth that we have only one sun—that, no matter where we are, we all see the same sun.

"Although it is difficult for me to understand the languages of the western world, still I can understand the hearts of the people. This book [*Anno's Italy*] has no words, yet I feel sure that everyone who looks at it can understand what the people in the pictures are doing, and what they are thinking and feeling.'' [Mitsumasa Anno, *Anno's Italy*, Collins & World, 1980.[5]]

The following year Anno and his son, Masaichiro, designed a picture book entitled *Anno's Magical ABC*. The technique used in the book, known as anamorphosis, was used by ancient Greek mural painters and by Renaissance portrait artists. Anno wrote the text and drew the pictures and his son drew the letters.

1982. Travelled through the United States, mostly by car. ''. . . It is almost impossible for the average Japanese to realize how big America is. Driving from Atlanta to New Orleans, for example, I saw cotton fields for miles and miles and then corn fields which seemed to go on endlessly. I was excited at first, but after a while I had the urge to escape from the same scenery.

''It was my original plan to go to the West Coast and back to Japan. But when I got as far as Albuquerque, I felt I had to go to St. Louis. As a child I loved Tom Sawyer and Huckleberry Finn, and Mark Twain meant America to me. So I just had to meet them before going back to Japan.

''Going all the way from Boston to Albuquerque, I still could not realize the enormous size of the continent. So I headed for St. Louis, driving alone. An American said that I was brave, but I was only ignorant. On the first day's drive I felt that I had had enough. There was nothing but desert. Ahead of me was one horizon, and in the back mirror I saw an identical horizon. I told myself that because I had come this far from the horizon behind me, I would perhaps be able to reach the horizon ahead of me. Comforted by that thought, I went on. As I learned later, the distance between Albuquerque and St. Louis is greater than the whole length of Japan. If I had known that, I certainly wouldn't have started out.

''But as I got nearer to Kansas, a few trees and pasture land appeared. To my surprise I suddenly began to wish for the desert again, for I saw the trees as disturbing my clear vision. Anyway, I reached St. Louis at long last; I 'met' Mark Twain and saw the Mississippi River and was satisfied. Then I flew to San Francisco and returned to Japan.''[1]

Anno continues to design books. He is also a renowned artist, having exhibited his paintings in museums throughout the world. ''Once someone said, upon seeing my pictures, 'You amuse yourself by fooling people; you can't draw without a mischievous spirit.'

''I really wanted to counter by saying, 'The spirit of noble humanity causes me to do so.' If, however, I had to admit it, I should say that his words were correct. The more I think of playing tricks on my audience, the better I can concentrate power in my pictures.

''My pictures are like maps, which perhaps only I can understand. Therefore, in following my maps there are some travellers who get lost. There are those who become angry when they discover they have been fooled; but there are also those who enter into the maze of my maps willingly, in an attempt to explore their accuracy for themselves. [Mitsumasa Anno, ''Postscript,'' *The Unique World of Mitsumasa Anno: Selected Works (1968-1977)*, Philomel Books, 1980.[6]]

About his work habits, Anno said: ''I try to work very thoroughly on whatever I have in hand. For example, I am constantly asked to create many different kinds of small pieces. Often these coincide with a major idea of mine, but as I'm always worried about getting things done by a deadline, these small works are inclined to get finished first. Then I feel free to concentrate on what I want to do myself.

(From *Anno's Alphabet: An Adventure in Imagination* by Mitsumasa Anno. Illustrated by the author.)

''My room is full of piles of unfinished work which is in fact already completed in my mind. What stimulates its completion is a phone call asking whether some work is ready or not. After giving an affirmative answer, I go back to the particular work and finish it off.

''My atelier looks terribly crowded and messy, but I like it that way, for I can see everything to be done and also what's in progress, and I don't have to hunt for things. Everything is visible! . . .''[1]

FOR MORE INFORMATION SEE: Scientific American, December, 1971; *Horn Book*, February, 1972, April, 1983; *Times Literary Supplement*, April 6, 1973; *New York Times Book Review*, March 9, 1975, November 9, 1980; *Bulletin of the Center for Children's Books*, April, 1975; *Children's Literature Review*, Volume 2, Gale, 1976; Doris de Montreville and Elizabeth D. Crawford, editors, *Fourth Book of Junior Authors and Illustrators*, H. W. Wilson, 1978; *Time*, December 3, 1979; *Contemporary Authors, New Revision Series*, Volume 4, Gale, 1981; *Washington Post Book World*, November 9, 1980, May 10, 1981.

(From *Anno's U.S.A.* by Mitsumasa Anno. Illustrated by the author.)

(From the filmstrip "Anno's Journey." Produced by Weston Woods, 1984.)

ARMITAGE, David 1943-

BRIEF ENTRY: Born in 1943. David Armitage has illustrated numerous picture books for children, many in collaboration with his wife, author Ronda Armitage. The Armitages' work as a husband-and-wife team has been deemed "fanciful, humorous, and lively" by critics who have recognized their contribution to children's reading. Their first book, *The Lighthouse Keeper's Lunch* (Deutsch, 1977), won the Esther Glen award in 1978 for the most distinguished contribution to New Zealand children's literature. In this story about a group of thieving seagulls, David Armitage reveals his visual perceptiveness through his illustrations. *Booklist* commented, "This light-hearted tale is nicely illustrated with bright, whimsical pictures that offer some pretty images of seascapes."

Ice Creams for Rosie (Deutsch, 1981), written by Ronda Armitage, also highlights her husband's artistic hand. *Times Literary Supplement* described his illustrations as having a "life of their own" while *School Library Journal* further added, "Picture layout includes vignettes and changes in perspective, all of which give a brisk rhythm to this watercolor picture book." Armitage displays a touch of comedy in *Don't Forget Matilda!* (Deutsch, 1979), also written by his wife. His illustrations express the frustrating, yet comic, side of absent-mindedness. "The lively, full-color illustrations," *Booklist* observed, "executed in a scrawly, appealing style, extend humor in a story that smoothly captures a small child's subter-

fuges. . . ." Armitage has also recently co-authored *Grandma Goes Shopping* (Deutsch, 1983) with his wife. Other books illustrated by Armitage include Lorna Hinds's *Beds* (F. Watts, 1975) and Jonathan P. Rutland's *Chairs* (F. Watts, 1975), both illustrated with Sandra Biggs; Freda Linde's *The Singing Grass* (Oxford University Press, 1975); John C. Siddons's *Fun with Electricity* (Kaye & Ward, 1976); *The Trouble with Mr. Harris* (Deutsch, 1978) and *The Bossing of Josie* (Deutsch, 1980, published as *The Birthday Spell*, Scholastic Book Services, 1981), both written by Ronda Armitage. *Home:* Old Tiles Cottage, Church Lane, Hellingly, East Sussex BN27 4HA, England. *For More Information See: Twentieth-Century Children's Writers*, 2nd edition, St. Martin's, 1983.

ARMITAGE, Ronda (Jacqueline) 1943-

BRIEF ENTRY: Born March 11, 1943, in Kaikoura, New Zealand. Armitage's belief that picture books are to be read aloud make her particularly aware of the flow and rhythm of every sentence in her children's stories. All her books have been illustrated by her husband, David Armitage, and their joint work has been praised by critics. Their first book, *The Lighthouse Keeper's Lunch* (Deutsch, 1977) won the Esther Glen Award in 1978, given for the most distinguished contribution to New Zealand literature for children. The story focuses on Mr. Grinling's lunch and the seagulls that continually try to steal it. Armitage offers the young reader detailed specifics of the food and the various schemes Mr. and Mrs. Grinling use to hinder the hungry seagulls. "Although her stories are simple, her style is never simplistic," *Twentieth-Century Children's Writers* commented. "It is distinguished by fluid, literate sentences which rather than condescend, happily include words like "brusque" or "irascible" when these are ones which best suit their context."

Armitage engages very vivid and vital characters into her stories, creating one of her best in *The Bossing of Josie* (Deutsch, 1980). Feeling dominated by the members of her family, Josie's "magic" birthday present allows her to momentarily imagine her family away. "Young listeners will identify immediately with Josie," *Booklist* commented, "a middle child who is bossed by everyone in her family. . . . In this nicely real account of a preschooler's sense of frustration and compensating fantasies of power, Josie is engagingly spunky and resilient." Other books by Armitage include *Don't Forget Matilda!* (Deutsch, 1979), *The Trouble with Mr. Harris* (Deutsch, 1978), *Ice Creams for Rosie* (Deutsch, 1982), and *One Moonlit Night* (Deutsch, 1983). *Home:* Old Tiles Cottage, Church Lane, Hellingly, East Sussex BN27 4HA, England. *For More Information See: Twentieth-Century Children's Writers*, St. Martin's, 2nd edition, 1983.

ASH, Jutta 1942-

PERSONAL: Born December 12, 1942, in Hamburg, West Germany; married wife, c.1967; children: Two. *Education:* Attended Werkkunstschule, Hamburg, Germany.

CAREER: Artists, author and illustrator of books for children. Has worked as an artist/designer for an advertising agency.

WRITINGS: Bella (juvenile), Longman, 1972.

Illustrator; all for children: Kenneth McLeish, reteller, *Chicken Licken*, Longman, 1973, Bradbury, 1974; Nathaniel Benchley, *Feldman Fieldmouse*, Abelard (London), 1975 (Ash was not associated with earlier edition); Delia Huddy, *The Ship That Sailed Away*, Kestrel Books, 1975; Mabel Esther Allan, *Trouble in the Glen*, Abelard, 1976; Peter Hartling, *Oma*, translated by Anthea Bell, Harper, 1977; Pat Barton, *A Week Is a Long Time*, Abelard, 1977, Academy Press-Santa, 1981; Marion Green, *The Last Surving Dragon*, Andersen Press, 1979; *Biminy in Danger*, edited by Andersen Press and Hutchinson Publishing Group, Andersen Press, 1980; Brothers Grimm, *Rapunzel*, Andersen Press, 1981, Holt, 1982.

SIDELIGHTS: "My ideas about art are not set, as, with every new picture, a new process starts, which adds to, or changes, my previous knowledge." [Lee Kingman and others, compilers, *Illustrators of Children's Books: 1967-1976*, Horn Book, 1978.]

FOR MORE INFORMATION SEE: Lee Kingman and others, compilers, *Illustrators of Children's Books: 1967-1976*, Horn Book, 1978.

AULT, Rosalie Sain   1942-
(Roz Ault)

PERSONAL: Born April 22, 1942, in Abington, Pa.; daughter of Fletcher D. (a surgeon) and Ertie (Warren) Sain; married Charles Michael Ault (a graphic designer), June 22, 1963; children: Michael Christopher, Benjamin Jeremy. *Education:* Wellesley College, B.A., 1963; Simmons School of Library Science, M.L.S., 1976. *Home:* 26 Mystic Valley Parkway, Winchester, Mass. 01890.

CAREER: Hardy Elementary School, Arlington, Mass., librarian, 1976—.

WRITINGS: (With Liz Uraneck; under name Roz Ault) *Kids Are Natural Cooks* (juvenile; illustrated by Lady McCrady), Houghton, 1974; *BASIC Programming for Kids*, Houghton, 1983.

SIDELIGHTS: "When my sons entered nursery school, under the creative teaching of Liz Uraneck, we discovered how much fun it could be for grownups and kids to share experiences in the kitchen. We like to approach a recipe not as a cut-and-dried set of orders, but as an opportunity for a new experience—as an idea-starter for going off in our own direction. I hope *Kids Are Natural Cooks* is encouraging other families and classrooms to have some of the same kinds of happy cooking times together.

"As a school librarian, I'm spending more time with books and less with cooks. But whether we're reading recipes or reference books, I always enjoy the good times I have working with boys and girls. Lately I've been transferring the approach we use with cooking to the exciting new area of computer programming. Here, too, kids and grownups can have fun exploring, experimenting, and learning together."

HOBBIES AND OTHER INTERESTS: Camping, photography.

ROSALIE SAIN AULT

JIM AYLESWORTH

As she drove along the windy road,
she sang this little song:

"My looks have got me down.
So, I'm going into town.
There I'll trade this stuff of mine,
And I'll dress myself up fine."

(From *Mary's Mirror* by Jim Aylesworth. Illustrated by Richard Egielski.)

AYLESWORTH, Jim 1943-

PERSONAL: Born February 21, 1943; married Donna LaPuzza (an interior designer); children: John, Daniel. *Education:* Miami University, Oxford, Ohio, B.A., 1965; Concordia College, River Forest, Ill., M.A., 1978. *Home:* 213 North Elm St., Hinsdale, Ill. 60521.

CAREER: Hatch School, Oak Park, Ill., teacher of first grade, 1971—. *Awards, honors:* Award for excellence from Illinois Office of Education, 1975.

WRITINGS: Hush Up! (juvenile; illustrated by Glen Rounds), Holt, 1980; *Tonight's the Night* (juvenile; illustrated by John Wallner), A. Whitman, 1981; *Mary's Mirror* (juvenile; illustrated by Richard Egielski), Holt, 1982; *Siren in the Night* (juvenile; illustrated by Tom Centola), A. Whitman, 1983.

WORK IN PROGRESS: "I always have things in the mail, and I always have my fingers crossed."

SIDELIGHTS: "I'm a first grade teacher. I've been one for more than twelve years. At the end of almost every day, I read picture books aloud to my kids. I have come to know that picture books belong to the reader every bit as much as to the author or to the illustrator. In fact, the reader often makes or breaks the book.

"I've tried to write picture books that the reader can dig into, and call their own."

BAHR, Robert 1940-

PERSONAL: Born October 29, 1940, in Newark, N.J.; son of Robert (an electrician) and Catherine (Kuebler) Bahr; married Alice Harrison (a librarian), 1971; children; Keith, Aimee, James. *Education:* King's College, Briarcliff Manor, N.Y., B.A., 1964. *Office:* 1104 Walnut St., Allentown, Pa. 18102. *Agent:* Dominick Abel, 498 West End Ave., New York, N.Y. 10024.

CAREER: Rodale Press, Emmaus, Pa., editor, 1964-72; free-lance writer, 1972—. Lecturer. *Member:* American Society of Journalists and Authors, Authors' Guild, Society of Children's Book Writers.

WRITINGS: The Virility Factor, Putnam, 1976; *Least of All Saints*, Prentice-Hall, 1979; *The Great Blizzard* (juvenile), Dandelion Press, 1979; *The Blizzard*, Prentice-Hall, 1980; *Blizzard at the Zoo* (juvenile; illustrated by Consuelo Joerns), Lothrop, 1982; *Kreskin's Fun Way to Mind Expansion*, Doubleday, 1984; *Good Hands: Massage for Total Health*, New America Library, 1985. Contributor to *Parade, Smithsonian, Science Digest, Writer's Digest, Popular Mechanics, Playboy, Boys' Life, Success Unlimited, Kiwanis, Scouting, Runner's World, Sports Illustrated, TV Guide, Let's Live, Prevention*, and other periodicals. Contributor to *Family Health Guide and Medical Encyclopedia, Family Legal Guide, Eat Better—Live Better, Home Improvements Manual.*

WORK IN PROGRESS: Adult novel, *Jodi.*

SIDELIGHTS: "I never read a book until I was thirteen years old. One day, my English teacher, Mr. Wilkes, took the class to the library to select a book for a book report. He found me looking for the smallest book I could find—I didn't care what it was about, as long as it was small.

"'Here, read this,' he told me, handing me a *gigantic* volume.

"'I'm looking for a small one,' I said.

"'Read *this*,' he demanded. So I had to do it.

"The book was *The Black Stallion* by Walter Farley. Once I started, there was no stopping, and I read and read. Then, I read another Farley book, and another, and then for some reason *The Good Earth* by Pearl Buck. Since then, I knew I was going to write books, although I didn't know if I could make a living at it. In fact, it's turned out to be a good living.

"I don't think there's anything more important than being able to write a book that helps young people to learn more about themselves and the world. Most of my books are for adults, and most of the letters I receive from my readers are from adults. But it seems the most interesting questions and comments usually come from young people about the age I was when I read my first book—and that's exciting."

Even the buffalo, who played in the snow, frisking and tossing great piles of it about with their heads, had been fed by the animal keepers. ■ (From *Blizzard at the Zoo* by Robert Bahr. Illustrated by Consuelo Joerns.)

ROBERT BAHR

BERENDS, Polly Berrien   1939-

BRIEF ENTRY: Born December 1, 1939, in Chicago, Ill. Author and pastoral counselor. A graduate of Skidmore College, Berends earned master's degrees from both Union Theological Seminary and Columbia University. She began her career as a picture book editor for Golden Press and worked for almost ten years as a children's book editor with Random House. Since 1975, she has written six children's books and a book for adults entitled *Whole Child/Whole Parent* (Harper, 1975, revised edition, 1982). *Publishers Weekly* called her bed-time story, *Ladybug and Dog and the Night Walk* (Random House, 1980), "quiet and warm as a hug," while *Booklist* took note of the story's "unpretentious gentleness" and Cyndy Szekeres's "soft-edged" drawings. In *The Case of the Elevator Duck* (Random House, 1973), Berends presents a humorous mystery about Gilbert, a boy who finds a lost duck in a housing project where no pets are allowed. Her other books for children are *Who's That in the Mirror?* (illustrated by Lilian Obligado; Random House, 1968), *I Heard Said the Bird* (Random House, 1969), *Vincent, What Is It?* (Random House, 1969), and *Ladybug and Dog Tales* (Lothrop, 1983). She is currently working on two additional children's books, *Baby Bear's Perfect Christmas* and *The Star Child*. *Residence:* Westchester County, N.Y. *For More Information See: Contemporary Authors*, Volume 108, Gale, 1983.

(From *The Goodbye Painting* by Linda Berman. Illustrated by Mark Hannon.)

BERMAN, Linda 1948-

PERSONAL: Born May 25, 1948, in Hempstead, N.Y.; daughter of Alexander (a lawyer and judge) and Regina (Goldberg) Berman; married Harold Pskowski, January 15, 1972 (divorced, 1978). *Education:* Boston University, B.A., 1972; University of Massachusetts, M.A., 1973; University of California, Berkeley, graduate study, 1982-83. *Politics:* Left, 60's liberal. *Religion:* Jewish. *Home address:* Rt. 1, Box 301, Hume, Va. 22639.

CAREER: Worked as a teacher for emotionally disturbed pre-school children. Social worker at a community health center in Northern Virginia, 1984—.

WRITINGS: The Goodbye Painting (juvenile fiction; illustrated by Mark Hannon), Human Sciences Press, 1982.

WORK IN PROGRESS: "A children's book about the 'blended' family, for example, the problems step-families have in coming together and functioning as a family."

SIDELIGHTS: "I am very interested in bibliotherapy—using literature to help young children cope with and better understand a variety of life crises. I believe very strongly that affective education has an important role in early childhood education and see books as being an important part of this curriculum."

LINDA BERMAN

BOLES, Paul Darcy   1916-1984

OBITUARY NOTICE—See sketch in *SATA* Volume 9: Born March 5, 1916, in Ashley-Hudson, Ind.; died May 4, 1984, in Atlanta, Ga. Author of novels, short stories, plays, and criticism. A high-school dropout, Boles was a self-taught writer who began writing stories at the age of nine. He held a variety of jobs and toured Europe before working as a radio program director and in advertising. His first novel, *The Streak,* published in 1953, was followed by several other award-winning works, including *Parton's Island* for which Boles received the 1959 Friends of American Writers' award. He was the author of two collections of short stories for young adults, *A Million Guitars* and *I Thought You Were a Unicorn.* In 1969 *A Million Guitars* received the Indiana University Writers' Conference award for most distinguished work of young adult fiction. That same year, Boles was awarded the Georgia Writers' Association literary achievement award for his entire body of work. Boles's short stories appeared in American and European periodicals, such as *Ladies' Home Journal, McCall's, Saturday Evening Post,* and *Cosmopolitan,* and were also anthologized in several collections, including *Best Post Stories* and *Seventeen's Stories. For More Information See: Contemporary Authors, New Revision Series,* Volume 4, Gale, 1981. *Obituaries: New York Times,* May 6, 1982.

BOWDEN, Joan Chase   1925-
(Joan Chase Bacon; Jane Godfrey, Charlotte Graham, Kathryn Kenny)

BRIEF ENTRY: Born May 1, 1925, in London, England; came to the United States, 1953; became a naturalized citizen, 1960. Since 1969 Bowden has been a full-time author of books for children under the name Joan Chase Bacon and various pseudonyms. Prior to that time she worked as a secretary in her native England and in Canada. Although she sold her first children's book fairly easily, she relates: "It took me another two years to discover what I had done right! I learned, at last, by applying the old adage—seat of the pants to seat of the chair." She has since written over twenty-five juvenile books, including *A New Home for Snowball* (1974), *Elizabeth and the*

Magic Lamp (1975), *The Backward Picnic* (1976), and *Little Gray Rabbit* (1979), all published by Golden Press, *Why the Tides Ebb and Flow* (Houghton, 1979), and *Strong John* (Macmillan, 1980). Many of Bowden's books are aimed at the beginning reader. She believes that "if a child can't read . . . he is handicapped for the rest of his life. . . . I'm trying to beckon and encourage the child to read on to discover for himself what happens next." *Address:* c/o Macmillan Publishing Co., 866 Third Ave., New York, N.Y. 10022. *For More Information See: Contemporary Authors,* Volumes 89-92, Gale, 1980.

BOYNTON, Sandra   1953-

BRIEF ENTRY: Born April 3, 1953, in Orange, N.J. Cartoonist, illustrator, author, and stationery products executive. Boynton has rapidly become well-known for her greeting cards that feature a variety of unlikely but irresistible animals, most notably, an over-indulgent hippopotamus. A master of comic illustration whose humorous cards sold over 100 million in 1981, Boynton is also an author who combines her talents as a cartoonist with clever and skillfully written texts. *Chocolate: The Consuming Passion* (Workman Publishing, 1982) has received much critical attention for its unique and sentimental, if not intimate, look at chocolate. "The author tells the inside and outside stories of boxed chocolates," *Publishers Weekly* observed, "presents several recipes, and examines the physiology and psychology of 'chocophilia,'" all of which add up to what the *New York Times Book Review* described as "a delightful little bonbon of a book. Sometimes playful, sometimes perfectly serious. . . ."

Boynton has written numerous books for younger children, including *Hippos Go Berserk* (Little, Brown, 1979) in which she reveals her fine ear for nonsense rhyme. Not only a counting book but a visual tool as well, *Hippos Go Berserk* was described by *Wilson Library Journal* as " . . . a small, unpretentious book, but a special one in terms of overall unity, not to mention its warmth and whimsicality. . . . The total effect is light, airy, and tender." The old adage of "try, try again" is spotlighted in *If At First . . .* (Little, Brown, 1980). The desperate attempts of an orange mouse to push a purple elephant up a hill sets the stage for a book that can be enjoyed as much by adults as by children.

Other children's books written and illustrated by Boynton include *Hester in the Wild* (Harper, 1979), *Moo Baa La La La* (Simon & Schuster, 1982), *Opposites* (Simon & Schuster, 1982), *The Going to Bed Book* (Simon & Schuster, 1982), *But Not the Hippopotamus* (Simon & Schuster, 1982), and *A Is for Angry: An Adjective and Animal Alphabet* (Workman Publishing, 1983).

BRADFORD, Ann (Liddell)   1917-

BRIEF ENTRY: Born November 9, 1917, in San Leandro, Calif. A professor of early childhood education and author of books for adults and children, Bradford graduated from California State University, Fresno. She later received her masters degree from the same university and earned a Ph.D. in education from the University of Maryland, College Park. Her eleven books for young people, all written with Kal Gezi, include a mystery series featuring the "Maple Street Five."

Published by Child's World, the titles include *The Mystery in the Secret Club House*, 1978, *The Mystery of the Missing Dogs*, 1980, *The Mystery of Misty Falls*, 1980, and *The Mystery of the Square Footprints*, 1980. In *Beebi, the Little Blue Bell* (Child's World, 1976), and *One Little White Shoe* (Child's World, 1976), Bradford invites readers to participate in supplying the story's ending. She is a member of the National Association for Education of Young Children, the California Teacher's Association, and the California Professors of Early Childhood Education. *Home:* 686 Riverlake Way, Sacramento, Calif. 95831. *For More Information See: Leaders in Education*, 5th edition, Bowker, 1974; *Who's Who of American Women 1981-82*, 12th edition, Marquis, 1981.

BROEKEL, Rainer Lothar 1923- (Ray Broekel)

PERSONAL: First syllable of surname rhymes with "rock'; born March 24, 1923, in Dresden, Germany; son of Eugene (a horticulturist) and Hedwig (Hartmann) Broekel; married Margaret McNeely, May 6, 1944; children: Peggy Rae, Randall Ray. *Education:* Illinois College, B.A., 1947; graduate study at Stanford University, 1948-50, and Wesleyan University, 1955. *Religion:* Episcopalian. *Home and office:* 6 Edge St., Ipswich, Mass. 01938.

CAREER: Junior high school science teacher in Murrayville and Jacksonville, Ill., 1950-56; Junior Science Museum, Jacksonville, Ill., founder and director, 1954-56; Wesleyan University, Middletown, Conn., member of department of school services, 1956-64; Xerox Education Publications, Middletown, Conn., editor, and publishing supervisor of "My Weekly Reader" publications, 1957-66; Silver Burdett Co., Morristown, N.J., senior editor, 1966-67; Addison-Wesley Publishing Co., Reading, Mass., editor-in-chief of juvenile division, 1967-75; author, free-lance editor, and educational consultant, 1975—; North Shore Regional Vocational School, Beverly, Mass., English teacher, 1976-77; Institute of Children's Literature, Redding Ridge, Conn., instructor, 1979—; North Shore Community College, Beverly, Mass., instructor, 1980—. *Military service;* U.S. Air Force, 1943-46. *Member:* National Association of Science Writers, Author's Guild, Mystery Writers of America, Society of Children's Book Writers, International Reading Association, National Science Teachers Association, Council of Elementary Science International, Mensa. *Awards, honors:* L.H.D., Illinois College, 1979; *Even the Devil Is Afraid of a Shrew* was included in the Children's Book Showcase, 1973 and *The Painter and the Bird* was included, 1976.

WRITINGS—Under name Ray Broekel: *The True Book of Tropical Fishes*, Childrens Press, 1956, published as *The Junior True Book of Tropical Fishes*, Muller, 1959; *You and the Sciences of Plants, Animals, and the Earth*, Childrens Press, 1956; *You and the Sciences of Mankind*, Childrens Press, 1956; *"I Have a Green Nose," Said Zanzibar*, Seale, 1963; *Rodney Bounced Too Much on Monday*, Seale, 1965; *Pangborn, the Peanut Bear, and His Tummy-Drum*, Seale, 1965; *Hugo the Huge*, Doubleday, 1968.

The Saga of Sweet Basil, Doubleday, 1970; (adapter) *Even the Devil Is Afraid of a Shrew* (illustrated by Richard Brown), Addison-Wesley, 1972; (adapter) *The Flying Orchestra*, Addison-Wesley, 1974; (adapter) *The Traffic Stopper*, Addison-Wesley, 1974; (adapter) *One, Two, Three*, Addison-Wesley, 1974; (adapter) *The Color Trumpet*, Addison-Wesley, 1974;

RAINER LOTHAR BROEKEL

(adapter) *Our Bird Friends*, Addison-Wesley, 1975; (translator) Max Velthuijs, *The Painter and the Bird*, Addison-Wesley, 1975; (with others) *The Underwater Adventure Book*, Random House, 1978; (with Laurence B. White) *The Trick Book*, Doubleday, 1979; (with L. B. White) *Now You See It: Easy Magic for Beginners* (illustrated by Bill Morrison), Little, Brown, 1979; *The Holiday Dragon*, I Discover Books, 1979.

The Mystery of the Funny Money, Carolrhoda, 1980; *The Twist Tie Riddle*, Carolrhoda, 1980; *The President Jackson Case*, Carolrhoda, 1980; *The Shoelace Solution*, Carolrhoda, 1980; *The Moustache Pickpocket*, Carolrhoda, 1980; *The Mystery of the Stolen Base*, Carolrhoda, 1980; *Pack of Fun Facts*, Xerox Paperback Bookclub, 1980; *Volcanoes and Other Disasters*, Xerox Paperback Bookclub, 1980; (with L. B. White) *The Surprise Book: Seventy-Seven Stupendously Silly Practical Jokes You Can Play on Your Friends* (illustrated by Will Winslow), Doubleday, 1981; *The New True Book of Fire Fighters*, Childrens Press, 1981; *The New True Book of Police*, Childrens Press, 1981; *The New True Book of Trains*, Childrens Press, 1981; *The New True Book of Snakes*, Childrens Press, 1982; *The New True Book of Storms*, Childrens Press, 1982; *The New True Book of Baseball*, Childrens Press, 1982; *The New True Book of Football*, Childrens Press, 1982; (with L. B. White) *Abbra-Ca-Dazzle: Easy Magic Tricks* (illustrated by Mary Thelan), A. Whitman, 1982; *The New True Book of Aquariums and Terrariums*, Childrens Press, 1982; *The New True Book of Trucks*, Childrens Press, 1983; *The New True Book of Sound Experiments*, Childrens Press, 1983; *The New True Book of Maps and Globes*, Childrens Press, 1983; *The New True Book*

And with Thomas waving his baton, they marched through the town to play in the park. ■
(From *The Flying Orchestra* by Ulf Löfgren. Adapted by Ray Broekel.)

of Gerbil Pets and Other Small Rodents, Childrens Press, 1983; (with L. B. White) *Hocus Pocus: Magic You Can Do*, A. Whitman, 1984; *The Baseball Book*, Child's World, in press; *The Basketball Book*, Child's World, in press; *The Soccer Book*, Child's World, in press; *The Football Book*, Child's World, in press; *If You Were a Mummy*, Xerox, in press.

Textbooks and workbooks: *Balloons, Birds, and Balls*, Hayes Book, 1976; *Smiles the Clown*, Hayes Book, 1976; *Meg and the Animals*, Hayes Book, 1976; *The Sunnyside News*, Hayes Book, 1976; *Mystery Island*, Hayes Book, 1976; *Hot Dogs, Pigeons, and Fish That Walk*, Hayes Book, 1976; *Gremlins, Mermaids, and Mousetraps That Fly*, Hayes Book, 1976; *Motorcycles, Swimming, and Dog Detectives*, Hayes Book, 1976; (editor with others) *The Spirit of God*, Sadlier, 1976; (with others) *Multiple Reading Skills Series*, Lowell & Lynwood, 1976; *Airplanes, Pet Stories, and Fire Trucks*, Hayes Book, 1977; (editor with others) *Earth and Universe*, Cambridge Book Company, 1977; (with others) *Elementary Science Series*, Addison-Wesley, 1977; *Word Problem Drill, Grade 5*, Hayes Book, 1977; *Word Problem Drill, Grade 6*, Hayes Book, 1977; *Solving Science Mysteries*, Hayes Book, Books 1, 2, and 3, 1977, Book 4, 1979; *Reading: Everyday Survival Skills*, Hayes Book, 1978; (with others) *Daystreaming*, Economy Company, 1978; (with others) *Forerunners*, Economy Company, 1978; (editor with others) *Jesus and His Friends*, Sadlier, 1978; *Language Arts and Science*, Delta Books, 1978; (editor with others) *Elementary Science Series*, Houghton, 1979; (editor) *Environmental Education*, eight volumes, Bedford, 1979.

(With others) *Keys to Reading*, Economy Company, 1980; *Everyday Survival Skills*, three volumes, Hayes Book, 1980;

(editor) *Environmental Education Evaluation Packet*, Bedford, 1980; (with others) *Reading about Science*, seven volumes, McGraw, 1981; (editor) *Project Business Student Manual*, Junior Achievement, 1981; (editor) *Project Business Consultant's Manual*, Junior Achievement, 1981; (editor) *Project Business Consultant's Binder*, Junior Achievement, 1981; *Real Life Math*, eight volumes, Instructo Corporation, 1981; (and editor) *Elementary Science, Grade 5*, D. C. Heath, 1981; (with others) *Elementary Science, Grade 6*, D. C. Heath, 1981; *Math: Everyday Survival Skills*, Hayes Book, 1981; *Problem Solving, Grades 5-6*, School Zone Publishing, 1981; (with others) *The Children's Book Market*, Institute of Children's Literature, 1981; *Sounds of Science: Environmental Module*, University of Oklahoma, 1982; *Improving Composition Skills—Nonfiction*, Hayes Book, 1982; *Improving Composition Skills—Fiction*, Hayes Book, 1982; (editor) *Mathco*, University of Oklahoma, 1982; *The People, North Carolina, Grade 4*, Ginn, 1982; (editor) *Gateways to Science, Grade 5*, McGraw, 1983; *Gateways to Science, Grade 3*, McGraw, 1983; *Gateways to Science, Grade 3, Teacher's Edition*, McGraw, 1983.

Adult: *The Great American Candy Bar Book*, Houghton, 1982.

Contributor of over 1,000 stories and articles to children's magazines and other periodicals, including *Cricket, Cobblestone, Ranger Rick, Highlights for Children, Jack and Jill, Child Life, Reader's Digest, Instructor, Saturday Review, Current Science, My Weekly Reader, Science Teacher*, and *Nation's Schools*.

WORK IN PROGRESS: More Abra-Ca-Dazzle Magic for Whitman; *The Home Run Kid; Writing for Young Readers; Your First Puppy; Your First Kitten; Desert Isles and Candy Bars;*

The South Boulevard Alley Cats; Sweet Nickel Nostalgia, for adults.

SIDELIGHTS: "I was born on a farm in Germany, raised in Illinois, married in Texas. My wife and I have also lived in South Carolina, Massachusetts, California, and Connecticut. We love all areas of the country.

"My favorite city? New Orleans for the great food and great music. Second favorite city? Vancouver British Columbia—what an environment—wow!

"I have lots of hobbies. I collect records and albums, specializing in the classics, Big Band nostalgia, and Dixieland Jazz. I'm an avid mystery/fantasy reader. My favorite old-time authors arc Cornell Woolrich and H. P. Lovecraft. I love nothing better then having a good mystery to read at the beach on a sunny day. (Beaching is another hobby.)

"I've always been involved and interested in sports. I played semi-pro softball for a few years. I was known as a screwball lefty pitcher, and one year ended the season with twenty-one wins and no losses. (The next year, however, the batters really shellacked me.) One of my hobbies is connected with baseball, as I collect baseball cards.

"I've always been interested in politics, and I collect political campaign buttons (have about 5,000). I'm a rabid gardener, raising all kinds of vegetables that taste 'nifty keen' fresh, with the excess stocking the freezer for wintertime. And finally, I'm acknowledged as the #1 expert in the country on candy bars as a result of a book I wrote on the history of the candy bar.

"My wife and I have been married for over forty years, and we've both wondered how we've stood each other so long. As she says, 'It's probably because we both are so lovable, ha, ha.' (My wife has a great sense of humor, and she's a great person, too.)

"We have two grown children, a daughter who's a nurse, and a son, who's a lumberyard foreman. Our biggest baby is still at home. She's our dog, Fergus, whose two loves in life are chasing tennis balls and barking at squirrels. (Fergus, by the way, is a left-pawed dog, no joshing.) She's quite a thoughtful dog, too. Each day, after I've done my stint at the typewriter, Fergus takes me out for a walk in the late afternoon.

"Physically, I'm in great shape: I have arthritis, hypertension, a sinus condition, floating bone chips, etc. Everything is under control, however, as I face each day with a smile when I creak out of bed at 4:45 each morning. (No, I'm not crazy. I just have an early morning biological clock.) I sit down at my typewriter at 7:00 to bang away at manuscripts."

FOR MORE INFORMATION SEE: The New York Times Book Review, June 17, 1979.

O you that are so strong and cold,
O blower, are you young or old?
Are you a beast of field or tree,
Or just a stronger child than me?
  O wind, a-blowing all day long,
  O wind, that sings so loud a song!
          —Robert Louis Stevenson

BROWNE, Richard 1917-
(Dik Browne)

BRIEF ENTRY: Born August 11, 1917, in New York, N.Y. Cartoonist. Since 1954 Browne has collaborated with Mort Walker on the popular syndicated comic strip "Hi and Lois," featuring the gentle humor of a typical suburban family. Browne is also the creator of the equally popular strip "Hägar the Horrible" which began publication in 1973. Its bushy-bearded hero is described by *People* as "history's average Viking: He loots, pillages, drinks and gets in trouble at home." Browne's career as a cartoonist began as a side-step from the profession he had originally intended to pursue—newspaper reporter. As a teenager, he landed a job as copyboy with the *New York Journal.* It was during the trial of gangster Lucky Luciano that Browne made the crossover from newsroom to art department. Having acquired a reputation as a "doodler," he was sent by the city editor to draw pictures of the trial when cameras were barred from the courtroom. In 1941, with the incentive of a larger salary, he joined *Newsweek* as staff artist. After serving in the Army during World War II, he began his association with the Johnstone & Cushing advertising agency where he was responsible for redesigning the Campbell Soup Kids and creating the Chiquita Banana.

Browne is the first cartoonist to have received Reuben awards from the National Cartoonists Society for different comic strips, one each for "Hi and Lois" and "Hägar the Horrible." He is also the recipient of the Banshees Silver Lady award and the Elzie Segar award. Both strips have appeared in their own series of books, under titles such as: *Hi and Lois Family Ties, Hi and Lois in Darkest Suburbia, Hi and Lois: Beware Children at Play, Hägar the Horrible and the Golden Maiden, Hägar's Knight Out, Hägar the Horrible: Sacking Paris on a Budget,* and *The Wit and Wisdom of Hägar the Horrible.* Browne is also the illustrator of two "cautionary" tales for children written by partner Mort Walker, *Most* and *The Land of Lost Things. Address:* c/o King Features, 235 East 45th St., New York, N.Y. 10017. *For More Information See: Authors in the News,* Volume 1, Gale, 1976; *The World Encyclopedia of Comics,* Chelsea House, 1976; *People,* December 11, 1978.

BURNFORD, Sheila (Philip Cochrane Every) 1918-1984
(S. D. Burnford; Sheila Burnford Louisburgh)

*OBITUARY NOTICE—*See sketch in *SATA* Volume 3: Born May 11, 1918 in Scotland; emigrated to Canada in 1951; died of cancer, April 20, 1984, in Bucklers Hard, Hampshire, England. Author of *The Incredible Journey,* the international best-seller that was made into a movie with the same title by Walt Disney. The novel describes the adventures of three animals as they travel across Canada in search of their owners. The book received numerous awards, including the American Library Association's Aurianne Award, 1963, and a Lewis Carroll Shelf Award in 1971. Burnford's other book for children is *Mr. Noah and the Second Flood.* She also wrote *Without Reserve, One Woman's Arctic, Bel Ria,* and *The Fields of Noon,* a collection of autobiographical essays. *For More Information See: Profiles,* Canadian Library Association, 1971; *Children's Literature Review,* Volume 2, Gale, 1976; *Fourth Book of Junior Authors and Illustrators,* H. W. Wilson, 1978; *The Writers Directory 1984-86,* St. James Press, 1983; *Twen-*

tieth-Century Children's Writers, 2nd edition, St. Martin's, 1983. *Obituaries: Washington Post,* May 1, 1984.

CANFIELD, Jane White 1897-1984

*OBITUARY NOTICE—*See sketch in *SATA* Volume 32: Born April 29, 1897, in Syracuse, N.Y.; died of cancer, May 23, 1984, in Bedford, N.Y. Sculptor and author. Canfield studied sculpture in New York City at the Art Students League and in Paris with A. Bourdelle. Her work has been exhibited at the Whitney Museum and the Cornell University Museum; it is also featured in many private collections. Canfield was affiliated with the American Red Cross Arts and Skills Unit, Planned Parenthood, and the Margaret Sanger Bureau. She wrote two children's books, *The Frog Prince: A True Story* and *Swan Cove. For More Information See: Who's Who in American Art,* 15th edition, Bowker, 1982. *Obituaries: New York Times,* May 24, 1984.

CAVIN, Ruth (Brodie) 1918-
(Sally Brodie, Jennie Soble)

PERSONAL: Born October 15, 1918, in Pittsburgh, Pa.; daughter of Abraham Jacob (a salesman) and Jennie (Soble) Brodie; married Bram Cavin (a writer and editor), November 26, 1946; children: Anthony, Emily, Nora. *Education:* Carnegie Institute of Technology (now Carnegie-Mellon University), B.S., 1941. *Politics:* Independent Socialist. *Religion:* None. *Home:* 2 Upland Ter., White Plains, N.Y. 10604. *Agent:* John Schaffner Associates, 425 East 51st St., New York, N.Y. 10022. *Office:* Walker & Co., 720 Fifth Ave., New York, N.Y. 10019.

CAREER: Employed as newsletter editor, public relations writer, researcher for dictionary publisher, and vacuum tube handler, 1942-68; administrative assistant, Longacre Press, 1968-73; Two Continents Publishing Group, New York City, editorial director, 1973-76, vice-president in charge of publicity, 1976-78; Walker & Co., New York City, senior editor, 1979—. *Member:* Authors League of America, Authors Guild.

*WRITINGS—*Juvenile, except as indicated: *Complete Party Dinners for the Novice Cook* (adult), Macmillan, 1965; *Best Restaurants of the United States* (adult), revised edition, Sun River Press, 1970; (adapter) Hans Manz, *Wheeler!* (illustrated by Werner Hofmann), Quist, 1971; (adapter) Ilse Noor, *The House on the Hill,* translated by Carola Lepping, Quist, 1971; *Timothy the Terror,* Quist, 1973; *1 Pinch of Sunshine, ½ Cup of Rain: Natural Food Recipes for Young People* (illustrated by Frances Gruse Scott), Atheneum, 1973; *Trolleys: Riding and Remembering the Electric Interurban Railways* (adult), Hawthorn, 1976; *A Matter of Money: What Do You Do with a Dollar?,* S. G. Philips, 1978; (adapter under pseudonym Sally Brodie) *The Tree Outside My Window,* Cypress, 1978; (adapter under pseudonym Jennie Soble) *Presto!,* Cypress, 1978; *Crossing the Puddle,* Cypress, 1978; (ghost-writer) *New York Divorce Book* (adult), Delacorte, 1980; *Simply Christmas,* Walker, 1980; *Wedding Album,* Walker, 1981; *The Famous Brands Cookbook,* Hammond, 1982.

"Make-a-Books" series: *Picnic Pickles,* Sun River Press, 1974; *The Day It Snowed Colored Snow,* Two Continents, 1974; (under pseudonym Sally Brodie) *Litter, Rubbish, Trash,* Sun

In the Middle Ages . . . all the food that came their way went into a big pot that was kept simmering on the fire all day. ∎ (From *1 Pinch of Sunshine, ½ Cup of Rain* by Ruth Cavin. Illustrated by Frances Gruse Scott.)

River Press, 1975; (under pseudonym Jennie Soble) *Houses That Keep the Weather Out*, Sun River Press, 1975.

Also contributor to *Feasting on Raw Foods*, Rodale; adapter of "Great To-Do" series, Quist. Contributor of articles to *Good Housekeeping*.

WORK IN PROGRESS: A trade book on management.

SIDELIGHTS: "I feel that I am a crafts person, rather than 'a writer,' never having written anything I would particularly admire as more or less literature if I read it somewhere else. The one area in which I really do want to write seriously is playwriting. I have done that (with not an unexpected lack of success) in the past; then it seemed that the American theatre had passed me by, but now we seem to be getting back to the beginning-middle-end play, and I hope to be working on something for the stage very soon. It's percolating at present, in spaces between a quite demanding editing job day-by-day and a number of additional free-lance assignments I unwisely take on.

"I never set out to write for children; it just happened. A friend who is a kind of one-man children's book publishing operation and who produces beautiful books with glorious art in them enlisted my editing help several times. Then he came to me with some books he had bought in foreign languages—the American rights, that is, or English language rights or whatever—and found he hated the text when it was translated for him, but was very happy with the art. I therefore wrote a new story around the existing art. I did this for several of his books; some with author credit; others with 'adapted by' somewhere on the copyright page.

"The four Two Continents/Sun River Press titles on my juvenile list are part of a series I conceived called 'Make-a-Books' Story. 'Make-a-Books' give the reader a text and plenty of white space on each page for the child's own illustrations—drawn, painted, scribbled, cut and pasted, or whatever. Picture 'Make-a-Books' give a series of related pictures with room for a written or dictated text. The young author or artist's name goes on the cover and title page as well."

HOBBIES AND OTHER INTERESTS: Acting (community theater), travel, printing and production, drawing, and the theater.

CHRISTELOW, Eileen 1943-

PERSONAL: Born April 22, 1943, in Washington, D.C.; daughter of Allan (a historian and business executive) and Dorothy (an economist; maiden name, Beal) Christelow; married Albert B. Ahrenholz (a potter), December, 1965; children: Heather. *Education:* University of Pennsylvania, B.A., 1965; graduate study, University of California, Berkeley. *Address:* P.O. Box 1, Marlboro, Vt. 05344. *Agent:* (Illustrations) Dilys Evans, 40 Park Ave., New York, N.Y.

CAREER: Free-lance photographer in Philadelphia, Pa., 1965-71, and graphic designer and illustrator in Berkeley, Calif., 1973-81; author and illustrator of books for children. *Member:* Society of Children's Book Writers. *Awards, honors:* Little Archer Award (Wisconsin), 1983, for *Henry and the Red Stripes.*

WRITINGS—All for children; all self-illustrated: *Henry and the Red Stripes* (Junior Literary Guild selection), Clarion, 1982; *Mr. Murphy's Marvelous Invention* (Junior Literary Guild selection), Clarion, 1983; *Henry and the Dragon* (Junior Literary Guild selection), Clarion, 1984; Thomas Rockwell, *Oatmeal Is Not for Mustaches,* Holt, 1984; Sue Alexander, *Dear Phoebe,* Little, Brown, 1984.

Illustrator: Barbara Dana, *Zucchini* (juvenile), Harper, 1982. Photographs have appeared in *Progressive Architecture, Colloque, Ford Foundation, Home, Media and Method, New York Times Book Review, Pennsylvania Gazette, Youth, Teacher,* and in various textbooks.

WORK IN PROGRESS: Jerome, the Babysitter (self-illustrated) for Clarion; a project for Lothrop.

SIDELIGHTS: "I majored in architecture at the University of Pennsylvania in Philadelphia. While I was there, I discovered the darkroom in the graphics department. I spent more time there than I should have, taking photographs. After graduation, I earned my living as a free-lance photographer, photographing buildings rather than designing them. I also photographed in the Philadelphia public school classrooms, skid row, and Chinatown. I took several trips with my cameras across the United States and one trip to Mexico. My photos appeared in various magazines and textbooks.

"In 1971 my husband and I moved to Cornwall, England, where he apprenticed to potter Michael Cardew. That was also the year our daughter Heather was born.

"When we came back to the United States in 1972, we moved to Berkeley, California, where my husband established a pottery. I found that I was tired of constantly looking at the world through a camera lens, so I began to learn about type, graphic design, and illustration. I eventually started freelancing as a designer producing ads, brochures, catalogues, and books.

"When my daughter was fourteen months old, I decided that I wanted to write and illustrate picture books for young children. For several years my daughter and I researched the problem together, taking weekly trips to the library and reading at naptime and bedtime. I found the picture book format a fascinating and frustrating challenge. I learned about pacing and I learned to keep my text spare. I also found that the years I'd spent as a photographer, trying to capture one photo that would tell an entire story, were invaluable to the process of creating stories with pens and pencils.

"The result of all the years of work and research was that my daughter and I collected a large library of books, she learned to read and write, and at the age of seven wrote and illustrated a book called *The Robbery of Dancer Dog* which won the local

"Perhaps an evil spell was cast on him!" said Mrs. Fox.

"That's more nonsense!" said Mr. Fox.

"I won't cook this rabbit!" shouted Mrs. Fox, stamping her foot. ■ (From *Henry and the Red Stripes* by Eileen Christelow. Illustrated by the author.)

Eileen Christelow and daughter.

library's 'Newcott-Caldeberry' award. And I wrote and illustrated several books—one of which is *Henry and the Red Stripes*.

"The idea for *Henry and the Red Stripes* first came to me when I was half asleep in a hot steamy bath. It had been percolating in the back of my mind for months as I researched and illustrated a poster picturing twenty-six insects, reptiles, birds, and mammals camouflaged in a forest setting. That poster, combined with observing my daughter and her friends decorating themselves with paints and magic markers, led to the creation of Henry Rabbit.

"In 1981 we moved to Marlboro, Vermont, where I continue to take hot steamy baths and to write and illustrate picture books for young children."

CLAMPETT, Bob   1914(?)-1984

OBITUARY NOTICE: Born May 8, about 1914, in San Diego, Calif.; died May 2, 1984, in Detroit, Mich. Cartoonist, animator, writer and director of animated films, lecturer, and author. Creator of the popular cartoon characters Beany and Cecil, Clampett began his career in 1931 as an animator on "Looney Tunes" and "Merry Melody" cartoons for Warner Brothers. Bugs Bunny, Daffy Duck, Tweety Pie, and Porky Pig were among the cartoon characters he helped create. In 1940 he produced "Horton Hatches the Egg," a cartoon adapted from the popular children's book by Dr. Seuss. After resigning from Warner Brothers in 1946, Clampett began working out of a studio in his home. There he created "Time for Beany," a television program using hand puppets to represent cartoon-like, seafaring characters such as Beany Boy, Cecil the Seasick Serpent, Captain Huffenpuff, and the evil Dishonest John. The show ran for five years and was succeeded by the animated cartoon series "The Beany and Cecil Show." The same characters were also featured in a book written and illustrated by

Clampett entitled *Beany*. Clampett received numerous awards for his work as an animator, including three Emmys and an Annie Award from Association Internationale du Film d'Animation. He was also named one of the eight greatest animators by *Mediascene*. *For More Information See: Authors in the News,* Volume 1, Gale, 1976; *New York Times Encyclopedia of Television,* New York Times Book Co., 1977; *The World Encyclopedia of Cartoons,* Volume 1, Gale, 1980; *Who's Who in America,* 42nd edition, Marquis, 1982. *Obituaries: Los Angeles Times,* May 4, 1984.

CLAVERIE, Jean   1946-

PERSONAL: Born January 4, 1946, in Beaune, France; son of Marcel and Jacqueline (Gauthronet) Claverie; married Michelle Nikly (author and illustrator of children's books), July 17, 1973; children: Louis, Francois. *Education:* Attended Ecole des Beaux–Arts de Lyon, 1967, and Arts décoratifs de Genève, 1968-72. *Home:* Montée des Chavannes, Poleymieux au Mont d'or, 69250 Neuville sur Saone, France.

CAREER: Illustrator; artist. Ecole Nationale des Beaux Arts, Lyon, France, professor, 1972—. *Exhibitions:* Children's Book Fair, Bologna, Italy, 1977, 1978; The 13th Exhibition of Original Pictures of International Children's Books, Tokyo, Japan, 1978, The 15th Exhibition, 1980; "L'enfant Lecteur," Bibliotheque de la Part-Dieu, Lyon, France, 1979; "L'illustration dans le livre pour enfants," Maison de la Culture, Saint-Etienne, France, 1979; "L'illustration pour enfants," Maison de la Cul-

JEAN CLAVERIE

(From *Puss in Boots,* retold by Kurt Baumann. Illustrated by Jean Claverie.)

ture, La Rochelle, France, 1979; "10 illustrateurs ou l'art im-aginaire dans l'edition enfantine," C.A.C. Theatre, Angou-leme, France, 1980; "Gens d'images," Espace Lyonnais D'Art Contemporain, Lyon, France, 1981; Centre Georges Pompidou Beaubourg, Paris, France, 1982; Bibliotheque, Chalon S/Saone, France, 1982; Biennale of Illustration, Bratislava, 1986; Bien-nale of Graphic Design, Czechoslovakia, 1986. *Military ser-vice:* French Air Force, 1967-68. *Member:* Syndicat National des Peintres Illustrateurs. *Awards, honors:* Prix Graphique, Loisirs Jeunes, 1982, for *The Princess on the Nut;* award from Bratislava Biennale of Illustration, 1983, for *Three Fairy Tales.*

ILLUSTRATOR: Kurt Baumann, *Le Joueur de Flûte de Ha-melin,* Lotus, 1978, published in America as *The Pied Piper of Hamelin,* Methuen, 1979; Michelle Nikly, *Le Village vert se rebiffe* (title means "Revolt in the Green Village"), Gal-limard, 1978; Jean Tardieu, *Il était une fois, deux fois, trois fois* (title means "Once, Twice . . . upon a Time"), illustrator with J. Tardieu, Gallimard, 1978; K. Baumann, *Le Prince et le luth,* Lotus, 1980, published as *The Prince and the Lute,* Gollancz, 1980; Oscar Wilde, *Le Prince heureux,* Editions Nord-Süd, 1980, published in America as *The Happy Prince,* Oxford University Press, 1981; Isaac Bashevis Singer, *L'Au-berge de la peur* (title means "The Inn of Fear"), Hachette, 1980; Xavier Bied Charreton, *Les Boutons de Bérangère* (title means "Bérangère's Spots"), Bayard–Presse, 1980; Nicole Schneegans, *Le Pêcheur d'oiseaux* (title means "The Bird Fisherman"), Bayard-Presse, 1980; M. Nikly, *La Princesse sur une noix ou le marriage problèmatique du fils de la prin-cesse au pois,* Editions Nord-Süd, 1981, translated by Lucy Meredith published in America as *The Princess on the Nut: or, The Unusual Courtship of the Son of the Princess on the Pea,* Faber & Faber, 1981; K. Baumann, reteller, *Puss in Boots,* Faber & Faber, 1982; Ludwig Bechstein, *Trois Contes,* Edition Nord-Süd, 1982, published as *Three Fairy Tales,* Hutchinson, 1982; Michel Tournier, *Que ma Joie demeure,* Gallimard, 1982; René Escudié, *Les Peurs de Petit-Jean* (title means "Little John's Fears"), Bayard-Presse, 1982; Nicholas de Hirsching, *Le Mot interdit* (title means "The Forbidden Word"), Bayard-Presse, 1982; M. Nikly, *Jeanne et les mots* (title means "Jeanne and the Words"), Albin Michel, 1983; Laurence Ottenheimer, and others, *L'Été* (title means "Sum-mer"), Gallimard, 1984.

WORK IN PROGRESS: Illustrations for Peter Dickinson's *Mole Hole,* Mathew Price's *Peak-a-Boo!,* Hans Christian Andersen's *La Vieille Maison* ("The Old House"), Daniele Monneron, and others' *Un Etonnant Secret* ("The Astonishing Secret"), and Anne Marie Chapouton's *Jeremie peur de rien* ("Jeremie Is Never Frightened"); writing and illustrating a children's story about a little black child living in the U.S. during the 1920s and 1930s who plays the piano and aspires to become a jazzman (tentative title, *Little Lou*).

SIDELIGHTS: "To communicate with children one must either communicate with the child you have been, or communicate with society's image of a child. Since in the last case there is a risk of the message becoming a product, I look for pictures for the child I was. Unfortunately, just like waking after a wonderful dream, I cannot wholly remember myself as a child. How much I would give for one hour with myself at the age of six or eight!

"What recollections are left to me—some intuitions and some pictures—help to build new images. Very often my 'best' pictures fit well with today's children; my children as well as others. Unfortunately they're rare: two or three in a book; the others are only fillers.

"The whole book should become fundamental. I am still far from that, but perhaps I shall reach it by becoming an author? My surroundings are a big help in this search for improvement. I live with Michelle, my wife, who writes the texts I like, and with our children, Louis and Francois, in a tiny village near Lyon."

FOR MORE INFORMATION SEE: Pomme d'Api, August, 1980; *10 Illustrateurs: Arts Imaginaires,* Comité d'Animation Culturelle d'Angouleme, 1980; *Elac Magazine,* October, 1982.

COUSTEAU, Jacques-Yves 1910-

PERSONAL: Born June 11, 1910, in St. Andre-de-Cubzac, France; son of Daniel P. (a lawyer) and Elizabeth (Duranthon) Cousteau; married Simone Melchior, July 12, 1937; children: Jean-Michel, Philippe (deceased). *Education:* French Naval Academy, graduated, 1933. *Residence:* Monaco. *Office:* Cousteau Society, 930 West Twenty-first St., Norfolk, Va. 23517.

CAREER: Undersea explorer, photographer, inventor, and writer. Entered French Navy in 1930; became interested in diving in 1936; began working on underwater breathing apparatus, and with Emile Gagnan developed the aqualung in 1942; founder and head, with Philipe Taillez, of Groupe d'Etudes et Recherches Sous-Marines (Undersea Research Group) of French Navy, 1946-56; Campagnes Océanographiques Francaises, Marseilles, France, founder, president, and chairman, 1950—; Centre d'Etudes Marines Avancées, Marseilles, founder, president, and chairman, 1952—; Institute Océanographique et Musée (Oceanographic Institute and Museum), Monaco, director, 1957—; US Divers Co., Santa Ana, Calif., chairman, 1957—. After World War II founded various marketing, manufacturing, engineering, and research organizations that were incorporated as Cousteau Group in 1973; director of Conshelf Saturation Dive program, 1962—; general secretary of International Commission for the Scientific Exploration of the Mediterranean, 1966—; chairman of Eurocean, 1971-76; founder and president, Cousteau Society, 1973—; corresponding member of the Hellenic Institute of Marine Archaeology, 1975. Inventor of numerous undersea devices, including diving saucers, the Bathygraf cinecamera, deepsea camera sleds, and mini-submarines.

JACQUES-YVES COUSTEAU

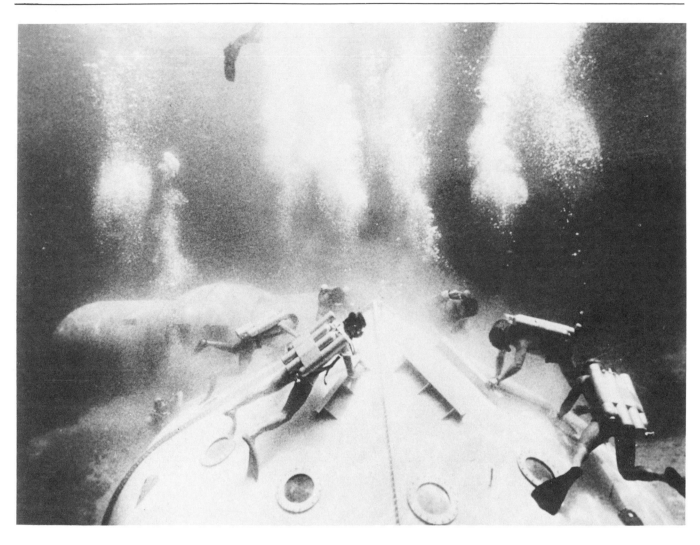

(From the movie "World without Sun," which won the 1964 Academy of Arts and Sciences "Oscar" for best documentary feature.)

Leader of oceanographic research expeditions throughout the world in cooperation with many research institutes and universities, including National Geographic Society, French National Research Center, National Aeronautics and Space Administration, and Texas A & M University. *Military service:* French Navy, 1930-57; resigned with rank of lieutenant commander; member of French underground during World War II; received Croix de Guerre with palm; named Commander, Legion of Honor. *Member:* National Academy of Sciences (United States), Club des Explorateurs of Paris, Indian Academy of Sciences (honorary member).

AWARDS, HONORS: Berthault Prize of the Academy of Sciences, 1958; Gold Medal, National Geographic Society, 1961; Gold Medal, Royal Geographic Society (London), 1963; Washburn Medal, Museum of Science (Boston), 1965; Bradford Prize, Boston Museum of Science, 1965; Potts Medal, Franklin Institute, 1970; D.Sc., Brandeis University, 1970, University of California, Berkeley, 1970, Rensselaer Polytechnic Institute, 1979, Harvard University, 1979, University of Gent, 1983; Gold Medal, Grand Prix d'Océanographie Albert Ier, 1971; Grand medaille d'or (Gold Medal), Société d'encouragement au progrès, 1973; New England Aquarium award, 1973; Prix de la Couronne d'Or, 1973; La Polena della Bravura San Remo, Medaille d'Or avec plaque "Arts-Sci-

ences-Lettres," both 1974; Manley Bendall Prize from Marine Academy, 1975; International Environmental Prize, United Nations, co-recipient, 1977; Gold Medal, New York Zoological Society; named Officier des Arts et Lettres, Officier du Mérite Maritime, Officier du Mérite Agricole, Commandeur du Mérite Sportif; Jean Sainteny Prize and Kiwanis International Prize, both 1980; Lindbergh Award and Neptune Award from American Oceanic Organization, both 1982; Bruno H. Schubert Foundation Prize from the Bruno H. Schubert Foundation and the Wildlife Fund of Germany, 1983.

Film awards, include: Cannes Film Festival awards, 1946, for "Epaves," and 1956, for 'Le Monde du silence''; Motion Picture Academy of Arts and Sciences (Oscar) Awards, 1957, for "The Silent World," 1960, for "Golden Fish," and 1964, for "World without Sun"; National Academy of Television Arts and Sciences (Emmy) Awards, 1970, for "The Desert Whales," 1971, for "The Tragedy of the Red Salmon," "Lagoon of Lost Ships," "The Dragons of Galapagos," "Secrets of the Sunken Caves," and "The Unsinkable Sea Otter," 1972, for "A Sound of Dolphins," 1974, for "Beneath the Frozen World"; Learning Magazine, A.V. (audiovisual) Awards, first place, junior high science level, 1976, and U.S. Industrial Film Festival Gold Camera Award, 1978, both for "Return to the Sea" and "The Liquid Sky"; Gold Cindy Award from the

Information Film Producers of America, 1976, for "To Save a Living Sea"; nominated for the National Academy of Television Arts and Sciences (Emmy) Award, 1977-78, for Outstanding Informational Series, "Oasis in Space"; Chicagoland Film Festival, first place, and Chris Bronze Plaque award, Columbus Film Festival, 1977, both for "The Power Game"; finalist, Black Orca Film Festival, 1978, for "Population Time Bomb" and for "Troubled Waters"; finalist, American Film Festival, 1978, for "Troubled Waters"; Silver Cindy Award from the Information Film Producers of America, 1978, for "The Invisible Multitude."

WRITINGS—All illustrated with own photography; (With Philippe Taillez and Frederic Dumas) *Par dix-huit métres de fond: Histoire d'un film* (title means "Sixty Feet Down: The Story of a Film"), Durel, 1946; *La Plongeé en schaphandre* (title means "Scuba Diving"), Elzevir, 1950; (with F. Dumas) *The Silent World* (Reader's Digest Book Club selection; Book-of-the-Month Club selection), Harper, 1953; (with Jacques Bourcart) *La Mer* (title means "The Sea"), Larousse, 1953; (contributor) John Oliver LaGorce, editor, *Book of Fishes*, National Geographic Society, 1958; (editor with James Dugan) *Captain Cousteau's Underwater Treasury*, Harper, 1959.

(With J. Dugan) *The Living Sea*, Harper, 1963; (compiler) *Bibliographie de la sismique marine* (title means "Bibliography of Marine Seismology"), Oceanographic Institute (Monaco), 1964; *Le Monde sans Soleil*, Hachette, 1964, English-language version edited by J. Dugan, published as *Jacques-Yves Cousteau's World without Sun*, Harper, 1965; (with Y. Paccalet) *Saumons, Castors et Loutres*, Flammarion, 1978; (with Y. Paccalet) *La Vie au bout du Monde*, Flammarion, 1979; (with Y. Paccalet) *Les Surprises de la Mer*, Flammarion, 1980; *Le Monde des Océans*, Robert Laffont, 1980; (with Y. Paccalet) *A la recherche de l'Atlantide*, Flammarion, 1981; *Pianeta Mare* (title means "Water Planet"), Fabbri, 1981; *Almanach Cousteau de l'Environnement*, Robert Laffont, 1981; (with H. Jacquier) *Francais, on a volé ta mer*, Robert Laffont, 1981; (with Y. Paccalet) *Le destin du Nil*, Flammarion, 1982; (with Y. Paccalet) *Fortunes de Mer*, Flammarion, 1983; *Jacques Cousteau's Calypso*, Abrams, 1983; *Jacques Cousteau's Amazon Journey*, Abrams, 1984.

"Undersea Discovery" series; all published by Doubleday, except as noted: (With son, Philippe Cousteau) *Les Requins*, Flammarion, 1970, translation by Francis Price published as *The Shark: Splendid Savage of the Sea* (ALA Best Young Adult Book), 1970; (with Philippe Diole) *Un Trésor englouti*, Flammarion, 1971, translation by J. F. Bernard published as *Diving for Sunken Treasure*, 1971; (with P. Diole) *La Vie et mort des coraux*, Flammarion, 1971, translation by J. F. Bernard published as *Life and Death in a Coral Sea* (ALA Best Young Adult Book), 1971; (with P. Diole) *Nos Amies les baleines*, Flammarion, 1972, translation by J. F. Bernard published as

They swim round and round, butting the trap. It rolls away with its unattainable inmates. We can sit in the front row of this farce and the big ones pay no attention to us. If fish can be angry, these are madder than hornets. ■ (From *Jacques-Yves Cousteau's World without Sun*, edited by James Dugan.)

The Whale: Mighty Monarch of the Sea, 1972; (with P. Diole) *Pieuvres: La Fin d'un malentendu,* Flammarion, 1973, translation by J. F. Bernard published as *Octopus and Squid: The Soft Intelligence,* 1973; (with P. Diole) *Trois Aventures de la Calypso,* Flammarion, 1973, translation by J. F. Bernard published as *Three Adventures: Galapagos, Titicaca, the Blue Holes,* 1973; (with P. Diole) *Compagnons de la plongée,* Flammarion, 1974, translation by J. F. Bernard published as *Diving Companions: Sea Lion, Elephant Seal, Walrus,* 1974; (with P. Diole) *Les Dauphins et la liberté,* Flammarion, 1975, translation by J. F. Bernard published as *Dolphins,* 1975; *The Ocean World,* Abrams, 1979; (with the Cousteau Society staff) *The Cousteau Almanac,* 1981.

"The Ocean World," encyclopedia series; all published by World Publishing, 1972-74, except as noted; all revised editions published by Abrams, 1975, except as noted: Volume I: *Oasis in Space;* Volume II: *The Act of Life;* Volume III: *Quest for Food;* Volume IV: *Window in the Sea;* Volume V: *The Art of Motion;* Volume VI: *Attack and Defense;* Volume VII: *Invisible Messages;* Volume VIII: *Instinct and Intelligence;* Volume IX: *Pharoahs of the Sea;* Volume X: *Mammals of the Sea;* Volume XI: *Provinces of the Sea;* Volume XII: *Man Reenters the Sea;* Volume XIII: *A Sea of Legends: Inspiration from the Sea;* Volume XIV: *The Adventure of Life,* Volume XV: *Outer and Inner Space;* Volume XVI: *The White Caps;* Volume XVII: *Riches of the Sea;* Volume XVIII: *Challenges of the Sea;* Volume XIX: *The Sea in Danger;* Volume XX: *Guide to the Sea and Index;* Volume XXI: *Calypso,* Abrams, 1978.

THEATRICAL FILMS: "Par Dix-huit Mètres de fond," 1942; "Epaves," 1945, released in U.S. as "Danger under the Sea," 1952; "Paysages du silence," 1947; "Autour d'un récif," 1948, released in U.S. as "Rhythm on the Reef," 1952; "Carnets de plongées," 1949; "Une Plongée de rubis," 1949; "Le Monde du silence," 1956, released in U.S. as "The Silent World"; (and producer) "Histoire d'un poisson rouge," 1960, released in U.S. as "Golden Fish"; "Le Monde sans soleil,"

1964, released in U.S. as "World without Sun"; "The Undersea World of Jacques-Yves Cousteau," 1967; "Voyage to the Edge of the World," 1975.

Writer of "Pulse of the Sea" monthly column, *Saturday Review,* 1976—; contributor to magazines, including *National Geographic.*

TELEVISION: "The World of Jacques-Yves Cousteau," CBS Special, April 28, 1966.

"The Undersea World of Jacques Cousteau" a series based on Cousteau's expeditions around the world, ABC-TV, 1968-76: "Sharks," January 8, 1968; "The Savage World of the Coral Jungle," March 6, 1968; "Search in the Deep," April 15, 1968; "Whales," November 15, 1968; "The Unexpected Voyage of Pepito and Cristobal," January 13, 1969; "Sunken Treasure," March 4, 1969; "The Legend of Lake Titicaca," April 23, 1969; "The Desert Whales," December 4, 1969; "The Night of the Squid," January 15, 1970; "The Return of the Sea Elephant," February 8, 1970; "Those Incredible Diving Machines," February 20, 1970; "The Water Planet," March 28, 1970; "The Tragedy of the Red Salmon," November 23, 1970; "Lagoon of Lost Ships," January 11, 1971; "The Dragons of Galapagos," February 24, 1971; "Secrets of the Sunken Caves," March 19, 1971; "The Unsinkable Sea Otter!," September 26, 1971; "Octopus, Octopus," December 21, 1971; "The Forgotten Mermaids," January 24, 1972; "A Sound of Dolphins," February 25, 1972; "The Smile of the Walrus," November 15, 1972; "500 Million Years Beneath the Sea," January 11, 1973; "Hippo!," February 16, 1973; "The Singing Whale," March 12, 1973; "South to Fire and Ice," November 29, 1973; "The Flight of Penguins," January 21, 1974; "Beneath the Frozen World," March 3, 1974; "Blizzard at Hope Bay," March 22, 1974; "Life at the End of the World," November 14, 1974; "Beavers of the North Country," January 6, 1975; "The Coral Divers of Corsica," February 21, 1975; "The Sleeping Sharks of Yucatan," April 6, 1975; "The Sea

. . . Headquarters building, . . . "Starfish House," . . . is 35 feet in diameter, sleeps eight, and contains kitchen, dining space, biological laboratory and photo lab. ■ (From *Jacques-Yves Cousteau's World without Sun,* edited by James Dugan.)

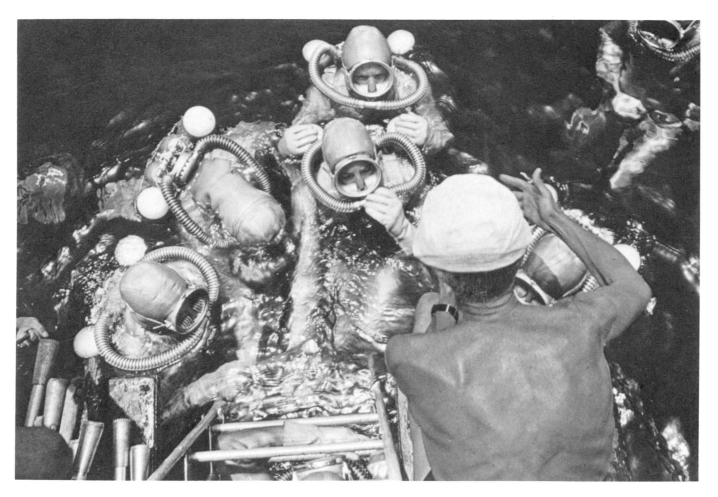

The Oceanauts in silver suits listen to Captain Cousteau's final instructions . . . . They wear shining silver in order to be picked out quickly in torch beams during night dives . . . . ■ (From *Jacques-Yves Cousteau's World without Sun,* edited by James Dugan.)

Birds of Isabela,'' December 8, 1975; ''Mysteries of the Hidden Reefs,'' April 18, 1976; ''The Fish That Swallowed Jonah,'' May 23, 1976; ''The Incredible March of the Spiny Lobsters,'' May 30, 1976.

''Oasis in Space'' series, PBS-TV, 1977: ''What Price Progress?''; ''Grain of Conscience''; ''Troubled Waters''; ''Population Time Bomb''; ''The Power Game''; ''Visions of Tomorrow.''

''The Cousteau Odyssey'' series, PBS-TV, except as noted, 1977-84: ''Calypso's Search for the Britannic,'' November 22, 1977; ''Diving for Roman Plunder,'' March 14, 1978; ''Calypso's Search for Atlantis,'' Part I, May 1, 1978, Part II, May 2, 1978; ''Blind Prophets of Easter Island,'' December 6, 1978; ''Time Bomb at Fifty Fathoms,'' March 6, 1979; ''Mediterranean: Cradle or Coffin?,'' May 27, 1979; ''The Nile,'' Part I, December 9, 1979, Part II, December 10, 1979; ''Lost Relics of the Sea,'' March 12, 1980; ''Clipperton: The Island Time Forgot,'' 1981; ''The Warm-Blooded Sea: Mammals of the Deep,'' March 24, 1982; ''Calypso Countdown: Rigging for the Amazon,'' Turner Broadcasting System, 1982; (with the National Film Board of Canada) ''Cries from the Deep,'' 1982; (with the National Film Board of Canada) ''St. Lawrence: Stairway to the Sea,'' 1982; ''Cousteau/Amazon Voyage to a Thousand Rivers,'' 1984; ''Cousteau/Amazon,

The New El Dorado: Invaders and Exiles,'' 1984; ''Cousteau/Amazon River of the Future,'' 1984.

ADAPTATIONS—Selected films and filmstrips derived from Cousteau television films: ''The Undersea World of Jacques Cousteau,'' 21 shortened versions of the television series, available with study guides, Churchill Films, 1977, including: ''Beneath the Frozen World''; ''Coral Jungle''; ''Desert Whales''; ''500 Million Years Beneath the Sea''; ''The Flight of Penguins''; ''The Green Sea Turtle''; ''The Legend of Lake Titicaca''; ''The Night of the Squid''; ''Octopus, Octopus''; ''The Return of the Sea Elephants''; ''The Sea Birds of Isabela''; ''Seals''; ''Sharks''; ''The Singing Whale''; ''The Sound of Dolphins''; ''Sunken Treasure''; ''Those Incredible Diving Machines''; ''The Tragedy of the Red Salmon''; ''The Unsinkable Sea Otter''; ''The Water Planet''; ''Whales.''

Filmstrips produced by Walt Disney Production, 1981: ''Cousteau Oceanography'' series: ''The Water Planet,'' Set I, five filmstrips with five cassettes or records and a teacher's guide (includes ''Return to the Sea,'' ''To Save a Living Sea,'' ''The Liquid Sky,'' ''A Sea of Motion,'' and ''The Invisible Multitude''), Set II, five filmstrips with five cassettes or records and a teacher's guide (includes ''Anatomy of an Ocean,'' ''The Infinite Variety,'' ''The Act of Life,'' ''Time and the Sea,'' and ''The Survivors''); ''Undersea Exploration,'' four film-

(From the documentary film "Cries from the Deep," which aired as an episode of the television series "The Cousteau Odyssey." Presented on PBS-TV, April, 1982.)

strips with four cassettes and a teacher's guide (includes "Man Enters the Sea," "Conquest of the Depths," "Freedom Underwater," and "Living Under the Sea"); "Rivers: Roots of the Ocean," five filmstrips with five cassettes and a teacher's guide (includes "The River Falls: The Amazon," "The River Returns: The Thames," "The River Begins: The Colorado," "The River Rises: The Nile," and "The River Flows: The Mississippi"); "The Life of Fishes," six filmstrips with six cassettes and a teacher's guide (includes "The Shaping of Life," "The Range of Life," "The Undersea Ecosystems," "Survival," "The Roots of Intelligence," and "The Fragile Balance").

Filmstrips produced by Walt Disney Productions, 1982: "Island Earth: Lessons in Human Ecology," ten filmstrips with ten cassettes and a teacher's guide (includes "Connections Among Living Things," "How Nature Cycles Material," "How Valuable is Nature?," "Growth of Living Communities," "National Limits to Growth," "Sharing a Natural Resource," "Using a Resource Wisely," "Balancing Ecology with Development," "Protecting Natural Diversity," and "Managing Resources in the Future").

SIDELIGHTS: **June 11, 1910.** Born in St. André-de-Cubzac, a village near Bordeaux, France. The little town was chosen as Cousteau's birthplace because his parents had both been born there.

1920. Father brought the family to New York for a year, where Cousteau learned to play baseball, went to summer camp in Vermont, and learned fluent English. Even as a boy, Cousteau was inventive. At the age of eleven, he built a four-foot model of a 200-ten marine crane, adding a movement to the crane that was a patentable improvement.

1930. Entered the French Naval Academy.

1932. Midshipman on board the *Jeanne d'Arc*.

1933-1935. Took part in numerous campaigns in the Far East aboard the cruiser *Primauguet*.

1935. Trained to become a Navy flier until a serious car accident ended his career in aviation.

1936. Served as a gunnery officer, using his free time to start a series of diving experiments.

1937. Married Simone Melchior, the daughter of a French naval officer. The couple lived in a modern apartment in Toulon. As Cousteau's wife recalled: "It didn't stay neat and clean long. In ten months Jean-Michel [first son] came along. And Jacques was experimenting with underwater rubber suits which smelled awful. One day two nuns collecting for charity rang our bell. Jacques opened the door wearing a white rubber diving suit. The poor things ran away screaming." ["She Lives with Adventure," *McCall's*, January, 1956.[1]]

1942. Joined the French Underground after the fall of France during World War II. His work for the Allies won him the Legion d' Honneur and the Croix de Guerre. While serving the Allies, Cousteau continued to dive in the Mediterranean, spying on the Germans and working to perfect his diving gear. "The Germans considered me a harmless nut. And I did all I could to reinforce the impression." ["The Wet World of Jacques-Yves Cousteau," *The Saturday Evening Post*, November/December, 1973.[2]]

That same year he developed with Emile Gagnan the first regulated, compressed air-breathing device for deep-sea diving (the aqualung). ". . . When I dive in the clearest of sea waters the greatest distance at which I can identify an object is 100 feet. With or without any kind of artificial light a diver is imprisoned, as far as vision is concerned, in a bubble of perception only a few dozen feet in diameter. Most fish, most marine animals, are at best in the same situation, but they have developed other senses to extend tremendously their 'spheres of perception,' and those senses are mainly based on acoustics, pressure waves, or smell.

"Underwater man has good hearing, but no echo-location system, no nerves sensitive to slight pressure waves, no smell at all. When diving, man suddenly realizes and appreciates how overwhelmingly dependent his race is upon its sense of vision. He realizes why nothing else—not the loss of hearing, not the loss of an arm or a leg—can be compared with the loss of sight.

"Years of direct or indirect visual exploration of the seas with Aqualung, with photographic sleds, with Diving Saucers or bathyscaphs or with Dr. Harold Edgerton's automatic cameras have revealed to me that the ocean is like a gigantic layer-cake with occasional raisins or cherries included in it. The overall horizontal stratification of the sea comprises layers of water, transparent or turbid, that are either of a different temperature and salinity, or in which dead particles remain in suspension, or in which planktonic creatures struggle for their miniscule lives. The fruits of the cake are concentrations of larger living creatures, like schools of squid or clouds of shrimp, each one a rare oasis in a three-dimensional liquid desert. But the concentrations disperse and regroup farther away, and the layers constantly move up and down, under the influence of the sun. Everywhere in the ocean, at dawn, trillions of tons of creatures sink from the surface to the 'twilight zone' hundreds of meters below, as if shy of light. After sunset all the multitude rushes back to the surface. This huge daily vertical migration, the 'pulse of the oceans,' is triggered by light alone, light mother of life through photosynthesis, light manufacturer or our oxygen, light architect of beauty." [Jacques Cousteau, *The Ocean World of Jacques Cousteau*, Volume IV: *Window in the Sea*, World Publishing, 1973.[3]]

1944-1949. Organized the first French undersea unit, which revolutionized and perfected free diving techniques and underwater photography.

1950. Formed a non-profit organization which bought the ship *Calypso*, a 360-ton, converted British navy minesweeper. It is crammed with laboratories, diving gear, cranes, diving saucers, cameras, and, for much of the year it cruises the world, exploring the seas. "*Calypso* was ready for her first working cruise in the autumn of 1951. We had long since decided that the maiden voyage would take her to the Red Sea. It was virtually unexplored, transparent, and not too far away. It had the reputation of being a nice hot bathtub full of sharks, and it was a coral sea. We sought out scientists who would like to use divers and submarine photography on a Red Sea project. Such an offer appeared to be completely unheard-of; for the first time a research ship was looking for scientists rather than vice versa.

"On this first voyage *Calypso* acquired a buoyant personality that has never left her. I decided from the beginning that those on board were companions in the adventure, whatever their jobs might be. There was no officers' mess; we all ate together. During the tumultuous and jocose mealtimes we discussed plans,

(From the movie "The Golden Fish," which won the Academy of Arts and Sciences "Oscar" for best live-action short-subject film in 1960. Produced by Jacques Cousteau. Released by Columbia Pictures, 1959.)

made decisions, and learned from each other. No one shouted orders, and no one wore anything resembling a uniform. Pride of outfit began to develop, expressed in customs of our own: a bawdy *Calypso* song, a perpetual funny-hat contest, and a distinctive cry of recognition that sounded something like *Hooooooo* (falsetto) *Hop!* (guttural)—copies from the call of a Fiji Island bird. We borrowed the latter from a friendly Marseilles bark, *Hou-Hop,* that sometimes joined *Calypso* on diving stations. We greeted each other as *'Professeur'* or *'Docteur,'* unless the person addressed held such a degree, in which case he was called *'Monsieur.'*

"Our godfather was the Napoleonic marshal Pierre Combronne, whose portrait hung in the mess. We chose him because of his reply to Wellington's demand for the surrender of the Old Guard at Waterloo. *'Merde,'* said Cambronne. It had no nationalistic meaning for us; it simply expressed the attitude with which we tried to meet adversity.

"*Calypso* lacked certain ship's traditions, including rats. We have never seen one aboard, although once we had a rat scare. We were back in Toulon from the Indian Ocean, and Henri Plé was alone on board. He heard gnawing sounds belowdecks and traced them to the bilge. He found a big red coconut crab eating a champagne crate. The crab was from the Seychelles Islands, five thousand miles away. It had consumed six crates during the voyage, but could not broach the bottles to wash them down.

"*Calypso* carried a three-ton stainless-steel wine tank, which amused foreign oceanographers, some of whom travel on wretched craft without a drop aboard. Calypsonians could drink as much as they liked: average daily wine consumption per capita was about a pint.

"I wanted *Calypso* to be an international exploring ship with a French cadre. James Dugan was the first of many Americans

to sail with us. Dr. Melville Bell Grosvenor of the National Geographic Society, a seasoned salt-water sailor, became interested in our work. The Research and Exploration Committee of the society voted financial support of Calypso Expeditions, which has been renewed annually in the decade since. The Edo Corporation, a key U.S. firm in aviation and marine electronics, contributed its elegant UQN sonar apparatus after its president, Noel McLean, read *The Silent World* and thought we should have one." [Jacques Cousteau and James Dugan, *The Living Sea,* Harper, 1963.[4]]

1951. Collaborated with André Laban to perfect the first underwater camera equipment for television. The following year Cousteau created the Centre d'Etudes Marines Avancées, a corporation designed to develop underwater equipment.

1953. *The Silent World* published. The book has been published in twenty-two languages and has sold more than three million copies in the English language alone. "The sea is a most silent world. I say this deliberately on long accumulated evidence and aware that wide publicity has recently been made on the noises of the sea. Hydrophones have recorded clamors that have been sold as phonographic curiosa, but the recordings have been grossly amplified. It is not the reality of the sea as we have known it with naked ears. There are noises under water, very interesting ones that the sea transmits exceptionally well, but a diver does not hear boiler factories.

"An undersea sound is so rare that one attaches great importance to it. The creatures of the sea express fear, pain and joy without audible comment. The old round of life and death passes silently, save among the mammals—whales and porpoises." [Captain J. Y. Cousteau and Frederick Dumas, *The Silent World,* Harper, 1953.[5]]

In 1956 a film of the same title and based on his book won the grand prize of the Cannes International Film Festival and in 1957 the film won a Motion Picture Academy award. "Since the early years still and motion-picture photography have come a long way both above and below the sea's surface. After 1943 the Aqualung gave divers freedom and mobility and allowed them time to make true motion pictures underwater.

"With fast film and strong artificial lights it became possible to make them in color. In 1956 our first full-length underwater color film released commercially, *The Silent World,* introduced movie audiences to the startling beauty of the sea's inhabitants and landscapes. Today underwater photography is the hobby of thousands and an invaluable tool for marine scientists studying underwater life, geological formations, and other subaquatic phenomena."[3]

1957. Retired from the Navy with the rank of Captain of Corvette. Devoting himself full time to various marine interests, he was elected director of the Musée Océanographique of Monaco.

1959. With Jean Mollard invented the "Diving Saucer," a round, highly maneuverable submarine, capable of diving to a depth of 350 meters, permitting two passengers to film and observe the ocean. "Although the Aqualung had enabled us to explore the ocean down to the 'twilight zone,' it did so for too short a time and didn't let us go deep enough. In pondering these problems we realized the need for a unique and specialized undersea vehicle. The result was the 'Diving Saucer' or *soucoupe plongante*—a radical departure from the traditional submarine and one that would enable us to explore deeper and longer than the Aqualung could and still to be almost as ma-

Jacques Cousteau (left) with son, Philippe.

neuverable as a diver. The six-foot diameter, five-foot high circular vehicle has ten eyes—three optical ports for overhead viewing, two forward-looking ports for pilot and passenger, two photo ports, and three sonar ports—beamed up, down, and forward. Jet nozzles powered by special batteries provide propulsion and lateral steering in any direction, while mercury ballast helps steer the Saucer upward or downward. The pilot lies comfortably on a mattress with all controls at fingertips, including buttons for cameras, lights, and tape recorder. To see, to explore, the pilot can 'turn the Saucer' almost as easily as a diver can turn his head.''[5]

1962. Developed his first home under the sea, ''Conshelf One'', in the area of Marseilles. This first deep-sea experimental ''house'' was a 17-by-8-foot steel cylinder, 33 feet deep in the Mediterranean, which housed two men for a week. It was followed by another experimental ''home,'' which sheltered five men for a month 36 feet below the Red Sea in June, 1963. ''Conshelf Two'' consists of four prefabricated steel structures, several fish pens, and some antishark cages. Above us rides our utility ship *Rosaldo,* which suppies the undersea hamlet with compressed air, electricity, fresh water, food, and medical care—in short, with life. Above us also is our research vessel *Calypso,* serving as liaison ship.

''This is the second Conshelf experiment we have conducted. In Conshelf One . . . two men lived and worked for a week

in much smaller quarters. . . . Now we have launched a much more ambitious expedition, with more men. . . .

''We chose to plant Conshelf Two in the inhospitable Red Sea because it was far away, hot, and hard to supply. If we could build and maintain a sea-bottom station there, we could do it almost anyplace in the world'' [Capt. Jacques Cousteau, ''At Home in the Sea,'' *National Geographic,* April, 1964.[6]]

The third ''house under the sea,'' Conshelf Three was manned in 1965 and permitted six men to live and work during three weeks at a depth of 100 meters.

1964. Wrote *World without Sun,* which was adapted into an award-winning motion picture.

1968. First of over fifty television films about Cousteau's expeditions around the world was shown on ABC-TV. The television series, ''The Undersea World of Jacques Cousteau,'' became the highest rated documentary series in broadcasting history. ''My decision to go into television entailed a sacrifice. An esthetic sacrifice, compared to what can be done in full-length motion pictures. But one television show reaches more people in three months than ten years of 'Gone with the Wind.'

''It's a way to reach many more million of people; and when one person, for whatever reasons, has a chance to lead an

(From *Jacques-Yves Cousteau's World without Sun,* edited by James Dugan.)

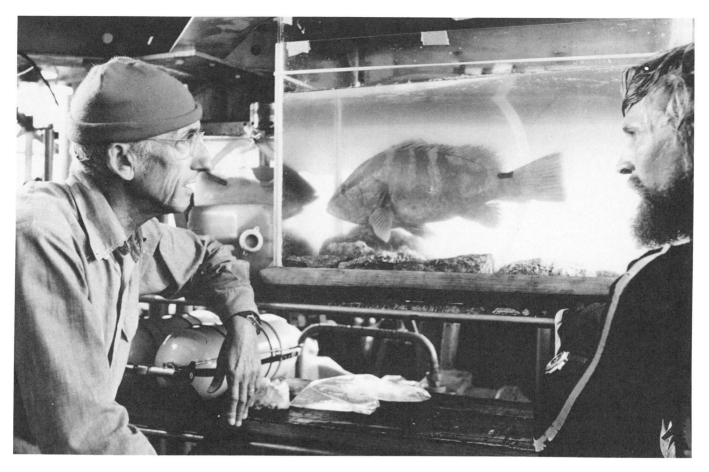

(From "The Fish That Swallowed Jonah" episode of the television series "The Undersea World of Jacques Cousteau." Presented on ABC-TV, May 23, 1976.)

exceptional life, he has no right to keep it to himself!'' [Dan Rosen, ''A Week Aboard the *Calypso*,'' *TV Guide*, April 24, 1976.[7]]

1973. Founded the Cousteau Society in order to foster public opinion about the need to save the oceans from pollution. ''. . . Just now, in our generation, when after many thousands of years of ignorance and superstitions man is at last beginning to learn about managing and exploiting the vast resources of 70 per cent of earth's surface, he finds himself in a race against time to rescue it from his own spoilations.

''. . . The ocean can die—and . . . we want to make sure that it doesn't. Man exists only because his home-planet, Earth, is the one celestial body we know of where life is at all possible. And life is possible on earth because earth is a 'water planet'—water being a compound itself probably as rare in the universe as life, perhaps even synonymous with life. Water is not only rare, not only infinitely precious—it is peculiar, with many oddities in its physical and chemical make-ups. It is out of this unique nature of water, interacting with the dynamics of the world 'water system' of which the sun and the ocean are the motors, that life originated. The ocean is life.'' [Jacques Cousteau, *The Ocean World of Jacques Cousteau*, Volume I: *Oasis in Space*, World Publishing, 1972.[8]]

The Cousteau Society is a non-profit, membership-supported, environmental organization dedicated to the protection and im-

provement of life. The society believes that only an informed and alerted public can best make the choices to provide a healthier and more productive way of life for itself and for future generations. To this end, the society produces television films for national and public networks, filmstrips and books for high schools and colleges, books on important marine and environmental issues for the public; it organizes lectures throughout the United States and publishes articles and columns in various periodicals for distribution throughout the world. The society also conducts educational programs in the marine sciences that involve on-the-scene exploration of ocean habitats.

1977. *Calypso* completed the first survey of the entire Mediterranean basin—a ''health report'' that will serve as a base line for future comparison. Cousteau Society crews teamed up with scientists from the eighteen-country International Commission for the Scientific Exploration of the Mediterranean to complete this study.

1979. A scientific investigation and survey of the Venezuelan coastline delta area, and Maracaibo Lake region was completed. The extensive study will help determine policy for coastline development and fishing regulations. It has implications for the health of the entire Caribbean region, since the principle Atlantic currents feeding this tropical sea pass along the Venezuelan coast before entering the Caribbean.

June 28, 1979. Son, Philippe, died in a seaplane accident near Alverca, Portugal, at the age of thirty-nine.

1980. *Calypso* visited a critical waterway, the St. Lawrence Seaway system, and examined the life and health of this freshwater highway from its headwaters in the Great Lakes to the Gulf of St. Lawrence and beyond to the region of the Atlantic near Newfoundland where it merges with the sea.

1981. Creation of the Foundation Cousteau in France, a nonprofit environmental organization, having the same goals as The Cousteau Society in the United States.

1982. Began a fifteen-month expedition to study the plant and animal life of the Amazon. ''This is the greatest and most difficult expedition I have ever undertaken, surpassing even my Antarctic trip [1972].'' [*New York Times*, January 10, 1982.[9]]

''If we can bring back answers to what nature is without men, what it is with men and in what extent Indian tradition of nature exploitation has influenced it, then we may be able to provide better means to develop the region.'' [*New York Times*, June 7, 1982.[10]]

1983. The *Calypso* and Captain Cousteau explored the Mississippi River. ''The river cannot be separated from the people who live with it and the culture it supports. Our film about the Mississippi will be a story of the river told by the people themselves.

''We humans are a young species on earth, experimenting and learning about our surroundings. The objective of The Cousteau Society is to witness what Americans have learned from their great Mississippi experiment and to determine how this information can help all of our fellow voyagers on our water planet.'' [''Cousteau Society News,'' *Calypso Log Dispatch*, Volume 5, Number 5, edited by Judith Anderson, October, 1983.[11]]

The Cousteau Society developed and designed a windship, *Moulin à Vent*. The catamaran, bearing the aspirated-cylinder prototype propulsion system developed by the Cousteau team, made its first Transatlantic test voyage in 1983.

1984. ''Journey to a Thousand Rivers,'' the first of a three-part series for television, was shown. The television specials were based on the Amazon expedition of 1982-1984.

FOR MORE INFORMATION SEE—Books: Captain J. Y. Cousteau and Frederick Dumas, *The Silent World*, Harper, 1953; James Dugan, *Undersea Explorer: The Story of Captain Cousteau* (juvenile), Harper, 1957; Philip Dunaway and George De Kay, editors, *Turning Point*, Random House, 1958; Frederick Wagner, *Famous Underwater Adventurers*, Dodd, 1962; Jacques Cousteau and James Dugan, *The Living Sea*, Harper, 1968; Muriel Guberlet, *Explorers of the Sea*, Ronald, 1964; Terry Shannon, *Saucer in the Sea* (juvenile), Golden Gate, 1965; John Canning, editor, *100 Great Adventures*, Taplinger, 1969; Ross R. Olney, *Men Against the Sea*, Grosset, 1969; Robert Elliot, *Banners of Courage* (juvenile), Platt & Munk, 1972; Jacques Cousteau, *The Ocean World of Jacques Cousteau*, Volume I: *Oasis in Space*, World Publishing, 1972, Volume IV: *Window in the Sea*, World Publishing, 1973.

Articles: *Science Illustrated*, December, 1948; *Life*, November 27, 1950; *New York Herald Tribune Book Review*, February 22, 1953; *New York Times Book Review*, February 22, 1953, April 28, 1963; *Seventeen*, February, 1955; *Holiday*, September, 1955; *McCall's*, January, 1956; *Nature*, January 12, 1957;

Time, March 28, 1960; *Cosmopolitan*, January, 1960; *New York Times Magazine*, April 21, 1963; *Christian Science Monitor*, April 25, 1963, October 13, 1981; *New York Herald Tribune*, April 28, 1963; *National Geographic*, April, 1964, December, 1981; *l'Express*, August 4-10, 1960; *Best Sellers*, November 15, 1970; *Reader's Digest*, November, 1973; *Detroit Free Press*, December 16, 1973, May 26, 1976; *The American Way*, August, 1974; *Pittsburgh Press*, March 2, 1975; *Parade Magazine*, March 16, 1975; *People*, September 15, 1975; *TV Guide*, April 24, 1976; *Saturday Review*, July 10, 1976; *New York Times*, January 10, 1982, June 7, 1982; *Calypso Log Dispatch*, Volume 5, Number 5, edited by Judith Anderson, October, 1983.

CROOK, Beverly Courtney

PERSONAL: Born in Baltimore, Md.; daughter of Robert A. (a stockbroker) and Edith (a store owner; maiden name, Lamberth) Courtney; married Compton N. Crook (a professor; died, 1981); children: Judy, Stephen, Leslie. *Education:* Towson State University, B.S., Johns Hopkins University, M.L.A. 1973. *Politics:* Independent. *Religion:* Protestant. *Home:* 2829 Merryman's Mill Rd., Phoenix, Md. 21131.

CAREER: Elementary schoolteacher in Baltimore City Public Schools, Baltimore, Md.; Towson State University, Alumni Association, Towson, Md., executive director and editor, about 1960-70. Has also been employed as a tutor and instructor in writing and typing. Active in numerous conservation groups. *Member:* Authors Guild, Society of Children's Book Writers.

BEVERLY COURTNEY CROOK

(Jacket illustration by Tom Huffman from *Invite a Bird to Dinner* by Beverly Courtney Crook.)

WRITINGS—All for young readers: *April's Witches* (fiction), Steck, 1971; *Invite a Bird to Dinner: Simple Feeders You Can Make* (craftsbook; illustrated by Tom Huffman), Lothrop, 1978; *Fair Annie of Old Mule Hollow* (fiction), McGraw-Hill, 1978. Also contributor of short stories to various children's magazines.

WORK IN PROGRESS: "Since the long illness and subsequent death of my husband, I have been unable to write. However, ideas are now beginning to stir."

SIDELIGHTS: "I am a native Marylander who has traveled widely, but all roads have led back to Maryland. I now live in the middle of a woods that is a wildlife refuge. Although it is a lovely setting, there are drawbacks: wild critters of various sorts have been encouraged to take up residence here, but when raccoons turn over the trash cans, groundhogs burrow in the bean patch, and deer nibble the lettuce, I am tempted to pull in the welcome mat. Still, that is a small price to pay for living so close to nature. Actually the local politicians are a much bigger problem. They persist in believing that 'progress' means a shopping mall on every corner.

"In my travels, I like to get away from cities and into remote areas. I especially like to visit Africa where I can observe the wildlife in its natural habitat—before it vanishes.

"When I was first married, my husband, an underpaid biology teacher at the time, worked for the National Park Service during summer vacations. From June until September, we lived high in the Rockies in a tiny one-room cabin with a big wood stove, one cold-water faucet—and an outhouse over the hill. (A trip there at night, with the possibility of meeting a bear along the way, was not undertaken lightly.) But the magnificent surroundings more than compensated for lack of any creature comforts, and awakened in me a deep interest in conservation. It is not surprising that this interest colors my writings, and I hope that some of it rubs off on my readers.

"I have always liked to write, but most of my writing was job-related nonfiction. Then my husband, who wrote fiction under a pen name, urged me to try writing for children. I finally took his advice and discovered, rather belatedly, that this was the type of writing that I really wanted to do.

"My primary goal in writing is to entertain, but with the hope that perhaps a new awareness or understanding will come about through the entertainment."

CROSS, Gillian (Clare)   1945-

PERSONAL: Born December 24, 1945, in London, England; daughter of (James) Eric (a scientist and musician) and Joan (an English teacher; maiden name, Manton) Arnold; married Martin Cross (an examinations director of the Royal Society

GILLIAN CROSS

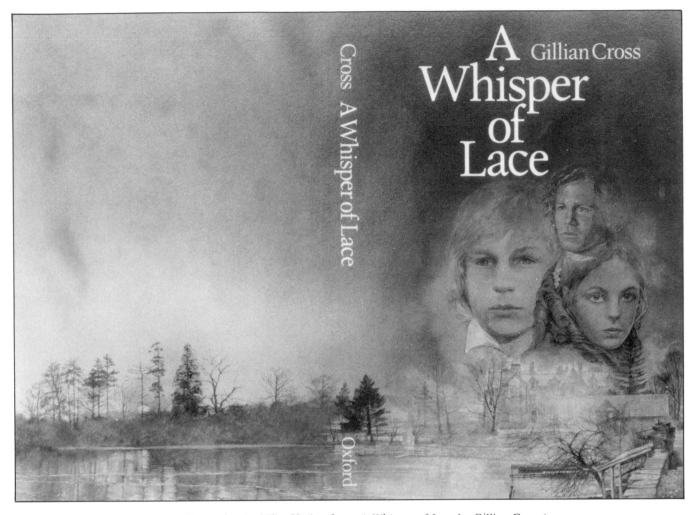

(Jacket illustration by Mike Heslop from *A Whisper of Lace* by Gillian Cross.)

of Arts), May 10, 1967; children: Jonathan George, Elizabeth Jane, Colman Anthony Richard. *Education:* Somerville College, Oxford, B.A. (first class honors), 1969, M.A., 1972; University of Sussex, D. Phil., 1974. *Home:* 41 Essex Rd., Gravesend, Kent DA11 OSL, England.

CAREER: Author of books for young people. Has also worked variously as a teacher, assistant to an old-style village baker, and as an assistant to a member of Parliament. *Member:* Society of Authors.

*WRITINGS—*All juvenile fiction: *The Runaway* (illustrated by Reginald Gray), Methuen, 1979; *The Iron Way* (illustrated by Tony Morris), Oxford University Press, 1979; *Revolt at Ratcliffe's Rags* (illustrated by T. Morris), Oxford University Press, 1980; *Save Our School* (illustrated by Gareth Floyd), Methuen, 1981; *A Whisper of Lace,* Oxford University Press, 1981, Merrimack, 1982; *The Dark behind the Curtain* (illustrated by David Parkins), Oxford University Press, 1982, Merrimack, 1984; *The Demon Headmaster* (illustrated by Gary Rees), Oxford University Press, 1982, Merrimack, 1984; *The Mintyglo Kid* (illustrated by G. Floyd), Methuen, 1983; *Born of the Sun* (illustrated by Mark Edwards), Oxford University Press, 1984; *On the Edge,* Oxford University Press, 1984; *The Prime Minister's Brain,* Oxford University Press, 1985. Regular contributor of children's book reviews to *British Book News* and *Times Literary Supplement.*

SIDELIGHTS: "When I was a child, for as far back as I can remember, there was always a great divide between the 'official' writing I did for school and the 'private' writing that I did for myself.

"At school, I was busy being a model student, studying English Literature, French, History, and Latin as my main subjects. Then I went to University to take an English degree and write a doctoral thesis.

"But, in private, I scribbled. I remembered having a tremendous lust for clean, blank sheets of paper. When I was fifteen that's what I asked everyone to give me for my birthday and, to this day, I find it difficult to pass a stationer's shop without going in and buying something. But I never finished anything I wrote. There was always the shadow of the other books— the great books that I studied at school—to remind me how bad my own writing was.

"I told stories as well. When my brother was small, I told him cowboy stories and when I had to travel to school on the train for half an hour every day I told my friends an endless serial story—it was very popular, because *they* were the heroines.

"But it never occurred to me that I wanted to be a writer. I thought that everyone else wrote in secret too, and I assumed that they all did it better. So I just scrawled my half-stories and my 'Chapter One's' and kept quiet about them.

"Then, when I was nineteen, things started to happen to me. Between school and University, I worked as a volunteer in England, helping on a course for educationally-subnormal teenagers and teaching in a fairly poor part of London, quite different from the suburbs where I had always lived. I began to see that life was more varied and more demanding than I had realized. I married early, while I was still at University, and took a year off to have my first child. During that year, I worked for an old-style baker in a village outside Oxford, helping him to make the bread. I used this experience later on, to describe the Victorian village bakery in *The Iron Way.*

"What really made me into a writer was finishing my doctoral thesis. Suddenly, I was no longer a student. For the first time in my life I had lots of free time and no 'official' writing to do. And I was up to the knees in stories. I had two children by then, and I was always making up stories for them and making them small illustrated books. I'd also helped to start a Children's Book Group in Lewes, the small town where I was living. So I decided it was time I had a go at some proper writing. Thanks to my thesis, I knew how to handle something long and, very tentatively, I began my first real book. It has never been published (quite rightly!) but by the time I'd finished it I was hooked and I went straight on to the next one. Four years later, when I had five finished books and a whole host of rejection slips, two of my books were accepted, simultaneously, by two different publishers.

"I have often asked myself why it took me so long to begin properly. Partly, I think, it was the effect of studying English Literature. I enjoyed it immensely and learnt a vast amount from it, but it was very intimidating. But I was also put off by sheer lack of time. Until I was nearly twenty-eight, I was a student, and for most of my grownup life I'd been a student with small children. I could have written short stories—and that's where aspiring authors are often told to begin. I think it's very bad advice. Writing good short stories is a very special skill, and it's not one that interests me at all. I like to be absorbed in a *long* story. I like the fascinating contrast between the wide sweep of the structure and the small details, both of which effect each other.

"It's very important to me that the writing I do now is 'private' writing and not 'official' writing. Writing fiction is the one thing that anyone can do. The quality is not the crucial thing. The crucial thing is that you control it *yourself* and decide exactly what you want to do and how you want to do it. A sort of freedom.

"I like to write for children and young people because then I feel free to write about important things: love, death, moral decisions. I find a lot of adult fiction is cynical and despairing, concerned to illustrate the powerlessness and unimportance of ordinary people. I believe that ordinary people *are* important and that everyone has the power to influence his own life. I think the young know that too.

"I have done one or two other things since I began writing seriously. For a while I taught part-time at a university and I spent some time as assistant to a member of Parliament. But although I enjoyed these things, writing was my major activity. Now I am able to do it for a large part of every day. In my spare time, I play the piano—very badly—and go orienteering, which involves running round strange forests, map and compass in hand, looking for control flags. I'm not very good at

finding my way and I take lots of wrong turnings and get stuck in lots of thorny bushes, but I usually get there in the end. A bit like writing a book really. . . ."

CROWLEY, Arthur M(cBlair) 1945-

PERSONAL: Born September 19, 1945, in Dallas, Tex., son of Arthur Aloysius and Elizabeth (McBlair) Crowley. *Education:* Attended Washington and Lee University, 1963-65; University of Texas, B.A., 1968; University of Missouri, Kansas City, M.A., 1977. *Home and office:* 8130 Garland Rd., Dallas, Tex. 75218.

CAREER: Public school teacher in "Head Start" program in Kansas City, Kan., 1969-80; Winston School, Dallas, Tex., teacher, 1980-82; writer, 1980—. *Member:* Authors Guild, Philtain Society.

WRITINGS—All juvenile: *The Boogey Man* (illustrated by Annie Gusman), Houghton, 1978; *Bonzo Beaver* (illustrated by A. Gusman), Houghton, 1980; *The Wagon Man* (New England Book Club selection), Houghton, 1981; *The Ugly Book* (illustrated by A. Gusman), Houghton, 1982.

WORK IN PROGRESS: "*Fairy Tale,* my tribute to the fairy tale genre and the mystique of story-telling in general, in which 'Friendship,' 'Bravery,' 'True Love,' 'Magic' and 'Fun' pre-

ARTHUR M. CROWLEY

(From *The Ugly Book* by Arthur Crowley. Illustrated by Annie Gusman.)

vail over 'Wickedness' in a bizarre yet traditional tale-within-a-tale which is otherwise reasonably indescribable."

SIDELIGHTS: "I love reading reviews of my work. It reminds me that none of us knows what he is doing."

DeARMAND, Frances Ullmann 1904(?)-1984

OBITUARY NOTICE—See sketch in *SATA* Volume 10: Born about 1904 in Springfield, Mo.; died April 14, 1984, in New York, N.Y. Editor and author. During the 1930s and 1940s, DeArmand was employed as editor of *Calling All Girls* and *Parents' Magazine* as well as executive editor of *Child Study*. She later served as encyclopedia managing editor at Doubleday and executive editor for the Junior Literary Guild. She was the author of two books, *Girl Alive!* and *A Very, Very Special Day*. Among the books she edited are *Never to Be Forgotten, The Encyclopedia of Child Care and Guidance,* and *When Mother Was a Girl: Stories She Read. For More Information See: Authors of Books for Young People,* 2nd edition, Scarecrow, 1971. *Obituaries: New York Times,* April 28, 1984.

DEEGAN, Paul Joseph 1937-

BRIEF ENTRY: Born March 19, 1937, in Mankato, Minn. Publishing executive and author of books for young readers.

After graduating from the University of Minnesota in 1959, Deegan began his professional career as a reporter and editor for newspapers in several Minnesota cities. In 1969 he became editorial director at Creative Education, Inc. and then, in 1973, president of Children's Book Co. Deegan is the author of numerous books, most of them about sports. He has written instructional books focusing on particular sports, biographies and notable sports figures, and fictional works that revolve around sports life in high school. Among his titles are: *Tom Seaver, Jerry West, Jack Nicklaus: The Golden Bear,* and *Bill Russell* (all Creative Education, 1973); *Important Decision, Almost a Champion, Dan Moves Up,* and *Close But Not Quite* (all Amecus Street, 1975); *Pitching, Skates and Skating,* and *Tennis* (all Creative Education, 1976). *Home:* 139 Eastwood Dr., Mankato, Minn. 56001. *For More Information See: Contemporary Authors,* Volume 102, Gale, 1981.

DENZEL, Justin F(rancis) 1917-

BRIEF ENTRY: Born January 15, 1917, in Clifton, N.J. Denzel attended New Jersey State Teacher's College (now William Peterson College of New Jersey), and the University of California. He has worked as a field naturalist for the American Museum of Natural History, collected marine life in Alaska, and worked as a scientific librarian with Hoffman La Roche in Nutley, N.J. Although Denzel has written biographies about historical figures, much of his juvenile literature features animals. Most of these books weave together the spirited and explosive personality of the animal and the determination of the child protagonist to know and love it. Denzel has been cited by the New Jersey Institute of Technology for seven of his literary contributions. One of these, *Jumbo: Giant Circus Elephant* (Garrard, 1973), is the true story of the famous and irresistible performing animal that stole the heart of America. *School Library Journal* noted that Jumbo and his trainer Scotty are "believably characterized" as Denzel recounts the elephant's short career and tragic death. Denzel has also contributed over one hundred short stories and articles to periodicals including *Coronet* and *Frontiers*. Other books written by Denzel and cited by the New Jersey Institute of Technology include *Genius with a Scalpel: Harvey Cushing* (Messner, 1971), *Black Kettle: King of the Wild Horses* (Garrard, 1974), *Wild Wing: Great Hunting Eagle* (Garrard, 1975), *Snowfoot: White Reindeer of the Arctic* (Garrard, 1976), *Scat: The Movie Cat* (Garrard, 1977), and *Sampson: Yankee Stallion* (Garrard, 1980). *Home:* 73 Livingston St., Clifton, N.J. 07013. *For More Information See: Contemporary Authors, New Revision Series,* Volume 4, Gale, 1981.

EGYPT, Ophelia Settle 1903-1984

OBITUARY NOTICE—See Sketch in *SATA* Volume 16: Born February 20, 1903, in Clarksville, Tex.; died of lung disease, May 25, 1984, in Washington, D.C. Educator, social service administrator, and author. Formerly the director of a home for black, unwed mothers and a probation officer with the juvenile court in Washington, D.C., Egypt founded one of the capital's first birth-counseling clinics, the Parklands Neighborhood Clinic, in 1957. By 1981 the clinic was serving some 1,800 clients and was renamed the Ophelia Settle Egypt Clinic. Egypt was also an educator, serving as an instructor in social sciences at Fisk University and as an assistant professor and field work supervisor in the medical school at Howard University. After she retired from the birth control clinic in 1968, Egypt devoted her time to writing. She issued *James Weldon Johnson*, a juvenile biography of the black poet and social activist, and *Unwritten History of Slavery*, a collection of interviews the author conducted with former slaves during her travels in Kentucky and Tennessee from 1929 to 1931. At the time of her death Egypt was preparing a children's edition of the latter book. *Obituaries: Washington Post*, June 1, 1984.

ELMORE, (Carolyn) Patricia 1933-

PERSONAL: Born November 21, 1933, in Miami, Fla.; daughter of Thomas Henry (a grocer) and Winona (Harper) Elmore. *Education:* Attended Winthrop College, 1951-54; University of South Carolina, A.B., 1955; graduate study at University of Miami, New School for Social Research, and San Francisco University. *Residence:* Berkeley, Calif. *Agent:* Marcia Amsterdam, 41 West 82nd St., New York, N.Y. 10024.

CAREER: Teacher at elementary schools in Florida, 1955-59; publicity writer and editor at various locations in New York, N.Y., 1959-64; Xerox Education Division (formerly Basic Systems, Inc.), New York City, training specialist, 1964-67; freelance writer and editor, 1967-69; Far West Lab for Educational Research and Development, San Francisco, Calif., editor, 1969-73; substitute teacher at elementary schools in Oakland, Calif., 1974-78; free-lance training specialist, writer, and editor, 1978—. *Member:* Women's National Book Association, American Society for Training Development, Mystery Writers of America, Society of Children's Book Writers, Sierra Club.

PATRICIA ELMORE

WRITINGS—Fiction for young readers: (With Cynthia Chase) *Ginny, the Office Assistant* (vocational; illustrated by John Martinez), McGraw-Hill, 1967; *Susannah and the Blue House Mystery* (illustrated by John Wallner), Dutton, 1980; *Susannah and the Poison Green Halloween* (illustrated by Joel Schick), Dutton, 1982.

WORK IN PROGRESS: A third book in the "Susannah" series, tentatively entitled, *Susannah and the Case of the Golden Dragon*.

SIDELIGHTS: "I decided to become a writer in the third grade, after composing my first poem and discovering the joy of playing with words. My mother wrote poetry, and both my parents took my ambition seriously. Perhaps I particularly valued written words because I hadn't learned to read until well into second grade.

"I don't think I read very many contemporary children's books, except mysteries, but I loved the stories in my father's *Saturday Evening Post*. Later, I became interested in authors like Alcott, Stevenson, Scott, and especially Dickens. I read all Shakespeare's comedies before high school.

"My favorite games as a child were pretend ones. I made up all sorts of characters and situations for the neighborhood gang to play. In one game, we were detectives solving mysteries we made up as we went along. I once tried writing a play for

Even before anybody got poisoned and the police started grilling us about the Eucalyptus Arms, that Halloween was a bummer. ▪ (From *Susannah and the Poison Green Halloween* by Patricia Elmore. Illustrated by Joel Schick.)

us to perform, a murder mystery in which all the suspects did it.

"I worked on the junior high and high school newspapers, and in my junior and senior years, on our local paper, the *Florence (S.C.) Morning News,* writing a weekly column on high school activities plus occasional features. I thought I'd like to become a journalist, so in college I worked toward a journalism minor and an English major. Even though I didn't become a journalist, the journalism courses were valuable training.

"I ended up writing training materials in New York, as I still do in California. I like the work; it's very satisfying to organize and write information simply and clearly to help others learn a job as easily as possible.

"I tried writing fiction for adults long before I discovered that I really wanted to write for children. I never thought of writing mysteries until one day I had a character I couldn't think what else to do with. I didn't think I could write a mystery, but I gave it a try, and the result was *Susannah and the Blue House Mystery.*

"In writing for children, I try to adhere to my standards for adult mysteries. I want the child detective, no less than the adult one, to solve the mystery through reasoning, not by accident. A good mystery should give the reader all the clues, but keep him guessing and just one step behind the detective. At the same time, I want my characters to be real people. Mystery, I think, is a form of fantasy and, like all good fantasy, must have believable characters to work. Above all, I write to please the child in me."

ENDERLE, Judith (Ann) 1941-

PERSONAL: Surname is pronounced *En*-der-lee; born November 26, 1941, in Detroit, Mich.; daughter of Theodore P. (an engineer) and Ellenore (a teacher; maiden name, Tanner) Ross; married Dennis Joseph Enderle (a vice-president and controller), August 18, 1962; children: Kevin Dennis, Brian Peter, Monica Ann. *Education:* University of Detroit, Certificate in Secretarial Business, 1962; also attended University of California, Los Angeles. *Residence:* Malibu, Calif. *Agent:* Andrea Brown, 1064 Madison Ave., #7, New York, N.Y. 10028.

(Jacket illustration by Mort Engle from *S.W.A.K., Sealed with a Kiss* by Judith Enderle.)

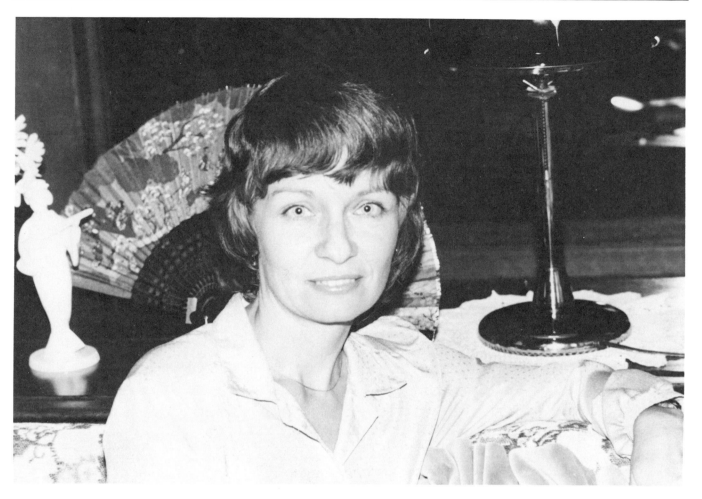

JUDITH ENDERLE

CAREER: Ford Motor Co., Wixom, Mich., secretary, 1963-65; Santa Monica Emeritus College, Santa Monica, Calif., teacher of writing for children, 1981-82. *Member:* Society of Children's Book Writers, Authors Guild, Southern California Council on Literature for Children and Young People. *Awards, honors:* International Reading Association/Children's Book Council Children's Choice Book award, 1982, for *Good Junk.*

WRITINGS: Good Junk (juvenile; illustrated by Gail Gibbons), Elsevier-Nelson, 1981; *Cheer Me On!* (juvenile), Tempo Books, 1982; *Someone for Sara* (juvenile), Tempo Books, 1982; *S.W.A.K., Sealed with a Kiss* (romance), Tempo Books, 1983; *Programmed for Love* (romance), Tempo Books, 1983; *When Wishes Come True* (romance), Tempo Books, 1983; *With Love, Lark* (romance), Dutton, 1983; *Sing a Song of Love* (romance), Tempo Books, 1984; *Will I See You Next Summer?* (romance), Tempo Books, 1984; *T.L.C., Tender Loving Care* (romance), Tempo Books, 1984; *Secrets* (romance), Silhouette, 1984; *Sixteen Sure Ways to Succeed with Boys* (romance), NAL, 1984; *A Little Love Dust* (romance), NAL, 1985; *Kisses for Sale* (romance), Scholastic, 1985; (with Stephanie Gordon Tessler) *The Journal of Emily Rose* (ghost story), Berkley/Tempo, 1985.

"Bayshore Medical Center" series; all with Stephanie Gordon Tessler; all published by Walker: *Andrea Whitman: Pediatrics,* 1983; *Monica Ross: Maternity,* 1983; *Elizabeth Jones: Emergency,* 1984; *Gabriella Ortiz: Crisis Center/Hotline,* 1984.

Contributor to *Highlights for Children.*

WORK IN PROGRESS: Let's Be Friends Again; Kisses for Terri; with S. G. Tessler, *Jacquelyn,* a historical romance for Scholastic.

SIDELIGHTS: "I was born and grew up in Detroit, Michigan, the elder of two girls. My earliest memory of writing is learning to print my name on a blackboard—the color which existed before green. This blackboard was not a tiny slate, but framed in red-painted wood to stand like an easel. The board folded down to make a desk for coloring and other creative activities. Above the board was a paper scroll which could be turned with a little knob, and it spun around like a player piano roll filled with delightful pictures of flags, animals, presidents, fruits, vegetables, letters, and numbers. I learned to print well, though my *J*s were often backward; and I can still find my 'signature' in the front, back and sometimes the middle of my childhood books.

"I was a reader because my parents were readers. My childhood reading included some of my mother's childhood favorites, such as the 'Mother McGrew' stories published in 1917. These were rhymes about animals who didn't behave, such as the donkey who once had short ears, but because he eavesdropped Mother McGrew made his ears grow. There were 'Golden Books,' my favorite being *The Lively Little Rabbit,*

The Pokey Little Puppy, and *The Shy Little Kitten.* There were also 'the Bobbsey Twins,' 'Honeybunch,' 'Maida,' and the 'Nancy Drew' series.

"My very favorite stories were the fairy tales. And when the bookmobile came, my first acquaintance with a library, I read every fairy-tale book I could find on the shelf. Other favorite authors when I was young were Estes and Enright. I discovered the Moffits and the Saturdays the year I was reading through the library in alphabetical order. I'm not sure I ever passed *E* because I reread those books so often.

"I grew up, and I fell in love several times—experiences which are of great value in the books I'm currently writing. After attending the University of Detroit, where I met my husband Dennis, I worked at the Ford Motor Company until my first son was born. It was after this that I first tried writing for publication. However, a second son followed shortly thereafter, then came a move to California, and with my hands full with moving and a daughter born in California, the writing was put under the bed to wait.

"Finally, when all three children were in school, a friend who was writing, suggested that we get together with a few other neighbors who were struggling to be published writers. Six months after our first writers' group meeting, I sold my first story, 'Mr. Purple's Christmas Stocking,' to *Highlights for Children.* There were a few more magazine sales, then my first book, *Good Junk.*

"Time to take some classes. I studied at the University of California with Sue Alexander and with Eve Bunting, both excellent teachers, both sharing their experiences with a novice writer.

"A set of guidelines received from the editor of Tempo Books encouraged me to try a proposal for a longer book. A phone call a short time later brought me my first contract for a teen romance. And I've written a number of them since.

"Interested in sharing my experiences with other aspiring writers, I proposed a class to the local community college. Teaching the craft of writing made an amazing impact on my own work. There was something about saying the rules out loud that reinforced them in my mind, so that I look at my manuscripts with a different eye.

"One cannot be an absolute judge of one's own work, however. The final judgment comes from the reader. A writer of books for young people hopes the reader will find some tidbit of recognition of those books—a feeling of 'that's exactly how I feel,' or 'that person has my problem and acted' or 'that person is like someone I know; now I understand.'

"Two of my favorite themes are friendship and the importance of communication. Growing up in today's world is often difficult. If I can sympathize a lot, help a little, and make a few people smile, I'll feel I've been a successful writer.

"Still living in California with the same husband, my children growing up and soon to be on their way, a horse grazing in the backyard and a cat at the door demanding to be petted and fed, I know that writing—though draining and demanding—is also very, very, satisfying. The days when I could put my writing under the bed and forget about it are long past."

HOBBIES AND OTHER INTERESTS: Reading, gardening.

ESPELAND, Pamela (Lee)   1951-

BRIEF ENTRY: Born August 19, 1951, in Oak Park, Ill. Freelance editor and author of children's books. Espeland attended both Harvard University and the University of Minnesota prior to receiving her B.A. from Carleton College. She is the author of ten books for children, eight of which are retellings of stories taken from ancient mythology. All published by Carolrhoda, these include *The Story of Cadmus,* 1980, *The Story of King Midas,* 1980, *The Story of Pygmalion,* 1981, and *The Story of Narcissus and Echo,* 1983. She also wrote *Why Do We Eat?* (Creative Education, 1981) and *How to Play Word Games* (Creative Education, 1982). Espeland is the editor of five books, including *A Frog Jumped Up* (Black Willow, 1982), a collection of children's poems by Halfdan Rasmussen. She is currently working on *James Made Himself Invisible,* another collection of poems for children. *Home and office:* 5704 Nicollet Ave. S., Minneapolis, Minn. 55419. *For More Information See: Contemporary Authors,* Volume 107, Gale, 1983.

ESPY, Willard R(ichardson)   1910-

PERSONAL: Born December 11, 1910, in Olympia, Wash.; son of Harry Albert (a rancher) and Helen (Richardson) Espy; married Hilda Cole, October 17, 1940 (divorced, 1962); mar-

WILLARD R. ESPY

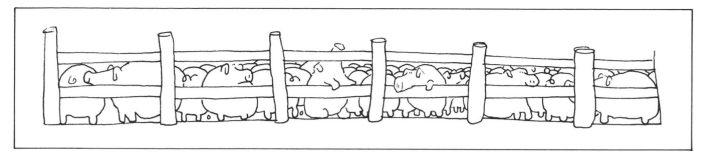

(From *A Children's Almanac of Words at Play* by Willard R. Espy. Illustrated by Bruce Cayard.)

ried Louise Manheim (a researcher), July 10, 1962; children: (first marriage) Mona Margaret (Mrs. Eugene Shreiber), Freddy Medora (Mrs. George Ames Plimpton), Joanna Page, Cassin Richardson, Jefferson Taylor. *Education:* University of Redlands, B.A., 1930; graduate study at Sorbonne, University of Paris, 1930-31. *Politics:* Independent. *Religion:* Protestant. *Home and office:* 529 West 42nd St., New York, N.Y. 10036; and Oysterville, Wash. 98641.

CAREER: Reporter for California daily newspaper, 1932-33; *World Tomorrow,* New York City, promotion director, 1933-35; *Nation,* New York City, correspondent, 1935-37; *L'Agence Havas,* New York City, reporter, 1937-40; *Reader's Digest,* Pleasantville, N.Y., promotion director and public relations manager, 1941-57; producer and interviewer for syndicated radio program, ''Personalities in Print,'' 1957-58; creative advertising director, Famous Artists' Schools, 1958-63; president and publisher, Charter Books, 1960-66; free-lance writer in communications, 1967-75. *Member:* P.E.N., Authors Guild, National Book Critics Circle, New England Society of New York; Century Association, Coffee House Club, Dutch Treat Club (all New York City). *Awards, honors:* Recipient of Governor's award for contribution to cultural life of Washington, 1973-76; Captain Robert Gray medal from Washington Historical Society, 1979, for his ''outstanding contribution to the history of Washington and the Pacific Northwest.''

WRITINGS: Bold New Program, Harper, 1951; *The Game of Words,* Peter Wolfe, 1971, Grosset, 1972; *Omak Me Yours Tonight,* Seattle Book, 1974; *An Almanac of Words at Play,* C. N. Potter, 1975; *Oysterville: Roads to Grandpa's Village,* C. N. Potter, 1977; *The Life and Works of Mr. Anonymous,* Hawthorn, 1977; *O Thou Improper, Thou Uncommon Noun,* C. N. Potter, 1978; *Say It My Way,* Doubleday, 1980; *Another Almanac of Words at Play,* C. N. Potter, 1980; *Have a Word on Me,* Simon & Schuster, 1981; *Espygrams,* C. N. Potter, 1982; *A Children's Almanac of Words at Play* (juvenile; illustrated by Bruce Cayard), C. N. Potter, 1982; *Word Puzzles,* Dembner Books, 1983; *The Garden of Eloquence: A Rhetorical Bestiary,* Harper, 1983; *Words to Rhyme With,* Potter, 1985. Contributor to magazines. Panelist, *Harper Dictionary of Contemporary Usage,* 1976; contributing editor, *Harvard* magazine, 1978—.

WORK IN PROGRESS: A Hippomonstroesquipedalian Account of the Misspent Life of the Late Unlamented Isaac Walter Kibble, Jr., to be illustrated by Roy McKie.

SIDELIGHTS: ''I spent my childhood in the village of Oysterville, on the coast of Washington, where, at the age of five or thereabouts, I mastered the skill of tying a double bow knot.

Though I have forgotten many things since then, I can still tie a neat double bow; there are those, indeed, who consider my dexterity in this regard the one substantial accomplishment of a generally undistinguished life. I do not go so far, however, as to claim to have perfected the art; while I handily tie my shoe laces in a double bow, I cannot tie a bow tie, and have to buy the sort that comes already knotted.

''Oysterville had about fifty inhabitants when I was a boy, and still has, but with a few doddering exceptions they are not the same people; those I knew back then have removed long since to the graveyard on the hill, which is much more densely populated than the village.

''By my time the oysters that had made Oysterville the center of a thriving business in the last half of the nineteenth century were pretty much gone, but enough remained so that my father could bring home a supply from the tide flats when we had guests for dinner. We served first oyster cocktails, then oysters on the half shell, then oyster soup, then, as a main course, fried oysters or oyster stew; I am quite certain we had oysters also for dessert, perhaps sweetened with sugar and cream.

''Oysterville sits on the bank of an arm of the ocean that was first called Shoalwater Bay, and for good reason. It was so shallow that I never learned to swim; instead I mud-crawled, which means that while I kicked vigorously for show, my hands were on the bay bottom pulling me along. My inability to swim bothered me less than my inability, despite the buoyancy of the salt water, to float; when I lay back, my body would gradually submerge, feet first, until only my head remained above the surface. It occurs to me as I look back that this may have been an early indication of the light-headedness that is charged against me so unfairly by some of my friends.

''It was in those long-ago days at Oysterville that I discovered the magic of words—not just at home, where the walls were lined with books, but at the one-room school where we sang schoolyard rhymes, and chanted skip-the-rope verses, and exchanged secrets in pig Latin. Words were central to all of us, and marvelous fun.

''My home was in New York City for more than half a century, and I refuse to hear a word against it; but I am back in Oysterville more and more nowadays. It is a good, quiet place for writing, though probably I spend more time than I should looking out over the bay, watching the soft changes of color in mudflats and water and distant hills and sky. The colors changed the same way when I was a child. Perhaps that is what set me to thinking of doing a book for children, which came out as *A Children's Almanac of Words at Play.*

"I am sure that words are no less enchanting and exciting to children today then they were back in the first quarter of this century. I'd feel ridiculously proud and pleased if I could write something that would help keep that fun alive and well through grammar school and high school and college and, indeed, forever afterward."

ETCHEMENDY, Nancy   1952-

PERSONAL: Born February 19, 1952, in Reno, Nev.; daughter of Fredrick Lewis (a public school teacher) and Barbara Fay (Nelson) Howell; married John William Etchemendy (a professor of philosophy), April 14, 1973. *Education:* University of Nevada, B.A., 1974. *Home and office:* 410 French Court, Menlo Park, Calif. 94025. *Agent:* Carol Mann Literary Agency, 1968 Pacific St., Brooklyn, N.Y. 11201.

CAREER: Western Industrial Parts, Reno, Nev., lithographer, 1970-75; Sutherland Printing, Reno, worked in art, stripping, and camera, 1975-76; Menlo Graphics and Lithography, Menlo Park, Calif., art director, 1976-78; Etchemendy Commercial Graphics, Palo Alto, Calif., sole proprietor, 1978-81; writer, 1981—.

WRITINGS—All juvenile science fiction: *The Watchers of Space* (illustrated by Andrew Glass), Avon, 1980; *Stranger from the Stars* (illustrated by Teje Etchemendy), Avon, 1983; *Osmyrrah,* Avon, 1985.

WORK IN PROGRESS: Figgy's Wings, a fantasy novel for young readers about a boy who discovers and helps a race of people who have wings; in collaboration with Nina K. Hoffman, *Apples and Incense* (tentative title), a novel for young

She was silent for a moment, scrutinizing the box as though, if she looked hard enough, she might see through the cover. ▪ (From *Stranger from the Stars* by Nancy Etchemendy. Illustrated by Teje Etchemendy.)

readers about the adventures of two children, one of whom is a ghost.

SIDELIGHTS: "From the time my sister and I were four or five years old until we were teenagers, my dad used to read to us on a regular basis. He always had a passion for science fiction, so we heard a lot of it during our evening story time. Tom Swift, the Tom Corbett series, and even judicious amounts of Jules Verne and Ray Bradbury all found places on Dad's reading list. By the time I was eight years old, I *knew* that I was going to live in space when I grew up. Other little girls talked about becoming nurses or stewardesses or mommies when they grew up. But I wanted to be an astronaut, or a brave settler on some far–flung and mysterious world.

"At the same time, I was rapidly discovering a second love— the love of words, and the thrill of making them leap and dance to a tune of my own. I learned the alphabet; I discovered the miraculous connection between marks on a sheet of paper and the thoughts inside my head; and I began to write stories and poems.

NANCY ETCHEMENDY

"For a long time I hoped I could be a writer *and* an astronaut. It didn't seem too farfetched. Surely they were going to need somebody to chronicle all those adventures we were going to have. But then several things happened. John Kennedy died. We found ourselves in a seemingly endless war in Southeast Asia. And our social priorities began to change. People started saying things like, 'Why are we spending all this money on the moon when the masses are starving right here on Earth?' and 'Look at the mess we've made of this planet. Do you want and same thing to happen to the other planets?' and 'Why don't we solve the problems of this world before we worry about solving the problems of space travel?'

"Feeling very bleak indeed, I watched the space program fizzle to a smoldering stump, like a big roman candle that turned out to be a dud. To make matters worse, I was getting old. And I knew that sooner or later I was going to have to find a way to pay the rent and keep potatoes in the pot. Writing was fun, but you couldn't rely on the income. So basically I chickened out. I went to work in a printshop, and that's how I came to be a graphic designer writing science fiction novels on my lunch hours.

"Eventually it became clear to me that no matter what happened, I was going to be dead or too old to make the trip by the time the call went out for space colonists. But I was never able to shake the conviction that mankind belongs in space; that it is in fact our best hope for civilized survival in a dangerous age. As I recently explained to a young fan, 'Why do I write science fiction? It's a lot of fun to consider scientific possibilities. It's important for people to think about all the different things science means to us, and how it might effect our lives. That's partly because scientific inventions can be very dangerous if we use them without thinking about them. I believe it's especially important for today's kids to think about science, particularly space science, because I think that space is the future home of mankind and that we should start exploring it as soon and as fast as possible.''

"It's a joy to write for kids. As a group they're more sincere and concise about things than any other people I can think of. If you've missed the mark, they'll tell you so—plainly and candidly, without any intention of either sparing you or hurting you. But if you're on target, and a child somewhere begins to think about what you've said, then in a small way you've really affected eternity.''

HOBBIES AND OTHER INTERESTS: "I wish I could say that I'm still a rock climber, but I've given that up for safer pursuits. I'm a dedicated dabbler—these days particularly in anthropology, archaeology, and paleontology. I like to travel, especially in warm climates; I have a particular love for the deserts of the North American West. Whatever time is left over, I usually spend in the garden where I grow lilies, my favorite of all the flowers.''

ETCHISON, Birdie L(ee)   1937-
(Leigh Hunter, Catherine Wood)

PERSONAL: Born June 22, 1937, in San Diego, Calif.; daughter of Leland H. (an aircraft inspector) and Naomi E. (an artist; maiden name, Brumwell) Leighton; married William R. Tucker, May 28, 1955 (divorced March 25, 1971); married Vernon L. Etchison (a cashier), August 14, 1971; children: (first marriage) William R., Jr., Tamela Cia, Naomi Leanne, Barbara Tucker Kowalski; (second marriage) Matthew, Sarah. *Education:* Attended University of Oklahoma. *Politics:* Democrat. *Religion:* Church of God. *Home:* 6306 Southeast 19th Ave., Portland, Ore. 97202.

CAREER: Burke Marketing Research, Portland, Ore., supervisor, 1973-78; *Oregonian-Oregon Journal,* Portland, typist-salesperson in classified advertisements, 1978-79; free-lance writer, 1979—. Member of staff of Warner Pacific Christian Writers Conference, 1978-82, Mount Herman Christian Writers Conference, and Willamette Writers Conference. *Member:* Oregon Association of Christian Writers (president). *Awards, honors:* Writer of the Year award in juvenile fiction, 1982, from Warner Pacific Writer's Conference.

WRITINGS: Me and Greenley (juvenile novel; illustrated by James Converse), Harold Press, 1981; *Strawberry Mountain* (juvenile novel; illustrated by J. Converse), Herald Press, 1982; (with Diane Nason) *The Celebration of Family,* T. Nelson, 1983; *Don't Drop the Sugar Bowl in the Sink,* Radiant Book, 1984.

Author, under pseudonyms Catherine Wood and Leigh Hunter, of personal experience articles.

Contributor of more than three hundred fifty articles and stories to magazines.

WORK IN PROGRESS: A romance novel, under pseudonym

BIRDIE L. ETCHISON

Ben froze. Someone had a hold of him—a tight, firm grip—and it hurt. ■ (From *Strawberry Mountain* by Birdie L. Etchison. Illustrated by James Converse.)

Leigh Hunter, tentatively titled *Cane Hill; Cassie's Choice;* two young adult romance novels: *My Sister—My Aunt* and *The Impossible Summer; A Dog for Darcy; Wheels of Danger; 227 Miles to John Day; Summer's End; The Disappearing Footprints; My Husband—My Friend.*

SIDELIGHTS: "I began writing in May, 1963. Over the next several years I sold fifty confession stories to various magazines, and in 1974 turned almost exclusively to the Christian writing field. My articles, fillers, and stories have now been published in approximately sixty-five different publications.

"In order to stay at home and make it as a full-time free-lance writer, I must keep about two hundred pieces circulating at all times, and still work on my fiction books for young teens. Speaking at writers conferences has been a means of support, as has the inspiration and fellowship of other writers and editors.

"Why do I write for children?

"My fondest memories are of snuggling up with a good book—usually a mystery—and nights spent reading by flashlight under the covers, to avoid detection, of course. To this day I cannot go to sleep unless I read first.

"I expect I was the typical child who becomes a writer. I kept a diary, jotted down poems, and told scary ghost stories to cousins who stayed overnight. I dreamt of how my name would look on the dust jacket of a book.

"So, when did my dreams become realities? After marriage and mothering four children, the inclination to put words down on paper hit again, and since my children were avid listeners, I wrote for them.

"The main character in my first published book, *Me and Greenley,* is really me. I was a tomboy; couldn't stand make-up, dresses or pantyhose. Life was more fun when you didn't have to worry about your hair. Robin's best friend is the boy next door.

"Each June, when school was out, found me on my uncle's strawberry farm in Sublimity, Oregon. Since there were animals on the farm, and it was quite primitive with no running water or electricity, I was constantly busy, but the change of pace was refreshing. It was this farm, this life I wrote about in my second book, *Strawberry Mountain.* Though I had never been a foster child, I could write about Ben's failure at milking cows, his reluctance to ride a horse, and his catastrophe while learning to drive a tractor. The abandoned house on the hill across the hollow, was another reality, and though I heard about ghosts, I never ran into one, but Ben did. A kind ghost, I might add.

"In *Cassie's Choice* [work in progress], Cassie's best friend is her grandfather. While everyone else thinks grandpa is senile, he and Cassie enjoy a special relationship.

"Who do I write for children? They are constantly curious, and I guess I will never grow up, because I am constantly curious, too."

EZZELL, Marilyn   1937-

BRIEF ENTRY: Born March 11, 1937, in Teaneck, N.J. Author of mystery books for young readers. Ezzell was employed as a registered nurse and teacher of nursing in New Jersey before the publication of her first book in 1982. She is the author of seven novels comparable to the popular Nancy Drew series in format. Ezzell's heroine is Susan Sand, a mystery writer who acts as a sleuth on the side. All published by Pinnacle Books, the titles are: *The Mystery at Hollowhearth House, The Secret of Clovercrest Castle, The Clue in Witchwhistle Well, The Riddle of Raggedrock Ridge* (all 1982), *The Phantom of Featherford Falls* (1983), *The Password to Diamonddwarf Dale* (1983), and *The Search for the Snowship Songs* (1984). Anticipated is the eighth book in the series, *The Mystery of Beggarbay Bluff. Residence:* New York, N.Y. *For More Information See: Contemporary Authors,* Volume 109, Gale, 1983.

I'll tell you a story
About Jack a Nory—
And now my story's begun;
I'll tell you another
About Johnny, his brother—
And now my story is done.

—Mother Goose

FALLS, C(harles) B(uckles)   1874-1960

PERSONAL: Born December 10, 1874, in Fort Wayne, Ind.; died April 15, 1960, in New York, N.Y.; married Bedelia M. Croly, March 15, 1917; children: Bedelia (Hughes); *Education:* Self-taught artist. *Residence:* Falls Village, Conn.

CAREER: Book and magazine illustrator, painter, muralist, designer. Began career in an architect's office in Chicago, Ill.; member of art staff, *Chicago Tribune,* Chicago, Ill.; instructor, Art Students League and the School of Disabled Soldiers, New York City; free-lance artist. Murals displayed at the American Radiator Building and the Players Club, New York City, and the State Office Building, Albany, N.Y. *Military service:* U.S. Marine Corps., served during World War I in Haiti; became sergeant. *Member:* Society of Illustrators (honorary), Artists Guild (honorary president), Guild of Free-lance Artists (founder), Players Club (honorary), Dutch Treat Club (New York City, honorary), Century Club. *Awards, honors:* First prize in a poster competition, 1920, for "Victory Hall" poster; illustrator of Newbery honor books, 1946, Katherine Shippen's *New Found World,* 1952, Elizabeth Baity's *Americans before Columbus,* and 1953, Ann Weil's *Red Sails to Capri; New York Herald Tribune's* Spring Book Festival award, 1943, for *Vast Horizons,* 1945, for *New Found World,* and 1951, for *Americans before Columbus;* Clinedinst Medal from the Artists Fellowship, 1959, for his contributions to the art of illustration.

*WRITINGS—*All for children; all self-illustrated: *The ABC Book,* Doubleday, Page, 1923, reissued, 1972, also published as *The Modern ABC Book,* John Day, 1930; *The First 3000 Years: Ancient Civilizations of the Tigris, Euphrates, and Nile River Valleys and the Mediterranean Sea,* Viking, 1960.

C. B. FALLS

On the eighth day, a Moor appeared riding a white camel.... ■ (From *Vast Horizons* by Mary Seymour Lucas. Illustrated by C. B. Falls.)

Illustrator: Maurice P. Maeterlinck, *Old Fashioned Flowers and Other Out-of-Door Studies,* Dodd, 1905; Bert L. Taylor, *The Pipesmoke Carry,* Reilly & Britton, 1912; Jessie B. White, adapter, *Snow White and the Seven Dwarfs: A Fairy Tale Based on the Story of the Brothers Grimm,* Dodd, 1913; Donn Byrne, *Messer Marco Polo,* Century, 1921; Oliver Herford, editor, *Poems from "Life",* Macmillan, 1923; Theodore Dreiser, *The Color of a Great City,* Boni & Liveright, 1924; *Mother Goose,* Doubleday, 1924; Walter R. Bowie, reteller, *When Jesus Was Born,* Harper, 1928; *The Story of the Birth of Jesus Christ, According to the Gospel of Saint Matthew and Saint Luke,* Marchbanks, 1929; Robert Louis Stevenson, *Two Mediaeval Tales,* Limited Editions, 1930; Ik Marvel (pseudonym of Donald G. Mitchell), *Reveries of a Bachelor; or, A Book of the Heart,* Morrow, 1931; Laura E. Richards, *What Shall the Children Read?,* Appleton-Century, 1939.

Mary S. Lucas, *Vast Horizons,* Viking, 1943; Merritt P. Allen, *White Feather,* McKay, 1944; Katherine B. Shippen, *New Found World,* Viking, 1945, revised edition, 1964; R. L. Stevenson, *Treasure Island,* World Publishing, 1946, new edition, 1972; K. B. Shippen, *The Great Heritage* (ALA Notable Book), Viking, 1947; R. L. Stevenson, *Kidnapped,* World Publishing, 1947; Louisa M. Alcott, *Eight Cousins; or, The Aunt-Hill,* World Publishing, 1948; Elizabeth C. Baity, *Americans before Columbus* (ALA Notable Book), Viking, 1951, revised edition, 1961; K. B. Shippen, *Bridle for Pegasus,* Viking, 1951; Ann Weil, *Red Sails to Capri* (ALA Notable Book), Viking, 1952; Enid L. Meadowcroft, *Story of Davy Crockett,* Grosset, 1952, E. C. Baity, *America before Man* (ALA Notable Book), Viking, 1953; Gene Lisitzky, *Four Ways of Being Human,* Viking, 1956.

A pen and ink gouache by C. B. Falls.

Illustrator of James Hunecker's "Lively Arts" column in *Puck*, late 1910s. Also illustrator of *Man Is a Weaver* (ALA Notable Book) published by Viking; of decorations for *Our Friend the Dog* by Maurice Maeterlinck, published by Dodd, 1904, and *The East Window* by Bert Leston Taylor, published by Knopf, 1924; of cover decoration for *Catalogue of the Paintings and the Art Treasures of the Players,* published by the Players Club, 1925; and of frontispiece of *All's Fair in Love* by Josephine C. Sawyer, published by Dodd, 1904.

SIDELIGHTS: Born in Fort Wayne, Indiana in 1874, Falls originally intended to become a lawyer. He went to Chicago when he was twenty-one. There he began his career in an architect's office. After a year he landed a job as a sketch artist on the art staff of the *Chicago Tribune*. In the days before news photographers, the sketch artist was an integral part of the news-covering team. Here he gained training in the use of spontaneous line and form and learned his basic art craft.

Following a wage dispute, Falls left the paper and moved to New York City. Several months of job-hunting and meager

living followed, until he landed a job with an art studio called "The Decorative Designers," where he designed book covers or cover designs for magazines.

Falls left the commercial studio to free-lance, and for the rest of his life was seldom without a commissioned project. During his long and varied career he produced a large volume of work in advertising, book and magazine illustration, mural decoration, scenic and costume design, and printmaking.

It was in poster designing, however, that he won prominence in the field of American art. Falls first began designing posters in 1910. "My first show posters were made for vaudeville houses—Proctor's Fifth Avenue and the Palace. In all, I made between twenty and thirty. It may interest you to know that for each of these I was paid fifteen dollars and two tickets for the show . . . there was a saving grace, however, I was allowed to do anything I liked (in the way of motif). Often the manager didn't see the poster until it was on the billboards. I was . . . happy about the entire arrangement.

"At first, the wood blocks for my posters were cut in the printing shops that specialized in making theatrical posters, and while the *general* effect was good, what the boys could do to a face was agonizing. So, after I had seen two or three of their efforts, I took over and cut the blocks myself—even the eight-sheet ones!. . . Among the players I posterized were such notables as Cissy Loftus, Lillian Russell, Bert Williams, Harry Lauder, the clown Slivers, and Ruth St. Denis," [Norman Kent, "C. B. Falls, 1874-1960: A Career in Retrospect," *American Artist,* February, 1962.[1]]

During the period preceding World War I, Falls also conceived the idea of publishing a sixteen-page pamphlet containing short stories, poems, and drawings from regular contributors. Most of the contributors to this pamphlet, entitled

I came to the bay at last, more dead than alive . . . . ∎
(From *Kidnapped* by Robert Louis Stevenson. Illustrated by C. B. Falls.)

Here we see the army of Hannibal, . . . descending the Alps into Italy, led by enormous African elephants. ■ (From *The First 3000 Years: Ancient Civilizations of the Tigris, Euphrates, and Nile River Valleys, and the Mediterranean Sea* by C. B. Falls. Illustrated by the author.)

1910, later became famous. Included on the list of regular contributors were Theodore Dreiser, Montague Glass, Walter Fawcett, and Boardman Robinson. As editor and publisher, Falls filled in the empty spaces with his own designs.

During World War I Falls' posters for the Marines and War Bond drives played an important part in informing the American people. He served as a sergeant in the Marines in Haiti. The tropical isle sojourn influenced Falls' art for many years.

One of his earliest ventures in book illustration was done for his little daughter, Bedelia Jane. To help his daughter learn her alphabet, Falls designed and illustrated for her *The ABC Book,* which has become a classic in children's books through the years. When the book first appeared in 1923, Anne Carroll Moore, the famous children's librarian, stated: "We may well feel proud that an ABC book so admirable in design and in color printing has been produced on this side of the Atlantic. Mr. Falls designed the book for his little three-year-old daughter who likes a big book with lots of pictures. The drawings

are cut on wood blocks and printed from four-color plates, and the artist has personally superintended the reproduction of them. The imagination of a child or grown-up is left free to capture by its own thrill of recognition the familiar in a new-old medium where color has not obscured the outline nor played too many tricks with nature.

"The book will take its own place in the art departments of schools and libraries, but the fact that it was designed for a living child for whose mentality the artist had such evident respect stamps it first of all as a children's book which bids fair to exert a very considerable influence on American picture books." [Taken from the book jacket of *The ABC Book* by C. B. Falls, Viking, 1972.[2]]

During sixty-five years as an artist, Falls illustrated many books (most of them for children), produced numerous magazine covers, illustrations, and advertisements. He also taught at the Art Students League, was a scenic and costume designer, a fabric and furniture designer, and a designer of woodcuts. He was one of the founders of the Artists Guild. When he began his

"Angelo! Angelo, look! A boat!" ■ (From *Red Sails to Capri* by Ann Weil. Illustrated by C. B. Falls.)

art career in the late nineteenth century, commercial art was not a lucrative profession. During his many years in the field, he saw art turn into a highly paid business. "Indeed many of the younger generation look upon art, not as a radiant and beautiful maiden to be wooed, but as an old woman with a lot of money."

Falls died in New York City on April 15, 1960. "New York artists of today are business men. They have to be business men and to deal with business men if they expect success." ["Charles Falls, Illustrator, Dies; Aided Book Drives in Two Wars," *New York Times*, April 16, 1980.³]

FOR MORE INFORMATION SEE: Anice Page Cooper, *About Artists,* Doubleday, 1926; Anice Page Cooper, *Authors and Others,* Doubleday, 1927, Books for Libraries Press, 1970; *Contemporary Illustrators of Children's Books,* Bookshop for Boys and Girls, Women's Educational and Industrial Union, 1930, reprinted, Gale, 1978; *Illustrators of Children's Books: 1744-1945,* Horn Book, 1947; *American Artist,* February, 1947, February, 1957, February, 1962; *Junior Book of Authors,* sec-

ond edition, H. W. Wilson, 1951. *Obituaries: New York Times,* April 16, 1960.

FARBER, Norma 1909-1984

OBITUARY NOTICE—See sketch in *SATA* Volume 25: Born August 9, 1909, in Boston, Mass.; died of a vascular disease, March 21, 1984, in Cambridge, Mass. Singer, actress, poet, and author. Farber wrote several volumes of poetry and nearly twenty books for children. Her best known work, *As I Was Crossing Boston Common,* won a National Book Award and a Children's Book Showcase Award, and her poetry was often cited by the Poetry Society of America. Also a noted soprano, Farber received the Premier Prix in singing from the Jury Central des Etudes Musicales in Belgium in 1936. Her writings for children include *This Is the Ambulance Leaving the Zoo* (a Junior Literary Guild selection), *Did You Know It Was the Narwhale?, How the Hibernators Came to Bethlehem,* and *How to Ride a Tiger.* She also wrote the young adult novel *Mercy Short: A Winter Journal, North Boston, 1692-93.* Two additional books will be published posthumously. *For More Information See: Language Arts,* April, 1981; *Who's Who in America,* 42nd edition, Marquis, 1982; *Twentieth-Century Children's Writers,* 2nd edition, St. Martin's 1983. *Obituaries: Globe & Mail* (Toronto), March 24, 1984; *Publishers Weekly,* May, 1984; *School Library Journal,* May, 1984.

FARMER, Peter 1950-

PERSONAL: Born November 3, 1950, in Loton, Bedfordshire, England; son of Kenneth Carl (a hat manufacturer) and Phylis (a flower arranger; maiden name, Burnase) Farmer. *Education:* Central School of Art, diploma in theatre design. *Home:* 15 Holland Mews, Hove, Sussex, England.

CAREER: Free-lance illustrator, painter and ballet designer. *Exhibitions:* Work has appeared in numerous one-man exhibitions, including Lasson Gallery, London, England, 1977.

ILLUSTRATOR: Ian Serraillier, *Enchanted Island: Stories from Shakespeare,* Walck, 1964; Eileen Dunlop, *Elizabeth, Elizabeth,* Holt, 1977; Alexandre Dumas, *When Pierrot Was Young,* Oxford University Press, 1978. Illustrated the cover of *Tom's Midnight Garden* by Philipa Pearce. Contributor of illustrations to magazines.

PETER FARMER

Her face was aching with the effort of smiling carelessly, and every few minutes she felt the hot discomfort of tears stinging behind her eyes . . . . ■ (From *Elizabeth* by Eileen Dunlop. Illustrated by Peter Farmer.)

SIDELIGHTS: "I feel the best work to be done is the work to be done tomorrow. I have a desire to work in all fields of design."

FISHER, Lois I. 1948-

PERSONAL: Born December 8, 1948, in Bronx, N.Y.; daughter of John Bryant (a postal worker) and Frances (Warren) Fisher. *Education:* Attended public schools in New York, N.Y., and business school. *Residence:* Bronx, N.Y.

CAREER: Author. Has been variously employed as a secretary. *Member:* Society of Children's Book Writers.

WRITINGS—All juvenile fiction: *Sarah Dunes, Weird Person* (Junior Literary Guild selection), Dodd, 1981; *Wretched Robert,* Dodd, 1982; *Puffy P. Pushycat, Problem Solver* (illustrated by Dale Payson), Dodd, 1983; *Little Miss,* Bantam, 1983; *Little White Lies,* Bantam, 1983; *I Can't Forget You* (young adult romance novel), Bantam, 1984; *Rachel Vellars, How Could You?,* Dodd, 1984; *Drive-Time Robert* (a sequel to *Wretched Robert*), Dodd, 1985. Also contributor of short stories to numerous periodicals for children and young adults, such as *The Friend, Wee Wisdom,* and *Chidren's Playmate.*

WORK IN PROGRESS: "There's always at least one book pestering me. Right now, I have many ideas and proposals for young adult romances. I'm also trying something a little different for me—a serious young adult mystery."

SIDELIGHTS: ''Not long ago, I attended a conference of romantic book writers. The very nice people were all amazed that I wrote for teenagers. 'How do you write for young people?' I smiled and replied, 'I remember what it was like. Vividly.' A little voice inside me also asked, 'How do *you* write for adults?' I still wonder what they would have answered. Actually, I'd like to write in both fields. Young people do grow up. It would be lovely if we followed each other.

''I was an only child, ill much of the time, growing up in a city housing project in the Bronx. My parents read to me until their voices gave out. Then my imagination took over and I told myself stories. In the fourth grade, again ill, I wrote my first story (long since forgotten as far as plot) and gave it to my mother as a birthday gift. From then on, I never stopped writing.

''It wasn't until 1973 that I decided to write professionally. Sold my second short story on its first trip out. And from there on . . . it got harder and harder! But I never grew up. At times, people viewed my tenacity as either grand stupidity or incredible vanity. Determination won out over all their remarks. And there was a great deal of determination involved; my first book, *Sarah Dunes, Weird Person,* went to fifteen publishers in three years before Dodd, Mead purchased the novel on the sixteenth time out. What a wonderful, glorious feeling! Those who believed me stupid or vain now all agreed, 'Well, she's a writer. She's entitled to her eccentricities.'

''The idea for *Sarah* came as I was drifting off to sleep one night. There she was, with Gayle, Connie, and her Aunt Rhoda and all the problems, including the tag line, Weird Person. Needless to say, sleep was delayed, as the plot and other characters jumped into my head. Most of my writing ideas pop in unannounced and in full bloom. Sarah's wariness about reading fat, nubby-covered, maroon or hunter-green-jacketed books was an anxiety I had as a young teenager. Although an avid reader, I hesitated when faced with a book over three hundred pages that simply looked smarter than me!

''Sometime between eleven and fourteen, a kid who has always been like everybody else suddenly seems different, not just to others but to herself. Sarah is confronted with this scary and very real feeling. She's alienated from her friends and family. As terrified as she is by her weirdness, she manages to handle a great deal of it with a sense of humor. I hope the kids who read the book feel a little less weird and can smile about it!''

''Books usually arrive unannounced, full-blown, with characters, plot, theme, and bits of dialogue into my thoughts, pushing out all other business in my brain. It's exciting because I'm never sure when a book will strike.

''I'm not going to get killed playing hockey.''

''But you could lose your teeth. And what boy wants to kiss a girl with false teeth?'' ■ (Jacket illustration by Robert T. Handville from *Sarah Dunes, Weird Person* by Lois I. Fisher.)

LOIS I. FISHER

"My favorite kind of novel, to read and to write, is an 'identity' story. The main character isn't quite sure who he or she really is, or how to act/react in important situations. I like to see the character grow, change, feel, rebel, or experience whatever emotions are necessary to the story. Real people change all the time. Characters should, too.

"I also like mysteries and suspense stories. Puzzles of all sorts, especially crosswords, cryptic messages, and crostics, keep me busy for hours.

"Another hobby is collecting rock recordings from the 1960s. I was a teenager during that period and loved the music, particularly the British invasion of the 1964 to 1966 era (Beatles, Dave Clark Five, Stones, Kinks, Animals . . . I could go on for pages!). Someday, I hope to write a book about a young person enjoying *and* suffering through the very exciting time. However, that story hasn't struck yet. When it does . . . I can hardly wait!"

When at home alone I sit
And am very tired of it,
I have just to shut my eyes
To go sailing through the skies—
To go sailing far away
To the pleasant Land of Play;
To the fairy land afar
Where the little people are;
Where the clover-tops are trees,
And the rain-pools are the seas,
And the leaves, like little ships,
Sail about on tiny trips;
And above the daisy tree
   Through the grasses,
High o'erhead the Bumble Bee
   Hums and passes.

—Robert Louis Stevenson

FRANCO, Marjorie

PERSONAL: Born in Chicago, Ill.; daughter of Claus F. and Martha (Rehn) Peterson; married Daniel Franco, Jr. (an elementary school principal); children: Douglas, Joyce, Peter. *Education:* Attended Northwestern University. *Home:* 105 Linden Ave., Glencoe, Ill. 60022. *Agent:* Aaron M. Priest Literary Agency, 344 East 51st St., New York, N.Y. 10022; and Internation Press Agency, P.O. Box 149A, Surbiton, Surrey, KT6 5HJ, England.

CAREER: Full-time writer. Also instructor of creative writing at several writers' conferences, including Indiana University Writers' Conference and Midwest Writers' Conference. *Awards, honors:* Children's Book Award from the Society of Midland Authors, 1984, for *Love in a Different Key.*

WRITINGS—Novels for young adults: *So Who Hasn't Got Problems?,* Houghton, 1979; *Love in a Different Key,* Houghton, 1983.

Other: *Genevieve and Alexander,* Atheneum, 1982. Also contributor of short stories and articles to periodicals, including *Redbook, McCall's, Good Housekeeping, The Writer, Writer's Digest,* and others.

WORK IN PROGRESS: An adult novel.

MARJORIE FRANCO

Suddenly he smiled an extraordinary smile that lit up his face . . . . To Neenah it was the most genuine smile she'd ever seen . . . . ■ (Jacket illustration by Donna Diamond from *Love in a Different Key* by Marjorie Franco.)

SIDELIGHTS: "Although I have written many serious stories, I consider myself a humor writer. I like humor with serious undertones. If I emphasize the comic, it doesn't mean I have ignored the tragic. I have simply treated a subject in another way. Indeed, without tragedy there could be no comedy."

FOR MORE INFORMATION SEE: The Writer, April, 1980, June, 1982.

FRASER, Eric (George) 1902-1983

PERSONAL: Born June 11, 1902, in Westminster, London, England; died in 1983; son of George James and Matilda (Peartree) Fraser; married Irene Lovett, 1925; children: three sons, one daughter, Mary. *Education:* Attended Westminster City School; Goldsmiths' College of Art, London, 1919-24. *Home:* Penn's Place, 9 Church St., Hampton, Middlesex, England. *Office:* 4 Denmark St., London WC2H 8LP, England.

CAREER: Camberwell School of Art and Crafts, London, England, instructor in figure composition and commercial design, 1928-40; Berlin Reimann School, London, instructor in fashion

design, mid-1930s; free-lance advertising and book illustrator, muralist, and stained-glass designer. Executed various commissions, including World War II maps for the Ministry of Information (now Central Office of Information); murals for Babcock House, London, England; and stained-glass windows for St. Mary's Church, Hampton, England. Work has been exhibited at various locations, including Royal Academy, London, England; Society of Scottish Artists, Edinburgh, Scotland; British Empire Exhibition, Wembley, England, 1923; Glasgow, Scotland, 1938; Festival of Britain, London, England, 1951; Brussels Exhibition, 1958; and elsewhere. *Wartime service:* Air-raid warden, Hampton, England, 1939-45. *Member:* Society of Industrial Artists and Designers (fellow), Art Workers' Guild.

ILLUSTRATOR—Of interest to young readers: Henry Bett, *English Legends,* Batsford, 1950; Powys Mathers, translator, *The Book of the Thousand Nights and One Night,* Volume I, Folio Society, 1958 (Fraser was not associated with other volumes); John Hampden, reteller, *Sir William and the Wolf, and Other Stories from the Days of Chivalry,* Dutton, 1960; Barbara L.

"Ha-ha!" mocked the giant, as a second head instantly sprang on his shoulders. "You didn't know I have more than one head, did you?" ■ (From "Hassan the Brave" in *Egyptian and Sudanese Folk-Tales,* retold by Helen Mitchnik. Illustrated by Eric Fraser.)

ERIC FRASER

Picard, reteller, *Tales of the British People*, Criterion, 1962; Navin Sullivan, *Pioneer Germ Fighters*, Atheneum, 1962 (published in England as *Pioneers against Germs*, Harrap, 1962); Sullivan, *Pioneer Astronomers*, Atheneum, 1964 (published in England as *Pioneers in Astronomy*, Harrap, 1964); Charles Kingsley, *The Golden Fleece, with Theseus [and] Perseus*, Blackie & Son, 1965; Thomas Bulfinch, *The Age of Fable*, Dent, 1969; *Folklore, Myths and Legends of Britain*, Reader's Digest Association, 1973; James Reeves, reteller, *The Voyage of Odysseus: Homer's Odyssey*, Blackie & Son, 1973; Patricia Hill, *Joan of Arc*, Oxford University Press, 1975; William Barclay, *A Life of Christ*, Harper, 1977; Helen Mitchnik, reteller, *Egyptian and Sudanese Folk-Tales*, Oxford University Press, 1978; Nigel Sustins, *The Scent of Freedom*, CIO, 1982.

Other: Edmund G.V. Knox, *Here's Misery!*, Methuen, 1928; Maurice L. Norcott, *Up the Aerial; or, Ten Million Listeners Must Be Wrong*, Grayson & Grayson, 1933; *Complete Works of Shakespeare*, Collins, 1951; *Nero*, Folio Society, 1952; Ippolito Nievo, *Castle of Fratta*, translated by Lovett F. Edwards, Folio Society, 1954; *The Ephesian Story*, Golden Cockerel Press, 1975; Maria de Zayas Sotomayer, *A Shameful Revenge and Other Stories*, translated and introduced by John Sturrock, Folio Society, 1963; Alessandro Manzoni, *The Betrothed*, translated by Archibald Colquhoun, Folio Society, 1969; Ovid, *The Art of Love*, translated by B. P. Moore, Heritage Press, 1971; Richard Wagner, *Der Ring des Nibelungen/ The Ring* (text in German and English; translated from the German by Andrew Porter), Dawson, 1976; (with the Queen of Denmark) J.R.R. Tolkien, *The Lord of the Rings*, Folio Society, 1980.

Also illustrator of *The Story of Mond Nickel*, 1951 and J.R.R. Tolkien's *The Hobbit*, Folio Society; illustrator of book jackets; contributor of illustrations to periodicals, including *Radio Times, Harper's Bazaar, Vogue, Listener, Arts and Industry, Studio, Nash's, Leader, Punch*, and others.

SIDELIGHTS: Fraser began his career as an illustrator in the advertising field, later turning to both magazine and book illustration. His drawings first met the public eye in 1923 with publication of his work in a Christmas catalogue of a Kensington, England store. Since then, his artwork has been the medium through which a number of companies have reached the potential customer, including British Rail, United Steel, J. Arthur Rank, Atlas Copco, Bowaters, and many others. Fraser was best known, however, for his many illustrations of *Radio Times*, the journal of the British Broadcasting Corporation, which he had provided for over fifty years. The covers exemplify his highly detailed style in black-and-white drawings, displaying a richness and depth rendered with pen, brush, and scraper.

FOR MORE INFORMATION SEE: Print, August, 1951; Alec Davis, *The Graphic Work of Eric Fraser*, Uffculme Press, 1974.

FRENCH, Michael 1944-

BRIEF ENTRY: Born December 2, 1944, in Los Angeles, Calif. Novelist. French graduated from Stanford University in 1966 and received his M.S. from Northwestern University the following year. Employed as a full-time writer since 1982, French admits to being influenced by author Arthur Hailey while producing his first two adult novels, *Club Caribe* (Fawcett, 1977) and *Abingdon's* (Doubleday, 1979). As he explains: "... I was despairing because I couldn't get any of my fiction published, and I started reading Hailey for the first time. ... I told myself I could do a pretty decent job in this genre. ... It looked like a fair challenge, even fun." One of the books French had had difficulty getting published was a young adult novel entitled *The Throwing Season*. Later published by Delacorte in 1980, it relates the story of Henry Chevrolet (better known as Indian), a high school shot-putter who views his athletic ability as a means of obtaining a college scholarship. The young half-Cherokee encounters the obstacles of small town prejudice, bribery attempts, and betrayal by a teammate. *New York Times Book Review* described Indian as "superbly drawn . . . one of the genre's most interesting and unusual characters," calling the book ". . . a fascinating introduction to this special sports world of brute strength and psychological warfare."

In a second young adult novel, *Pursuit* (Delacorte, 1982), French explores the relationships that develop amongst four teenage boys on a hiking trip in the Sierra mountains. When one of the boys deliberately severs the safety rope of another, causing his death, the outing quickly becomes more than just a friendly excursion. *Horn Book* described the book as "a tautly paced story of survival. . . . [with] vivid wilderness descriptions [that] add to the immediacy of a suspenseful adventure story." *Booklist* took note of French's adept characterization, adding that ". . . the novel's pacing and slick culmination have been carefully manipulated for maximum effect." French is also the author of two storybooks adapted from motion pictures, *Flyers* (Random House, 1983) and *Indiana Jones and the Temple of Doom* (Random House, 1984). *Home:* 951 Acequia Madre, Santa Fe, N.M. 87501. *For More Information See: Contemporary Authors*, Volumes 89-92, Gale, 1980.

I have a little shadow that goes in and out with
  me,
And what can be the use of him is more than I
  can see.
He is very, very like me from the heels up to the
  head;
And I see him jump before me, when I jump into
  my bed.
                        —Robert Louis Stevenson

GARFIELD, James B. 1881-1984

OBITUARY NOTICE—See sketch in *SATA* Volume 6: Born September 19, 1881, in Atlanta, Ga.; died of pneumonia, May 23, 1984, in Valdosta, Ga. Actor, broadcaster, and author. An actor on Broadway and then in vaudeville during the early 1900s, Garfield became a free-lance writer and actor for radio during the 1930s, playing in more than twenty-five hundred soap opera episodes. Though blindness ended his acting career, Garfield continued to work in radio, broadcasting and the weekly public service program "A Blind Man Looks at You" from 1947 to 1967. He wrote stories, poems, and articles for juvenile magazines and gained acclaim for his novel, *Follow My Leader*, about a seeing eye dog and his master. After the book's publication, Garfield earned recognition as a classroom speaker and expert on the blind. He was appointed to the California State Commission for the Blind by former California Governor Edmund G. Brown. *Obituaries: Washington Post*, May 28, 1984.

GOUDGE, Elizabeth (de Beauchamp) 1900-1984

OBITUARY NOTICE—See sketch in *SATA* Volume 2: Born April 24, 1900, in Wells, Somerset, England; died April 1, 1984, near Henley-on-Thames, England. Educator, artist, and author of books for children and adults. Although Goudge had aspired to a writing career from childhood, her parents believed it expedient that she be trained in a more secure profession. Thus, she studied art for two years at Reading University and became a teacher of handicrafts. Her first writing efforts were for the theater, followed by the publication of her novel, *Island Magic*. In both her stories for children and adult novels, Goudge was known for creating an aura of romantic enchantment while capturing life in British small towns through accurate descriptions of individuals and locations. Throughout her long career, she produced ten books for children and fifteen novels, as well as several collections of short stories.

In 1947 Goudge was the recipient of the Carnegie Medal for her best-known children's book, *The Little White Horse*. The story was praised by critics for its unique blend of reality and fantasy, complete with images of unicorns, moonlight, and haunting countrysides. Included among her other juvenile works are *Smoke-House, The Well of the Star, Henrietta's House*, and *Linnets and Valerians*. Of her adult novels, the most notable is *Green Dolphin Country* for which she received both the 1944 Metro-Goldwyn-Mayer Literary Award and the Literary Guild Award. The book was successfully adapted as a motion picture in 1947. Goudge's other novels include *Towers in the Mist, The Rosemary Tree, The White Witch*, and *The Child from the Sea*. Her autobiography, *The Joy of the Snow*, was published in 1974. *For More Information See: The Who's Who of Children's Literature*, Schocken, 1968; *Third Book of Junior Authors*, H. W. Wilson, 1972; Elizabeth Goudge, *The Joy of the Snow: An Autobiography*, Coward, 1974; *Contemporary Authors, New Revision Series*, Volume 5, 1983; *Twentieth-Century Children's Writers*, St. Martin's, 1983. *Obituaries: Times* (London), April 3, 1984; *New York Times*, April 27, 1984.

GRAHAM, Eleanor 1896-1984

OBITUARY NOTICE—See sketch in *SATA* Volume 18: Born in 1896 in London, England; died March 8, 1984. Critic, ed-

itor, and author. Throughout her career, Graham strived to raise the standard of children's literature. She headed the Bumpus Books children's department from 1927 until 1931 and then reviewed children's selections for the Sunday edition of the London *Times*. Graham later served as the first editor of Puffin Books, a position she held from 1941 until 1962 when she became children's book editor at Methuen. In 1973 she was the recipient of the Eleanor Farjeon Award for extraordinary achievement in children's books. Included among the numerous books she wrote are *The Children Who Lived in a Barn, The Story of Jesus, The Night Adventures of Alexis*, and *Kenneth Grahame*. Of the many she edited, the most notable is *A Puffin Book of Verse*. *For More Information See: The Who's Who of Children's Literature*, Schocken, 1968; *Contemporary Authors*, Volumes 73-76, Gale, 1978; *The Writers Directory: 1982-1984*, Gale, 1981; *Twentieth-Century Children's Writers*, 2nd edition, St. Martin's, 1983. *Obituaries: Times* (London), March 13, 1984.

GREENE, Laura 1935-

PERSONAL: Born July 21, 1935, in New York, N.Y.; daughter of Charles (in sales) and Ida (Katz) Offenhartz; married Victor Robert Greene (a professor of American history), February 21, 1957; children: Jessica, Geoffrey. *Education:* Boston University, B.S., 1958; University of Pennsylvania, M.A., 1963; also attended Kansas State University, 1963-72. *Home and office:* 4869 North Woodburn St., Milwaukee, Wis. 53217.

CAREER: Junior high school English teacher in Yeadon, Pa., 1961-62; high school English teacher in Haddonfield, N.J., 1962-63; Kansas State University, Manhattan, Kan., instuctor in English, 1963-72; teacher at religious schools in Milwaukee,

LAURA GREENE

When my jeans were new, they were much too long. Now they're old and much too short. Growing makes the difference. ■ (From *Change* by Laura Greene. Illustrated by Gretchen Mayo.)

Wis., 1973—. Member of teaching staff at University of Bremen, 1981, and University of Wisconsin—Milwaukee, 1982. *Member:* Society of Children's Book Writers, Council for Wisconsin Writers, Chicago Reading Roundtable. *Awards, honors:* Citation from National Council of Social Studies, 1979, and Wisconsin Writers Award runner-up, 1980, both for *I Am an Orthodox Jew;* Arthur Tofte Memorial Award from Council for Wisconsin Writers, 1981, for *Sign Language.*

WRITINGS—For children: *I Am an Orthodox Jew* (illustrated by Lisa C. Wesson), Holt, 1979; *I Am Somebody* (illustrated by Gerald Cross), Childrens Press, 1980; *Change: Getting to Know About Ebb and Flow* (illustrated by Gretchen Mayo), Human Sciences Press, 1981; *Help: Getting to Know about Needing and Giving* (illustrated by G. Mayo), Human Sciences Press, 1981; (with Eva Barash Dicker) *Sign Language: A First Book* (illustrated by Caren Caraway), F. Watts, 1981; *Careers in the Computer Industry,* F. Watts, 1983; *Computers in Business and Industry,* F. Watts, 1984; *Computer Pioneers,* F. Watts, 1985.

WORK IN PROGRESS: Children's picture books, fiction and non-fiction.

SIDELIGHTS: "Children's egos are very fragile things. What children think of themselves is an important factor in forming their egos and thus their personalities. One thing that affects children's self-images is the way they perceive their differences among people which are often a source of pain and prejudice, but I try to look at these differences as a potential source of pride.

"*I Am an Orthodox Jew* is about what it's like to be a member of a community which is different from that of the majority. *I Am Somebody* concerns a boy who isn't as good at sports as he'd like to be. The characters in both books are proud of what they are, even though they rub against their differences. *Help* and *Change* deal with the idea that we don't always have control over everything in life, yet, despite this, each of us can do significant things. *Sign Language* explains a language with a unique communication base to hearing children. It is my hope that children with hearing disabilities, who read this book, will feel a sense of pride in their own special language. I write about people and their feelings because I care very much about the hurt we inflict upon one another.

"I have just begun writing nonfiction. This too I find very rewarding. When I write nonfiction, I have the opportunity of investigating new subjects in depth. In this way I continue learning. Learning, to me, is one of the most exciting things about living. There are so many things I know nothing about and I'm curious to seek out the answers to questions I haven't even asked yet.

"As I continue to learn, I try to keep an open mind about new subjects and new points in view. There are some subjects, however, about which I feel especially strong. The women's movement is one of them.

"I support the Equal Rights Amendment and believe women should have the same opportunities, benefits, and responsibilities as men. Yet, I fear that in the struggle for this cause (which is so right), it is the children who are being hurt, as are the women who choose not to engage in out-of-home employment. I have two full-time jobs: writing and homemaking; I am committed to both with equal fervor."

HADLEY, Lee 1934- (Hadley Irwin, a joint pseudonym)

BRIEF ENTRY: Born October 10, 1934, in Earlham, Iowa. An assistant professor of English and author of books for young people, Hadley graduated from Drake University and received her masters degree from the University of Wisconsin, Madison. Under joint pseudonym Hadley Irwin, she has collaborated with author and co-worker Ann Irwin in writing five juvenile novels. Among these is *The Lilith Summer* (a Book-of-the-Month-Club selection; Feminist Press, 1979), the story of seventy-seven-year-old Lilith and twelve-year-old Ellen, who find themselves "sitting" each other for the summer. *Publishers Weekly* said it was "written with grace and wit," adding that "it teaches a lesson about the human condition." Other books by Hadley and Irwin include *Bring to a Boil and Separate* (A McElderry Book, 1980) and *What about Grandma?* (A McElderry Book, 1982). *Home address:* R.R.1, Madrid, Iowa 50156. *For More Information See: Contemporary Authors,* Volume 101, Gale, 1981.

I know a funny little man,
    As quiet as a mouse,
Who does the mischief that is done
    In everybody's house!
There's no one ever sees his face,
    And yet we all agree
That every plate we break was cracked
    By Mr. Nobody.

                   —Anonymous

HAMSA, Bobbie   1944-

BRIEF ENTRY: Born June 14, 1944, in Ord, Neb. Hamsa has worked as a junior underwriter for an insurance company, as a copywriter, and has written advertising copy for Mutual of Omaha's ''Wild Kingdom'' television show. A three-time recipient of the Cornhusker Addy Awards for advertising copy, Hamsa began writing books as a diversion from writing copy for her clients. She recalls ''busting brazenly over the transom,'' when she sent out her first three book manuscripts for the ''Far-Fetched Pet'' series, published by Children's Press. Her books for this series include background information about various animals while portraying each as a household pet. The combination is both educational and entertaining. Hamsa said that her philosophy for writing ''. . . is to make light of the world around me, turn the commonplace into the unexpected, and observe things in a new light.'' Books by Hamsa in the ''Far-Fetched Pet'' series include: *Your Pet Bear* (1980), *Your Pet Beaver* (1980), *Your Pet Elephant* (1980), *Your Pet Kangaroo* (1980), *Your Pet Camel* (1980), *Your Pet Penguin* (1980), *Your Pet Gorilla* (1980), *Your Pet Lion* (1981), *Your Pet Sea Lion* (1982), and *Your Pet Giraffe* (1982). *Home:* 2302 South 102nd St., Omaha, Neb. 68124. *For More Information See: Contemporary Authors,* Volume 106, Gale, 1982.

HARDCASTLE, Michael   1933-
(David Clark)

BRIEF ENTRY: Born February 6, 1933, in Huddersfield, England. Journalist and author of sports books for children. The strength of Hardcastle's books is found in the combination of interesting, substantial plots, and the concise and simple language he employs. As *School Librarian* observed, ''True stories, told in a simple journalistic style, about contemporary sports, life and death are bound to be compulsive reading for middle and secondary 'reluctant' readers.'' Although soccer is Hardcastle's most popular subject, he also writes about other sports including motocross, football, and cricket. The characters he creates are responsible for much of the appeal and attraction of these books, as readers find it easy to identify with the frustrations and struggles of the challenger. In *Roar to Victory* (Methuen, 1982), a story about look-alike brothers, Hardcastle deals with the problem of sibling rivalry and the meaning of confidence and perseverance. *Junior Bookshelf* commented that ''With Michael Hardcastle's books it is the underdog who wins through in the end, the bullies, the boasters, and the cheats having got their come-uppance along the way.'' In *The Gigantic Hit* (Pelham, 1982), a story about the game that ensues between a cricket club and its rival team, once more the underdog becomes the hero after scoring 499 runs. *Junior Bookshelf* again observed, ''The jigsaw of the plot fits snugly together with no outrageous flights of fancy or unacceptable twists. The final resolution is fairytale happiness all around . . . but it fits!''

In what is considered a difficult genre to write competently, *Twentieth-Century Children's Writers* commented on Hardcastle's adept hand, and summed up his talent by saying, ''Sporting fiction . . . has not yet reached the point where individual writers may be acclaimed as masters of the genre. But Michael Hardcastle's football novels clearly demonstrate that he must be seriously regarded as a writer of children's fiction and not simply as a successful author of football stories.'' Included among Hardcastle's books are: *Dive to Danger* (Benn, 1969), *Strike!* (Benn, 1970), *In the Net* (Methuen, 1971), *Playing Ball* (Heinemann, 1972), *The Demon Bowler* (Hei-

nemann, 1974), *The Saturday Horse* (Methuen, 1977), *Soccer Special* (Methuen, 1978), *Top of the League* (Heinemann, 1979), *Go for the Goal* (Benn, 1980), and *Fast from the Gate* (Methuen, 1983). He has also written several books under the pseudonym David Clark, including *Goalie* (Benn, 1972), *Top Spin* (Benn, 1973), and *Roll Up* (Benn, 1975). *Home:* 17 Molescroft Park, Beverly, North Humberside HU17 7EB, England. *For More Information See: Contemporary Authors,* Volumes 25-28, revised, Gale, 1977; *Twentieth-Century Children's Writers,* 2nd edition, St. Martin's, 1983.

HARTMAN, Evert   1937-

PERSONAL: Born July 12, 1937, in Avereest, Netherlands; son of Coendert and Henny (van Housselt) Hartman; married Tjitske Medema, June 11, 1963; children: Theo, Julius. *Education:* Graduated, Rijksuniversiteit te Utrecht, 1965. *Religion:* Calvinist. *Home:* Eddingtonlaan 4, 7904 EE Hoogeveen, Netherlands.

CAREER: Menso Alting College, Hoogeveen, Netherlands, instructor in geography, 1962—. *Military service:* Dutch Army, 1956-58, became sergeant.

WRITINGS—Fiction; of interest to young readers: *Oorlog zonder vrienden,* Lemniscaat (Rotterdam, Netherlands), 1979, translation by Patricia Crampton published as *War without Friends,* Crown, 1982; *Vechten voor overmorgen* (title means ''Fighting for the Day after Tomorrow''), Lemniscaat, 1980;

EVERT HARTMAN

(Jacket illustration by Michael Garland from *War without Friends* by Evert Hartman.)

Het onzichtbare licht (title means "The Invisible Light"), Lemniscaat, 1982; *Gegijzeld* (title means "Hijacked"), Lemniscaat, 1984.

Adult fiction: *Signalen in de nacht* (title means "Signals in the Night"), J. H. Gottmer (Haarlem, Netherlands), 1973; *Machinist op dood spoor* (title means "Engine Driver on a Dead Track"), J. H. Gottmer, 1975; *De laatste stuw* (title means "The Last Dam"), J. H. Gottmer, 1977.

WORK IN PROGRESS: A book about personal freedom, for young readers.

SIDELIGHTS: "By the time I was sixteen, I intended to be a writer, but it was another sixteen years before I wrote my first book, an adventure novel about World War II (*Signalen in de nacht*). The two books following it (*Machinist op dood spoor* and *De laatste stuw*) are also adventure novels.

"Only after these books did I start writing juvenile literature. The first book of this genre (*Oorlog zonder vrienden*) again takes place during World War II but deals with a subject never written about before—the situation of a boy growing up in the social setting of the NSB (Dutch National Socialist Movement, in collaboration with the occupying German forces). The boy is treated scornfully by his peers and lives through a difficult period. Issues in this book are: following a political conviction blindly, loneliness, and the question of whether or not we should make children responsible for the actions of their parents.

"The setting of my second juvenile book (*Vechten voor overmorgen*) is in the near future, the principal theme being the issue of how much authorities may lay down rules and legislation without endangering individual freedom.

"My third book for young people (*Het onzichtbare licht*) is about a clairvoyant thirteen-year-old girl, and is based mainly on the experiences of a real schoolgirl. The theme deals with the belief in phenomena that cannot be observed or be scientifically explained.

"My fourth book for juveniles, *Gegijzeld,* is about a situation in a school, where four pupils and a teacher are captured by two terrorists from a foreign country. After the hijacking has lasted for several days, understanding grows between the hijackers and their victims, especially when one of the terrorists tells his own story of what happened to him as a fourteen year old boy. . . .

"My fifth book for young readers (still in progress) has 'personal freedom' for its subject. Everybody has the right to think and act differently from his classmates, neighbors, and members of his family. There is no need to belong to a special group and to behave in accordance with the belief or ideology of that group."

His studies were pursued but never effectually overtaken.

—H.G. Wells

Because of the look on her face, the Bear reached out his paw, but Megan did not move. Randall stirred awake and wondered where he was. ■ (From *South Star* by Betsy Gould Hearne. Illustrated by Trina Schart Hyman.)

HEARNE, Betsy Gould   1942-

PERSONAL: Born October 6, 1942, in Wilsonville, Ala.; daughter of Kenneth (a doctor) and Elizabeth (Barrett) Gould; married Michael Claffey; children: Joanna Hearne, Elizabeth Claffey. *Education:* Wooster College, B.A., 1964; University of Chicago, M.A., 1968; graduate study, 1979—. *Residence:* Chicago, Ill. *Agent:* Philippa Brophy, The Sterling Lord Agency, Inc., 660 Madison Ave., New York, N.Y. 10021. *Office:* American Library Association, 50 East Huron St., Chicago, Ill. 60611.

CAREER: Wayne County Public Library, Wooster, Ohio, children's librarian, 1964-65; University of Chicago Laboratory Schools, Chicago, Ill., children's librarian, 1967-68; *Booklist,* Chicago, editor of children's books, 1973—. Judge, National Book Awards, 1975 and American Book Awards, 1981. *Member:* American Library Association (member, Mildred Batchelder Committee, 1973-77, Newbery-Caldecott Award Committee; consultant, Notable Books Committee), Children's Reading Round Table. *Awards, honors:* Agnes Sayer Klein Award for Graduate Study, American Library Association, 1979; Children's Reading Round Table Award, 1982.

WRITINGS: South Star (juvenile fiction; illustrated by Trina Schart Hyman), Atheneum, 1977; *Home* (juvenile fiction; illustrated by T. S. Hyman), Atheneum, 1979; (editor, with Marilyn Kaye) *Celebrating Children's Books: Essays on Children's Literature in Honor of Zena Sutherland* (adult reference book), Lothrop, 1981; *Choosing Books for Children: A Commonsense Guide* (adult reference book), Delacorte, 1981. Also contributor of articles, reviews, and editorials to periodicals such as *Library Quarterly* and *Signal.*

Recordings: "Evaluating Children's Books," Children's Book Council, 1979.

WORK IN PROGRESS: Beauty and the Beast: A Study of Aesthetic Survival.

BETSY GOULD HEARNE

HELLBERG, Hans-Eric   1927-

PERSONAL: Born May 11, 1927, in Borlaenge, Sweden; son of Eric and Hanna Hellberg; married; children: Asa Erica. *Home:* Vasagatan 12 a, S-781 50 Borlaenge, Sweden.

CAREER: Journalist, 1957—; art editor, 1957—; publisher, 1979—. *Member:* Swedish Union of Authors. *Awards, honors:* Nils Holgersson Plaque from Swedish Library Association, 1971, for collected works; certificate of honor from International Board on Books for Young People, 1971, for *Bogserbaaten;* Astrid Lindgren Prize from Raben & Sjoegren Publishers, 1975, for lasting contribution to children's literature; diploma of honor from Swedish Academy of Detection, 1976.

WRITINGS—All for children; all translated from the Swedish by Patricia Crampton, except as indicated: *Bjoern med trollhatten,* Bonnier, 1965, translation published as *Ben's Lucky Hat* (illustrated by David Parkins), Methuen, 1980, Crown, 1982; *Morfars Maria,* Bonnier, 1969, translation published as *Grandpa's Maria* (illustrated by Joan Sandin), Morrow, 1974; *Martins Maris,* Bonnier, 1970, translation published as *Maria and Martin* (illustrated by Trevor Stubley) Methuen, 1975; *Jag aer Maria jag,* Bonnier, 1971, translation published as *I Am Maria* (illustrated by T. Stubley), Methuen, 1978; *Da enoegda banditerna,* Raben & Sjoegren, 1972, translation published as *The One-Eyed Bandits* (illustrated by Annabel Spenceley), Andersen Press, 1978; *J & J,* Bonnier, 1972, translation by Joan Tate published as *Follow My Leader,* Macmillan, 1977.

In Swedish; all published by Bonnier, except as indicated: *Jan faar en vaen* (title means "A Friend for Jan"), 1958; *Jan och Ann-Charlotte faar en ide* (title means "An Idea from Jan and . . ."), 1959; *Aelvpirater* (title means "River Pirates"), 1960; *Hemligheten* (title means "The Secret"), 1961; *Joakim, kallad jocke* (title means "Joakim, Called Jocke"), 1962; *Ung man med kamera* (title means "Young Man with a Camera"), Prisma, 1962; *Miks fiende* (title means "Mik's Enemy"), 1963; *Soeren och silverskrinet* (title means "Sören and the Silver Box"), 1964; *Kalle Karolina* (title means "Charlie Caroline"), 1965, revised edition, 1978; *Annika paa en soendag* (title means "Annika on a Sunday"), 1966; *Jonas haemnd* (title means "The Revenge of Jonas"), 1967; *Men mars aer kall och blaasig: En thriller paa skoj* (title means "Mars, Cold and Windy"), 1968.

Bogserbaaten (title means "The Tug"), Raben & Sjoegren, 1970; *Kram* (title means "Hug"), 1973; *Upp genom luften* (title means "Into the Air"), Raben & Sjoegren, 1973; *Aelskade Maria* (title means "Beloved Maria"), 1974; *Skuggan som foell* (title means "The Shadow that Fell"), Raben & Sjoegren, 1974; (with Elvira Birgitta Holm) *Foerbjudet* (title means "Forbidden"), Foerfattarfoerlaget, 1974; (with Holm) *Tillaatet* (title means" Allowed"), Foerfattarfoerlaget, 1975;

Would she look like Agnes when she was old? You get fat and white and lumpy and then you die and end up in the graveyard. ■ (From *Grandpa's Maria* by Hans-Eric Hellberg. Illustrated by Joan Sandin.)

HANS-ERIC HELLBERG

Raedda paradiset (title means "Save Paradise"), Raben & Sjoegren, 1975; *Puss* (title means "Kiss"), 1975; *Som vaenner* (title means "Being Friends"), 1976; *Paeivi dyker ned* (title means "Päivi Dives Down"), Raben & Sjoegren, 1976; *Baklaenges* (title means "Backwards"), Raben & Sjoegren, 1977; *Love Love Love*, 1977; *Behaall dej* (title means "Keep Well"), 1977; *Framlaenges* (title means "Forwards"), Raben & Sjoegren, 1978; *Nedbrottslingarna* (title means "Villains"), Raben & Sjoegren, 1979; *Aelskar, aelskar inte* (title means "Love Me, Love Me Not"), 1979; *BUSungen* (title means "The Mischievous Kid"), Tvaa Skrivare, 1979; *BUSligan* (title means "The Rowdy Gang"), Tvaa Skrivare, 1979; *BUSfroeet* (title means "Young Ragamuffin"), Tvaa Skrivare, 1980; *BUSvisslaren* (title means "The Rowdy Whistler"), Tvaa Skrivare, 1980; *Maria kär* (title means "Maria, in Love"), 1982; *Pojken som hade tur* (title means "Boy Lucky"), Tvaa Skrivare, 1983; *Det är jag som är Gry* (title means "I am Gry"), Tvaa Skrivare, 1983; *Osynlig närvaro* (title means "Invisible Presence"), Tvaa Skrivare, 1984; *Gry i Amerika* (title means "Gry in America"), Tvaa Skrivare, 1985.

Also author of "Skuggornas klubb" (television play; title means "The Club of Shadows"), 1959, "Bogserbaaten" (television serial), 1973, "Vaennerna," 1974, and "Jag aer Maria" (film).

SIDELIGHTS: Hellberg revealed the inspiration for his writing in the following letter addressed to children. "I have a secret. I know something. I know how to do things which I don't dare to do.

"You have a few cherished dreams, right? They are secret dreams, right?

"One of mine is to lie comfortably on a cloud, slowly drifting above the rooftops.

"Another dream is about a flying saucer. One day it lands in my garden, and a fellow not bigger than my thumb climbs down. He is small, but he has immense power. I am a small child and have no power at all. Now this fellow tells me that

I am chosen by a Universal Empire to do a great deed: the Empire gives me power to bring everlasting peace on earth. But I am going to die in the process. Am I willing? And I answer with a high, steady voice: Yes! Give me power, glory, and death!

"Also, I am a daring young man who knows perfectly well how to deal with girls and headmasters—I am the opposite of Charlie Brown. I am always winning, always doing the right thing, saying the right words, telling the little red-haired girl that I like her, and telling Lucy to go bury herself.

"Here is the secret: You write the dreams down. It's that simple. Writers do that. But luckily you don't need to be a writer to have this fun. You just put down your most secret dreams, your innermost wishes, on paper.

"Believe me, it's a thrilling business." ["Meet Your Author: Hans-Eric Hellberg," *Cricket*, June, 1976.]

FOR MORE INFORMATION SEE: Cricket, June, 1976.

HIRSHBERG, Al(bert Simon)   1909-1973

PERSONAL: Born May 10, 1909, in Boston, Mass.; died April 11, 1973, apparently of a heart attack, in Sarasota, Fla.; son of David Walter and Alice (Lilienthal) Hirshberg; married Marjorie Littauer, August 21, 1939 (died, 1970); married Bert Milstone Cohen, November 12, 1971; children: (first marriage) Judy (Mrs. Paul Marandett), Albert S., Jr. *Education:* Boston University, B.S., 1932. *Agent:* Sterling Lord Agency, 660 Madison Ave., New York, N.Y. 10021.

CAREER: Writer. *Boston Post*, Boston Mass., columnist, 1930-52; *Boston Herald-Traveler*, Boston, sports writer, 1964-68. Part-time lecturer, University of Southern Florida, 1962-67. Chairman of board, National Foundation for Eye Research, 1950-69; member of corporation, Perkins School for the Blind. *Military service:* U.S. Naval Reserve, 1943-45; became lieutenant. *Member:* Authors League, Society of Magazine Writers, Baseball Writers Association of America, Authors Guild, Fernald League for Retarded Children, Sigma Delta Chi. *Awards, honors:* E. P. Dutton sports writing award, 1952; Distinguished Alumni Award, Boston University, 1966.

WRITINGS: (With Joe McKenney) *Famous American Athletes of Today*, Page, 1947, reprinted, Books for Libraries Press, 1972; *The Red Sox, the Bean and the Cod*, Waverly House, 1947; *The Braves, the Pick and the Shovel*, Waverly House, 1948; (with Jim Piersall) *Fear Strikes Out: The Jim Piersall Story*, Atlantic, 1955; *The Battery for Madison High* (juvenile), Atlantic, 1955; *Varsity Double Play* (juvenile), Atlantic, 1956; (with Sammy Aaronson) *As High as My Heart*, Coward, 1957; (with Bob Cousy) *Basketball Is My Life*, Prentice-Hall, 1958, revised edition, J. L. Pratt, 1963; (with Ralph Pfau) *Prodigal Shepherd*, Lippincott, 1958.

The Jackie Jensen Story (juvenile), Messner, 1960; *The Eddie Mathews Story* (juvenile), Messner, 1960; (ghost written for Arthur Wilson) *Thy Will Be Done*, Dial, 1960; *The Man Who Fought Back: Red Schoendienst* (juvenile), Messner, 1961; (with Bernice F. Davis) *The Desperate and the Damned*, Crowell, 1961; *From Sandlots to League President* (juvenile), Messner, 1962; (with Clinton T. Duffy) *88 Men and 2 Women*, Doubleday, 1962; *Basketball's Greatest Stars*, Putnam, 1963; (with Russ Hodges) *My Giants*, Doubleday, 1963; *Bill Russell*

(Jacket illustration by George Loh from *Basketball's Greatest Teams* by Al Hirshberg.)

of the Boston Celtics (juvenile), Messner, 1964; *The Al Kaline Story* (juvenile), Messner, 1964; (with C. T. Duffy) *Sex and Crime*, Doubleday, 1965; *Basketball's Greatest Teams*, Putnam, 1965; (ghost written for Angeline Tucker) *He Is in Heaven*, McGraw, 1965; *Baseball's Greatest Catchers*, Putnam, 1966; (with Lindsey Nelson) *Backstage at the Mets*, Viking, 1966; (with Curt Gowdy) *Cowboy at the Mike*, Doubleday, 1966; (with James W. Turpin) *Vietnam Doctor: The Story of Project Concern*, McGraw, 1966; (with Carl Yastrzemski) *Yaz*, Viking, 1968; *The Glory Runners* (juvenile), Putnam, 1968; *Henry Aaron: Quiet Superstar* (juvenile), Putnam, 1969, revised edition published as *The Up-to-Date Biography of Henry Aaron, Quiet Superstar*, 1974; (with Ken Harrelson) *Hawk*, Viking, 1969.

(With J. W. Turpin) *A Faraway Country: The Continuing Story of Project Concern*, World Publishing, 1970; *The Greatest American Leaguers* (juvenile), Putnam, 1970; (with Ted Green) *High Stick*, Dodd, 1971; (with James DeWitt) *Addict: A Doctor's Odyssey*, Cowles, 1972; (with C. Yastrzemski) *Batting*, Viking, 1972; *What's the Matter with the Red Sox?*, Dodd, 1973; *Frank Robinson: Born Leader* (juvenile), Putnam, 1973; *Frank Howard, the Gentle Giant* (juvenile), Putnam, 1973; (with Jack Kelley and Milt Schmidt) *Hockey: Bantam to Pro*, Allyn & Bacon, 1974; *Bobby Orr: Fire on Ice* (juvenile), edited by Frank Orr, Putnam, 1975.

Contributor of aricles to *Saturday Evening Post, Look, Sport,*

Reader's Digest, and *Sports Illustrated.*

For More Information See: (Obituary) *New York Times*, April 13, 1973.

HOARE, Robert J(ohn)   1921-1975
(Adam King)

PERSONAL: Born November 5, 1921, in Manchester, England, died August 30, 1975; son of John William (a journalist) and Margaret (Giles) Hoare; married Eileen Mary Hodgkinson, July, 1952; children: Clare Susan, Zoe Therese, Lois Joanne. *Education:* Alsager Training College, Cheshire, England, Ministry of Education teaching certificate; University of Reading, diploma in advanced study of education. *Politics:* "Undecided." *Religion:* Catholic. *Home:* "Karina," Wells Lane, Ascot, Berkshire, England.

CAREER: Allied Newspapers (later Kemsley Newspapers), Manchester, England, sub-editor, 1937-41, 1946-48; St. Cuthbert's Senior Mixed School, Manchester, assistant master, 1949-56; St. Peter's Primary School, Marlow, Buckinghamshire, England, assistant master, 1956-59; St. Mary's College, Twickenham, Middlesex, England, tutor and librarian, 1959-75. Author of juveniles and texts. *Military service:* Royal Air Force, 1941-46; became leading aircraftsman. *Member:* Association of Training Colleges and Departments of Education, Society of Authors, Simmarian Athletic Club.

*WRITINGS—*Juveniles: *Wings over the Atlantic*, Phoenix House, 1956, Branford, 1957; *The Sinister Hoard*, Parrish, 1958; *The First Book of Aviation*, Cassell, 1958; *The Second Book of Aviation*, Cassell, 1958; *Desperate Venture*, Parrish, 1958; *The Story of Aircraft and Travel by Air*, A. & C. Black, 1958, 4th edition, 1968, Dufour, 1982; (with Jim Peters) *Spiked Shoes*, Cassell, 1959; *Rangi to the Rescue*, Hamish Hamilton, 1960; *Secret of the Sahara*, Parish, 1960; *Temba Becomes a Tiger*, Hamish Hamilton, 1960; (compiler) *True Stories of Capture and Rescue* (anthology), Hamish Hamilton, 1960, new edition, 1961; *Travel by Sea*, A. & C. Black, 1961, Dufour, 1965, 2nd edition, A. & C. Black, 1967; (editor) Margaret Hyde, *Flight Today and Tomorrow*, Brockhampton Press, 1961; *First Person: An Anthology of Achievement*, Odhams, 1963; *Deep Waters*, Ginn, 1966; *The High Peaks*, Ginn, 1966; *Southwards*, Ginn, 1966; *Christianity Comes to Britain*, Geoffrey Chapman, 1968; *The Old West*, Muller, 1969; *Messages*, Muller, 1969; *Cowboys and Cattle Trails*, Hulton Educational, 1971; *True Mysteries*, Carousel, 1971; *Men of the Old West*, Chatto & Windus, 1972; *Saints*, Chatto & Windus, 1972; *Sporting Giants*, Heinemann, 1973; *More True Mysteries*, Carousel, 1974; (under pseudonym Adam King) *Who Wants to Be a Dead Hero?*, Macmillan, 1974; *At the Bottom of the Deep Blue Sea*, Heinemann, 1975; *Gold*, Muller, 1975; *Underwater*, Muller, 1975; *Giant Escapes of World War II*, Carousel, 1976; *When the West Was Wild*, A. & C. Black, 1976.

"Champion Library" series, published by Macmillan: *Four-Minute Miler and the Boy from Bowral*, 1962; *The Fighting Marine and the Boy Who Loved Horses*, 1962; *Queen of Tennis and She Jumped to Fame*, 1962.

Textbooks: "Planned Composition" series, five books, Odhams, 1957-61; "Understanding" series, four books, Longmans, Green, 1961; "Modern Age Readers" Books 1-4, Odhams, 1962, Books 5-8, Ginn, 1966; (co-author) "Catholic Workbooks," four books, Macmillan, 1963-64; *From the Ear-*

liest Times to the Assyrian Empire, Macmillan, 1963; *From the New Babylon to the Time of Christ*, Macmillan, 1964; (with Sean D. Healy) *From the Roman Empire to the Crowning of Harold*, Macmillan, 1964; (with A. M. Dyer) *From the Norman Conquest to the Flight of James II*, Burns & Oates, 1964; (with F. C. Price) *From William and Mary to the Mechanical Age*, Burns & Oates, 1965; "Planned English" series, four books, Ginn, 1966; (with Adolf Heuser) *Christ through the Ages: A Church History for Secondary Schools*, Geoffrey Chapman, Volume 1: *From the Beginning to the Fifteenth Century*, 1966, Volume II: *From the Reformation to Second Vatican Council*, 1966; "Our Saints" series, eight books, Longmans, Green, 1967; "Write Away" series, four books, Longmans, Green, 1969; "Words in Action" series, four books, Philograph Publications, 1970; *Topic Work with Books*, Geoffrey Chapman, 1971; *World War I: An Illustrated History in Colour*, William Macdonald, 1973; *World War II: An Illustrated History in Colour*, William Macdonald, 1973; *Turn of the Century: An Illustrated History in Colour, 1899-1913*, Macdonald Educational, 1975; "Beginning Write Away" series, two books, Longman, 1976: *A Dictionary of People*, Longman, 1976.

Contributor to *Times Educational Supplement, Teachers World, Teacher, School Librarian, Books for Your Children, Bookseller*.

ADAPTATIONS: The Sinister Hoard was broadcast in installments on British Broadcasting Corp. "Children's Hour," 1960.

SIDELIGHTS: True Mysteries and *Great Escapes of World War II* were published in German. *At the Bottom of the Deep Blue Sea* was published in Africaans.

HOBBIES AND OTHER INTERESTS: Running, swimming.

HOPPER, Nancy J. 1937-

PERSONAL: Born July 24, 1937, in Lewistown, Pa.; daughter of David L. (a school superintendent) and Joyce (Beaver) Swartz;

NANCY J. HOPPER

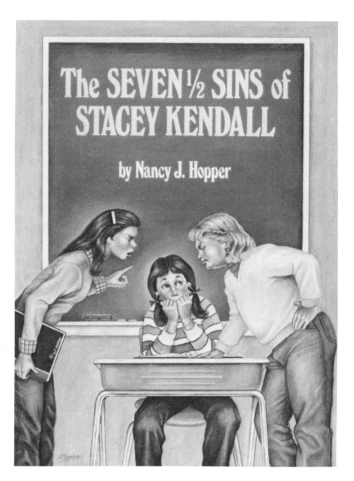

(Jacket illustration by Jim Spence from *The Seven ½ Sins of Stacey Kendall* by Nancy J. Hopper.)

married James A. Hooper (a professor and artist), August 20, 1960; children: Christopher J., Jennifer A. *Education:* Juniata College, B.A., 1959. *Home:* 2341 Ridgewood, Alliance, Ohio 44601.

CAREER: Teacher of English at public schools in Tyrone, Pa., 1959-60, and Freeport, N.Y., 1960-62. *Member:* Authors League of America, Authors Guild.

WRITINGS—Fiction; of interest to young readers: *Secrets*, Elsevier/Nelson, 1979; *The Seven½ Sins of Stacey Kendall*, Dutton, 1982; *Just Vernon*, Lodestar, 1982; *Hang On, Harvey!*, Dutton, 1983; *Lies*, Lodestar, 1984; *Ape Ears and Beaky*, Dutton, 1984.

WORK IN PROGRESS: Currently working on a manuscript for young readers.

SIDELIGHTS: "I like to work from character, the character coming first, the story happening at least partially as a result of that character. The largest part of my writing is both for and about people between the ages of nine and sixteen because I find individuals this age to be fascinating. They have a fresh, critical eye on life, and are quite often endowed with a great sense of humor. Also, they are engaged in the all-encompassing battle to grow up, to mature; and I think that is to a great extent what life is about at either age one month or eighty years: to mature, to grow, to understand. It seems to me that between the ages of nine and sixteen, individuals make a frontal attack on this issue, acting with determination, courage, and a willingness to take their bumps and to write off their losses. This enables them as real people, and as people in books, to move in and out of situations that offer much in the way of opportunity for excitement, and, best of all, to regard life as what it really is: an adventure.''

HOBBIES AND OTHER INTERESTS: Reading, bird watching, walking, bicycling, going to concerts and to the movies, and making Ukranian eggs.

IRWIN, Ann(abelle Bowen)   1915-
(Hadley Irwin, a joint pseudonym)

BRIEF ENTRY: Born October 8, 1915, in Peterson, Iowa. Educator, playwright, and author of books for young people. A graduate of Morningside College, Irwin received a M.A. from the University of Iowa. She began teaching English in 1937, and, since 1970, has been an associate professor at Iowa State University. With fellow staff member Lee Hadley, she has written five novels under the joint pseudonym Hadley Irwin. Among these are *The Lilith Summer* (a Book-of-the-Month Club selection; Feminist Press, 1979), *We Are Mesquakie, We Are One* (Feminist Press, 1980), and *Moon and Me* (Atheneum, 1981). She also wrote four books with Bernice Reida, including *Moon of the Red Strawberry* (Aurora, 1977) and *Until We Reach the Valley* (Avon, 1979). She is sole author of *One Bite at a Time* (F. Watts, 1973), which relates the story of one day in the life of a teenage girl as she struggles with an overweight problem. Irwin's other works are *Successful Treatment of Stuttering* (Walker, 1980) and the one-act plays, ''And the Fulness Thereof'' (Pioneer) and ''Pieces of Silver'' (Eldridge Publishing). *Office:* Department of English, Iowa State University, 347 Ross Hall, Ames, Iowa 50011. *For More Information See: Contemporary Authors,* Volume 101, Gale, 1981.

JOHNSON, Spencer   1938-

BRIEF ENTRY: Born November 24, 1938, in Watertown, S.D. Author. Soon after earning his M.D. from the Royal College of Surgeons in 1968, Johnson decided that he would be of more service to people through the written word rather than on an individual basis. From 1970 to 1977 he was employed in communications at corporations in Minnesota and California. Currently, he is chairman at Candle Communications in La Jolla, Calif. Johnson's first venture as an author was the ''Valuetales'' series, a collection of thirteen books for children that emphasize basic tenets using well-known historical figures as role models. Published by Value Communications between 1976 and 1979, the titles include: *The Value of Patience: The Story of the Wright Brothers, The Value of Believing in Yourself: The Story of Louis Pasteur, The Value of Imagination: The Story of Charles Dickens,* and *The Value of Fantasy: The Story of Hans Christian Andersen.*

Although the ''Valuetales'' series proved successful in its field, Johnson gained nationwide attention with the publication of his book for adults entitled *The One Minute Manager* (Morrow, 1982). Written with Kenneth Blanchard, it remained on the bestseller list for over a year and was followed by *The One Minute Father: The Quickest Way to Help Children Learn How to Like Themselves and Want to Behave Themselves* as well as *The One Minute Mother* (both Morrow, 1983). His current projects include *Who Moved My Cheese,* a book, as he explains, about ''dealing with unexpected change,'' *Peaks 'n'*

Valleys, ''a philosophy of living,'' and *Patroled,* about ''non-accountability in American society.'' *Office:* Candle Communications Corp., 1250 Prospect St., Ocean Level, La Jolla, Calif. 92037. *For More Information See: Publishers Weekly,* August 26, 1983; *Contemporary Authors,* Volume 110, Gale, 1984.

JOHNSON, William R.

PERSONAL: Born in Minneapolis, Minn.; son of Carl A. and Anna M. (Anderson) Johnson; married Pauline Doten; children: William R., Jr., Jill Anne. *Education:* Attended Dartmouth College and Jean Morgan School of Art, New York, N.Y. *Religion:* Lutheran. *Home:* 10656 Riverview Pl., Coon Rapids, Minn. 55433.

CAREER: Free-lance artist, cartoonist, and writer in New York, N.Y., 1957-65. and Coon Rapids, Minn., 1965—; Trend Enterprises, Inc., St. Paul., Minn., art director and artist, 1971-78; Founder and proprietor of BLIP Productions, Minneapolis, Minn., 1978—. Former member of board of directors and baseball manager, Levittown (N.Y.) Boys Club. *Military service:* U.S. Naval Reserve, active duty, 1942-46. *Awards, honors:* Freedoms Foundation honor certificate for editorial cartoon; selections from, ''Letters from the Twins'' placed in the Baseball Hall of Fame, 1984.

WRITINGS—All self-illustrated: *Holiday Funtime,* Doubleday, 1964; *Dinosaur Funbook,* Troubador Press (San Francisco), 1979; *Famous Monsters Funbook,* Troubador Press, 1981. Author of sports cartoon column ''Letters from the Twins,'' *St. Paul Dispatch.*

Illustrator: P. Werner, *How Many Angels in the Sky?,* Augsburg, 1965.

WORK IN PROGRESS: A novel.

SIDELIGHTS: ''I write out of an impelling desire to create— to use more of my creative instincts and more of what has been passed on to me by my birthright and all the other contributors

WILLIAM R. JOHNSON

(From "King Kong" in *Famous Monsters Funbook* by William R. Johnson. Illustrated by the author.)

to my life and education. I feel I owe all that I can do to my family before me, my teachers and associates who have worked with me, and to my present family and progeny to follow. I was impelled first to pursue my art but I found that professionally it was often less creative than I hoped for—until I finally managed to use my art in direct alliance with my writing. My most successful writings seem to come out as 'funbooks' of some kind; they were fun for me and I hear they are fun for my readers (and publishers). Most of my creative instincts have gone into these but my biggest work is still in progress . . . a novel, I do hope it will not be too serious to be a *fun book*."

JUDSON, Clara Ingram   1879-1960

PERSONAL: Born May 4, 1879, in Logansport, Ind.; died May 24, 1960, in Evanston, Ill.; daughter of John Carl (a banker) and Mary (Colby) Ingram; married James McIntosh Judson (an oil company official), June 26, 1901 (died, 1944); children: Alice Colby (Mrs. Gordon Canning), Mary Jane McIntosh (Mrs. Kingsley Loring Rice). *Education:* Graduated from Girls' Classical School, Indianapolis, Ind., 1898. *Residence:* Evanston, Ill.

CAREER: Author, lecturer, and teacher. Judson began her career following the publication of her stories as a daily column in a local newspaper; she was soon the author of a newspaper feature for children, "Bed Time Tales," published and syndicated by the *Indianapolis Star;* she later published two other columns, "Read It to Me Now" and "Woodland Fairies"; in 1915, she published the first of seventy-nine books for children; during World War I, she lectured for the U.S. Government about war bonds in Illinois high schools, and following the war, lectured to various women's clubs and adult education classes throughout the country on various topics, including home economics and household budget planning; also did con-

siderable radio work, beginning in 1928 with her own program about child training and homemaking. *Member:* Illinois Woman's Press Association, Society of Midland Authors (former director and treasurer), Chicago Authors' Club, Theta Sigma Phi, Chicago Woman's Club, Evanston Country Club, Pieran Club, Woman's City of Chicago Club, Cordon Club, Evanston Woman's Club.

AWARDS, HONORS: Newbery honor book, 1951, for *Abraham Lincoln, Friend of the People,* 1954, for *Theodore Roosevelt, Fighting Patriot,* and 1957, for *Mr. Justice Holmes;* recipient of the first Children's Reading Round Table award, 1953, for outstanding achievement in children's literature; Thomas Alva Edison Mass Media Award, 1957, for *Mr. Justice Holmes;* Indiana Authors' Day award, 1958, for *Benjamin Franklin,* and 1960, for *St. Lawrence Seaway;* Laura Ingalls Wilder Award, 1960, for lasting contribution to children's literature; the Clara Ingram Judson Award was established in her name by the Society of Midland Authors in 1961.

*WRITINGS—*Juvenile fiction: *Flower Fairies* (illustrated by Maginel W. Enright), Rand McNally, 1915; *Good-Night Stories* (illustrated by Clara P. Wilson), A. C. McClurg, 1916; *Billy Robin and His Neighbors,* Rand McNally, 1917; *Tommy Tittlemouse,* [Chicago], 1918; *The Camp at Gravel Point,* Houghton, 1921; *Foxy Squirrel,* Rand McNally, 1921; *Garden Adventures of Tommy Tittlemouse* (illustrated by Frances Beem), Rand McNally, 1922; *Jean and Jerry, Detectors,* Rand McNally, 1923; *Virginia Lee* (illustrated by Charles L. Wrenn), Barse & Hopkins, 1926, reissued as *Virginia Lee's Bicycle Club,* 1939; *Alice Ann* (illustrated by John M. Foster), Barse & Co., 1928; *Foxy Squirrel in the Garden,* Rand McNally, 1929; *Play Days* (illustrated with photographs by Arthur Dailey), Grosset, 1937; *People Who Come to Our House* (illustrated by Marjorie Peters), Rand McNally, 1940; *People Who Work Near Our House* (illustrated by Keith Ward), Rand McNally, 1942; *Peo-*

CLARA INGRAM JUDSON

ple Who Work in the Country and in the City (illustrated by K. Ward; Junior Literary Guild selection), Rand McNally, 1943; *Summer Time* (illustrated by Polly Jackson), Broadman Press, 1948.

Nonfiction; for children, except as indicated: *Cooking without Mother's Help: A Story Cook Book for Beginners*, Nourse, 1920; *The Junior Cook Book*, Barse & Hopkins, 1920; *Business Girl's Budget Book* (adult), [Chicago], 1921; *Sewing without Mother's Help: A Story Sewing Book for Beginners*, Nourse, 1921; *Household Budget Book* (adult), [Chicago], 1922; *Business Man's Budget Book* (adult), [Chicago], 1923; *Garden Adventures in Winter*, [Chicago], 1923; *My Household Day Book* (adult), P. V. Volland, 1923; *Child Life Cook Book*, Rand McNally, 1926; *The Mighty Soo: Five Hundred Years at Sault Ste. Marie* (illustrated by Robert Frankenberg), Follett, 1955; *St. Lawrence Seaway* (illustrated by Lorence F. Bjorklund), Follett, 1959, revised edition, 1964; *The Collector's Encyclopedia of Antique Marbles*, Collector Books, 1972.

Juvenile biography: *Pioneer Girl: The Early Life of Frances Willard* (illustrated by Genevieve Foster), Rand McNally, 1939; *Boat Builder: The Story of Robert Fulton* (illustrated by Armstrong Sperry), Scribner, 1940; *Railway Engineer: The Story of George Stephenson* (illustrated by Eric M. Simon), Scribner, 1941; *Soldier Doctor: The Story of William Gorgas* (illustrated by Robert Doremus), Scribner, 1942; *Donald McKay, Designer of Clipper Ships* (illustrated by John O. Cosgrave), Scribner, 1943, reprinted as *Yankee Clippers: The Story of Donald McKay* (illustrated by Yukio Tashiro), Follett, 1965; *Reaper Man: The Story of Cyrus Hall McCormick* (illustrated by Paul Brown), Houghton, 1948, reissued, Follett, 1959; *Abraham Lincoln, Friend of the People* (illustrated by R. Frankenberg), Wilcox & Follett, 1950, an edition for younger readers published as *Abraham Lincoln* (illustrated by P. Jackson), Follett, 1961; *City Neighbor: The Story of Jane Addams* (illustrated by Ralph Ray), Scribner, 1951; *George Washington, Leader of the People* (illustrated by R. Frankenberg), Wilcox & Follett, 1951, an edition for younger readers published as

Then he organized the Union Fire Company, which was an immediate success. ■ (From *Benjamin Franklin* by Clara Ingram Judson. Illustrated by Robert Frankenberg.)

Occasionally a trader came by the lower lakes and the St. Lawrence. But most still used the Ottawa route. . . . ■ (From *St. Lawrence Seaway* by Clara Ingram Judson. Illustrated by Lorence F. Bjorklund.)

George Washington (illustrated by Bob Patterson), Follett, 1961; *Thomas Jefferson, Champion of the People* (illustrated by R. Frankenberg; ALA Notable Book), Wilcox & Follett, 1952; *Theodore Roosevelt, Fighting Patriot* (illustrated by L. F. Bjorklund), Wilcox & Follett, 1953; *Andrew Jackson, Frontier Statesman* (illustrated by L. F. Bjorklund), Follett, 1954; *Mr. Justice Holmes* (illustrated by Robert Todd), Follett, 1956; *Benjamin Franklin* (illustated by R. Frankenberg; ALA Notable Book), Follett, 1957; *Christopher Columbus* (illustrated by P.

Jackson), Follett, 1960, an edition for younger readers published as *The Picture Story and Biography of Admiral Christopher Columbus* (illustrated by W. T. Mars), Follett, 1965; *Andrew Carnegie* (illustrated by Steel Savage), foreword by Mary Jane Judson Rice, Follett, 1964.

''Mary Jane'' series: *Mary Jane: Her Book*, Barse & Hopkins, 1918; *Mary Jane—Her Visit*, Varse & Hopkins, 1918; *Mary Jane's Kindergarten* (illustrated by Frances White), Barse & Hopkins, 1918; *Mary Jane Down South*, Barse & Hopkins, 1919; *Mary Jane's City Home*, Barse & Hopkins, 1920; *Mary Jane in New England*, Barse & Hopkins, 1921; *Mary Jane's Country Home*, Barse & Hopkins, 1922; *Mary Jane at School*, Barse & Hopkins, 1923; *Mary Jane in Canada* (illustrated by

C. L. Wrenn), Barse & Hopkins, 1924; *Mary Jane's Summer Fun* (illustrated by C. L. Wrenn), Barse & Hopkins, 1925; *Mary Jane's Winter Sports*, Barse & Hopkins, 1926; *Mary Jane's Vacation*, Barse & Hopkins, 1927; *Mary Jane in England* (illustrated by C. L. Wrenn), Barse & Co., 1928; *Mary Jane in Scotland* (illustrated by C. L. Wrenn), Barse & Co., 1929; *Mary Jane in France* (illustrated by C. L. Wrenn), Barse & Co., 1930; *Mary Jane in Switzerland*, Barse & Co., 1931; *Mary Jane in Italy* (illustrated by Marie Schubert), Grosset, 1933; *Mary Jane in Spain* (illustrated by M. Schubert), Grosset, 1937; *Mary Jane's Friends in Holland* (illustrated by G. Foster), Grosset, 1939.

''They Came From'' series: *They Came from Sweden* (illustrated by Edward C. Caswell), Houghton, 1942, reprinted as *Sod-House Winter*, Follett, 1957; *They Came from France* (illustrated by Lois Lenski; Junior Literary Guild selection), Houghton, 1943, reprinted as *Pierre's Lucky Pouch*, Follett, 1957; *They Came from Scotland* (illustrated by Mary A. Reardon), Houghton, 1944, reprinted as *Bruce Carries the Flag*, Follett, 1957; *Petar's Treasure* (illustrated by Ursula Koering; Junior Literary Guild selection), Houghton, 1945, reprinted as *Petar's Treasure: They Came from Dalmatia*, Follett, 1958; *Michael's Victory: They Came from Ireland* (illustrated by El-mer Wexler), Houghton, 1946; *The Lost Violin: They Came from Bohemia* (illustrated by Margaret Bradfield), Houghton, 1947; *The Green Ginger Jar: A Chinatown Mystery* (illustrated by P. Brown), Houghton, 1949.

Also author of *Billy Robin*, 1916; *Bed Time Tales, Sun-Yat-Sen*, and *Simon Bolivar*. Contributor of short stories and articles to numerous periodicals, including *Ladies' Home Journal, Women's Home Companion, Child Life, St. Nicholas, Youth's Companion, Banker's Life, Industrial Banker, Farmer's Life, Fruit Garden and Home, American Legion, Country Gentleman*.

SIDELIGHTS: Judson was born in Logansport, Indiana in 1879. Very little is known about her early years, which were spent with her three brothers in Indianapolis. After attending public school, Judson graduated from the Girls' Classical School. She taught in public school and in Sunday schools.

After her marriage to James McIntosh Judson, an oil company official, the couple settled in Evanston, Illinois, where they raised their two daughters, Mary Jane and Alice. Judson's career as a writer began while rearing her children. She sent her stories to a local newspaper whose editor liked them so much that he urged Judson to write more stories for a daily column, which was eventually syndicated as a national newspaper feature.

Her first book, *Flower Fairies*, published in 1915, claimed the distinction of being one of the very earliest "modern" fairy tales, a forerunner of the stories now known as realistic (rather than sentimental) stories.

During World War I, Judson gained a reputation as a lecturer and an authority on family finance. She lectured throughout the country on war savings stamps, time and money budgets, and financial training for children. Besides housekeeping and lecturing, Judson continued writing many juvenile books.

In 1928 she had her own radio program, thus making her one of the first women broadcasters. As an authority on personal finances, she also served as consultant to two banks.

Her success in the field of children's books came with the nineteen books in the "Mary Jane" series, followed by her juvenile biographies. Judson wrote over seventeen biographies about such famous Americans as Abraham Lincoln, Robert Fulton, Andrew Jackson, and Andrew Carnegie (the last published posthumously in 1964).

Although these books were fictionalized biographies, Judson spent much time researching records, diaries, letters, localities, and personalities of people who were associated with the subjects of her books. "When I first began writing, my purpose, expressed in many ways, was to show that life is more useful and rewarding when lived harmoniously with ourselves and with those around us. Then . . . I had what in an earlier era would have been called a vision. I had been speaking at the University of Nebraska in adult education meetings, and I had met many fine Americans, many of whom were foreign born. Returning home on the train that night, I was thinking of these people. I thought of the countless fine people who had come, bringing their skills and their choicest treasures, to make a new world.

In the afternoon he gave himself to the children. All the remaining years of his life there were children at Monticello. Martha's family of eleven boys and girls grew up there. ■ (From *Thomas Jefferson, Champion of the People* by Clara Ingram Judson. Illustrated by Robert Frankenberg.)

"Surely the land they made was no melting pot—a phase happily heard less often now. But what did they make? I thought of a beautiful tapestry made of threads of many kinds and colors—a tapestry that was beautiful because the threads were varied and different. The cross threads were the people; the up and down threads the leaders who made the pattern and gave strength to the whole.

"These thoughts so moved me that I resolved, that night, to study and to write books that would show young readers the work, the hopes, the ideals, that were woven into the making of the New World. And I resolved to write biographies of the leaders whose dedication and lofty aims guided the pattern of living. . . ." [Clara Ingram Judson, "Acceptance," *Horn Book*, October, 1960.[1]]

Her "They Came From" series was an extension of that interest. "During twenty years of lecturing and broadcasting I had the good fortune to come in contact in person or by letter with many who had recently come to this country. (We call these 'foreign-born.' I hope we remember that the term is one of degree. All but Indians were 'foreign born' in our ancestry.) I found them open-minded, eager to learn American ways, happy to have their children educated. They were frightened sometimes, naturally enough, and hence stiff and shy and proud in their poverty and ignorance of language. Often their children too rapidly learned new freedoms and scorned anything old. This was especially hard to bear because at school English was acquired more quickly than was possible for the stay-at-home mother. But once one got past the shyness, one found warm response and eagerness to learn.

"One day . . . in Iowa, I helped a busy mother, my hostess, finish her ironing so she could go to a farm meeting at which I was to speak. I smoothed the beautiful hand-woven linens and embroideries and listened to her talk of old recipes (she was a marvelous cook, as I had reason to know) and new fashions, especially in hats, her gratitude for the free school and delight in the new methods she and her husband were learning from farm and home advisers. But she voiced a concern, too. She wanted to hold tight the family group with its joys and its disciplines, to keep the music and handcrafts and devotion to church. It was plain that her spiritual heritage was wide and deep.

"Suddenly a new thought came to me. How wonderful it would be if we all appreciated the strength and idealism brought to this country! If we understand these varied peoples. Perhaps in knowing them better we would gain a new knowledge of ourselves and of the people overseas who did *not* have strength or ambition to leave the ancestral home. I resolved to study all this, to stand as it were at the side of the great tapestry that is America, ravel out the threads of which it is woven and write what I found in story form for readers.

"After some years of study, I felt ready to write on my project. I talked with several publishers, and Ira Kent, then in charge of children's books for Houghton Mifflin, Publishers, saw merit in my idea and told me to go ahead. Of six national groups which I offered to him, he chose the Swedish for my first book. And so the 'They Came Froms' began.

"Greater dramatic effect is gained when the time period is short, as all writers of children's stories know. I could not meander through the whole story of a migration. In my earlier studies I had made an over-all plan. The books should tell of different parts of the country and show different periods of national development so that when several were completed they would portray regional life in America. The newcomer's neigh-

Sleepy Hessians grabbed muskets and rushed out. ■
(From *George Washington, Leader of the People* by Clara Ingram Judson. Illustrated by Robert Frankenberg.)

bors were as important to me as the newcomer himself. To execute this plan I must be quite at home in a wide sense.

"For the Swedish story [*They Came from Sweden*] I must know who was the first Swede who came to America, where he settled, how he succeeded or why he failed. Who came later, where they settled (many Swedes did not stay where they first lived) and how he got along with his neighbors. With all this in mind, I must pick a place and a year.

"I chose Wisconsin and the year 1856. My family came by ship, train, packet and lake boat to Milwaukee. They walked to their new home by Pine Lake, carrying their meager possessions and leading a newly bought cow. They made a home, of a sort, but later thought it wise to move further west, so the place was sold, goods packed again and after a walk to the Mississippi they took a boat from Prairie du Chien to Red Wing and settled permanently near Vasa. Thousands of Swedes had a story similar to this. My tale is made up of incidents gathered from letters and personal histories recounted to me. Every secondary character in my story is a real person, mentioned by his true name and engaged in doing what he actually did that year. Doctors, ministers, lawyers, land agents, blacksmiths, boat captains and innkeepers are real people I found in county histories, church records and family letters. Every article of furniture, clothing, dishes, books mentioned in the book are things I have seen in private homes or in the very choice museum at Augustana College. A book in the Swedish

"In those days, we were laughingly called 'Beef-eaters,' " the guard explained, **"because beef was the cheapest of foods and the castle guards were fed on it."** ■ (From *Mary Jane in England* by Clara Ingram Judson. Illustrated by Charles L. Wrenn.)

Old People's Home in Evanston has a picture of the home by Pine Lake to which the Larssons came. Every detail in *They Came from Sweden* is carefully documented history.'' [Clara Ingram Judson, ''Writing Juveniles Isn't All Fun,'' *Library Journal*, August, 1947.[2]]

Judson's second book in the ''They Came From'' series was first published in 1943 under the title *They Came from France*, and was a Junior Literary Guild selection. The book was later reprinted in 1957 as *Pierre's Lucky Pouch*. ''The French immigration spread over a wide space and time so it was not easy to select my time and place. Should I take missionaries or explorers, settlers in the North or the South? Or where along the Gulf was the best spot, if that region was chosen? Only after long study did I decide on New Orleans exactly at the end of the Beinville (pioneer) period and the beginning of the colonial era under Vaudreuil 1741-43. It seemed unlikely, since this was so far away in time, that I could carry out my plan and have real people and things in this story. Two disastrous fires had burned most of early New Orleans records, I knew. But, to my delight, persistent study of such records as were available (in French, of course) disclosed a wealth of material.

''Here, as in the Swedish book, every dress, book and dish, small incidents and major events were revealed to me in wills, bills of sale, shipping lists and other documents, and I was able to weave my story about real people and events. The priests and professional men, the wigmakers and dressmakers, forgemen and merchants, even M. Bebe who came from France that very year—as though to oblige me!—all are real people. My

'family' is fiction only to the extent that this device allows me to assign to them the happenings to many.''[2]

The fifth book in ''They Came From'' series was about Irish immigrants. ''Defiance, Ohio, the scene of *Michael's Victory* is the town where my parents were born and where I often visited as a child. But childish recollections count for little beyond a love for a place. I engaged in years of correspondence with older residents and while writing the book stayed in Defiance to study locale and read newspapers. Defiance and one of the early Ohio railroads and the rails were laid by strong willing Irish hands. Some stayed, some followed the track. An old Irishman, nearing ninety told me about Flanagan. Contractor Phelps' daughter supplied me with data about railroad building and labor problems. The advertisement of the circus is copied from the *Defiance Crescent* and the lion actually did escape into Grant's barn. Dr. and Mrs. Colby are my maternal grandparents and the Indian story is not only cherished family tradition but is included in some Ohio histories. For my account of how Dr. Colby would treat an injured shoulder I searched the medical library of Northwestern University until I found a report of the Ohio Medical Society of April 1854 (the year of my story) which told me exactly how to proceed. Librarians, priests, old families all helped me and the mayor hunted out the water-damaged engraving from which the endpapers were drawn.

''In all these books I have chosen not to use dialect which might slow young readers and dampen full enjoyment of the content. I have assumed that, since my people spoke their native language well, I truthfully represented them in correct English. Instead of dialect, I have used native rhythms which are easy to read and yet have definite individuality. Each book has been checked by 'foreign–born readers' for this and other points.

''In a hundred small ways I have made my stories accurate. Even the weather, when mentioned, is the weather of that day and place. Much of this, I well know, is not important to a young reader. But it is important to me to know that materially and spiritually these books are true. Writing fiction is pleasant work, but this unraveling of history has been a more rewarding experience.''[2]

During her long career as homemaker, lecturer and author, Judson wrote over seventy-nine books, and it is estimated that these books sold over six million copies. Three of her fictionalized biographies were runner-ups for the John Newbery Medal. ''What is a book—I sometimes wonder? A thing of paper and ink inert, standing on its shelf. I fancy it is like a radio box of wood or plastic, silent, the cord dangling. But when you take this thing of paper and ink from the shelf and put it into the hands of a reader you plug it in, letting free a current of understanding between the mind of the author and of the reader. . . .

''One question is often asked me: What are the qualities that a writer must have?. . .

''The qualities are three:

''1. We must have a curiosity, a desire to know. Children have this eagerness to know; we must foster it in them and in ourselves, for it is the breath of life.

''2. We must have a sense of time. Perhaps time is the only true equality we experience—whether we are rich or poor, old or young, bright or dull, we each have 24 hours every day

No sick men were allowed to leave; no new ones were landed unless they were healthy. Tropical disease was not to spread to the United States if he could help it. And it didn't. ■ (From *Soldier Doctor* by Clara Ingram Judson. Illustrated by Robert Doremus.)

with which to make a life. Yet how strangely we speak of time! We say we must 'find time'—you cannot find time. Time is. We say we must 'save time'—we cannot, time passes. Only one thing can be done with time. We can use it. Of course we cannot in a lifetime do all the things we wish we could do. But I believe we can do all we *want* to do.

Judson died quietly in her sleep at her home in Evanston, Illinois on May 24, 1960. She was eighty-one years old. At the time of her death she was working on a biography of Woodrow Wilson.

A month before her death she had received the Indiana Authors' Day award for her book *St. Lawrence Seaway*. She had also been notified that she was to be the recipient of the Laura Ingalls Wilder Award for her contribution to children's literature, and was working on her acceptance speech. "I feel so deeply that as we help children to understand our neighbors, we help in understanding of world problems. Peace, real lasting peace, is a growth from the hearth and spreads to the neighborhood, the community, the town, the country and some day throughout the world, and our hope lies in the children." [Nina

Brown Baker, "Clara Ingram Judson," *Wilson Library Bulletin*, June, 1948.[3]]

In 1961 the Clara Ingram Judson Award was established by the Society of Midland Authors. The award, a prize of $500, is given annually to the most outstanding book written for children by an author from the Midwest. Judson's works are included in the Kerlan Collection at the University of Minnesota.

FOR MORE INFORMATION SEE: New York Times Book Review, October 13, 1940, January 30, 1949, September 27, 1964; *New York Herald-Tribune Weekly Book Review*, January 10, 1943, September 12, 1948, October 9, 1949; Clara Ingram Judson, "Writing Juveniles Isn't All Fun," *Library Journal*, August, 1947; *Christian Science Monitor*, August 28, 1947; *Wilson Library Bulletin*, June, 1948; *Indiana Authors and Their Books, 1816-1916*, Wabash College, 1949; *New York Herald-Tribune Book Review*, November 27, 1950, September 28, 1952; Stanley J. Kunitz and Howard Haycraft, editors, *Junior Book of Authors*, H. W. Wilson, 1951; *Chicago Sunday Tribune*, April 19, 1959; C. I. Judson, "Acceptance," *Horn Book*, October, 1960; Mariam Hoffman and Eva Samuels, *Authors and Illustrators of Children's Books*, Bowker, 1972.

Obituaries: *New York Times*, May 25, 1960; *Publishers Weekly*, June 13, 1960; *Britannica Book of the Year*, 1961.

KAHL, Virginia (Caroline) 1919-

BRIEF ENTRY: Born February 18, 1919, in Milwaukee, Wis. Kahl's decision to write and illustrate children's books was a result of her work as an army librarian in Austria after World War II. The picturesque landscape of the country inspired the simplicity of her illustrations; and the humor and warmth of the Austrian people inspired the personality of her characters. Full of slapstick and bumbling comedy, each story begins with a small event that erupts into exaggerated chaos. Kahl's most popular book with readers and critics alike is *The Duchess Bakes a Cake* (Scribner, 1955). It was chosen as an honor book in the 1955 Spring Book Festival and received the Lewis Carroll Shelf award in 1972. In a fantasy that balances the rational and the absurd, Kahl describes the catastrophe that ensues when too much yeast is added to a cake dough. *Twentieth-Century Children's Writers* noted that, "The winning combination of this book is apparently the clarity with which silliness and logic have been joined." Kahl uses couplets to tell the story, which is based on a true incident from her own life. The chaos continues as the same duchess and her thirteen daughters find themselves with an unusual pet on their hands in *How Many Dragons Are There Behind the Door?* (Scribner, 1977). Kahl's illustrative excellence is highlighted here as the daughters are shown smuggling a dragon into the castle. *Publishers Weekly* observed, "The tale is told in brisk verses, enhanced immeasurably by Kahl's fond touches in the pictures of the scenes, painted the shades of green and the vivid red which are hallmarks of the noble family."

Especially effective and expressive are the illustrations in *Whose Cat Is That?* (Scribner, 1979), the story abut a cat that manages to belong to seven people at the same time. *Publishers Weekly* commented, "Kahl's application of undimmed primary colors to lots of white in her drawings captivates the readers as much as her sassy tale." Summarizing her own expectations as a writer, Kahl says, "I hope that the children who read my books have put them down with sighs of contentment, knowing that their expectations of cheerful, uncomplicated tales with happy endings have been vindicated.'' Other books written and illustrated by Kahl and published by Scribner include: *Away Went Wolfgang* (Spring Festival honor book, 1954; 1954), *Plum Pudding for Christmas* (1956), *The Perfect Pancake* (1960), *The Baron's Booty* (1963), *How Do You Hide a Monster?* (1971), *Gunhilde's Christmas Book* (1972), *Giants, Indeed!* (1974), and *Gunhilde and the Halloween Spell* (1975). *Office:* Alexandria Public Library, Alexandria, Va. *For More Information See: More Junior Authors*, H. W. Wilson, 1963; *Illustrators of Children's Books: 1957-1966*, Horn Book, 1968; *Books Are By People*, Citation Press, 1969; *Contemporary Authors, New Revision Series*, Volume 2, Gale, 1981; *Twentieth-Century Children's Writers*, St. Martin's, 2nd edition, 1983.

KANETZKE, Howard W(illiam) 1932-

PERSONAL: Born February 25, 1932, in Racine, Wis.; son of Henry William (an electrician) and Margaret (Sweetman) Kanetzke; married Lucetta Bloedow (a bookstore manager), September 15, 1957; children: Laurel, Neil. *Education:* Attended Augustana College, 1950-52; University of Wisconsin, Madison, B.S., 1958, graduate study, 1958-59. *Religion:* United Church of Christ. *Home:* 5726 Elder Place, Madison, Wis. 53705. *Office:* State Historical Society of Wisconsin, 816 State St., Madison, Wis. 53706.

CAREER: Mt. Horeb Public Schools, Mt. Horeb, Wisc., teacher, 1959-60; State Historical Society of Wisconsin, Madison, school consultant, 1960—. President, Wisconsin Housing Coopera-

HOWARD W. KANETZKE

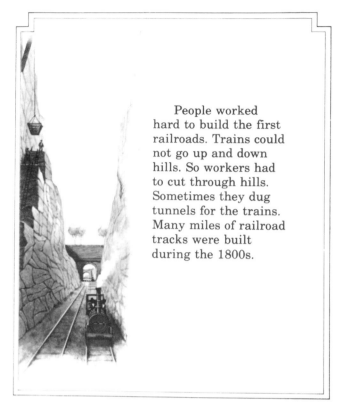

People worked hard to build the first railroads. Trains could not go up and down hills. So workers had to cut through hills. Sometimes they dug tunnels for the trains. Many miles of railroad tracks were built during the 1800s.

(From *Trains and Railroads* by Howard W. Kanetzke.)

tive, 1960-65; officer and member of board, Wisconsin Central Hospital Volunteers. *Military service:* United States Army, 1952-54. *Member:* Wisconsin Council for the Social Studies.

WRITINGS—All nonfiction for children: *Trains and Railroads*, Raintree, 1978; *The Story of Cars*, Raintree, 1978; *Airplanes and Balloons*, Raintree, 1978. Also author of over fifty books in the ''Badger History'' series for State Historical Society of Wisconsin; author of student and teacher manuals on American Indians; author of classroom manual for the educational television series ''Wisconsin Then and Now,'' 1983; author of guide booklet ''Wisconsin Then,'' for intermediate level. Contributor of *Thirtieth Star*, a supplemental newsletter on American history for high-school students.

WORK IN PROGRESS: A history of Pilgrim Camp on Green Lake in Wisconsin.

SIDELIGHTS: ''My training is in history, and I have become more and more aware of how important the history of each city and town is to our national story. I am excited by stories and events that happen in places throughout our country. All of these prove that all of us are a part of the history of our nation.''

HOBBIES AND OTHER INTERESTS: Music, gardening, antiques.

The school system has much to say these days of the virtue of reading widely, and not enough about the virtues of reading less but in depth.

—John Ciardi

KING-SMITH, Dick 1922-

BRIEF ENTRY: Born March 27, 1922, in Bitton, Gloucestershire, England. Author of books for children. King-Smith worked as a farmer for twenty years before earning his B.Ed. from Bristol University in 1975. For the following seven years he taught primary school near Bath, Avon, England. A full-time writer since 1982, King-Smith's novels for children have been praised by critics for their warmth, sensitivity, and humor. The characters of his books are animals, anthropomorphized to reflect human foibles and strengths. According to *Times Literary Supplement,* King-Smith "builds his earthy comic inventions on the hard facts of farmyard life." In his first novel, *The Fox Busters* (Gollancz, 1978), the fowls of Foxearth Farm band together against the menace of local foxes. *Times Literary Supplement* described the book as "a good, fast-moving story,. . . funny without condenscension or whimsicality."

King-Smith's next two novels emphasize his inclination toward creating an underdog hero who makes good. In *Daggie Dogfoot* (Gollancz, 1980), a deformed piglet manages to escape a slaughterhouse fate and become a savior of his farm. *Publishers Weekly* observed: "It's impossible to remain unmoved by the queer little pig. . . . The author's dialogue creates immense empathy. . . ." Published in the United States as *Pigs Might Fly* (Viking, 1982), the novel was chosen runner-up for the 1981 Guardian award. In *The Mouse Butcher* (Viking, 1982), the hero is a butcher's cat who wins the heart of a high society feline while defeating Great Mog, a ferocious wildcat. *Horn Book* called it "a comic animal fantasy . . . witty in style, clear in expression, and swift in movement. . . ." Devoted to writing children's literature, King-Smith believes that "an ounce of fantasy is worth a pound of reality," adding, "I couldn't possibly write a modern sort of novel for grown people—I should get the giggles." His latest novels are *Magnus Powermouse* (Gollancz, 1982) and *The Queen's Nose* (Gollancz, 1983). *Home:* Diamond's Cottage, Queen Charlton, Avon, England. *For More Information See: Contemporary Authors,* Volume 105, Gale, 1982; *Twentieth-Century Children's Writers,* 2nd edition, St. Martin's, 1983.

KLEVIN, Jill Ross 1935-

BRIEF ENTRY: Born September 7, 1935, in Brooklyn, N.Y. An author of novels for young adults, Klevin explains that her works are about ". . . young people interacting in and coping with our complex modern society." Her first book, *The Summer of the Sky Blue Bikini* (Scholastic Book Services, 1978), was followed by *That's My Girl* (Scholastic Book Services, 1980), the story of a sixteen-year-old figure skater who aspires to the Olympic team. In *The Best of Friends* (Scholastic Book Services, 1981), Kelvin describes the trade-off that occurs between two girls faced with the situation of "beauty, no brains" and "brains, no beauty" as they help strengthen each other's weaknesses.

When four twelve-year-olds put their heads together, kids and capitalism are a successful combination in *The Turtle Street Trading Company* (Delacorte, 1982). Ingenuity results in a flourishing junk-trading business that firmly establishes the residents of Turtle Street in the free enterprise system. *School Library Journal* noted, "The book succeeds because of its simplicity: The kids-to-tycoons story, always fascinating to children, is all the more appealing here because there are few digressions from it." In its sequel, *Turtles Together Forever!* (Delacorte, 1982), Klevin takes a closer look at the individual characters when one of the children is forced to move with his divorced mother to another city. *School Library Journal* again observed that "as a representation of a child's view of his parents' divorce and second marriages, this book is one of the best, with its simple, fresh approach." Currently in press are two additional books featuring the Turtle Street residents, *Turtles Triumphant* and *Turtles in TV Land,* as well as two novels, *Miss Perfect* and *Spoiled Rich Kids.* Klevin is now working on a screenplay entitled "Little Victories." *Home:* 4011 Blackbird Way, Calabasas, Calif. 91302. *For More Information See: Contemporary Authors,* Volume 111, Gale, 1984.

KRASILOVSKY, Phyllis 1926-

PERSONAL: Born August 28, 1926, in Chappaqua, N.Y.; daughter of Richard and Florence Manning; married William Krasilovsky (attorney, lecturer, and author), September 14, 1947; children: Alexis, Jessica, Margaret, Peter. *Education:* Attended Brooklyn College (evenings), and Cornell University, 1949-50. *Home:* 1177 Hardscrabble Rd., Chappaqua, N.Y. 10514.

CAREER: Writer of children's books. Marymount College, Tarrytown, N.Y., teacher of children's literature, 1969-70.

PHYLLIS KRASILOVSKY

She never stood up straight so everyone could see how lovely she really looked. ■ (From *The Shy Little Girl* by Phyllis Krasilovsky. Illustrated by Trina Schart Hyman.)

WRITINGS: The Man Who Didn't Wash His Dishes (illustrated by Barbara Cooney), Doubleday, 1950; *The Very Little Girl,* Doubleday, 1953; *The Cow Who Fell in the Canal,* Doubleday, 1957; *Scaredy Cat* (illustrated by Ninon), Macmillan, 1960; *Benny's Flag,* World, 1960; *Susan Sometimes,* Macmillan, 1962; *The Very Little Boy,* Doubleday, 1964; *The Girl Who Was a Cowboy,* Doubleday, 1965; *The Very Tall Little Girl,* Doubleday, 1969; *The Shy Little Girl* (illustrated by Trina Schart Hyman), Houghton, 1972; *The Popular Girls Club,* Simon & Schuster, 1972; *L. C. Is the Greatest* (young adult novel), T. Nelson, 1975; *The Man Who Tried to Save Time,* Doubleday, 1979; *The May Who Entered a Contest* (illustrated by Yuri Salzman), Doubleday, 1981; *The First Tulips in Holland* (illustrated by S. D. Schindler), Doubleday, 1982; *The Man Who Cooked for Himself* (illustrated by M. Funai), Parents Magazine Press, 1982. Contributor to *New York Times, American Home, Better Homes and Gardens,* and various women's magazines. Writer of travel articles for several newspapers and travel magazines.

ADAPTATIONS: ''The Cow Who Fell in the Canal'' (filmstrip and record), Weston Woods, 1957; ''The Man Who Didn't Wash His Dishes'' (filmstrip and record), Weston Woods, (book and cassette), Doubleday, 1969; ''The Man Who Tried to Save Time'' (filmstrip and cassette), Educational Enrichment Materials, 1980.

WORK IN PROGRESS: A novel.

SIDELIGHTS: Born **August 28, 1926** in Chappaqua, New York and raised in Brooklyn, New York. ''I had a very bad emotional background because I came from a split home. On the other hand, there were all the wonders of childhood—roller skating, jumping rope, making friends. Underneath, however, there was always a layer of sadness because of the problems we had as a family. My parents were never happy together.

''I have two sisters. My older sister was like an aunt to me, because she is nine and a half years older. She was a very good influence—a real reader, always bringing home many special books from the library.

''My mother was my strongest influence. She came from a lower east side family, and belonged to an east side settlement house. She was a member of a group of thirty-five girls, led by a teacher who taught them about all the finer things of life, took them to theater, and read them books. As a result, my mother became very culture conscious, which of course rubbed off on us. We saw plays and went to museums. To this day I could walk around the Brooklyn Museum blindfolded; I went so many times as a child.

''*L. C. Is the Greatest,* my young adult novel, was really about that time. In the beginning it was an adult novel, but after four editors turned it down, I decided to reduce it by taking out all of the things I felt young people might not understand, and then published it as a young adult novel. A lot of me is in that book.

''We lived in a lower middle class neighborhood, had our own house, and in a sense had a life which was much different from our neighbors. That made it hard to make friends. My best friend was Marie, an Irish girl who lived on the end of the street. Her father was in jail because he'd tried to rob a gas station. Marie dropped all of her 'g's,' when she spoke. She said 'goin . . . talkin,' etc. I loved her even though she didn't care about books. She didn't even go to church. On Sundays she came to our house to skip mass. Afterwards, she and I

She was smaller than all the other little girls she played with. ■ (From *The Very Little Girl* by Phyllis Krasilovsky. Illustrated by Ninon.)

(From the filmstrip "The Cow Who Fell in the Canal."
Produced by Weston Woods, 1970.)

"I always wrote. A terrible thing happened to me when I was young. I was quite unhappy with the situation between my parents, and so, I started a notebook as a release. I put the notebook away in a cupboard, and my mother, who never gave us enough privacy, read it and confronted me. That incident scared me away from writing for a long time. I think writing is a kind of subterranean force which must break through and surface.

"I always wanted praise from my mother, but she wasn't a giver. I remember ten years ago, the Chappaqua Library had a Phyllis Krasilovsky day, during which they held a special showing of the movie 'The Cow Who Fell in the Canal.' All the mothers came with their children. I invited my relatives, gave a talk at the library, and afterwards, they all lined up for me to autograph their books. My mother came up and told me how proud of me she was. I was over forty years old then, and the terrible thing was, by that time, I just didn't care.

"I used to tell her when I was a little girl, washing the dishes, 'Someday, I'm going to write about you in the *New York Times Book Review*.' 'When I see it, I'll believe it,' she'd say.

"After the notebook incident, I didn't write for about a year. Then, at eight, I wrote my first book. Mother's Day was coming up, and I had only ten cents with which I bought a black and white composition book. I compiled all of my best school compositions and poems. When I ran out of material, I went

would use her collection money to play the slot machine in the corner candy store. My mother was very fidgety about our friendship. To a certain extent, my mother turned me into a literary snob. It took a lot of repair to turn me into a person.

"My book, *Popular Girls Club*, probably has something to do with that aspect of my childhood, but the main character becomes friends with a girl who has different interests than the other girls at school. My friends didn't really have interests, or anything to care about. I remember during our adolescence, Marie was interested in boys, wanted to smoke cigarettes and put on lipstick, but she didn't share my interest in movie stars—Katherine Hepburn, in particular.

"I had 152 pictures of Hepburn pasted all over the ceiling of my room. She was the epitome of everything I dreamed of being—elegant and graceful. She was tall, as was I, but I was very self-conscious of my height. During the war, Hepburn was in a play in New York. I crept backstage, where she was busy at the stage door signing autographs for American soldiers. She wouldn't give me the time of day, which would have meant so much to me."

An avid reader since childhood, Krasilovsky recalls: "I read all the classics. I started out with *Heidi,* then moved on to *Pollyana*, and *Little Women*. But *Little Women* was my Bible. Later when I taught children's literature at Marymount College, I read all of those books again. I remember I just wanted to research certain passages of *Heidi*. I was sitting on a hard kitchen chair, and before I knew it, I'd read the whole book. I cried. It was just like reading it as a little girl.

"We were not allowed to read comic books, which was another difference between myself and the other children in the neighborhood. They all read comic books and talked about them. I didn't know what was going on or who Dick Tracy was. We never missed them because we loved books so much.

He wanted his flag to be like the stars he dreamed by—gold stars spread out like the Big Dipper in the blue sky. ■ (From *Benny's Flag* by Phyllis Krasilovsky. Illustrated by W. T. Mars.)

to the neighborhood store, and copied all of the verse on Mother's Day cards until the manager kicked me out. That was my first book, and one that my mother really treasured. She gave it back to me a few years ago.

"When I graduated from grammar school I was twelve years old and reading *Gone with the Wind*. My sister had brought it home, and I used to sneak it to school because that was the only place I could read it freely.

"The Brooklyn public schools were like factories, but as I said before, the subterranean will surface. When we were given assignments as, 'write Aunt Sarah a thank you card for her birthday gift.' I was never satisfied writing like the other kids in my class. I would say 'The box was so wonderful and the ribbon I'll use for. . . .' I was always inventing things. I have to give my mother credit for that. She always said 'Be original.' I must have heard that ten million times a day. I used to think of it as a curse, but it really wasn't.

"I'm convinced that part of the reason people are ambitious is that at some time in their life they have been kept from something. I was a very aggressive person and determined to beat all the windows down. During high school with my mother and father divorced, I took a general course of study because I believed I would have to help support my mother. I did manage to get into a creative writing class. The teacher never paid any attention to my writing as she had a crush on one of the boys in the class. I think I felt that I was going to 'show her.' The terrible thing was, by the time I was ready to contact her, she had died.

"After high school I worked full time and attended Brooklyn College at night to study English literature. I worked at the *New Yorker* magazine and at the Brooklyn Museum. I always looked for the right scene."

1947. "I married early. My husband attended law school at Cornell, and I took history, Shakespeare, sociology and American literature courses. My husband was very idealistic. He wanted to go to Alaska to become a pioneer because it was the 'last frontier.' Before we left, my sister had given birth to a little girl. I was crazy about her and used to write things for her. I wrote her a birthday card once, and that turned into *The Very Little Girl*. *The Man Who Didn't Wash His Dishes* was written for a four year old boy we knew who was dying of cancer. Determined to get them published, I stormed into the office at Doubleday of editor Margaret Lesser and told her that she must read these stories immediately because I was leaving for Alaska in two weeks. She was impressed. Thinking back on it now, I think it helped that I was young and pretty. I didn't think so then, but I was. Ms. Lesser had a good sense of humor. While she was examining my work, I sat there, tapping my fingers on the table. She finished them in ten minutes and accepted both *The Very Little Girl* and *The Man Who Didn't Wash His Dishes*. I couldn't believe it. Because I had seen so many movies, I thought at that point I had better act tougher. So I took the manuscripts away and said, 'Well, I'll think about it.'" Krasilovsky was nineteen years old.

"I met my mother-in-law and my husband for lunch that day and told them what had happened. 'You dope, you'd better go back there right away,' was the response. I went. Lesser accepted the manuscripts and finally the day came for me to sign contracts. I brought along my husband, who had just graduated from law school, and he insisted on reading every word of small print. We were really a pair.

"Alaska was a dead end for Bill. We had some money saved, and decided to go to Europe. We left [our daughter] Alexis with my mother for two months and hitchhiked all over Europe. That's how I came to write *The Cow That Fell in the Canal*. The book still sells, is translated into fourteen languages, has been made into a record and filmstrip and has been included

He was too little to be   in the parade passing by.

(From *The Very Little Boy* by Phyllis Krasilovsky. Illustrated by Ninon.)

One Christmas she longed to be the littlest angel . . . . But she couldn't . . . because she was too tall . . . . ▪ (From *The Very Tall Little Girl* by Phyllis Krasilovsky. Illustrated by Olivia H. H. Cole.)

in many anthologies. It was the first book that Peter Spier ever illustrated. Now he's become so famous. I don't really collaborate with the illustrators of my books, but I do take a look at his work before I agree to let him work on my book. I was very concerned about the illustrations for *The Very Shy Little Girl*, because I knew it was a very sensitive book. I tore up a contract with one publisher because the illustrator wasn't right for the book. Then it took me over a year to hook up with Trina Schart Hyman, but it came out beautifully. When I saw the illustrations, I cried.''

Mother to four children and writer ''wasn't too difficult to handle. I have always been very organized and ambitious. My house is clean and everything is done by 9:00 a.m. so that the day belongs to me. And I always had good children. I'd set them up with crayons and toys and let them play. They didn't

need me around. When they were very little, I didn't write every day. I mostly baked cookies. But I remember sitting at my desk when Jessica was little. She would play under the desk with a drawer full of paper clips and everything sorting them out again and again. She was happy being there while I was writing at my desk, minding my own business.

''I was also writing lots of magazine articles and short stories. I wrote articles about everything that happened in my life. When we took the children out West, I wrote an article for *Redbook* magazine about traveling with children. I guess most writers feel as I do, I never wanted to waste anything. I tried to use up everything that was happening in my day, in my life, the lives of my children.

''Now I feel more like a writer than I did then, because I spend more time writing and I know more about what I am doing. Writing travel and newspaper articles sharpened my writing. I learned a lot about compression.

"When you're young, you think everything you write is great. You can't bear to part with a sentence or a word. Now I can cross out pages like a surgeon, realizing it's going to make the patient better in the long run. Sometimes I have to use a magnifying glass to read over all my corrections.

"I write at the typewriter, an electric, then I correct in longhand. I know I should get a word processor, but I like to look out my window, and how could I do that with one of those screens in my face? I guess I'm just set in my ways. I did go in for an hour's demonstration. It's very captivating—all those green letters—you feel like you're in Times Square. But I have to feel the juices flowing right through my own fingertips.

"There are days when I look at the typewriter and say 'oh, God,' and get up and polish the stove, because I can't bear to put my fingers on the keys. Other days, I come to it like a bride. When I hit it, well, it's like planting a flag on top of Mount Everest . . . WOW! Someone in business doesn't have to worry about expanding as much as a writer does. The expansion for a writer comes from within; he dictates growth."

Inspiration for her books comes from many sources. "I don't think my children really influenced my writing directly, except for *The Shy Little Girl* which is the life story of one of my daughters. She was shy and she suffered for it.

"*The Popular Girls Club* was inspired by a talk I had with a teacher I met. We were discussing how cruel children can be to one another and he told me that one girl in his class was having a party, and went around putting invitations on selected children's desks during class. That stayed in my mind and was the germ of the story.

. . . There wasn't one clean dish left! He was hungry enough to eat out of anything, so he ate out of the soap dish . . . . ■ (From *The Man Who Didn't Wash His Dishes* by Phyllis Krasilovsky. Illustrated by Barbara Cooney.)

"*Scaredy Cat* was actually a cat that my children had. He was terrible. He used to stand on a bookshelf and when I'd walk by, jump up at me."

"*The Shy Little Girl* is my favorite book. I really felt for that child. After that, I like *The Man* . . . series. I'm grateful to that man—he made me! I've been working on a book about a woman who lives alone. I was inspired by a little girl who asked me 'Why is it always the *Man* who lived all alone? Doesn't a woman ever live all alone?' I thought, 'Gee, these are the days of liberation.' I went home and wrote a story about a woman who lives all alone and tried to fix things that break. Now I'm having trouble selling it, which is interesting. I wonder if I'll have to change it into a man?'

Krasilovsky's character, the man, has been featured in five of her books. "The little man must be inside me someplace. I don't know how I discovered that character. He just happened. That's part of the mystique of writing.

"When the feminist organizations made a list of books for liberated children printed in *New York* magazine, they chose

"Apples! I love apples!" he said. Soon his pockets were bursting with them. ■ (From *The Man Who Cooked for Himself* by Phyllis Krasilovsky. Illustrated by Mamoru Funai.)

The Man Who Didn't Wash His Dishes. But when my daughter took a course in feminist studies at Yale, she came home one day and said 'Ha, ha! My professor says that the *Very Little Girl* is anti-feminist . . . kaput. . . .' I was shocked.''

Krasilovsky has visited 103 countries during her travels. "My kids spent a lot of time traveling with us. One summer, we rented our house to Alan Arkin, then used the money to go to Switzerland. When I was travel writing I took our son Peter everywhere with me—India, Turkey, Ireland, Greece, etc.

"Many of the countries I've visited I've returned to. I've been to Israel sixteen times. I've thought about living there because I made so many friends so quickly. And the climate is great. People are nervous wrecks but everyone I spoke to was interesting. They seem to have another dimension to their lives.

"I like the countries that begin with 'I,'—Israel, Ireland, Iceland. Iceland has more publishing houses per capita than any other country in the world. People sit on those ominous volcanoes and read their eyes out.

"I love literary pilgrimages. I like to visit the houses of writers and to try to imagine what it was like to live there. I must admit, I've seldom found inspiration in the houses themselves; I'm usually moved by something else: the parsonage and the moors at the Brontë's, or George Bernard Shaw's work hut. I could see how he could write so coldly and pettily sitting in that place.

"I don't regret all the travel writing I've done, but the last eight or nine years that I have been traveling has taken away a lot of the impetus for writing. I was too busy looking around and enjoying myself. Work as a travel writer is difficult. There are also plenty of moments when you are just sitting back, enjoying everything. In those sybaritic hours, I could have been employing my energies better. Now I'm older and I've lost a lot of the youthful drives I had.''

Krasilovsky lives and works at "Early Dawn," her home in Chappaqua, New York. "Our house was built in 1822. Thomas Wolfe's last editor, Edward Aswell lived there. When we first saw it, it was falling apart. Nobody wanted it. But I knew it was my house the minute I walked in.

"I write in a small room where Mr. Aswell used to work. The floor slants because that part of the house was built over the basement which is sinking. Every year, I notice the floor slope more and more. Outside my window are bushes and the little rooftop of a cottage across the way. It's not the best view, but I like it. I sit and watch the birds peck away at the berries.''

Mr. Hofstra pushed Hendrika into Pieter's wagon and drove her home. ■ (From *The Cow Who Fell in the Canal* by Phyllis Krasilovsky. Illustrated by Peter Spier.)

Sometimes she would peek through the window to see if he was passing by. ■ (From *The First Tulips in Holland* by Phyllis Krasilovsky. Illustrated by S. D. Schindler.)

Besides writing, Krasilovsky makes time to enjoy her many interests. "I'm a big gardener—vegetables as well as flowers. I cook a lot and bake too. I also like to draw, but I haven't sketched in a long time. I did a lot of drawings during my travels. I should have started years ago, so that I could illustrate my own work, but I lacked the confidence. One of my earlier ambitions was to do black and white drawings for the *New Yorker* magazine. They actually called me in one day. The editor asked me 'Why did you draw it this way?' and I answered 'Because I can't do it any other way.' That was dumb. I should have made up something esoteric."

In discussing and teaching her craft Krasilovsky explains: "When I speak to children I tell them about the magic of writing; how you can take a pencil and a piece of paper and create a whole world. Sometimes I feel like a madman sitting all by myself, making things happen sentence by sentence. It gives me such a sense of power, it's as if I were a miniature God. On the other hand, it's a lonely feeling. I realize my friends are out having a good time while I'm stuck in that little room playing God.

"I've put a lot into public speaking. When I taught children's literature for two years, I didn't write, but my students wrote every week, and four of them have published books. That's the way I am, I do everything intensely. Whether it be cooking or teaching or writing. I find that if I don't, nothing comes out right. Even if I'm writing a travel article, I must love the place, or it shows. You really put your heart on your paper every time.

"I don't believe writing can be taught, but I think you can germinate the seed and encourage people. Teaching writing developed my critical eye. Teaching at Marymount helped me to realize what education is all about. It doesn't matter whether you are teaching quantum mechanics or children's literature; what you are teaching people is how to *think*.

"I can't give any original advice to young people who'd like to be writers. Just work and follow your instincts. You have to be completely honest; you have to turn yourself inside out because if you are not honest; it shows. There is no way to fake it.

. . . Scaredy Cat opened his big green eyes and Mother saw it wasn't her muff at all! ■ (From *Scaredy Cat* by Phyllis Krasilovsky. Illustrated by Ninon.)

"We have a friend who's a singer. He said that he felt he had a gift and that he should use it. That's how I feel about writing. Sometimes I feel conscience-stricken when I am not writing enough. But undoubtedly, it is a gift. I don't know if I believe in God, but I do believe in the mystique of creativity."

HOBBIES AND OTHER INTERESTS: Travel and gourmet cooking.

FOR MORE INFORMATION SEE: Ladies' Home Journal, January, 1962; Muriel Fuller, editor, *More Junior Authors,* H. W. Wilson, 1963; *Publishers Weekly,* February 26, 1973; *Travel/ Holiday,* August, 1975, February, 1976, June, 1978; *New York Times,* September 8, 1979, July 11, 1982; *The Thomas Wolfe Review,* fall, 1983.

KROPP, Paul (Stephan) 1948-

PERSONAL: Born February 22, 1948, in Buffalo, N.Y.; son of Lloyd L. (an engineer) and Marjorie (Depew) Kropp; married Marsha Atwood (a teacher), December 22, 1968; children: Jason, Justin, Alexander. *Education:* Columbia College, New York City, B.A., 1970; University of Western Ontario, M.A., 1972. *Home:* 111 Maplewood Ave., Hamilton, Ontario, Canada L8M 1X1. *Agent:* Lucinda Vardey Literary Agency, 97 Maitland St., Toronto, Ontario, Canada M47 1E3.

CAREER: Hamilton Board of Education, Hamilton, Ontario, teacher, 1974—. Has also worked variously as a welder, bookseller, waiter, and photographer. *Awards, honors:* Honorable mention from the Young Adult Caucus of the Saskatchewan Library Association, 1981, for *Wilted.*

WRITINGS: Wilted (young adult novel), Coward, 1980; (translator) Jean Simard, *Le Cave,* Editions Fides, 1981.

"Series Canada I"; all juvenile; all published by Collier Macmillan, 1979, published as "Encounter" series, EMC Corp., 1982: *Burn Out* (illustrated by Tina Holdcroft); *Dope Deal* (illustrated by T. Holdcroft); *Runaway* (illustrated by Heather Collins); *Hot Cars* (illustrated by T. Holdcroft).

"Series Canada II"; all juvenile; all published by Collier Macmillan, 1980, published as "Encounter" series, EMC Corp., 1982: *Dean On* (illustrated by Elaine Macpherson); *Dirt Bike* (illustrated by Martin Springett and Paul McCusker); *No Way* (illustrated by Affie Mohammed); *Fair Play* (illustrated by H. Collins).

"Series Canada III"; all juvenile; all published by Collier Macmillan, 1982, published as "Encounter" series, EMC Corp., 1983; *Gang War* (illustrated by P. McCusker); *Wild One* (illustrated by E. Macpherson); *Snow Ghost* (illustrated by Mark Summers); *Baby, Baby* (illustrated by H. Collins).

WORK IN PROGRESS: An adult novel, based on Mozart's "Don Giovanni."

SIDELIGHTS: "When I first began to teach kids with reading problems at a local high school, it became apparent that there were very few books of any kind available for them and certainly no Canadian materials at all. Thus the first books in 'Series Canada' were written, I might say tailor-made, for the kids at Parkview Vocational School in Hamilton. That these books have a popularity far beyond their original intended readers is a considerable surprise to me, but certainly a pleasant surprise."

PAUL KROPP

I saw his back wheel slide sideways at the end of his skid. He was sliding on his leg as much as on his wheel. ■ (From *Dope Deal* by Paul Kropp. Illustrated by Tina Holdcroft.)

''After the original books in 'Series Canada' novels, in which the vocabulary was limited to 1200 words and where no sentence could possibly have more than two polysyllabic words or run even a quarter as long as this sentence, I naturally wanted to write a book where the needs of the reader made the writing less restrictive. The novel that resulted is *Wilted,* originally called 'Only Wilts Wear Glasses' until the publishers objected that many readers and prospective book-buyers also wear glasses.

''*Wilted* was originally based on a student who, like the character in the book, had some real problems dealing with parents, girls, and the violence within him. Both the character and the student got away from me before they had learned everything I intended for them; but that has something to do with the nature of both teaching and writing.''

FOR MORE INFORMATION SEE: Quill & Quire, October, 1980.

LAIRD, Jean E(louise) 1930-
(J. E. Drial, Marcia McKeever, Jean L. Wakefield)

PERSONAL: Born January 18, 1930, in Wakefield, Mich.; daughter of Chester A. and Agnes (Petranek) Rydeski; married Jack E. Laird (owner of retail lumberyards and investment companies), June 9, 1951; children: John E., Jayne E. Joan-An P., Jerilyn S., Jacquelyn T. *Education:* Duluth Business University, graduate, 1948; additional study at University of Minnesota, 1949-50, and Michigan State University, 1951. *Religion:* Roman Catholic. *Home:* 10540 South Lockwood Ave., Oak Lawn, Ill. 60453; Whitewood Ave., Grand Beach, Mich. 49117; and Lake Geneva, Wisconsin.

CAREER: Free-lance writer, mostly of nonfiction for magazines; Oak Lawn High School, Adult Evening School, Oak Lawn, Ill., journalism teacher, 1965-72; St. Xavier College, Chicago, Ill., instructor in journalism, 1973—. *Member:* Canterbury Writer's Club (Chicago; president, 1961; member of governing board, 1962-64), Oak Lawn Business and Profes-

JEAN E. LAIRD

sional Women's Club; St. Linus Guild, Mt. Assisi Academy, Marist, Queen of Peace (parents' clubs).

WRITINGS: Lost in the Department Store (juvenile), Denison, 1964; *Around the House Like Magic* (Book-of-the-Month Club selection), Harper, 1967; *Around the Kitchen Like Magic*, Harper, 1969; *The Plump Ballerina* (juvenile; illustrated by Robert L. Sweetland), Denison, 1970; *Hundreds of Hints for Harassed Mothers*, Abbey Press, 1971; *The Alphabet Zoo* (juvenile; illustrated by Barbara Furan), Oddo Press, 1972; *The Porcupine Story Book* (juvenile), Concordia Press, 1974; *Fried Marbles and Other Fun Things to Do* (juvenile), Scholastic Books, 1975; *The Homemaker's Book of Time and Money Savers*, Stephen Greene, 1979; *The Homemaker's Book of Energy Savers*, Stephen Greene, 1981.

Also author of *How to Get the Most from Your Apliances*, 1967, *The Book of Dollar Savers and Budget Stretchers*, and about 248 National Research Bureau booklets. Travel editor, *Travel/Leisure* (magazine) and former travel editor under pseudonym Marcia McKeever, *Oldsmobile Magazine;* author of hobby columns in *Modern Maturity* and *Vacations Unlimited;* author of monthly consumerism column for *Ladies' Home Journal;* author under pseudonym Jean L. Wakefield of beauty column "Ladylikes," *Ladycom* (magazine); author of columns "Around the House with Jean" and "A Woman's Work," 1965-70, "The World as I See It," *Chicagotown News*, 1969, and "Time and Money Savers," *Lady's Circle Magazine*,

1973—. Contributor of over 900 articles to periodicals, including *Popular Medicine, Good Housekeeping, Parents' Magazine, Coronet, Pageant, Modern Bride, Better Homes and Gardens, American Home, Family Digest, Chicago Tribune Magazine, Catholic Digest, Chicago Sun-Times Magazine, Reader's Digest*, and *Parade*.

SIDELIGHTS: Lost in the Department Store has been read on children's television shows, including "Three Top House," "Ray Raynor Show," and "Sesame Street." It is in its 37th printing.

FOR MORE INFORMATION SEE: Life and Health, March, 1964.

LANDAU, Jacob 1917-

PERSONAL: Born December 17, 1917, in Philadelphia, Pa.; son of Samuel (a poet and artist) and Deana (Kitaynick) Landau; married Amalia Fattori, c. 1941 (divorced, 1946); married Frances Paul (a psychotherapist), May 5, 1949; children: Stephan Paul, Jonas Michael. *Education:* Samuel S. Fleisher Art Memorial, 1931-36; Pennsylvania Museum and School of Industrial Art (now Philadelphia College of Art), certificate, 1938; attended New School for Social Research, 1948-49, 1952-53; Académie Julian, 1949-50; Académie de la Grande Chaumière, Paris, France, 1950-52. *Religion:* Jewish. *Home:* 2 Pine Dr., Roosevelt, N.J. 08555. *Agent:* (Prints) Associated American Artists. *Office:* Pratt Institute, Brooklyn, N.Y. 11205.

CAREER: Artist, educator, and illustrator of books for children and adults. Early in career, worked in the offices of *Jewish Day*, New York, N.Y.; School of Visual Arts, New York, N.Y., instructor, 1954-56; Philadelphia Museum School of Art (now Philadelphia College of Art), instructor in anatomy, graphics, and illustration, 1954-57; Pratt Institute, Brooklyn, N.Y., instructor, 1957-60, assistant professor, 1962-63, associate professor, 1964-68, chairman of department, 1964-68, professor of graphic arts, 1968-83, professor emeritus, 1983—. Founder and coordinator of integrative studies program at Pratt Institute; has also worked as a photographer, editor, and commercial illustrator. Visiting scholar, Memphis Academy of Arts, 1969, and University of Notre Dame, 1969; graphic arts panelist, New Jersey Arts Council, 1969, 1973; visiting artist, Skidmore College, 1971, and Brookdale College, 1976; panelist, New Jersey State Museum, 1973, New York University, 1974, Rutgers—The State University, 1976; consultant to the New Jersey Department of Higher Education, 1974—; artist-in-residence, University of Northern Iowa, 1977; teacher, Artist/ Teacher Institute, New Jersey State Council on the Arts, 1978—.

Recipient of numerous commissions, including sketches of participants at Pacem In Terris II, 1967; "Print of Peace," for the International Art Program, National Collection of Fine Arts, Smithsonian Institute, 1967; woodcut poster, "I, John Brown," for National Park Service, U.S. Department of the Interior, 1968; a cycle of ten stained-glass windows, "The Prophetic Quest," for Congregation Keneseth Israel, Elkins Park, Pa., 1970; a lithograph, "Meditation of Love and Death," for New Jersey State Arts Council, 1975; a lithograph, "But If the Cause," for Roten Galleries, Baltimore, Md., 1976; and commissions for International Graphic Arts Society, Associated American Artists Gallery, National Broadcasting Company, Inc., Limbach Co., and McGraw-Hill, Inc.

LION HOUND

BY JIM KJELGAARD

ILLUSTRATED BY JACOB LANDAU

HOLIDAY HOUSE, NEW YORK, N. Y.

(From *Lion Hound* by Jim Kjelgaard. Illustrated by Jacob Landau.)

EXHIBITIONS—One-man shows: Galerie LeBar, Paris, France, 1952; Art Alliance, Philadelphia, Pa., 1954, 1975; Samuel S. Fisher Memorial Gallery, Philadelphia, 1959; Associated American Artists Gallery, New York, N.Y., 1960, 1970; University of Maine, 1961; Cober Gallery, N.Y., 1961, 1963; Original Prints Gallery, San Francisco, Calif., 1964; Zora Gallery, Los Angeles, Calif., 1964; Gallery 100, Princeton, N.J., 1966; Earlham College, Richmond, Ind., 1967; St. Andrews Presbyterian College, N.C., 1967; The Other Gallery, Philadelphia, 1968; Art Gallery, University of Notre Dame, South Bend, Ind., 1969; Bertha Eccles Art Center, Ogden, Utah, 1969; Print Club, Philadelphia, 1970; Orpheus Ascending Gallery, Stockbridge, Mass., 1972; Galeria Pecanins, Mexico City, Mexico, 1972; Congregation Keneseth Israel, Elkins Park, Pa., 1974; ACA Galleries, New York, N.Y., 1976; Schneder–Sato Gallery, Karlsruhe, Germany, 1977; University of Arizona Museum, Tucson, 1979; New Jersey State Museum, Trenton, 1981; Utah State University, Logan, 1982; Mary Ryan Gallery, N.Y.; Western Carolina University, Cullowhee, N.C.; University of Athens, Ga., 1982; The Museum of Judaica, Philadelphia, Pa., 1983; and many others in cities including Philadelphia, Los Angeles, Chicago, New Orleans, and Washington, D.C.

Group shows: "Four Painters," Art Alliance, Philadelphia, Pa., 1961; "The Figure—Recent Paintings U.S.A.," Museum of Modern Art, New York, N.Y., 1962; "New Humanism,"

National School of Plastics Arts, University of Mexico, 1963; Smithsonian Invitational Exhibition, White House, Washington, D.C., 1966; "Prize Winning American Prints," circulating show, New York State Council on the Arts, 1967; "Three Artists View the Human Condition," New Jersey State Museum, Trenton, 1968; "Tamarind-Homage to Lithography," Museum of Modern Art, New York, N.Y., 1969; "Human Concern/Personal Torment," Whitney Museum of American Art, New York, N.Y., 1970; "Selections from the 50th Annual Society of American Graphic Artists," U.S.I.A. Near East Traveling Show, 1970; New Jersey Arts Council traveling show, 1972; Art Museum, Sao Paulo, Brazil, 1972; American Academy of Arts and Letters, 1975, 1976; American Color Print Society, 35th exhibition, Philadelphia, 1976; First Biennial of New Jersey Artists, 1977; Society of Illustrators, N.Y., 1979; Pratt Graphics Center, N.Y., 1979; The Philadelphia Print Club; Carnegie-Mellon University, Pittsburgh, Pa.; Nardin Gallery, N.Y., 1980; Worcester Art Museum, Mass., 1981; Ohio State University, Columbus, 1982; The Hirshhorn Museum and Sculptor Garden, Washington, D.C., 1983-84, and many others in cities throughout the United States.

Work is represented in permanent collections of numerous museums, including, Whitney Museum of American Art, New York, N.Y., Metropolitan Museum, New York, N.Y., Pennsylvania Academy of Fine Arts, Philadelphia, Library of Congress, Washington, D.C., and museums at Princeton University, Rutgers—The State University, University of Maine, University of Minnesota, Syracuse University, Yale University, University of Kentucky, University of Massachusetts, University of Florida, Columbia University, Butler Institute, Bibliotheque National, Paris, France, and in many private collections.

MILITARY SERVICE: U.S. Army Air Force, 1943-46, served in Mediterranean Theater of Operations; art editor, photographer and reporter of *At Ease,* Special Services magazine. *Member:* American Color Print Society, Society of American Graphic Artists, Visual Artists and Galleries Association, National Academy of Design. *Awards, honors:* Boys Club Junior Book Award, 1951, for *The Big Sky;* recipient of Lessing Rosenwald purchase award from the Print Club, Philadelphia, 1955, 1959; woodcut prize from Print Fair of the Philadelphia Free Library, 1960; Louise Comfort Tiffany award, 1962; honorable mention from American Watercolor Society, 1962; Paul F. Norton and Associated American Artists awards from the Society of American Graphic Artists, 1962; honorable mention from the Audubon Artists, 1962; named one of New Jersey's finest curators and critics, 1962; Philadelphia Watercolor Prize from Pennsylvania Academy of Fine Arts, 1963; first award from the New Jersey Tercentenary Art Festival, 1963; Edna Pennypacker Stauffer prize from Society of American Graphic Artists, 1965; Tamarind Lithography Workshop fellow, 1965; recipient of grants from National Arts Council, 1966, New Jersey State Arts Council, 1974, Ford Foundation, 1975; *To Dream upon a Crown* was chosen one of American Institute of Graphic Arts "Children's Books," 1967-68; Guggenheim Foundation fellow, 1968-69; Vera List purchase prize from the Society of American Graphic Artists, 1972; Childe Hassam purchase award from the American Academy of Arts and Letters, 1973-74.

ILLUSTRATOR: Izola L. Forrester, *The Secret of the Blue Macaw,* Macrae, 1936; (contributor) *Three Stories by Robert Louis Stevenson,* Folio Club, 1937; John Henry Lyons, *Stories of Our American Patriotic Songs,* Vanguard Press, 1942; James A. Kjelgaard, *Snow Dog,* Holiday House, 1948; Doris Gates, *River Ranch,* Viking, 1949; Alfred B. Guthrie, *The Big Sky,* Sloane, 1950; Quentin James Reynolds, *The Wright Brothers, Pioneers of American Aviation,* Random House, 1950; Edgar Allan Poe, *The Gold Bug, and Other Tales and Poems,* Macmillan, 1953; Elsie R. Ziegler, *The Blowing-Wand: A Story of Bohemian Glassmaking in Ohio,* J. C. Winston, 1955; J. A. Kjelgaard, *Lion Hound,* Holiday House, 1955; Roland B. Gittelsohn, *Little Lower Than the Angels,* UAHC, 1955; Hughie Call, *The Rising Arrow,* Viking, 1955; Isabel C. McLelland, *Shadows on the Moor,* Holt, 1955; Carleton Beals, *Adventure of the Western Sea,* Holt, 1956; Jean Lee Latham, *This Dear-Bought Land,* Harper, 1957; Barbee O. Carleton, *The Wonderful Cat of Cobbie Bean,* J. C. Winston, 1957; Nathaniel Hawthorne, *The Scarlet Letter,* Libra Collection, 1960; Benjamin Appel, *Man and Magic,* Pantheon, 1966; Joanne S. Williamson, *To Dream upon a Crown,* Knopf, 1967; Albert H. Friedlander, *Out of the Whirlwind: A Reader of Holocaust Literature,* Doubleday, 1968; E. T. A. Hoffmann, *Selected Writings,* edited and translated by Leonard J. Kent and Elizabeth C. Knight, University of Chicago Press, Volume I: *The Tales,* 1969, Volume II: *The Novel,* 1969; Lloyd Alexander, *The Marvelous Misadventures of Sebastian,* Dutton, 1970.

Contributor of illustrations to magazines, including *Life, American Heritage,* and *Ladies' Home Journal;* advertisement illustrations for *T.V. Guide,* J. Walter Thompson and others;

record album covers for Columbia Records, Vanguard Records, and others.

WORK IN PROGRESS: Currently working on lithographs for *The Revelation of St. John* (New Testament).

SIDELIGHTS: "When I was a student, I was torn between treading the avant-garde path which, because of its links to French cultural tradition, seemed too art-for-art's-sakist, or following the social-realist path which, though closer to my experience of poverty, depression, anti-fascism, war, did not please me. One was too remote from the human condition, the other too simple-minded a reflection of it. After some years of fluctuating loyalties and tastes, I was able to transcend myself by choosing what some have called humanism, and which for me meant swallowing myself whole, my formal consciousness and my social concerns, my love for story-telling and my penchant for conceptualizing.

"Pressured by most of my teachers and peers into blind worship of Picasso and modernism, I found myself secretly and shamefacedly drawn to the northern Europeans, to Durer and Grunewald at first, later to Bosch, Grosz, Beckmann, Kollwitz. And Blake! And the Mexicans, above all Orozco! And Goya! And Daumier! I also adored Gustave Doré, Wyeth, Pyle, Beardsley, Rodin, Van Gogh, the decadents. And the one teacher who really counted, Franklin Watkins. Humanism became for me a concern for human values, not at the expense of other values, but in dialectical interplay with them. I was interested in revolution, in Beethoven (he was God and I was his prophet!), Marx, Paine, Whitman. The constants in the midst of change: the moral, spiritual, ecological, esthetic constants. Love. Justice. Truth. Beauty. Discovery. Humor. Invention. Ecstasy. Imagination. But also hate, violence, pain, suffering, hell, revolution, madness, death.

"Love is a relation based on the understanding that we can help others achieve their purposes. Art is love. Art enables us to see the world whole and undivided. Art cannot be proven true or false. Art is a composite of vital lies we tell ourselves. The lies of art reveal important truths. Art-making is myth-making. The intimate, social and cosmic connections are the three dimensions of art. We are caught between the birth of meaning (the awareness of our being) and the death of meaning (what happens after I am gone?). Art is a voice heard beyond the grave.

"Artists are people who need to create, to transcend. Others are people who have had the need suppressed. Those who can't create wish to destroy. Loss of the art sense in most is a loss of wholeness and meaning, a fall from grace. . . . Would we talk about putting the art back into education if we had not forgotton that learning is itself an art, and that it can't take place without love? Like taking all the nutritional information out of nature's bounty and 'enriching' it with a few token vitamins. Art is also subversive, stress, survival kit. It is 'disease,' displease. Humanism is knowing all this, not in our heads but in our gonads and follicles. Humanism in art knows that art must do more than entertain or please. Art not tied to individual growth, to humanity and life, is dangerous because it lulls or amuses without altering consciousness. The humanist path in art is human concern seeking its . . . necessary form.

"I believe that the crisis of our time is a crisis of consciousness and meaning. We have failed to produce the earthly paradise. We are prisoners of our own inventions, we feel powerless and corrupted. Powerlessness corrupts, absolute powerlessness corrupts absolutely.

"I am not naive enough to think of art as an efficient cause of social change. Neither am I cynical enough to feel that art, in the broad sense, has no contribution to make to the process of transformation. Every stress towards the human or spiritual is at least a probable cause. If established modernist theory no longer believes that art can make a difference in human life in an age which has all but succeeded in wiping out differences between the intended and the caused, then whole-person, whole-planet humanism can only reply that it still believes in the humanist intention, in art, in the artist, and indeed in the reawakening of art sense in all. Without it we are an endangered and endangering species."

Landau's works are included in the Kerlan Collection at the University of Minnesota.

HOBBIES AND OTHER INTERESTS: Conversation, chess, music.

FOR MORE INFORMATION SEE: Scholastic Magazine, April 28, 1934, April 27, 1935; *Philadelphia Bulletin,* April 28, 1934; *Saturday Review of Literature,* 1934; *Pencil Points,* November, 1934; *Pennsylvania School Journal,* Volume 83, June, 1935; *The Carnegie Magazine,* 1935; *New York Herald-Tribune,* June 7, 1953, May 15, 1960; *American Artist,* October, 1956, April, 1957; *The Philadelphia Inquirer,* November 15, 1959, May 21, 1961; *New York Times,* February 18, 1961, August 1, 1962, February 7, 1970; *Newark Sunday News,* February 19, 1961, March 17, 1963; *Aufbau,* February 24, 1961; *New Jersey Music and Art,* March, 1961, May, 1962, April, 1963; *Arts,* April, 1961; *Christianity in Modern Art,* Bruce, 1961; *Time,* May 25, 1962; *Woodcuts of Fifteen American Cities,* McGraw, 1962; *American Judaism,* Volume XII, no. 2, 1962-63; *Washington Star,* May 15, 1963; *New York Times Book Review,* August, 18, 1963; *Heritage,* March 26, 1964; *Los Angeles Times,* April 3, 1964; *Pratt Alumnus,* Volume 67, No. 1, December, 1964; *Prize-Winning Watercolors,* Allied Publications, 1964; *The Logic of Drawing,* Reinhold, 1965; *Art in America,* January-February, 1968; *The Philadelphia Inquirer Magazine,* November 3, 1968; *New York Times Magazine,* August 3, 1969; *Arts in Society,* spring-summer, 1971, fall-winter, 1972; Lee Kingman and others, compilers, *Illustrators of Children's Books: 1967-1976,* Horn Book, 1978; *Boston Globe,* June 10, 1980; *New Jersey Art Form,* March-April, 1980.

LANE, Margaret 1907-

BRIEF ENTRY: Born June 23, 1907, in Cheshire, England. Novelist and biographer, journalist, and author of books for children. Lane's career as a journalist began in 1928 and spanned ten years, including work for the *Daily Express,* International News Service, and *Daily Mail.* In 1935 she received the Prix Femina-Vie Heureuse for her first novel, *Faith, Hope, No Charity.* Her next novel, *At Last the Island,* was followed by a biography of her father-in-law entitled *Edgar Wallace: The Biography of a Phenomenon.* In succeeding years, Lane displayed her versatility as an author by producing an array of novels, biographies, and general nonfiction. Two of her biographies, *The Tale of Beatrix Potter* and *The Brontë Story,* were favorably received by critics for the insight they shed on the lives of these eccentric literary figures. A revised edition of *The Tale of Beatrix Potter* was published in 1968; ten years later Lane provided a second biography of the popular children's author, *The Magic Years of Beatrix Potter.*

In 1981 Lane ventured into yet another literary genre—books for children. She is the author of a series of books that introduce various members of the animal kingdom to young readers, describing basic physical characteristics, life cycles, and environments. Published in the United States by Dial, the titles include: *The Frog, The Squirrel, The Beaver, The Fish: The Story of the Stickleback* (all 1981), *The Fox,* and *The Spider* (both 1982). *Booklist* called the series "a standout," noting that "Lane packs a great deal of information into remarkably concise texts. . . . easily understood by primary-graders."

She has also written a picture book, *Operation Hedgehog* (Methuen, 1981), described by *Times Literary Supplement* as "a gentle little book prettily illustrated in soft watercolors." *Home:* Blackbridge House, Beaulieu, Hampshire, England. *For More Information See: World Authors,* H. W. Wilson, 1975; *Contemporary Authors,* Volumes 25-28, revised, Gale, 1977; *Who's Who: 1982-1983,* St. Martin's, 1982.

LANGONE, John (Michael) 1929-

BRIEF ENTRY: Born December 3, 1929, in Cambridge, Mass. Journalist, editor, and author. Because of his background in newspaper reporting and editing, Langone achieves a clarity and accuracy in his writing that defies popular jargon and rhetoric. This preciseness has not only gained critical approval, but has proved to be important to Langone's readers as well. His philosophy that "you can't send a reader to the dictionary on a crowded bus" is not only apparent in his adult books, but is especially obvious in those he has written for teenagers. Death, mental illness, love, and responsible drinking are only a few of the issues Langone discusses in his matter-of-fact and distinct manner. Critics have called Langone's treatment of these issues "objective and intelligent."

In *Like, Love, Lust: A View of Sex and Sexuality* (Little, Brown, 1980), Langone discusses the differences between like and love, as well as the meanings of pornography, homosexuality, and prostitution. "Langone does his usual good job of presenting important issues to teenagers in a clear, astute manner," *Booklist* commented. "Throughout, the author maintains a straightforward, objective, and nonexploitive tone and marshalls evidence to promote responsibility in sexual relationships. . . ." *Bulletin of the Center for Children's Books* further commented that Langone's exploration of values and emotions is "clear-eyed" and his writing style "direct and objective." In one of his earlier books, *Death Is a Noun: A View of the End of Life* (Little, Brown, 1972), Langone balances the obvious trauma of death, and a bit of positive philosophy, to present a concise look at dying through an unemotional treatment of the subject. *Bulletin of the Center for Children's Books* observed, "The book is written with dignity, and given diversity by the incorporation of the opinions and comments of many eminent people and the findings of many scientists." *New York Times Book Review* further added, "As a pioneer book, *Death Is a Noun* gets good marks for its candor and its spirit of enlightment." Other books for teenagers by Langone include *Goodby to Bedlam* (Little, Brown, 1974), *Bombed, Buzzed, Smashed, or Sober* (Little, Brown, 1976), and *Thorny Issues: How Ethics and Morality Affect the Way We Live* (Little, Brown, 1981). For adults Langone has written *Human Engineering: Marvel or Menace* (Little, Brown, 1978), *Women Who Drink* (Addison-Wesley, 1980), and *Chiropractors: A Consumer's Guide* (Addison-Wesley, 1982). *Home:* 28 Jarvis Ave., Hingham, Mass. 02043. *For More Information See: Contemporary Authors, New Revision Series,* Volume 1, Gale, 1981.

LASKER, David 1950-

PERSONAL: Born April 21, 1950, in New York, N.Y.; son of Joseph Leon (an artist and author) and Mildred (a teacher; maiden name, Jaspen) Lasker. *Education:* Yale University, B.A. (cum laude), 1972, M.M., 1974. *Politics:* Democrat. *Religion:* Jewish. *Home:* 23 Alloway Ave., Winnipeg, Manitoba, Canada R3G 0Z7.

CAREER: Instructor in double-bass, University of Bridgeport, and Westport schools, 1973; American String Teachers Association, performer and instructor, double-bass workshop, Bridgeport, Conn., 1973; Winnipeg Symphony Orchestra, and Canadian Broadcasting Corp., Winnipeg, Manitoba, double-bass player, 1974—. Assistant visiting professor, University of Massachusetts at Amherst, 1974; playwright-in-residence, Edward Albee Foundation, 1974; music critic, *Winnipeg Free Press*, 1981; traveling lecturer in writing, Manitoba Arts Council and the Canada Council, 1981-82. *Member:* Canadian Authors' Association. *Awards, honors: The Boy Who Loved Music* was named a notable book by the American Library Association, 1980; honorable mention, Canadian Authors' Association, 1981, for newspaper article "Don't Blame the Musicians, Blame the Conductor"; Manitoba Arts Council grant to write "Walking-tour Guide to Winnipeg Architecture," 1984.

WRITINGS: The Boy Who Loved Music (Junior Literary Guild selection; ALA Notable Book; illustrated by father, Joe Lasker), Viking, 1979.

WORK IN PROGRESS: Articles on various aspects of using classical music in bodybuilding competitions; articles on his life as a musician.

SIDELIGHTS: "I am the first professional musician in my family. I started piano at seven and took up the double bass in the ninth grade. I always loved the sound of the low instruments. I thought that the proper way to listen to hi-fi was to turn the bass all the way up and the treble all the way down. Nowadays I listen 'flat' and wouldn't be caught dead owning a pre-amplifier with tone controls.

"I wanted to play the bass because the bass, unlike the piano, was a 'cash' instrument. With it I won scholarships to art camps and music schools: Indian Hill (1965, 1966), Juilliard, and Aspen. I started right in as a Yale freshman playing in the New Haven, Bridgeport and Yale Symphonies, and the Yale Bach Society. I didn't have much time for homework but I needed the extra income to support my hi-fi and records 'habit'. I majored in art history and did well. But I couldn't see making a living at it and so, not wanting to break out of the Yale cocoon, I stayed on for a masters degree from the Yale School of Music.

"Playing in a symphony orchestra has its exciting moments: working under a really fine conductor, performing Bruckner's Seventh Symphony for the first time, reading a Stravinsky piece and finding that I can count all the intricate meter changes without messing up.

DAVID LASKER

A few days later the orchestra performed for Prince Nicolaus and his few remaining guests. ■
(From *The Boy Who Loved Music* by David Lasker. Illustrated by Joe Lasker.)

"But I was never satisfied with being just a musician. The public has the misconception that symphony musicians lead a glamourous, creative life. Well, perhaps composers, and to a lesser extent conductors and soloists do, but symphony musicians are 'executive' rather than 'creative,' we just execute what's written on the music sheet. It demoralizes me to think that I spend most of my professional life rehashing the same old warhorses. You have no idea how *sick* I am of Tchaikovsky's Fifth Symphony, Rimsky-Korsakov's 'Capriccio Espagnol' and the overture of Offenbach's *Orpheus in the Underworld.*

"One fine summer day, while practicing bass at the Aspen Music Festival, I got fed up with running through orchestra audition excerpts for the zillionth time. I saw the writing of a book as a welcome escape from that routine, and that is how I began writing *The Boy Who Loved Music.*

"My hobbies are bodybuilding and high fidelity. I have an exotic 'high end' sound system and an enormous record collection. I bought my present house for the fortunate acoustical properties of its hi-fi room (the entire third storey), When I have free time I indulge in listening to late German romantic symphonies and operas while following the score.

"Most of my writing pertains to music.

"I'm moved by history. If I can resurrect a Haydn or a Prince Esterhazy and make him come alive to young readers then, indeed, 'the dead shall be raised.'

"My philosophy of writing is summed up by the motto 'Gossip is the stuff of life.' Readers of *The Boy Who Loved Music* may not care that Marie Theresa was Empress of Austria or that

Nicolaus Esterhazy was Prince of Galanta, but they are endlessly titillated with that book's juicy tidbits about life in the 18th century: people rarely bathed, fashionable ladies glued their hair into tall mounds with bird's nests perched on top.

"I take a *verismo* approach to writing for children. When I wanted to depict the cruelty of life in 1772, I wrote in an early draft about that class of opera singers known as castrati. My editor cautioned me that this was a bit too 'heavy' for a children's book, so I turned instead to a description of how Prince Nicolaus dealt with poachers who hunted on his land. The text describing the fox hunt reads:

> 'Prince Nicolaus has set aside thousands of acres of woods as his private hunting preserve. Pity the countryman who dared to enter it to hunt for himself! Prince Nicolaus had no mercy.'

"In the accompanying illustration a peasant's corpse hangs from a tree. You may not notice it at first, but it's there. It was a discreet solution to a difficult problem.

"Writing for children is good training. It requires more discipline than writing for adults and forces one to cast about for that *bon mot* as if he were writing poetry. Ambiguity is not allowed."

We are now at the point where we must educate people in what nobody knew yesterday, and prepare in our schools for what no one knows yet but what some people must know tomorrow.

—Margaret Mead

There is not much left of Mynydd Blaena, just dark trees along the ridges of the hills, just a shadow of an older darkness . . . . ■ (Jacket illustration by Ronald Himler from *The Earth Witch* by Louise Lawrence.)

LAWRENCE, Louise 1943-
(Elizabeth Rhoda Holden)

PERSONAL: Born June 5, 1943, in Leatherhead, England; daughter of Fred (a bricklayer) and Rhoda Edith (a cook; maiden name, Cowles) Holden; divorced; children: Rachel Louise, Ralph Lawrence, Rebecca Jane. *Education:* Attended high school in Lydney, England. *Politics:* "Bewildered by." *Religion:* "Searching for." *Home:* Glenhalda, Forest Rd., Bream-near-Lydney, Gloucestershire, England. *Agent:* A. M. Heath & Co., 40-42 William IV St., London WC2N 4DD, England.

CAREER: Gloucestershire County Library, Forest of Dean Branches, Gloucestershire, England, assistant librarian, 1961-63, 1969-71; writer, 1971—.

WRITINGS—Of interest to young readers; science fiction novels: *Andra*, Collins, 1971; *The Power of Stars: A Story of Suspense*, Collins, 1972; *The Wyndcliffe*, Collins, 1974; *Sing and Scatter Daisies*, Harper, 1977; *Star Lord*, Pocket Books, 1980; *Cat Call*, Harper, 1980; *The Earth Witch*, Harper, 1981; *Calling B for Butterfly*, Harper, 1982; *The Dram Road*, Harper, 1983.

WORK IN PROGRESS: *The Prince of Jahn* and *Children of the Dust*, both for Harper.

SIDELIGHTS: "What motivated me into writing my first (unpublished) book at the age of twenty-two was fear of becoming a mental vegetable. What gave rise to that fear was being married with small children, totally isolated socially and environmentally in a remote farmhouse, with a husband who had no time for me. I didn't choose to become a writer. An idea came to me and I felt compelled to set it down, and in six weeks I had written a very bad book.

"I wrote for my own self-interest, to occupy my mind, as a hobby, as a way of escaping from reality into worlds of fantasy. I wrote because I was compelled to write . . . and it got a hold on me like a drug.

"When I left my husband I wrote to survive, and I have survived. Writing has become a process of self-realization, an expression of experiences, and ideas come to me unsought. I think it is not I who write books, but books that make me write them. Perhaps I'm an open mind and things flow through me, are channeled through my fingertips and into words.

"I have viewpoints on many subjects, but I find my opinions constantly change. I suppose like all people I search for truths and something to believe in, I ask questions that have no answers and want to know the purpose of human existence. My books are little inroads, blind alleys perhaps, excursions I have made into vast subjects. To me they are important, and I guess one day I would like to write a book that is important to other people, too. Fame is the spur? I'm not sure, but I think it is too deeply personal for that."

HORST LEMKE

(From *Als Ich Ein Kleiner Junge War* by Erich Kästner. Illustrated by Horst Lemke.)

LEMKE, Horst 1922-

PERSONAL: Born June 30, 1922, in Berlin, Germany; son of Max and Else (Teske) Lemke; married Richard Baumann, October 13, 1966; children: Natalie, Bettina. *Education:* Attended Staatliche Hochschule für Bildende Kunste, Berlin, Germany. *Home:* CH-6645 Brionc, S.M. Switzerland.

CAREER: Artist and illustrator of books for children. *Military service:* German Army, 1941-45. *Awards, honors:* Runner-up for the Hans Christian Andersen medal, 1960, for Denneborg's *Jan und das Wildpferd;* Lewis Carroll Shelf award, 1961, for Kästner's *When I was a Boy;* recipient of the Federal Merit Cross, first class, from the Republic of West Germany. *Member:* Society of Illustrators.

WRITINGS—All self-illustrated: *Das heitere Einmaleins,* C. Ueberreuter, 1968, translation published as *One Times One* (juvenile), F. Watts, 1969; *Von A-Z: Mein buntes Bilderwörterbuch* (juvenile; title means "From A-Z: My Colorful Picture and Words Book"), Bertelsmann, 1970; *Vierlerlei aus Stadt und Land* (juvenile), Bertelsmann, 1971, translation published as *Places and Faces,* Scroll Press, 1971.

Illustrator; all for children, except as indicated: Horst Wolfram Geissler, *Der Liebe Augustin* (title means "The Loving Augustin"), Sanssouci, 1948; Miguel de Cervantes Saavedra, *Don Quixote,* retold by Erich Kästner, translated by Richard Winston and Clare Winston, Messner, 1957; Heinrich Maria Denneborg, *Grisella the Donkey,* translated from the German by Emile Capouya, McKay, 1957; H. M. Denneborg, *Jan und das Wildpferd*, C. Dressler, 1957, translation by E. Capouya published as *Jan and the Wild Horse*, McKay, 1958; *Die Schildbürger*, retold by E. Kästner, translated by R. Winston and C. Winston published as *Simpletons*, Messner, 1957; E. Kästner, *Als ich ein kleiner Junge war*, C. Dressler, 1957, translation by Isabel McHugh and Florence McHugh published as *When I was a Little Boy*, J. Cape, 1959, and as *When I was a Boy*, F. Watts, 1961; H. M. Denneborg, *Das Wildpferd Balthasar*, C. Dressler, 1959, translation by E. Capouya published as *The Only Horse for Jan*, McKay, 1961; Arno Reissenweber, *Deutsche Volkssagen* (title means "German Folktales"), Keysersche Verlagsbuchhandlung, 1961; Inge Dreecken, *Fluss und Meeressagen* (title means "River and Ocean Tales"), Keysersche Verlagsbuchhandlung, 1961, H. M. Denneborg, *Kater Kasper* (title means "Casper the Cat"), C. Dressler, 1961; Manfred Hausmann, *Die Bremer Stadtmusikanten* (title means "The Bremen Town Musicians"), Bertelsmann, 1962; James Krüss, *Zehn kleine Negerlein*, Bertelsmann, 1963; E. Kästner, *Der Kleine Mann*, C. Dressler, 1963, translation by James Kirkup published as *The Little Man*, J. Cape, 1966; A. Reissenweber, *Deutsche Burgensagen* (title means "German Town

Tales"), Keyserche Verlagsbuchhandlung, 1965; Brothers Grimm, *Grimm Märchen* (title means "Grimm Fairytales"), Hoch-Verlag, 1965; J. Krüss, *Fahre mit durch ABC*, S. Mohn, 1965, English edition by Susan Bond published as *Ride Me through ABC*, Scroll Press, 1968; Fritz Notzoldt, *Liebe zu Mannheim* (adult travel book), Stadt Verwaltung Pressestelle, 1965; Max Kruse, *Der Löwe ist los* (title means "The Lion is Loose"), Hoch-Verlag, 1965.

M. Kruse, *Kommt ein Löwe geflogen* (title means "A Lion Comes Flying"), Hoch-Verlag, 1966; Christian Morgenstern, *Kindergedichte* (title means "Children's Poetry"), C. Ueberreuter, 1966; August Kopisch, *Die Heinzelmännchen von Köln* (title means "Fairies from Cologne"), Bertelsmann, 1967; Heinz Bundschuh, *Der Hut, der fliegen wollte* (title means "The Hat that Wanted to Fly"), Keller, 1967; M. Kruse, *Gut gebrüllt Löwe* (title means "Good Roaring Lion"), Hoch-Verlag, 1967; E.T.A. Hoffmann, *Die Automate* (title means "The Automat"), Arche-Verlag, 1967; E. Kästner, *Der kleine Mann und die kleine Miss* (title means "The Little Man and the Little

(From *Kindergedichte* by Christian Morgenstern. Illustrated by Horst Lemke.)

Omnibus drivers roar through traffic,
Swerving, curving – quite fantastic!

(From *Ride with Me through ABC* by Susan Bond. Illustrated by Horst Lemke.)

Miss''), C. Dressler, 1967; Klaus Reuter, *Pepermintje und die WA 123*, Hoch-Verlag, 1967; E. Mörike, *Mozart auf der Reise nach Prag* (title means ''Mozart on a Trip to the Prag''), Sanssouci, 1967; Irmtraud Herzmansky, *Die kleinen Köche* (juvenile cookbook), Deutscher Bucherbund, 1967; E. Kästner, *Der kleine Grenzverkehr* (title means ''Small Border Patrol''), Atrium-Verlag, 1967; E. Kästner, *Drei Männer im Schnee* (title means ''Three Men in the Snow''), Atrium-Verlag, 1967; E. Kästner, *Die verschwundene Miniatur* (title means ''The Vanished Miniature''), Artium-Verlag, 1968; Josef Göhlen, *Bill Bo*, Hoch-Verlag, 1968; H. W. Geissler, *Oydsseus und die Frauen* (title means ''Odysseus and the Women''), Sanssouci, 1968; New Testament, *Die Gute Nachricht* (title means ''Good News''), Deutsche Bibelstiftung, 1968; H. M. Denneborg, *Ein Schatz fallt nicht vom Himmel* (title means ''Treasures Don't Fall from Heaven''), C. Dressler, 1969; H. M. Denneborg, *Junker Prahlhans*, C. Ueberreuter, 1968, translation published as *Johnny and the Jester*, F. Watts, 1969; M. Kruse, *Löwegut—alles gut* (title means ''Lion-Good—All Good''), Hoch-Verlag, 1969; J. Göhlen, *Bill Bo und die geheimnisvollen Reiter* (title means ''Bill Bo and the Secretive Horseman''), Hoch-Verlag, 1969.

E. Kästner, *Der 35. Mai* (title means ''May 35th''), C. Dressler, 1970; H. Jaeger, *Der Drehorgelmann* (title means ''The

Organ Grinder''), Arche-Verlag, 1970; K. Reuter, *Alle gegen Jurgis* (title means ''All against Jurgis''), Hoch-Verlag, 1970; H. W. Geissler, *Odysseus und Penelope*, Sanssouci, 1970; E. L. Köngisburg, *Merkwürdiges aus dem Frankweiler-Archiv*, Bertelsmann, 1970; Gunter Adrian, *Hase und Igel*, Bertelsmann Jugendbuchverlag, 1970, translation and adaptation by Euan Cooper-Willis published as *Hare and Hodgehog*, Blackie & Son, 1971; M. Kruse, *Der Löwe kommt zuletzt* (title means ''The Lion Comes Last''), Hoch-Verlag, 1970; M. Kruse, *Don Blech und der goldene Junker* (title means ''Don Blech and the Golden Squire''), Hoch-Verlag, 1971; Polly van der Linde and Tasha van der Linde, *Around the World in Eighty Dishes*, Scroll Press, 1971; H. M. Denneborg, *Die Reise ins Schlaraffenland*, G. Ueberreuter, 1971, translation by Anne Rogers published as *A Trip to Lazibonia*, Kaye & Ward, 1971; H. M. Denneborg, *Die singende Säge* (title means ''The Singing Tale''), C. Dressler, 1971; M. Kruse, *Don Blech und der glutrote Vogel* (title means ''Don Blech and the Red Glowing Bird''), Hoch-Verlag, 1972; H. M. Denneborg, *Kasperle is überall* (title means ''Casper Is Everywhere''), C. Ueberreuter, 1972; M. Hausmann, *Wenn dieses alles Faultheit ist* (title means ''When All of This Is Laziness''), Bertelsmann Jugendbuchverlag, 1972; M. Krause, *Don Blech und der silberne Regen* (title means ''Don Blech and the Silver Rain''), Hoch-Verlag, 1973; O. Hassenkamp, *Bekenntnisse eines möblierten Herrn* (title means

"Familiarities of a Lodger"), Europäische Bildungsgemeinschaft, 1974; H. W. Geissler, *Der Geburtstag* (title means "The Birthday"), Sanssouci, 1973; Max Kolpenitsky, *Zoo ist das Leben: Satierische Verse* (title means "Zoo Is Life: Satirical Verse"; illustrated with Miroslav Sasek), Neureuter & Wolf, 1974; H. M. Denneborg, *Die Lügenlok*, C. Ueberreuter, 1974; Konrad Federer, *Immerwährender Drehorgel Kalender* (title means "Everlasting Street Organ Calendar"), Sanssouci, 1975; Barbara Noak, *Der Bastian*, Readers Digest, 1976; H. W. Geissler, *Das Orakel: Reisetagebuch eines andern* (adult travel book), Sanssouci, 1977; Eva Meinerts, *Das Liederbuch der Jugend* (title means "Songbook from Youth"), Bertelsmann, 1978; P. Zaunert, *Deutsche Märchen seit Grimm* (title means "German Fairytales since Grimm"), Hop Shuppan, 1979; H. W. Geissler, *Melodien der Landstrasse* (title means "Melodies of the Countryside"), Sanssouci, 1979.

Illustrator of German editions: P. L. Travers, *Mary Poppins*, C. Dressler, 1972; P. L. Travers, *Mary Poppins im Park*, C. Dressler, 1953; Astrid Lindgren, *Rasmus und der Landstreicher* (title means "Rasmus and the Tramp"), Oetinger, 1957; P. L. Travers, *Mary Poppins kommt wieder* (title means "Mary Poppins Comes Back"), C. Dressler, 1957; Jonathan Swift, *Gullivers Reisen* (title means "Gullivers Travels"), retold by E. Kästner, C. Ueberreuter, 1962; Mark Twain, pseudonym for Samuel Langhorne Clemens, *Tom Sawyer Abenteuer* (title means "Adventure of Tom Sawyer"), Bertelsmann, 1963; Paul Gallico, *Der Tag an dem des Meerschweinchen . . .* (title means "The Day the Guinea-Pig . . . "), 5 Volumes, Bertelsmann, 1964-67; M. Twain, *Die Abenteuer des Huckleberry Finn* (title means "The Adventures of Huckleberry Finn"), Bertelsmann, 1964; Roald Dahl, *James und der Riesenpfirsig* (title means "James and the Giant Peach"), Bertelsmann, 1968; P. Gallico, *Vom mütigen Manxmaus-Mäuserich*, Bertelsmann, 1970; Mark Twain, *Prinz und Bettelknabe* (title means "The Prince and the Little Beggar"), Hoch-Verlag, 1970; R. Dahl, *Charlie und die Schokoladenfabrik* (title means "Charlie and the Chocolate Factory"), Bertelsmann, 1971; R. Dahl, *Charlie und der gläserne Fahrstuhl* (title means "Charlie and the Great Glass Elevator"), Bertelsmann, 1972; A. Lindgren, *Rasmus, Pontus und der Schwertschluker* (title means "Rasmus, Pontus and the Swordswallower"), Oetinger, 1971.

SIDELIGHTS: "From the age of twelve, I wished to become a painter and was designing and painting all the time. My older brother procured for me reproductions of the French Impressionists which I copied. And to call forth new ideas, he provided me with books by writers such as Hoffmann, Poe, Dickens and Twain for the purpose of illustrating them. In September 1939, as war was declared and just half a year before my leaving examination, I was compelled to leave school because of a cartoon of mine representing the then Propaganda Minister Goebbels. Moreover, no further school was allowed to accept me. But, I had luck again and the High School of Plastic Arts admitted me. My teacher was Gerhard Ulrich to whom I owe very much. From 1941 to the end of the war I was a soldier. After the war I went to Heidelberg.

"In 1955, I bought a 400 year old farm house which looks over Lake Aggiore in the south of Switzerland and reconstructed it. I live in that little paradise where I can work undisturbed and in a wonderful quietness." [Lee Kingman and others, compilers, *Illustrators of Children's Books: 1957-1966*, Horn Book, 1968.[1]]

About his illustrations, Lemke categorized them as "entertaining, with good and sly humor. [I prefer] cheerful, dreamy and scurrilous books like Mark Twain, Dickens or the fairy tales of Grimm. For the black-and-white illustrations I am working with pen, brush and colored pencil. But for picture books I use tempera, water color, collage, pen, colored pencil and crayon. In the course of years, my stroke has become lighter and looser. I write my illustrations just as I would write a letter."[1]

Lemke's works are included in the Kerlan Collection at the University of Minnesota.

FOR MORE INFORMATION SEE: Lee Kingman and others, compilers, *Illustrators of Children's Books: 1957-1966*, Horn Book, 1968.

LINDGREN, Astrid 1907-

PERSONAL: Born November 14, 1907, in Vimmerby, Sweden; daughter of Samuel August and Hanna (Jonsson) Ericsson; married Sture Lindgren, April 4, 1931 (died, 1952); children: Lars, Karin (Mrs. Carl Olof Nyman). *Home:* Dalagatan 46, 113 24 Stockholm, Sweden.

CAREER: Writer of children's books, 1944—; Rabén & Sjögren (publishers), Stockholm, Sweden, children's book editor, 1946-70. *Member:* Union of Swedish Writers, League of the Nine, P.E.N. *Awards, honors:* Rabén & Sjögren's prize com-

She tied two scrubbing brushes on her bare feet and skated over the floor . . . . "I certainly should have been a skating princess," she said . . . . ■ (From *Pippi Longstocking* by Astrid Lindgren. Illustrated by Louis S. Glanzman.)

ASTRID LINDGREN

petition, second prize for books for girls ten to fifteen years old, 1944, for *Britt-Marie lättar sitt hjärta*, first prize for books for children six to ten years old, 1945, for *Pippi Laangstrump*, and shared first prize for detective books for youth, 1946, for *Mästerdetektiven Blomkvist; Svanska Dagbladet's* litteraturpris (Swedish newspaper literary prize), 1946, for *Pippi Laangstrump*; Nils Holgersson Medal, 1950, for *Nils Karlsson-Pyssling;* German Sonderpreis for Children's Books, 1956, for *Mio, min Mio;* Swedish State Award, 1957, for high literary standards; Hans Christian Andersen Award, 1958, for *Rasmus paa luffen,* and Boys' Clubs of America Junior Book Award, 1961, for American edition of same book, *Rasmus and the Vagabond; New York Herald Tribune* Children's Spring Book Festival Award (shared with Anna Riwkin-Brick), 1959, for *Sia Lives on Kilimanjaro.*

State Artist Award (Sweden), 1965; *Expressen's* (newspaper) "Heffaklump" award, 1970, for *Än lever Emil i Lönneberga;* Litteraturfrämjandets hederspris Guldskeppet (Literary Achievements honorary Golden Ship award), 1970; Lewis Carroll Shelf Award, 1970, for *The Tomten,* and 1973, for *Pippi Longstocking;* Swedish Academy's Gold Medal, 1971; Honorary Doctor of Philosophy from the University of Linköping (Sweden), 1973, Brooklyn Art Books for Children citation, 1973, for *The Tomten;* Bokhandelsmedhjälparnas plakett (Bookseller's Cooperative Plaque), 1974, and Janusz Korczak Literary Prize, 1979, both for *Bröderna Lejonjärta;* "Medalj

för leende" (Russian distinction), 1974, for a reading on Russian radio of *Karlsson paa taket* and *Pippi Laangstrump;* Litteris et Artibus Medal from the King of Sweden, 1975; International Writer's Prize from the Welsh Arts Council and Friedenspreis des Deutschen Buchhandels (German Peace Prize) from German publishers and book dealers, both 1978; Honorary Doctor of Letters from the University of Leicester (England), 1978; Mildred L. Batchelder Award, 1984, for *Ronia, the Robber's Daughter.*

WRITINGS—All Swedish books published by Rabén & Sjögren, all translations published in America by Viking, except where noted: *Britt-Mari lättar sitt hjärta* (title means "Britt-Mari Opens Her Heart"), 1944, 3rd edition, 1959; *Huvudsaken är att man är frisk: Kriminal komedi* (play; title means "The Most Important Thing in Life Is Health: Criminal Comedy"), Lindfors, 1945; *Pippi Laangstrump* (illustrated by Ingrid Vang Nyman), 1945, new edition, 1983, translation by Florence Lamborn published as *Pippi Longstocking* (illustrated by Louis S. Glanzman; ALA Notable book), 1950 [special edition illustrated with photographs from the film, "Pippi Longstocking," 1973]; *Kerstin och jag* (title means "Kerstin and I"), 1945, new edition, 1970.

Mästerdetektiven Blomkvist, 1946, new edition, 1981, large print edition (illustrated by Eva Laurell), Liber, 1967, translation by Herbert Antoine published as *Bill Bergson, Master*

(From *Pippi in the South Seas* by Astrid Lindgren. Illustrated by Louis S. Glanzman.)

Detective (illustrated by L. S. Glanzman), 1952; *Pippi Laangstrump gaar ombord* (illustrated by I. Vang Nyman), 1946, new edition, 1969, tranlsation by Marianne Turner published in England as *Pippi Goes Aboard* (illustrated by Richard Kennedy), Oxford University Press, 1956, translation by F. Lamborn published in America as *Pippi Goes on Board* (illustrated by L. S. Glanzman), 1957 [special edition illustrated with photographs from film, 1973]; *Pippi Laangstrumps liv och leverne: Lustpel för barn* (title means "Pippi Longstocking's Life: Comedy Play for Children"), 1946, 2nd edition, 1950; *Alla vi barn i Bullerbyn* (illustrated by I. Vang Nyman), 1947, new edition, 1975, translation by Evelyn Ramsden published in England as *The Six Bullerby Children* (illustrated by Ilon Wikland), Methuen, 1963; *Mästerdetektiven Blomkvist: Teaterpjäs för barn* (title means "Bill Bergson, Master Detective: Theater Play for Children"), 1948; *Pippi Laangstrump i Söderhavet* (illustrated by I. Vang Nyman), 1948, new edition, 1969, translation by M. Turner published in England as *Pippi in the South Seas* (illustrated by R. Kennedy), Oxford University Press, 1957, translation by Gerry Bothmer (illustrated by L. S. Glanzman) published in America, 1959; *Mera om oss barn i Bullerbyn* (title means "More about the Bullerby Children"; illustrated by I. Vang Nyman), 1949, new edition, 1975; *Nils Karlsson-Pyssling* (fairy tales; title means "Niels,

the Midget"; illustrated by Eva Billow), 1949, new edition, 1982.

Kajsa Kavat och andra barn (fairy tales; title means "Kajsa Kavat and other Children"; illustrated by I. Vang Nyman), 1950, 12th edition, 1969; *Kati i Amerika* (illustrated by Gobi, pseudonym of Margit Uppenberg), Bonnier, 1950, translation by M. Turner published in England as *Kati in America* (illustrated by Daniel Dupuy), Brockhampton, 1964; *Mästerdetektiven Blomkvist lever farligt* (illustrated by E. Laurell), 1951, new edition, 1981, translation by H. Antoine published as *Bill Bergson Lives Dangerously* (illustrated by Don Freeman), 1954; *Boken om Pippi Laangstrump* (title means "The Book about Pippi Longstocking"; contains several Pippi Longstocking stories; illustrated by I. Vang Nyman), 1952; *Bara roligt i Bullerbyn* (title means "Only Good Times in Bullerbyn"; illustrated by I. Vang Nyman), 1952, new edition, 1975; *Kati paa Kaptensgatan*, Bonnier, 1952, reissued as *Kati i Italien*, Rabén & Sjögren, 1971, published as *Kati in Italy* (illustrated by D. Dupuy), Grosset, 1961; *Kalle Blomkvist och Rasmus* (illustrated by Kerstin Thorvall), 1953, new edition, 1981, translation by F. Lamborn published as *Bill Bergson and the White Rose Rescue* (illustrated by D. Freeman), 1965; *Kati i Paris*, Bonnier, 1953, new edition, 1972, published as *Kati in Paris* (illustrated by D. Dupuy), Grosset, 1961; *Mio, min Mio* (illustrated by I. Wikland), 1954, new edition, 1983, translation by M. Turner published as *Mio, My Son*, 1956.

Lillebror och Karlsson paa taket (illustrated by I. Wikland), 1955, new edition, 1983, translation by M. Turner published in England as *Eric and Karlsson-on-the-Roof* (illustrated by R. Kennedy), Oxford University Press, 1958, translation by M. Turner published in America as *Karlsson-on-the-Roof* (illustrated by Jan Pyk), 1971; *Rasmus paa luffen* (illustrated by Eric Palmquist), 1956, new edition, 1982, translation by G. Bothmer published as *Rasmus and the Vagabond* (Junior Literary Guild selection), 1960 (translation by G. Bothmer published in England as *Rasmus and the Tramp*, Methuen, 1961); *Rasmus, Pontus och Toker* (title means "Rasmus, Pontus and Toker"; illustrated by E. Palmquist), 1957, new edition, 1980; *Barnen paa Braakmakargatan* (illustrated by I. Wikland; first published in *Klumpe Dumpe* Journal), 1958, new edition, 1982, translation by G. Bothmer published as *The Children on Troublemaker Street*, Macmillan, 1964 (translation by G. Bothmer published in England as *The Mischievous Martens*, Methuen, 1968); *Sunnanäng* (fairy tales; title means "The South Wind Field"; illustrated by I. Wikland), 1959, new edition, 1975.

Madicken (illustrated by I. Wikland), 1960, new edition, 1982, translation by G. Bothmer published as *Mischievous Meg* (illustrated by Janina Domanska), 1962 (translation by M. Turner published in England as *Madicken*, Oxford University Press, 1963); *Bullerbyboken* (consolidated volume; title means "The Bullerby Book"; illustrated by I. Wikland), 1961 [selections translated by F. Lamborn published as *The Children of Noisy Village*, 1962; selections translated by F. Lamborn published in England as *Happy Times in Noisy Village*, 1963; selections translated by F. Lamborn published in England as *Cherry Time at Bullerby*, Methuen, 1964; selections translated by F. Lamborn published in England as *Happy Days at Bullerby*, Methuen, 1965, translation by E. Ramsden and F. Lamborn published in England as *All about the Bullerby Children* (includes translations of *Alla vi barn i Bullerbyn, Mera om oss barn i Bullerbyn,* and *Bara roligt i Bullerbyn),* Methuen, 1970]; *Lotta paa Braakmakargatan* (illustrated by I. Wikland), 1961, new edition, 1983, translation by G. Bothmer published as *Lotta on Troublemaker Street*, Macmillan, 1963 (translation by G. Bothmer published in England as *Lotta Leaves Home*, Methuen, 1969); *Karlsson paa taket flyger igen* (illustrated by I. Wikland), 1962, new edition, 1983, adapted for the deaf by Helena Renvall published as *Emil*, Rabén & Sjögren, 1977, translation by Patricia Crompton published in England as *Karlson Flies Again*, Methuen, 1977; *Emil i Lönneberga* (illustrated by Björn Berg), 1963, new edition, 1980, translation by Lilian Seaton published as *Emil in the Soup Tureen*, Follett, 1970.

Vi paa Saltkraakan (illustrated by I. Wikland), 1964, new edition, 1979, translation by E. Ramsden published as *Seacrow Island* (illustrated by Robert Hales), Oliver & Boyd, 1968, Viking, 1969; *Nya hyss av Emil i Lönneberga* (illustrated by B. Berg), 1966, new edition, 1972, published as *Emil's Pranks*, Follett, 1971; *Karlsson paa taket smyger igen* (title means ''Karlsson-on-the-Roof Lurking Again''; illustrated by I. Wikland), 1968, new edition, 1983.

Än lever Emil i Lönneberga (illustrated by B. Berg), 1970, new edition, 1979, translation by Michael Heron published as *Emil and Piggy Beast*, Follett, 1973 (translation by M. Heron published in England as *Emil and His Clever Pig*, Brockhampton, 1974); *Allt om Karlsson paa taket* (consolidated volume; title means ''All about Karlsson-on-the-Roof''; illustrated by I. Wikland), 1972; *Bröderna Lejonhjärta* (illustrated by I. Wikland), 1973, new edition, 1983, translation by Joan Tate published as *The Brothers Lionheart* (illustrated by James Keaton Lambert), 1975; *Ronja Rövardotter* (illustrated by Trina S. Hyman), 1981, published in America as *Ronia, the Robber's Daughter*, 1983.

Picture books based on episodes from Lindgren's children's books; all published by Rabén & Sjögren: *Känner du Pippi Laangstrump?* (title means ''Do You Know Pippi Longstock-

ing?''; illustrated by I. Vang Nyman), 1947, new edition, 1968; *Sjung med Pippi Laangstrump* (title means ''Sing with Pippi Longstocking''; illustrated by I. Vang Nyman; music and songs by Per-Martin Hamberg), 1949; *Nils Karlsson-Pyssling flyttar in* (illustrated by I. Wikland), 1956, new edition, 1975, translation by M. Turner published in England as *Simon Small Moves In*, Burke, 1965; *Här Kommer Pippi Laangstrump* (title means ''Here Comes Pippi Longstocking''; illustrated by I. Vang Nyman), 1957; *Kajsa Kavat hjälper mormor* (illustrated by I. Wikland), 1958, new edition, 1975, adapted and translated by Kay Ware and Lucille Sutherland published in America as *Brenda Brave Helps Grandmother*, Webster, 1961 (translation by Marianne Helweg published in England as *Brenda Helps Grandmother*, Burke, 1966).

Jul i Bullerbyn (illustrated by I. Wikland), 1963, new edition, 1980, translation by F. Lamborn published in America as *Christmas in Noisy Village* (Junior Literary Guild selection), Viking, 1964, (published in England as *Christmas at Bullerby*, Methuen, 1964); *Vaar i Bullerbyn* (illustrated by I. Wikland), 1965, new edition, 1975, published in America as *Springtime in Noisy Village*, Viking, 1966 (published in England as *Springtime in Bullerby*, Methuen, 1981); *Barnens dag i Bullerbyn* (illustrated by I. Wikland), 1966, new edition, 1973, published in England as *A Day at Bullerby*, Methuen, 1967; *Skraallan och sjörövarna* (illustrated with photographs by Sven-Eric Delér and Stig Hallgren), 1967, translation by Gunvor Edwards published in England as *Scrap and the Pirates*, Oliver & Boyd, 1968, translation by Albert Read and Christine Sapieha published in America as *Skrallan and the Pirates*, Doubleday, 1969; *Pippi flattar in* (title means ''Pippi Moves In''; illustrated by I. Vang Nyman; first published in *Klumpe Dumpe Journal*), 1969; *Pippi ordnar allt* (title means ''Pippi Puts Ev-

... In through the window Karlsson buzzed like a giant bumble-bee. He hummed a happy little tune while he circled around the walls. ■ (From *Karlsson-on-the-Roof* by Astrid Lindgren. Translated by Marianne Turner. Illustrated by Jan Pyk.)

When Polly strode into the kitchen back home, she looked a bit mysterious. But nobody noticed. Jonas and Maria sat in their chairs crying, and Mother was busy comforting them. No one looked at Polly. ■ (From *Of Course Polly Can Do Almost Everything* by Astrid Lindgren. Illustrated by Ilon Wikland.)

erything in Order''; illustrated by I. Vang Nyman; first published in *Klumpe Dumpe* Journal), 1969.

Pippi är starkast i världen (title means "Pippi, the Strongest in the World"; illustrated by I. Vang Nyman; first published in *Klumpe Dumpe* Journal), 1970; *Pippi haaller kalas* (title means "Pippi Has a Party"; illustrated by I. Vang Nyman; first published in *Klumpe Dumpe* Journal), 1970; *Pippis maalarbok* (title means "Pippi's Coloring Book"; illustrated by I. Vang Nyman), 1970; *Pippi gaar till sjöss* (title means "Pippi Goes to Sea"; illustrated by I. Vang Nyman; first published in *Klumpe Dumpe* Journal), 1971; *Pippi vill inte bli stor* (title means "Pippi Doesn't Want to Grow Up"; illustrated by I. Vang Nyman; first published in *Klumpe Dumpe* Journal), 1971; *Paa rymmen med Pippi Laangstrump* (photographs by Bo-Eric Gybert), 1971, published in America as *Pippi on the Run*, Viking, 1976; *Visst kan Lotta cykla* (based on *Barnen paa Braakmakargatan;* illustrated by I. Wikland), 1971, published in America as *Of Course Polly Can Ride a Bike*, Follett, 1972 (published in England as *Lotta's Bike*, Methuen, 1973); *Den där Emil* (illustrated by B. Berg), 1972, translation by J. Tate published in England as *That Emil*, Brockhampton, 1973; *Allrakäraste Syster* (based on *Nils Karlsson-Pyssling;* illustrated by Hans Arnold), 1973, published in England as *My Very Own Sister*, Methuen, 1974; *När Emil skulle dra ut Linas tand* (illustrated by B. Berg), 1976, published in England as *Emil and Lina's Bad Tooth*, Brockhampton, 1977; *Visst kan Lotta nästan allting* (illustrated by I. Wikland), 1977, published in America as *Of Course Polly Can Do Almost Everything*, Follett, 1978 (published in England as *Lotta's Christmas Surprise*), Methuen, 1978.

Picture books by Anna Riwkin-Brick; all with photos by A. Riwkin-Brick; all published by Rabén & Sjögren; all translations published in America by Macmillan, except as noted: *Eva möter Noriko-San*, 1956, new edition, 1970, published as *Eva Visits Noriko-San*, 1957 (published in England as *Noriko-san, Girl of Japan*, Methuen, 1958); *Sia bor paa Kilimandjaro*, 1958, published as *Sia Lives on Kilimanjaro*, 1959; *Mina svenska kusiner*, 1959, published as *My Swedish Cousins*, 1960; *Lilibet, cirkusbarn*, 1960, published in England as *Circus Child*, Methuen, 1960, published in America as *Lilibet, Circus Child*, 1961; *Marko bor i Jugoslavien*, 1962, published as *Marko Lives in Yugoslavia*, 1962; *Jackie bor i Holland*, 1963, published as *Dirk Lives in Holland*, 1963; *Randi bor i Norge*, 1965, published as *Randi Lives in Norway*, 1965 (published in England as *Gerda Lives in Norway*, Methuen, 1965); *Noy bor i Thailand*, 1966, published as *Noy Lives in Thailand*, 1967; *Matti bor i Finland*, 1968, published as *Matti Lives in Finland*, 1969.

Picture books with Birgitta Nordenskjöld; all illustrated by B. Nordenskjöld; all published by Rabén & Sjögren: *Jag vill inte gaa och lägga* (title means "I Don't Want to Go to Bed"), 1947, new edition, 1969; *Jag vill ocksaa gaa i skolan*, 1951, new edition, 1959, published in England as *I Want to Go to School, Too*, Methuen, 1982; *Jag vill ocksaa ha ett syskon*, 1954, published as *I Want a Brother or Sister* (illustrated by I. Wikland), translated by Barbara Lucas, Harcourt, 1981.

Picture books with Harold Wiberg; all illustrated by H. Wiberg: *Jul i stallet*, Rabén & Sjögren, 1961, new edition, 1978, published as *Christmas in the Stable* (*Horn Book* honor list), Coward, 1962; (adapter) Viktor Rydberg, *The Tomten*, Coward, 1961, new edition, 1968; (adapter) Karl-Eric Forsslund, *The Tomten and the Fox* (ALA Notable Book), Coward, 1965 (published in England as *The Fox and the Tomten*, Constable, 1965).

Then we rushed up the stairs . . . and ran into the attic and hid behind the clothes. ■ (From *Happy Times in Noisy Village* by Astrid Lindgren. Illustrated by Ilon Wikland.)

Other translations from Swedish: *Lotta*, translation of *Barnen paa Braakmakargatan* and *Lotta paa Braakmakargatan* by G. Bothmer published in one volume in England, Penguin, 1972; *Mardie* (illustrated by I. Wikland), Methuen, 1979; *The World's Best Karlson* (illustrated by I. Wikland), Methuen, 1980; *That's My Baby* (illustrated by I. Wikland), Methuen, 1980.

Anthologies: *Sex pjäser för barn och ungdom* (title means "Six Plays for Children and Youth"), Rabén & Sjögren, 1950; (contributor) Aake W. Edfeldt, editor, *Bullerbybarnen* (title means "The Bullerby Children"), Ehlin, 1957, new edition, Liber, 1969; A. W. Edfeldt, editor, *Kajsa Kavats äventyr* (title means "Kajsa Kavat's Adventures"), Ehlin, 1957, new edition, Liber, 1969; A. W. Edfeldt, editor, *Tillbaka till Bullerbyn* (title means "Back to Bullerby"), Ehlin, 1958, new edition, 1969; *Pjäser för barn och ungdom: Första samlingen* (title means "Plays for Children and Youth: First Collection"), Rabén & Sjögren, 1959, 4th edition, 1971; *Salikons rosor: Sagor* (title means "Salikon's Roses: Fairytales"; illustrated by I. Wikland), Rabén & Sjögren, 1967; *Pjäser för barn och ungdom: Andra samlingen* (title means "Plays for Children and Youth: Second Collection"), Rabén & Sjögren, 1968; *Bullerbyn* (includes *Bullerbybarnen* and *Tillbaka till Bullerbyn;* illustrated by I. Wikland), Utbildningsförlaget, 1970; *Mina paahitt: Ett urval fraan Pippi till Emil* (title means "My Pranks: Selections from Pippi to Emil"; illustrated by I. Vang Nyman, I. Wikland, and B. Berg), Rabén & Sjögren, 1971; (contributor) *The Young America*, Lyons and Carnahan, 1972.

Other: *5 automobilturer i Sverige* (title means "Five Automobile Trips to Sweden"), Motormännens riksförbund, 1939; *Twenty-five Automobile Tours in Sweden*, Motormännens riksförbund, 1939, new edition, 1953; *Drei kleine Schweinchen*

(From the animated movie "The Tomten," adapted by
Astrid Lindgren. Produced by Weston Woods, 1982.)

im Apfelgarten (title means "Three Little Pigs in the Apple
Orchard"; translated by Karl Kurt Peters; illustrated by Ingrid
Jörg), Berliner Handpresse, 1972; *Samuel August fraan Sev-
edstorp och Hanna i Hult* (title means "Samuel August from
Sevedstorp and Hanna of Hult"), Bokvännerna, 1973, new
edition, Rabén & Sjögren, 1975.

ADAPTATIONS—Movies: "Mästerdetektiven Blomkvist" ("Bill
Bergson Master Detective"), S. Bauman-Produktion, 1947;
"Pippi Laangstrump" (Pippi Longstocking"), Sandrews, 1949,
Nord-Art, 1969; "Mästerdetektiven och Rasmus" ("Bill Bergson and the White Rose Rescue"), Artfilm, 1953; "Luffaren
och Rasmus" ("Rasmus and the Vagabond"), Artfilm, 1955,
produced as "Rasmus paa luffen" ("Rasmus and the Vagabond"), Artfilm/Svensk Filmindustri, 1981; "Rasmus Pontus
och Toker" ("Rasmus, Pontus, and Toker"), Artfilm, 1956;
"Mästerdetektiven lever farligt" ("Bill Bergson Lives Dangerously"), Artfilm, 1957.

"Alla vi barn i Bullerbyn" ("The Children of Noisy Village"),
Artfilm/Svensk Filmindustri, 1961; "Bara roligt i Bullerbyn"
("Only Good Times in Bullerbyn"), Artfilm/Svensk Filmin-
dustri, 1961; "Tjorven Baatsman och Moses," Artfilm, 1964;
"Tjorven och skraallan," Artfilm, 1965; "Tjorven och My-
sak," Artfilm, 1966; "Skraallan Ruskprick och Knorrhane,"
Artfilm/Svensk Filmindustri, 1967; "Vi paa Saltkraakan"
("Seacrow Island"), Artfilm/Svensk Filmindustri, 1968; "Pippi
Laangstrump paa de sju haven", Artfilm/Svensk Filmindustri,
1969, released in the U.S. as "Pippi in the South Sea," G.
G. Communications Films, 1974.

"Paa rymmen med Pippi Laangstrump", Artfilm/Svensk Fil-
mindustri, 1970, released in the U.S. as "Pippi on the Run,"
G. G. Communications Films, 197(?); "Emil i Lönneberga"
("Emil in the Soup Tureen"), Artfilm/Svensk Filmindustri,
1971; "Nya hyss av Emil i Lönneberga" ("Emil's Pranks"),
Artfilm/Svensk Filmindustri, 1972; "Emil och Griseknoen"
("Emil and Piggy Beast"), Artfilm/Svensk Filmindustri, 1973;
"Världens bästa Karlsson" ("Karlsson on the Roof"), Art-
film/Svensk Filmindustri, 1974; "Bröderna Lejonhjärta" ("The
Brothers Lionheart"), Artfilm/Svensk Filmindustri, 1977; "Du
är inte klok Madicken" (sequel to "Madicken"), Artfilm/Svensk
Filmindustri, 1979; "Ronja Rövardotter" ("Ronia, The Rob-
ber's Daughter"), Artfilm/Svensk Filmindustri, 1984.

Plays: "Pippi Longstocking," first performed at Oscars Theatre, Stockholm, Sweden, 1948, a later, revised production
was performed at Folkan Theatre, Sweden, 1980; "Mästerdetektiven Blomkvist" ("Bill Bergson Master Detective"),
first performed at Oscars Theatre, Sweden, c. 1950; "Karlsson
on the Roof," first performed at Dramaten Theatre, Sweden,
1969, later productions included performances at Folkan Theatre, Sweden, 1978, and in various theaters in Sweden in 1983;
"Mio, min Mio," ("Mio, My Son"), first performed at Folkan
Theatre, Sweden, 1980; "Emil i Lönneberga," Limabrall AB,
Sweden, February 18, 1984.

Television productions: "Mästerdetektiven Blomkvist paa nya
äventyr" ("Blomkvist, The Master Detective's New Adventures"), [Sweden], December 26, 1966.

Television series: "Alla vi barn i Bullerbyn" ("The Children
of Noisy Village"), 13-part series, Artfilm, 1960-61; "Bara
roligt i Bullerbyn" ("Only Good Times in Bullerbyn"), Art-
film, 1962; "Mästerdetektiven lever farligt" ("Bill Bergson
Lives Dangerously"), Artfilm, 1963; "Mästerdetektiven och
Rasmus" ("Bill Bergson and the White Rose Rescue"), Art-
film, 1963; "Luffaren och Rasmus" ("Rasmus and the Va-
gabond"), Artfilm, 1963; "Vi paa Saltkraakan" ("Seacrow
Island"), 13-part series, Artfilm, 1964; "Pippi Laangstrump"
("Pippi Longstocking"), 13-part series, Sveriges Radio/Svensk
Filmindustri, 1969; "Pippi Laangstrump paa de sju haven"
("Pippi on the Seven Seas"), Artfilm/Svensk Filmindustri,
1972; "Paa rymmen med Pippi Laangstrump" ("Pippi on the
Run"), Artfilm/Svensk Filmindustri, 1975; "Madicken"
("Mischievous Meg"), 10-part series, Artfilm/Svensk Filmin-
dustri, 1979.

Filmstrips; all produced by Weston Woods, except as noted:
"Christmas in Noisy Village" (with cassette), Miller-Brody,
1964; "The Tomten," 1965; "Christmas in the Stables," 1965;
"The Tomten and the Fox," 1973.

"Pippi Longstocking" has also been adapted into a recorded
book (with record or cassette), read by Esther Benson, produced by Miller-Brody. Many of Lindgren's books have been
produced as cassette recordings and have been published in
braille editions in Sweden.

WORK IN PROGRESS: Film script based on *Ronja*.

SIDELIGHTS: ". . . In **November of 1907** . . . I was born in
an old red house with apple trees around it. I was child number
two to farmer Samuel August Ericsson and his wife Hanna,
born Jonsson. The farm we lived on was called —and is still
called Näs—and it was right outside the little town of Vimmerby, in Smaland [Sweden]. Näs has been a parsonage since
1411 and it still is today. My father was certainly not a vicar
but rather just a parsonage tennant at Näs, just like his father
before him and his son after him."

"My father . . . fell in love with my mother, Hanna, from
Hult, when he was thirteen years old and she was nine—and
she remained his 'devoted little beloved one' throughout their
life together. She died eight years before him—we thought
he'd die, too. But no. He said that some leave ahead, others
leave later, there's nothing you can do. He enjoyed living, and
was sure that one day he'd meet her again—and he continued
to love her and talk about her and to praise all her virtues.
They were strong believers, which my brother and sisters and
I were not. In the Bible, we read that there is no marriage in
Heaven, just angels. So I told my father 'the little angel Hanna,'
and he got quite angry at the thought that Hanna should be

there as an angel and not belong to him! I've written a memoir about my parent's love affair and about my childhood [*Samuel August from Sevedstorp and Hanna of Hult*, unpublished in English]. . . ." [Jonathan Cott, "Profiles: The Astonishment of Being," *New Yorker*, February 28, 1983.[1]]

"In the red house two more children were born. So altogether we were four children—Gunnar, Astrid, Stina and Ingegerd, and we lived a happy life at Näs, in many ways just like the children in the Bullerby (Noisy Village) books. . . . We went to school in Vimmerby which was so close we could walk there in a quarter of an hour. . . ."

Lindgren has described her childhood as a time that was filled with security and freedom to play, although she and her brother and sisters were expected to share the daily chores with the farmhands. "It was fun and it was instructive for a child to grow up, as I did, with people of varying habits and types and ages. Without their knowing it and without my knowing it myself, I learned something from them about the conditions of life and how complicated it can be to be a human being. I learned other things as well, for these were outspoken people, who did not keep anything back just because children happened to be around. And we were around, my brother and sisters and I, for we had to bring them coffee while they were working in the fields. That is what I remember best—the coffee breaks, when they were all gathered, sitting there at the edge of a ditch, drinking coffee and dunking their rye-bread sandwiches and exchanging thoughts about this and that.

"It is true that we were disciplined with order and the fear of God, as was the tradition of the time, but in our life of play we were wonderfully free and never controlled. And we played and played and played—it is a wonder we didn't play ourselves to death. We climbed like apes in trees and on roofs, we jumped from lumber piles and haylofts so hard that our innards complained, we crawled through our dangerous subterranean tunnels in the sawdust heap, we went swimming in the river long before we knew how to swim, totally forgetting the imperative by our mother not to go 'farther out than the navel.' But all four of us survived.

"Rocks and trees were so close to us as living beings, and nature protected and nurtured our playing and our dreaming. Whatever our imagination could call forth was enacted in the land around us—all fairy tales, all adventures we invented or read about or heard about, all of it happened there, and only there. Even our songs and prayers had their places in surrounding nature."[1]

. . . He talks to Caro in tomten language, a silent little language a dog can understand. ▪ (From *The Tomten* by Viktor Rydberg. Adapted by Astrid Lindgren. Illustrated by Harald Wiberg.)

While nature was a pervasive influence on Lindgren's childhood, books also played a major role in her development. Her introduction to the world of books came about when a girlfriend read her a fairy tale. ''This girl Edith—blessed be she now and forever—read to me the fairy tale about the Giant Bam-Bam and the fairy Viribunda, and thus set my childish soul moving in a direction and it has not yet completely ceased to follow. The miracle occurred in the kitchen of a poor farmhand, and from that day forth there was no other kitchen in the world.''[1]

When Lindgren eventually learned to read she would ask for books as Christmas presents. ''. . . Imagine, to be the sole owner of a book—I wonder I didn't faint for pure happiness! I can still remember how these books smelled when they arrived, fresh from the printer. Yes, I started by smelling them, and there was no lovelier scent in all the world. It was full of foretaste and anticipation.

''. . . All the wonderful books for girls. . . . There were so many girls in the world who were suddenly as close to oneself as ever any beings of flesh and blood! There was Hetty, the Irish whirlwind. And Polly, a jewel of a girl from New England. Pollyanna and Katy, not to mention Sara, the one with the diamond mines who became so wonderously poor and was freezing in her attic until Ram Dass came climbing across the roof with soup and warm blankets. And then, of course, Anne of Green Gables—oh, my unforgettable one, forever, you will be riding the cart with Matthew Cuthbert beneath the flowering apple trees of Avonlea! How I lived with that girl! A whole summer, my sisters and I played at Anne of Green Gables in the big sawdust heap at the sawmill. I was Diana Barry, and the pond at the manure heap was the Dark Reflecting Waves.''[1]

1917. Went to school where her classmates and teachers predicted that she would be an author when she grew up. ''That scared me so much that I made a firm decision—never to write a book! It says even in Ecclesiastes that there is no end to the writing of books, and I didn't feel that I would be the right person to increase the stacks of books. I stuck to that decision until March of 1944. . . .''[1]

1930s. After completing school, Lindgren went to Stockholm to find work. ''I went off to Stockholm where I took secretarial training and got a job in an office. Then I married and had two children, Lars and Karin, who always wanted me to tell them stories. So I told them stories. But I didn't write any books, no, because I had very early decided that I wouldn't. Most of the people who never write books probably don't make up their minds not to do so, but for me, it was in fact a decision. When I was going to school I was always hearing people say, 'You'll probably be a writer when you grow up.' I think that scared me, I didn't dare try, even though somewhere deep inside I probably thought it would be fun to write. . . .

There was a ring of eyes all around the stone, watching her, and she had not noticed anything. Never before had she seen eyes that shone in the darkness, and she did not like them. ■ (Jacket illustration by Trina Schart Hyman from *Ronia, the Robber's Daughter* by Astrid Lindgren. Translated by Patricia Crampton.)

''In **1941** my then 7-year-old daughter Karin was sick in bed with a pneumonia. Every evening when I sat by her bedside she would nag in that way children do: 'Tell me something!' And one evening, completely exhausted, I asked her: 'What should I tell?' She answered: 'Tell about Pippi Longstocking!' She had come up with the name right there on the spot. I didn't ask her who Pippi Longstocking was, I just began the story, and since it was a strange name, it turned out to be a strange girl as well. Karin, and later even her playmates, from the very beginning showed a strong love for Pippi, and I had to tell the story again and again. It went on like that for several years.

''One day in **March, 1944** it snowed in Stockholm, and in the evening as I was out for a walk, there was fresh snow covering a layer of ice. Well, I slipped and fell, spraining one of my ancles [sic]. I was forced to stay in bed for a time. To make time pass I started to take down the Pippi stories in short-hand—since my office days I've been a capable stenographer, and I still write all my books first in short-hand.

''In **May, 1944** Karin was to celebrate her tenth birthday and I decided I would write out the Pippi story and give her the manuscript for a birthday present. And then I decided to send a copy to a publisher. Not that I believed for one minute that they would publish it, but even so! The fact was, I was rather upset about Pippi myself, and I remember concluding my letter to the publisher with 'In the hope that you won't notify the Child Welfare Committee'—really because I had two children of my own, and what kind of a mother had they, who wrote such books!

''Just as I had thought, I got the manuscript back, but while I was waiting for it, I wrote another book and sent it to the publishing house of Rabén & Sjögren, which in 1944 announced a prize contest for girls' books. And it actually happened. I won second prize in the competition. I don't think I've ever been happier than on that autumn evening in 1944 when word came that I'd won.

''The next year, **1945,** the same publishing house had a contest for children's books. I sent in the Pippi manuscript, and I received first prize. Well, one thing followed another. Pippi became a success, even if there were some who were shocked over the book and thought that now children would go around behaving like Pippi. 'No normal child eats up a whole cake at a coffee-party,' wrote one indignant reader. And in fact it's true. No normal child lifts a horse straight up in the air either. But if you're one of those who can, then you're also the type who can pack away a whole cake.

''I write to amuse the child within me and I can only hope that in this way other children as well can have a little fun. I don't know any answer to what goes into a good children's book— I mean how come no one ever asks what a good grown-up book should look like? I try to be 'truthful' in the artistic sense of the word, when I write, that's about the only guideline I have. Why don't you ever write a book about being an unhappy child of separated parents living in a slum district? That's what I [am] sometimes . . . asked. And to that my own answer is: I can only write about what I know. I don't know how it is to be such a child of separated parents. I know exactly how it is—or to be more accurate—how it was to be a happy farm child in Smaland and to be a child in a small town, and that's why most of the things that 'happen' in my books take place in these settings.

''Do you get inspiration from your own children and grand-children, [I'm] often ask[ed]. And to that I can answer that

**The pigeons were like a white cloud around Sofia . . . .
It was exactly what a Queen of the Pigeons should
look like, I thought.** ■ (From *The Brothers Lionheart*
by Astrid Lindgren. Translated by Joan Tate. Illustrated by J. K. Lambert.)

there is no child that can inspire me but the child that I myself once was. It's not at all necessary to have children of one's own to be able to write children's books. All you need is to have once been a child yourself, and to recall more or less how it felt.''

It is Lindgren's hope that her books contribute a little bit toward 'instilling human kindness and a democratic outlook in the children who read them. Even books that seek only to provide a pure reading experience are valid. 'Thanks for brightening up a gloomy childhood,' said a message on a little scrap of paper pressed into my hand once by an unknown woman. That's enough for me. If I've been able to brighten up a single gloomy childhood, then I'm satisfied.''

About her writing habits, Lindgren said: ''When I write, I lie in bed and put the book down in shorthand, and I have the feeling that nothing outside exists—I'm just on my bed in my little room, and I can go and meet the people I want to''[1]

Now this was just what Lotta wanted. Mother would keep on coaxing . . . and Lotta wouldn't answer. It gave her a good feeling not to answer when Mother called. ■ (From *Lotta on Troublemaker Street* by Astrid Lindgren. Illustrated by Ilon Wikland.)

1958. Awarded the Hans Christian Andersen medal from the International Board on Books for Young People. In her acceptance speech, Lindgren revealed once again that the source of inspiration for her children's books is her own childhood. ". . . You yourself must become a child. It is useless to make a conscious effort to try and recall how things were. You have to relive your own childhood and *remember* with your very soul what the world looked like, and how it felt to the touch; what you laughed at, and what you cried over when you were a child. People have sometimes asked me: 'When you write, do you think all the time of the children who are going to read your book?' No, I don't. I don't think of them at all. I write for one child only; a child who is sometimes six, sometimes eight, and sometimes eleven years old. And yet it's always the same child . . . she was a girl and she lived on a farm in Sweden many years ago; it was during the Horse Age when it was so wonderful to be a child.

"This girl I write for is rather hard to please: she knows exactly what she wants, and what she doesn't want. When she is six I may tell a very simple little story about a boy who gets angry with his mother and moves out into the yard. When she is eight she might want to hear about an enormously strong girl who can lift a horse on one outstretched arm and eat a whole big cream cake all by herself. When she is eleven she suddenly wants to hear about a boy who wanders on the roads in the company of a tramp. 'But it must be exciting,' she says.

" 'Not *too* exciting,' I say.

" 'Yes, I want crooks,' she says, 'two terrible ones who nearly kill Rasmus.'

" 'You've got very poor taste,' I say, 'I think it was better when you were younger.'

" 'If my taste has got worse, perhaps it's because I'm growing up,' she says. 'I want my crooks.'

"I give in.

"It also happens that people ask me: 'Couldn't you write a book for grown-ups?' as if to say that now I've written so many children's books it's high time I got on to something better. No I don't want to write for grown-ups. I want to write for readers who can work miracles. Children work miracles when they read. They take our poor sentences and words and give them a life which in themselves they do not have. The author alone does not create all the mystical essence contained within the pages of a book. The reader must help. But the author of books for adults has no willing little helpers at his disposal as we have. His readers do not work miracles. It is the child and *only* the child who has the imagination to build a fairy castle if you provide him with a few small bricks.

"There is no substitute for the book to make a child's imagination grow. Present-day children see films, listen to the radio, watch television, read serial strips—this can all be quite pleasant but it has very little to do with imagination. A child, alone with his book, creates for himself, somewhere in the secret recesses of the soul, his own pictures which surpass all else. Such pictures are necessary for humanity. On that day that the children's imagination no longer has the strength to create them, on that day humanity will be the poorer. All great things that have happened in the world, happened first of all in someone's imagination, and the aspect of the world of tomorrow depends largely on the extent of the power of imagination in those who are just now learning to read. This is why children must have books, and why there must be people . . . who really care what kind of books are put into the children's hands. . . ." ["Astrid Lindgren's Acceptance Speech at the Conferment of the Hans Christian Andersen Medal," *Bookbird*, July, 1958.[2]]

Probably the most controversial of Lindgren's books, because it deals with the death of two brothers, is *The Brothers Lionheart*. ". . . The book came about in a very strange manner. You know how you walk around with diffuse thoughts, waiting for something to grow and to be real? I like to walk in cemeteries; it's very peaceful to go there and read the inscriptions. And one day I saw one that said, 'Here lie two little brothers.' And then I found other dead brothers lying together—never sisters—and that made me think of what had happened to them, that they had to die so young. So I had this feeling and didn't know what to do about it. And then, one early winter morning, on a train trip through Sweden, seeing a beautiful rose-colored sunrise over the snow, I suddenly knew what I wanted to write—more or less. I thought that this book might be a comfort to children who were afraid of death, as many children are. When I was little and was told that after you die you go to Heaven, I didn't find that very amusing, but thought it better then lying down in the earth and just being dead. But my grandchildren have no such belief. I felt that one of them was afraid of death, and when I showed him the manuscript he smiled and said, 'Well, we don't know how it is—it could just as well be like that.' And I get lots of letters about *The Brothers Lionheart*—many from adults. One was from a German woman doctor who had lost her nine-year-old daughter to leukemia. And this little girl had lived with the book the last years of her life, and it was her only comfort. When her two little rabbits died, the girl said, 'Oh, they're in Nangiyala now.' Many children have written me saying, 'Now I'm not afraid of death anymore.' Even if it's just a tale, why shouldn't they have some comfort?. . ."[1]

Lindgren's first published children's books are four decades old, but they still appeal to children, and the author continues

She made herself a beard out of spaghetti and trimmed it with a pair of scissors. Then she ate it. ∎
(From *Pippi on the Run* by Astrid Lindgren. Photographs by Bo-Erik Gyberg.)

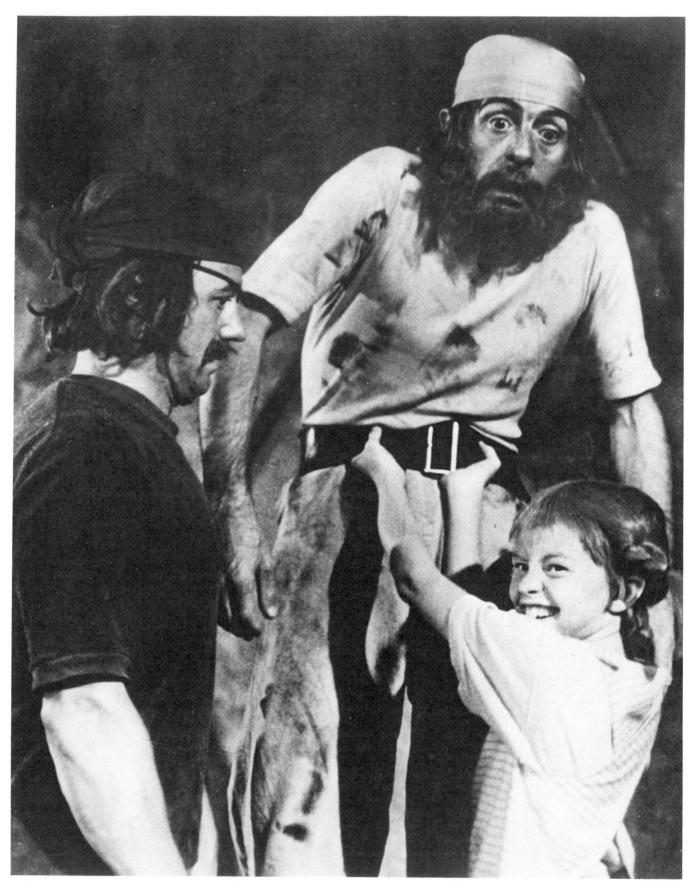

(From the movie "Pippi in the South Seas," starring Inger Nilsson. Released by G. G. Communications Films, 1974.)

to write stories that appeal to youngsters today. The internationally-acclaimed author feels that today's children can be damaged by an overdose of television. ''I'm afraid that children don't play the way we did as children and the way they do in my books. They participate in sports, but they don't *play*. Now they look at television. TV broadens the mind in one way but narrows it in another. It gives you more facts and words and information, but it limits your imagination. It's on a more superficial level than a book, because when a child reads a book he or she has to create his or her own pictures, which are more lovely and beautiful than anything you can ever see on TV. On the whole, I think TV is damaging if you can't control it. I met a mother in America who told me that her daughter had watched TV for eighteen hours one day. She must have been crazy at that point. And I'm sure that there are many homes in which parents don't speak to their children and children don't speak to their parents. I can't write for teen-agers now—I don't know enough about them. They're completely unlike the Bergson children—there's no resemblance at all. When I was a child, we didn't have cars, TV, radio, or even many films. So there was a lot of room for imagination.'' [1]

1978. Awarded the Peace Prize of the German Book Trade. ''The children of today will someday take over the chores of our world, if there is still something left of it. They are the ones who will decide about war and peace and in what kind of society they want to live. In a society where violence steadily increases or in one where people live together in peace and harmony. Is there even the slightest chance that today's children will someday establish a more peaceful world than we were capable of? And why were we so unsuccessful in spite of our good will?

''I can still remember very well what a shock it was for me— I was very young at the time—when it became clear to me that the men who were governing the world were not superior beings with supernatural talents and divine wisdom, that they were people with the same human weaknesses as I. But they had power and could at any time make fateful decisions depending on the impulses and forces which they were influenced by. If the circumstances were particularly unfortunate this could lead to war, merely because a single person was obsessed by power or revenge, by vanity or avarice, or—and this seems to be most common—by blind belief in violence as the most effective remedy in all situations. Accordingly, a good and level-headed individual could occasionally prevent catastrophes, for the very reason that he was good and level-headed and renounced violence.

''From this I could conclude only the following: It is always individual people who determine the fate of the world. But why weren't they all good and level-headed? Why were there so many who wanted only violence and strove for power? Were some evil by nature? I couldn't believe this at that time and I cannot believe it today either. Intelligence and the gifts of the mind are perhaps to a large extent inherent, but there is no seed slumbering in any newborn child from which good or evil necessarily sprouts. Whether a child grows up to be a warm-hearted, open-minded and trusting person with a feeling for public welfare or a cold, destructive, egotistic person is determined by those who are entrusted with the child in this world; it depends on whether they show him what love is or not. Goethe once said 'Everywhere you learn only from those whom you love' and there must be some truth to this. A child who is treated by its parents lovingly and who loves its parents, thereby establishes a 'loving' relationship to its environment and retains this attitude during its entire life. And this is good even if the child does not become one of those who govern

There was a farmhouse close by. Oscar had been there before and asked for permission to sleep in the hayloft. ■ (From *Rasmus and the Vagabond* by Astrid Lindgren. Illustrated by Eric Palmquist.)

the fate of the world. But if one day, contrary to expectations, the child should belong to those powerful people, then it is a joy for all of us if its attitude has been determined by love and not violence. Even the character of statesmen and politicians is formed before they are five years old—this is a horrifying fact, but it is true.

''. . . All of us, children and adults alike, need behavior standards, and through the examples that parents set, children learn more than by any other method. Certainly children should respect their parents, but parents should also respect their children and should never misuse their natural superiority. We can only wish that all parents and children would respect one another.

''I would like to tell those, however, who so loudly call for stricter discipline and tighter reigns what an old lady once told me. She was a young mother at a time when one still believed the saying from the Bible 'spare the rod and spoil the child.' At the bottom of her heart she really didn't believe this but one day her son did something for which, in her opinion, he had earned a sound thrashing, the first in his life. She directed him to go the garden and to find a rod himself which he should then bring to her. The little boy went out and did not return for a long while. Finally he returned crying and said 'I couldn't find a rod but here is a stone which you can throw at me.' Then the mother began to cry too, for suddenly she saw everything through the eyes of the child. The child must have thought: 'My mother really wants to hurt me and she can also do this with a stone.'

''She took her little son into her arms and then they both cried together for a while. She then placed the stone on a shelf in

(From the stage production of "Pippi Longstocking." Presented during the 1982-83 season at
The Children's Theatre Company and School. Photograph courtesy of George Heinrich.)

the kitchen and left it there as a constant reminder of the promise which she had made herself in this hour: 'Never violence!''' [Astrid Lindgren, ''Never Violence,'' *Bookbird*, 1979.³]

1983. Lindgren lives in an apartment in Stockholm where she is grandmother to seven children. Her books have been translated into more than fifty languages and films based on the Lindgren books have proven to be apt competitors in the international children's market. Perhaps the greatest reason for their international appeal is the fact that the author writes her books from her own memories—from the child that she was so long ago. ''Memory—it holds unknown sleeping treasures: fragrances and flavors and sights and sounds of childhood past!. . . I can still see and smell and remember the bliss of that rosebush in the pasture, the one that showed me for the first time what beauty means. I can still hear the chirping of the land rail in the rye fields on a summer evening, and the

hooting of the owls in the owl tree in the nights of spring. I still know exactly how it feels to enter a warm cow barn from biting cold and snow. I know how the tongues of a calf feels against a hand and how rabbits smell, and the smell in a carriage shed, and how milk sounds when it strikes the bottom of a bucket, and the feel of small chicken feet when one holds a newly hatched chicken. Those may not be extraordinary things to remember. The extraordinary thing about it is the intensity of these experiences when we were new here on earth.

''How long ago that must be! Otherwise, how can the world have changed so much? Could it all really become so different in just one short little half century? My childhood was spent in a land that no longer exists—but where did it all go?''¹

In Sweden an annual prize is awarded to a distinguished author of children's books called the ''Astrid Lindgren Prize.''

FOR MORE INFORMATION SEE: Bookbird, July, 1958, 1977, 1979; Huck and Young, *Children's Literature in the Elementary School,* Holt, 1961; *Horn Book,* April, 1962, October, 1964, April, 1969; *More Junior Authors,* edited by Muriel Fuller, H. W. Wilson, 1963; May Hill Arbuthnot, *Children and Books,* 3rd edition, Scott, Foresman, 1964; Martha E. Ward and Dorothy A. Marquardt, *Authors of Books for Young People,* Scarecrow, 1964; *The Children's Bookshelf,* Child Study Association of America, Bantam, 1965; Nancy Larrick, *A Teacher's Guide to Children's Books,* Merrill, 1966; *Books for Children, 1960-1965,* American Library Association, 1966; Miriam Hoffman and Eva Samuels, *Authors and Illustrators of Children's Books,* Bowker, 1972; Mary Orvig, ''A Collage: Eight Women Who Write Books in Swedish for Children,'' *Horn Book,* February, 1973; Astrid Lindgren, ''A Short Talk with a Prospective Children's Writer,'' *Horn Book,* June, 1973; M. Orvig, *En bok om Astrid Lindgren* (title means ''A Book about Astrid Lindgren''), Rabén & Sjögren, 1977; Jonathan Cott, *Pipers at the Gates of Dawn: The Wisdom of Children's Literature,* Random House, 1981; Jonathan Cott, ''Profiles: The Astonishment of Being,'' *New Yorker,* February 28, 1983; Astrid Lindgren, ''The Importance of Children's Books,'' *The Quarterly Journal of the Library of Congress,* summer, 1983.

CELIA LUCE

LUCE, Celia (Geneva Larsen) 1914-

PERSONAL: Born December 3, 1914, in Provo, Utah; daughter of B. F. (an artist and college professor) and Geneva (Day) Larsen; married Willard Luce (a writer and photographer), June 3, 1940; children: Willard Ray III, Loretta. *Education:* Brigham Young University, B.S., 1938. *Religion:* Church of Jesus Christ of Latter-Day-Saints (Mormons). *Home and office:* 710 North 600th W., Provo, Utah 84601.

CAREER: Elementary teacher in Utah public schools: Bear River City, 1936-37, Spring Lake, 1938-40, Orem, 1944-76. *Member:* League of Utah Writers. *Awards, honors:* With husband, Willard Luce, first place, Utah State Institute of Fine Arts Annual Original Writing Contest, 1978, for unpublished juvenile book, ''William Henry Jackson, Pioneer Artist and Photographer.''

WRITINGS—Juveniles; all with husband, Willard Luce: *Utah Past and Present,* Utah Color, 1955; *Timmy and the Golden Spike,* Deseret, 1963; *Jim Bridger: Man of the Mountains,* Garrard, 1966; *Sutter's Fort: Empire on the Sacramento,* Garrard, 1969; *Lou Gehrig: Iron Man of Baseball* (illustrated by Dom Lupo), Garrard, 1970; *Utah!,* Peregrine Smith, 1975.

Work has been anthologized in *Heroes of the Home Run,* edited by Bennett Wayne, Garrard, 1973; *Adventures in Buckskin,* edited by B. Wayne, Garrard, 1973. Contributor to magazines and newspapers, including *Relief Society Magazine, Household Magazine,* and *Denver Post.*

WORK IN PROGRESS: A biography about her father, B. F. Larsen.

SIDELIGHTS: ''My interest in writing started when I was young. I was a first class bookworm and dreamed of becoming a great poet. I had a story published when I was eleven years old—in the children's section of a church publication called the *Instructor.* That helped my dreams along.

''As I grew older I did a lot of writing, but it was just a hobby. I did win an essay contest and a play-writing contest in high school. In college and for a while after I wrote a lot of poetry, but nothing to qualify me as a 'great poet.'

''In 1940 I married Willard Luce, who also had writing as a hobby. We were both elementary school teachers. I gave up teaching. I had to. This was the depression and no married women were hired. That all changed when World War II came along and everyone who could work was needed as a worker. I taught three years during the war and our son went to nursery school. I quit for a while, then went back into teaching when our daughter started school, and I kept on teaching until I reached retirement age.

''The first four years after our marriage we lived in Blanding, Utah in San Juan County. It is the largest county in Utah, but had only four towns, two of them tiny, and the two large ones each had only a little over 1,000 people. We had lots of wilderness around us, with cliff dwellings in many of the little canyons and Navaho hogans just west of town. Both Navahos and Utes lived at or near Blanding.

''In 1944 we moved to Provo, in north central Utah and still live here. Utah has some outstanding scenery, and we have travelled the state again and again, taking pictures and writing articles. This also helped in our teaching since we each taught a fourth grade and the fourth grades study Utah.

''There was no fourth grade textbook on Utah, so we set about writing one, *Utah Past and Present.* Willard did most of the

John Bidwell first saw Sutter's Fort on a wet, dreary November day. ■ (From *Sutter's Fort* by Willard and Celia Luce. Illustrated by Paul Frame.)

actual writing, but I helped with the planning and read it over to make sure it said just what we wanted it to say. If I was not satisfied I had the job of writing parts of it over so it satisfied both of us.

"Later, after Willard retired, he wrote a much larger, better Utah book for the fourth grade. Once more I helped. One of my jobs was to go carefully over each word in the book, take out the hard words that we could, and put in easy words. With names of things and places we had to leave them in even if they were hard.

"I also worked on the index. This was a bigger job than I had anticipated, and it had to be done as fast as possible. We had to wait until the pages were printed so we could put in the page numbers. The printers were waiting for us so they could print the book. We called the book *Utah!* The fourth grades are using it.

"We worked together on several other books for children. My work alone has been articles for magazines. I am now working on a biography of my father, B. F. Larsen. He, too, did a lot of writing about what happened to him so the job is not hard. He was an artist and a college professor but he did a lot of writing, too."

HOBBIES AND OTHER INTERESTS: Photography, gardening, gathering rocks.

LUCE, Willard (Ray)   1914-

PERSONAL: Born September 18, 1914, in Price, Utah; son of Willard Ray (a salesman) and Rachel (Olsen) Luce; married Celia Larsen (a teacher and writer), June 3, 1940; children: Willard Ray III, Loretta. *Education:* Brigham Young University, B.S., 1947. *Religion:* Church of Jesus Christ of Latter-Day-Saints (Mormons). *Home and office:* 710 North 600th W., Provo, Utah 84601.

CAREER: Teacher in public elementary schools in Utah; East Summit, 1938-39, Blanding, 1939-43, Orem, 1944-45, 1947-54, 1956-73; physical education teacher in high school in Blanding, 1943-44; Brigham Young Univeristy, Provo, Utah, instructor in journalism, 1946-47; free-lance writer and photographer and owner of post card company, 1954-56; free-lance writer and photographer, 1973—. *Wartime service:* Served in Merchant Marine, 1945-46. *Member:* National Education Association, Utah Education Association, League of Utah Writers (past president). *Awards, honors:* With wife, Celia Luce, first place, Utah State Institute of Fine Arts Annual Original Writing Contest, 1978, for unpublished juvenile book, "William Henry Jackson, Pioneer Artist and Photographer."

WRITINGS—For children: (With wife, Celia Luce) *Utah Past and Present,* Utah Color, 1955; *Jerry Lindsey: Explorer to the San Juan* (illustrated by Farrell R. Collett), Deseret, 1958; *The Red Stallion,* Deseret, 1961; (with C. Luce) *Timmy and the Golden Spike,* Deseret, 1963; (with C. Luce) *Jim Bridger: Man of the Mountains,* Garrard, 1966; (with C. Luce) *Sutter's Fort: Empire on the Sacramento,* Garrard, 1969; (with C. Luce) *Lou Gehrig: Iron Man of Baseball* (illustrated by Dom Lupo), Garrard, 1970; *Birds That Hunt,* Follett, 1970; (with C. Luce) *Utah!,* Peregrine Smith, 1975.

Work has been anthologized in *Heroes of the Home Run,* edited by Bennett Wayne, Garrard, 1973; *Adventures in Buckskin,* edited by B. Wayne, Garrard, 1973. Photographs have been included in *Around the U.S.A. in a Thousand Pictures,* edited by A. Milton Runyon and Vilma F. Bergane, Doubleday, 1955, 2nd edition, 1965. Author of scripts and photographs for ten sound filmstrips for Creative Visuals, 1974; and three for Outdoor Pictures, 1975. Contributor of travel articles and photographs to magazines and newspapers, including *Natural History, Popular Photography, Ranger Rick's Nature Magazine, Ford Times, Dodge News,* and *Denver Post.*

WORK IN PROGRESS: "I'm working on articles and photo features mostly in the area of wildlife subjects."

SIDELIGHTS: "My wife, Celia, and I are now retired. Most of our teaching was in the fourth grade, and this was the age group for which we wrote our books. Our books are mostly non-fiction with historical and geographical accuracy. The fiction stories were usually based on historical events, such as *Timmy and the Golden Spike* which is about a boy who helped his father cut railroad ties for the Union Pacific Railroad. They later attended the 'Driving of the Golden Spike' celebration when the Union Pacific and the Central Pacific railroads were joined at Promontory, Utah in 1869. *The Red Stallion* was also based on an actual happening. Years ago Charlie Gibbons spent

WILLARD LUCE

months trying to capture a wild stallion. Finally he drove the animal to the top of what is now called Wild Horse Mesa. He blocked all escape routes off the mesa. Then, using several horses, he drove the stallion back and forth across the mesa until the animal became exhausted and was captured. I have met Charlie Gibbons and heard him tell the story. But so had Zane Gray and he had written a novel, *Wildfire,* about the happening. Because I was writing for boys and girls, I made the main characters two brothers who have to capture the wild stallion or it will be killed. They do it in a box canyon instead of on a mesa top.

"Writing *Utah!* probably took about thirty years. Nearly that long before the book was published, I taught my first fourth grade class. Since the study of Utah was one of the main subjects I soon learned how little I knew about the state and that there was nothing on the children's level that they could read. During those thirty years Mrs. Luce and I travelled throughout the state, taking photographs and learning Utah geography first hand. We studied history books and other books telling about human interest happenings. And during this time we wrote articles about Utah. Finally we wrote *Utah Past and Present.* It was fine but it wasn't long enough. And so finally *Utah!*

"We have often been asked how two people write one book. Sometimes it isn't easy! The most important part of any book is the planning. In non-fiction this is mainly deciding what comes first, what comes second, and what comes third. The actual writing might be done mainly by either writer or by both of them. One author might write one chapter while the other author writes a different chapter. As a final test, however, everything written must be approved by both writers. About one book we received an interesting comment from an editor. She was interested in play acting and felt that the book could easily be adapted for it. She especially liked chapter two and five. I had written chapter two and Celia had written chapter five.

"When *Utah!* was completed the reading level was found to be fifth grade. This was too hard and had to be made easier to read. Celia took the job of substituting an easy word for many of the hard words. For some words, however, there are no easy words. For these I worked the meanings into the text, sometimes supplying the diacritical markings. And, finally, there are many ways two people can work together compiling an index."

Utah Past and Present and *Utah!* are used as textbooks in the Utah elementary schools.

LUFKIN, Raymond H. 1897-

PERSONAL: Born January 29, 1897, in Salem, Mass. *Education:* Attended New School of Design, Boston, Mass. *Home:* Tenafly, N.J.

CAREER: Free-lance commercial artist in Boston, Mass., and New York, N.Y.; illustrator of books for children. Designed Treasury Department war bond posters and produced military maps during World War II. *Military service:* U.S. Army, World War II. *Awards, honors:* Illustrator of Newbery honor books, 1931, *Ood-le-uk the Wanderer,* and 1949, *The Story of the Negro; New York Herald Tribune*'s Spring Book Festival award honor book, 1943, for *Here Is Alaska.*

The time of surprises had now come. The state of Alabama gave a charter for a school in which colored teachers could be trained. ■ (From *Story of the Negro* by Arna Bontemps. Illustrated by Raymond Lufkin.)

ILLUSTRATOR—All for children, unless otherwise indicated: Alice Alison Lide and Margaret Johansen, *Ood-le-uk the Wanderer*, Little, 1930; Eric Philbrook Kelly, *Treasure Mountain*, Macmillan, 1937; Helene Ebeltoft Davis, *The Year Is a Round Thing*, Musson, 1938; E. P. Kelly, *At the Sign of the Golden Compass*, Macmillan, 1938; Caroline Dwight Emerson, *Magic Tunnel: A Story of Old New York*, McClelland, 1940; Ann Roos, *Man of Molokai: The Life of Father Damien*, Lippincott, 1943; (illustrator of maps) Evelyn S. B. Stefansson, *Here Is Alaska*, Scribner, 1943; Robert G. Cleland, *California Pageant*, Knopf, 1946; Adrienne Stone, *Hawaii's Queen, Liliuokalani*, Messner, 1947; Arna Wendell Bontemps, editor, *The Story of the Negro* (ALA Notable Book), Knopf, 1948, 3rd edition, 1958; Stephen Holt, *We Were There with the California Forty-Niners*, Grosset, 1956; Emma C. Sterne, *Mary McLeod Bethune* (ALA Notable Book), Knopf, 1957; Virginia T. Mosley, *Tenafly, 1894-1969* (adult), 75th Jubilee Committee, 1969.

Also illustrator of *American Rivers*, a series depicting events on twelve principal rivers of the United States.

SIDELIGHTS: As a child Lufkin spent much of his free time drawing. His first published work, a prize-winning pen and ink sketch, appeared in the *Boston Herald* when he was nine years old. After attending New School of Design in Boston, Lufkin began his career as a free-lance artist doing commercial work, first in Boston and later in New York. Lufkin's favorite medium was scratchboard.

FOR MORE INFORMATION SEE: Bertha E. Mahony and others, compilers, *Illustrators of Children's Books: 1744-1945*, Horn Book, 1947; Bertha E. Miller and others, compilers, *Illustrators of Children's Books: 1947-1956*, Horn Book, 1958.

LUZZATTO, Paola (Caboara) 1938-

PERSONAL: Born January 26, 1938, in Genoa, Italy; daughter of Lorenzo (a professor of philosophy) and Anna (a writer;

maiden name, Sogni) Caboara; married Lucio Luzzatto (a doctor and scientist), September 9, 1964; children: Stefano, Fatima. *Education:* University of Genoa, L.P., 1962; Columbia University, M.A., 1964; University of Ibadan, Ph.D., 1981; Goldsmith College, University of London, post-graduate diploma in art therapy, 1984. *Home:* 39 Grafton Rd., London W3 8PD, England.

CAREER: Western Nigeria Television, Ibadan, Nigeria, freelance television producer, 1968-72; Institute of African Studies, Ibadan, researcher, 1973-74; Department of Religious Studies, University of Ibadan, Ibadan, Nigeria, researcher, 1973-78; Institute of Historic-Religious Studies, University of Naples, Italy, researcher, 1978-80; Experimental High School, Naples, Italy, teacher of world religion, 1978-81; La Verne University, Naples, lecturer in world religion, 1980; art therapist, 1984—. *Member:* National Association of Journalists (Italy), BAAT (British Association of Art Therapists).

WRITINGS: (Reteller) *Tanto tempo fa quando la terra era piatta* (juvenile), Emme Edizioni (Milan), 1979, translation from the Italian published as *Long Ago When the Earth Was Flat: Three Tales from Africa* (illustrated by Aimone Sambuy), Philomel, 1980; (reteller) *La Principessa della Torre* (juvenile fairy-tale; illustrated by Graziano Gregori; title means "Princess of the Tower"), Emme Edizioni, 1982. Also author of television scripts for documentaries and children's programs. Contributor of articles to journals and Italian national newspapers.

PAOLA LUZZATTO

WORK IN PROGRESS: A biography of Austrian-born artist and African priestess, Susanne Wenger; publications of Ph.D. thesis "Saint-devotion in Naples"; a collection of myths for children; fairy-tales; *The Iron Man* for Collins.

SIDELIGHTS: "There is a thread in everyone's life, which may not be visible all the time, but somehow ties all events together.

"In my own case, although I have been living in different countries (Italy, USA, Nigeria, and now U.K.), and I have been working in different fields (production of TV programmes; research in African studies; teaching world religions; now working as an art therapist), this thread is perhaps my interest in symbolism.

"During my teens and 20s, I used to film, with my 8mm movie-camera, not family scenes, or travelling shots, as most people do, but rather unknown people in the street, anonymous objects, unusual nature-shots. I wanted to convey, I suppose (I don't think I was consciously aware of this), certain emotions, through symbolic images. People waiting at a bus stop; a leaf blown by the wind; children playing in the street. Chance; powerlessness; friendship.

"I was also interested in the meaning of symbols from a theoretical point of view. My thesis for the degree in philosophy was on the symbolic theory of the American woman-philosopher Susanne Langer, and specifically on symbolism in art and religion.

"When I was studying at Columbia University, majoring in 'Production of Television Programmes,' each student had to plan a series of educational programmes. I thought of a series on African mythology, because I was fascinated by some of the myths about the origin of earth, fire, sky, animals, man, rain, etc. Why do people have to phantasize on the origin of things? I never believed the theory that myths are naive scientific attempts. In myths about the origin of the sky, people do not really try to understand the astrophysical events involved. The sky is taken as symbol of something pure, light, powerful, distant and at the same time strangely close. I collected several myths about the origin of the earth and the sky, and that was the beginning of the book *Long Ago When the Earth Was Flat,* which was to be published many years later.

"When I actually did go to Africa, I produced for Western Nigeria Television a series of programmes for children on African traditional stories. But a book for children on African myths finally materialized after I had returned to Italy. I was struck by what a friend of mine, a high school teacher, said: 'When I suggest to my pupils to read myths and legends, in order to stimulate their interest toward other countries and other cultures, the opposite happens: they find the myths either too simple and childish, or too complicated and boring. In either case, they are put off, and they become convinced that they really have nothing to learn from traditional cultures.

"I had to agree. Most collections of myths are either funny tales for small children, or else academic studies. My small book comes out from my desire of bridging this gap: telling a myth in very simple words, but without giving the impression of saying something silly; instead, trying to convey the significant meaning that is beyond the story. When I wrote that the earth wanted to talk with the sky and so the mountains came to be; or that the sun was living on earth but the sea-water pushed him up; or that the fire was in the sky and man managed to get a piece of a star and take it home; I wanted

the readers to understand that these myths have something to do with very deep fundamental emotions: loneliness, friendship, love, fear, and joy.

"I now intend to do the same with some fairy-tales which I was told when I was a child. My aim is to retell these stories in such a way as to combine the simplicity of the language with the intensity of its meaning. The first of these fairy-tales has been published (*La Principessa della Torre*)."

MATCHETTE, Katharine E. 1941-

PERSONAL: Surname is accented on first syllable; born May 30, 1941, in Corvallis, Ore.; daughter of Jo Kenneth (contract logger) and Harriet (a bookkeeper; maiden name, Wright) Dingus; married Dennis Matchette (a printer), April 15, 1967. *Education:* Seattle Pacific College, B.A. (cum laude), 1963; graduate study at Oregon State University, 1965—. *Politics:* "Conservative Republican (Would prefer a good new party if someone would start one)." *Religion:* Protestant ("My closet association has been with 'holiness movement' churches"). *Home address:* 5265 S.W. Blueberry Dr., Corvallis, Ore. 97333. *Office:* Controller's Office, Oregon State Board of Higher Education, P.O. Box 488, Corvallis, Ore. 97333.

CAREER: Elementary school teacher in Hillsboro, Ore., 1963-64, in a Christian school in Eugene, Ore., 1964-65, and in a mission school in Tampa, Fla., 1965-66; Free Methodist Church of North America, World Headquarters, Winona Lake, Ind., promotional writer for General Missionary Board, 1966-70; Curry Public Library, Gold Beach, Ore., assistant librarian, 1971-72; Free Methodist Church of North America, World Headquarters, promotional writers for General Missionary Board, 1972; Evans Products Co., Corvallis, Ore., technical librarian, 1972-73; Oregon State Board of Higher Education, Corvallis, payroll clerk, 1974—. Piano and organ teacher, 1977—. *Member:* National Guild of Piano Teachers, Oregon Association of Christian Writers.

KATHARINE E. MATCHETTE

They began their meeting in front of the old hall. ∎
(From *Walk Safe through the Jungle* by Katharine E.
Matchette. Illustrated by Ivan Moon.)

WRITINGS: Walk Safe through the Jungle (illustrated by Ivant
Moon), Herald Press, 1974. Author of church school material
for Aldersgate Associates, 1970-73, and 1977-78. Author of
"Pitstop," a Bible column. Contributor of articles, poems,
and stories to magazines, including *Today's Girl, Young Teen
Power, Junior Counselor, Christian Reader, Purpose, The
Evangel,* and *Good News,* and to newspapers.

WORK IN PROGRESS: Feel with Faith's Fingers (tentative
title), an adult suspense novelette about the supernatural, dealing with the realities of evil and God's power; a historical
novel for young people, set in Southwestern Oregon; a biographical account of a girls' group foster home told from the
point of view of the housemother; research for several articles.

SIDELIGHTS: "By the middle of my third year of teaching
. . . I had discovered that in some developing countries people
actually forget how to read because they have no books or
magazines or newspapers available. I began to wonder if I

might fit in some kind of a mission literature program. To find
out, I took a brief orientation course from Evangelical Literature Overseas. With only this background, I accepted a job
as a writer. . . .

"Basically I am a 'story' person. Outside of writing I am deeply
interested in kids with problems and helping them. I have taken
part in volunteer work in a state girls' school, and with my
husband have done what I could to promote and help a group
foster home for girls in Corvallis. This theme shows up in
much of my writing."

HOBBIES AND OTHER INTERESTS: Reading historical novels, biographies, and history, music (plays piano and organ),
Oregon history, camping, hiking on the beach, pets. "Gardening, freezing and canning have become family hobbies."

MAYER, Jane Rothschild   1903-
(Clare Jaynes, joint pseudonym with Clara
Spiegel)

PERSONAL: Born December 30, 1903, in Kansas City, Mo.;
daughter of Louis P. and Nora (Westheimer) Rothschild; married David Mayer, Jr., December 28, 1927 (deceased); children: David III, Mary Jane Mayer Bezark, Philip. *Education:*
Vassar College, A.B., 1925. *Religion:* Jewish. *Home:* 1445
North State Parkway, Chicago, Ill. 60610.

CAREER: Field Enterprises Educational Corp., Chicago, Ill.,
editorial work, 1961-62. Free-lance writer. Member of Board

JANE ROTHSCHILD MAYER

of Education, Glencoe, Ill. *Member:* Authors League, Society of Midland Authors, Chicago Press Club, Arts Club (Chicago).

WRITINGS: Getting Along in the Family (monograph), Bureau of Publications, Teachers College, Columbia University, 1949; *Betsy Ross and the Flag* (juvenile), Random House, 1952; *Dolly Madison* (juvenile), Random House, 1954; *The Year of the White Trees* (novel), Random House, 1958.

With Clara Spiegel under joint pseudonym Clare Jaynes: *Instruct My Sorrows,* Random House, 1942, reissued as *My Reputation,* World Publishing, 1944; *These Are the Times,* Random House, 1944; *This Eager Heart,* Random House, 1947; *The Early Frost,* Random House, 1952. Author of short stories and articles on travel and child development.

SIDELIGHTS: "I started to think about writing when I was in the seventh grade. I liked reading and being in plays and on the school newspaper. My seventh grade teacher did some writing herself and encouraged us to write poetry and stories. In college I took writing courses. But I think the best way to learn how to write is to read a lot and to *write.*"

MAYHAR, Ardath 1930-
(Ravenna Cannon)

PERSONAL: Born February 20, 1930, in Timpson, Tex.; daughter of Bert Aaron (a farmer) and Ardath (a musician and farmer; maiden name, Ellington) Hurst; married Joe Mayhar

ARDATH MAYHAR

There was a change in the pressure of the air around us. All stood in one effortless upward thrust of trained muscles. ■ (Jacket painting by Yoshi Miyake from *Soul-Singer of Turnos* by Ardath Mayhar.)

(a salesman, mechanic, farmer and expressman), June 7, 1958; children: Frank Edward, James Anthony; (stepsons) Robert William, William Earl. *Politics:* Independent. *Religion:* Independent. *Home:* Route 1, Box 140, Chireno, Tex 75937. *Agent:* Vallarie Smith, Virginia Kidd, Literary Agent, 528 East Harford St., Milford, Pa. 18337.

CAREER: Partner in dairy farm in Nacogdoches County, Tex., 1942-57; owner and manager of book store in Nacogdoches, Tex., 1957-62; proofreader in Salem, Ore., 1968-75, and Nacogdoches, 1979-80; writer, 1980—. Raised chickens in Nacogdoches County, 1976-78. *Member:* Science Fiction Writers of America, Small Press Writers and Artists Organization.

WRITINGS: Journey to an Ending (poetry chapbook), South and West, 1965; *How the Gods Wove in Kyrannon* (fantasy), Doubleday, 1979; *The Seekers of Shar-Nuhm* (fantasy), Doubleday, 1980; *Soul-Singer of Tyrnos* (young adult fantasy), Atheneum, 1981; *Warlock's Gift* (fantasy), Doubleday, 1982; *The Runes of the Lyre* (juvenile), Atheneum, 1982; *Golden Dream: A Fuzzy Odyssey,* Ace, 1983; (with Marylois Dunn) *The Absolutely Perfect Horse* (juvenile), Harper, 1983; *Lords of the Triple Moons* (juvenile), Atheneum, 1983; *Khi to Freedom,* Ace, 1983; *Exile on Vlahil,* Doubleday, 1984; *The World Ends in Hickory Hollow,* Doubleday, 1985.

Work represented in anthologies, including *Mummy!*, Arbor House, 1980; *Amazon II*, DAW Book, 1982; *Stories To Be Read with the Lights On; Swords Against Darkness, Number Four*. Contributor of stories and poems to magazines, including *Fiction, Gothic, Weirdbook, Dark Fantasy,* and *Isaac Asimov's Science Fiction Magazine.*

WORK IN PROGRESS: "Feud at Sweetwater Creek," a western novel under pseudonym Ravenna Cannon; "Carrots and Miggle," a juvenile novel; "Snowlost," a science fiction novel; "The Strange War of Johnny Gann," a western novel.

SIDELIGHTS "I have spent most of my adult life shoveling manure, writing poetry, and looking up at the stars. At the age of forty-three, I 'reformed' and stopped writing poetry, took up yoga and writing fantasy novels, and haven't looked back in the years since. I have been influenced, to a greater or lesser extent, by Dickens, Shakespeare, Ayn Rand, Andre Norton, William Faulkner, and all the 'old heads' in the science fiction field.

"I earnestly believe that being upside down (yoga) directly stimulated my bursting forth into fantasy novels, short stories, and even a regular newspaper column.

"From the ages seventeen to twenty-seven, I ran my father's dairy. Not as some sort of lordly supervisor, but hand-to-hand (sometimes face-to-hoof) with the cows, the cruddy milking machines, the manure, the hay, the weather. In that time, I also studied Latin, Greek, German, French, Spanish, and Italian. At one time I read most of them with some ease, but I haven't kept my hand in. As I get older, time seems to telescope inward. In that time, I also mastered several forms of poetry. I was a very good poet, having work in many magazines (such as *Mark Twain Quarterly*). However, I finally realized that English teachers have destroyed any love of poetry that might remain in the English-speaking race.

"I escaped from the dairy into a bookstore. There I met my husband, for he worked just around the corner, and snared him infallibly with books. In the next few years we achieved two sons (he already had two), moved to Houston and Oregon. There I met mountains, yoga, and proofreading, all of which were seminal influences. We moved back to Texas in 1975, glad to have gone but gladder still to get back home to individualist country.

"Now we live in the mutilated edge of the Big Thicket, near Sam Rayburn Lake. We are so poor that church mice look affluent beside us, but we grow fine gardens and hear the wolves howl at night. Occasionally we see a bobcat. There are bear and deer and cougar in the woods around us. It is ideal for writing the sort of fantasy I do best, and I've written more than twenty books in the years since we moved here. I don't even count stort stories any more. If I ever quit writing, the U.S. Postal Service will go broke, for I buy enough stamps to keep them in business.

"I believe that hard work and early lack of success probably fitted me, more than anything else, to achieve what I wanted to; a control of my material which, whether it seems so or not, is deliberate. I have written some of my best poetry—stuff that won prizes—while shoveling manure. Many writers, I note, would be far better craftsmen for a closer acquaintance with actual, rather than metaphysical, manure. The combination of physical labor and wild imagination works extremely well for me.

"I am by nature a hermit. I do squeeze myself out of my burrow to go to science-fiction conventions, at times. I also, being a study in contradictions, love to speak to groups of intelligent people, so I do a bit of that. I am becoming pretty adept at pushing my own books, as big publishers don't give new authors any visible help at all. I am a hard-core independent. Worse yet, I am objective and logical. Sacred cows, I find, make excellent steak.

"A compulsive writer, I create my novels, both juvenile and adult, first of all for me. I write what I love to read, and I put into them everything I've learned about people, living, and understanding the world and the universe. Nothing that I've ever done, from milking cows to proofreading newspapers, has been wasted, for it's all grist for my mill.

"In science fiction and fantasy, I have a wonderful time creating my own worlds, with their strange denizens and conditions. . . , but I am strict about staying within my own 'rules' when writing about my own systems. The juvenile books that I have done are sharply divided between fantasy juveniles and East Texas juveniles. The East Texas ones incorporate into themselves much of my growing up on a dairy farm, my grandfather's big cotton and cattle farm, and my own oddball observations of the world as a very strange small child.

"I write every day, just as if I had to gussy up and drive to a job. On days when fiction lies there like a wart on a frog, I write letters to some of the many people with whom I correspond. When I go away to a science fiction convention or some such, I have real 'withdrawal symptoms' at leaving my typewriter, but I usually come back refreshed and ready for new worlds to conquer, quite literally."

FOR MORE INFORMATION SEE: Nacogdoches Daily Sentinel, October 10, 1979, July 10, 1980; *Beaumont Enterprise-Journal,* October 5, 1980.

MAYNES, J. Oscar, Jr. 1929- (Dr. J. O. Rocky Maynes, J. O. Rocky Maynes, Jr.)

PERSONAL: Born May 7, 1929, in El Paso, Tex.; son of J. Oscar, Sr. (a pharmacist) and Rae (Visconti) Maynes; married Mary Rebecca Sigworth, January 19, 1952; children: Jay, Robin, Christopher, Gina, Bridget, Fritz, Vito, Ingrid, Claudia and Kristin. *Education:* Arizona State University, B.A., 1952, M.A., 1955 and 1964, Ph.D., 1973; University of Colorado, certificate, 1959; Universidad de los Andes, diploma, 1960; Indiana University, certificate, 1966. *Home:* 5725 W. Belmont, Glendale, Ariz. 85301. *Office:* 1535 W. Jefferson, Phoenix, Ariz. 85007.

CAREER: Buckeye Union High School, Buckeye, Ariz., high school teacher of Spanish, 1952-57; Glendale High School, Glendale, Ariz., teacher of Spanish and chairman of department, 1957-66; Arizona Department of Education, Migrant Child Education and Foreign Languages Divisions, Phoenix, Ariz., director, 1966—. Instructor in Spanish, University of Nevada, summer, 1961-62, Phoenix College, 1962-66, San Jose State College, summer, 1963-65; participant, Foreign Language Supervisor's Institute, Indiana University, summer, 1966. *Member:* American Council of Teachers of Foreign Languages, American Association of Teachers of Spanish and Portugese (president, 1960-61), National Education Association, Arizona Foreign Language Association (president, 1957-58),

J. OSCAR MAYNES, Jr.

Arizona School Administrators' Association. *Awards, honors:* Fulbright fellowship from Universidad de los Andes, 1960, for teachers of Spanish to study the culture, language, literature, and people of Columbia, South America.

WRITINGS: Use and Misuse of Foreign Language Laboratories, Arizona State University, 1964; *Cancionero alegre* (title means "Cheerful Songbook"), Arizona Department of Education, 1968; *The Development of Guidelines for Model Child Care, Preschool, and Kindergarten Programs for Migrant Children,* Arizona Department of Education, 1971; (with Guillermina M. Supervia and Richard H. Sweet) *Actualidad hispánica* (title means "Hispanic World Today"), Allyn and Bacon, 1972; (under name J. O. Rocky Maynes, Jr., with Nicholas J. Silvaroli and Jann T. Skinner) *Oral Language Evaluation,* EMC, 1977; (under name Dr. J. O. Rocky Maynes, with Jay Maynes) *Cancionero Lindo* (title means "Beautiful Songbook"), Media Marketing, 1979.

(Under name J. O. Rocky Maynes, Jr., with Warren Wheelock) "Hispanic Heroes of the U.S.A." series; all juvenile biographies: all published by EMC Corp., 1976: *Raul H. Castro: Adversity Is My Angel; Tommy Nunez: NBA Ref.; Presenting, Vikki Carr!, Henry B. Gonzales: Greater Justice for All; Trini Lopez: The Latin Sound; Edward Roybal: Awaken the Sleeping Giant; Carmen Rosa Maymi: To Serve American Women; Roberto Clemente: Death of a Proud Man; Jose Feliciano: One Voice,* *One Guitar; Tony Perez: The Silent Superstar; Lee Trevino: Supermex; Jim Plunkett: He Didn't Drop Out.*

Also co-editor, *Forum,* 1966-68.

WORK IN PROGRESS: Two handbooks in English and Spanish for various professions as well as the general public.

MAYO, Margaret (Mary)   1935-

PERSONAL: Born May 10, 1935, in London, England; daughter of William John and Anna (Macleod) Cumming; married Peter Robin Mayo (a univeristy lecturer), July 28, 1958; children: Roderick, Katrina, Andrew. *Education:* University of Southampton, B.Sc. (with honors), 1956, certificate in education, 1957. *Home:* 85 Peacock Lane, Brighton, Sussex BN1 6WA, England.

CAREER: Teacher at numerous schools in England, 1957-61, 1969-71, 1973-75, and 1975-80; writer, 1974—. *Member:* Folklore Society, Society of Authors.

WRITINGS—Folktales for young people; all originally published by Kaye & Ward: (Compiler) *If You Should Meet a Crocodile* (illustrated by Carol Barker), 1974; (reteller) *The Book of Magical Horses* (illustrated by Victor Ambrus), 1976, Hastings House, 1977; (reteller) *The Book of Magical Birds* (illustrated by Fiona French), 1977; (reteller) *The Book of Magical Cats* (illustrated by V. Ambrus), 1978; *Saints, Birds, and Beasts* (illustrated by Cara Lockhart Smith), 1980; *The Italian Fairy Book* (illustrated by C. L. Smith), 1981; *Fairy Tales from France* (illustrated by C. L. Smith), 1983.

Then that fine steed said to Mirko, "My master, now you must find the saddle and bridle your father used when he rode in his youth . . . ." ■ (From "Prince Mirko" in *The Book of Magical Horses* by Margaret Mayo. Illustrated by Victor Ambrus.)

SIDELIGHTS: "My interests have centered on folklore and folktales. I am particularly fascinated by the motifs which recur in folktales throughout the world. This is seen in my collections on horses, birds, and cats. My later work is related more to my interest in the difference in style of telling and content of stories between one country and another. The stories which I used for the Italian collection were told with great verve and were full of lively dialogue and humor. The cruelty found in similar stories from other nations was softened and sometimes even eliminated.

"Though I use early written sources for retelling folktales, I am aware that they were originally passed on and adapted orally. So I pay particular attention to the sound and flow of words. I hope that not only will children read and enjoy for themselves, but that parents, teachers, and librarians will read aloud or use my version as a base for their own retelling. Thus my aim, in some part, is to help keep alive the great tradition of oral literature. For these are stories that have passed that most difficult of tests—the test of time—and they can still entertain and satisfy emotionally like no others. They are a precious part of our common heritage, and if our children are also to share it, then the tales must be told afresh to them."

McCAFFERY, Janet   1936-

PERSONAL: Born December 8, 1936, in Philadelphia, Pa.; daughter of Louis and Florence (Eisele) Metzger; divorced. *Education:* Attended Philadelphia College of Art, 1954-58, and School of Visual Arts, New York, N.Y. *Home and office:* 1 West 67th St., New York, N.Y. 10023.

CAREER: Mademoiselle, New York, N.Y., art promotion department, 1958-59; free-lance illustrator, 1959—.

WRITINGS: The Swamp Witch (juvenile; self-illustrated), Morrow, 1970.

Illustrator; all for young readers: Dale Everson, *Mrs. Popover Goes to the Zoo,* Morrow, 1963; Mary Calhoun, *The Witch of Hissing Hill,* Morrow, 1964; Robert M. Oksner, *The Incompetent Wizard,* Morrow, 1965; M. Calhoun, *The Runaway Brownie,* Morrow, 1967; M. Calhoun, *The Thieving Dwarfs,* Morrow, 1967; M. Calhoun, *The Goblin under the Stairs,* Morrow, 1968; M. Calhoun, *The Last Two Elves in Denmark,* Morrow, 1968; M. Calhoun, *The Pixy and the Lazy Housewife,* Morrow, 1969; M. Calhoun, *Traveling Ball of String,* Morrow, 1969; Doris H. Lund, *I Wonder What's Under,* Parents Magazine Press, 1970; M. Calhoun, *Mermaid of Storms,* Morrow, 1970; M. Calhoun, *Daisy, Tell Me!,* Morrow, 1971; Jan Wahl, *Cristóbal and the Witch,* Putnam, 1972; M. Calhoun, *The Flower Mother,* Morrow, 1972; M. Calhoun, *Mrs. Dog's Own House,* Morrow, 1972; M. Calhoun, *The Battle of Reuben Robin and Kite Uncle John,* Morrow, 1973; Lee B. Hopkins, compiler, *Hey-How for Halloween!,* Harcourt, 1974; James Still, *Way Down Yonder on Troublesome Creek: Appalachian Riddles and Rusties,* Putnam, 1974.

Carolyn Meyer, *The Needlework Book of Bible Stories,* Harcourt, 1975; J. Still, *The Wolfpen Rusties: Appalachian Riddles and Gee-Haw Whimmy-Diddles,* Putnam, 1975; Cynthia Basil, *Nailheads and Potato Eyes: A Beginning Word Book,* Morrow, 1976; J. Still, *Sporty Creek: A Novel about an Appalachian Boyhood,* Putnam, 1977; Eleanor Coerr, *Waza Wins at Windy Gulch,* Putnam, 1977; Gail K. Haines, *What Makes a Lemon Sour?,* Morrow, 1977; Vernon Pizer, *You Don't Say: How*

JANET McCAFFERY

People Communicate without Speech, Putnam, 1978; C. Basil, *Breakfast in the Afternoon: Another Beginning Word Book,* Morrow, 1979; C. Basil, *How Ships Play Cards: A Beginning Book of Homonyms,* Morrow, 1980.

WORK IN PROGRESS: Design and illustration for Elizabeth Arden Christmas wrap and porcelains.

SIDELIGHTS: Although McCaffery is presently engaged in designing and illustrating for packaging and *Better Homes and Gardens* magazine, she enjoyed the time when she illustrated children's books—"a time of delving and researching and coming up with an answer or a way of illustrating a story."

"It takes me about three months to finish a book and by the end of that time it has become like a member of the family. Each story has a life of its own and it takes a while to work it out. After reading a story many times I start doing experimental sketches in all different styles to try to find a way to contribute to the feeling of the story. To me this is the most creative period. I find inspiration and clues all around. A purple camel woven into a straw bag—hot dusty colors in the *National Geographic* Magazine—a gypsy woman's face on the subway—the clouds—the way a kid in a playground is standing. I do other kinds of illustration aside from books, but the feeling of doing a good job on a picture book is the most satisfying to me." [Lee Kingman and others, compilers, *Illustrators of Children's Books: 1967-1976,* Horn Book, 1978.]

McCaffery's works are included into the Kerlan Collection at the University of Minnesota.

HOBBIES AND OTHER INTERESTS: "Going to museums—and lots of shopping—and more work. I'm happiest when I'm working. I feel connected."

**The witch whirled around,
wove her arms into twists,
and began to murmur the spell.**

■ (From *The Witch of Hissing Hill* by Mary Calhoun. Illustrated by Janet McCaffery.)

McCOY, Lois (Rich) 1941-

PERSONAL: Born July 5, 1941, in Newark, N.J.; daughter of Harry (a merchant) and Ruth (Glassman) Rich; married Floyd W. McCoy, Jr. (an oceanographer); children: Mark, Jill, Brent, Elana. *Education:* Attended University of Miami, Coral Gables, Fla., 1964-66; Goddard College, B.S., 1971, M.S., 1972. *Home and office address:* Sneden's Landing, Palisades, N.Y. 10964; and Old Bottles, School St., Woods Hole, Mass. 02543. *Agent:* Christine Tomasino, RLR Associates, 7 West 51 St., New York, N.Y. 10019.

CAREER: Stockbroker with firms in Miami, Fla., 1962-65; Boston University, Boston, Mass., biologist in medical research, 1965-67; Marine Biological Laboratory, Woods Hole, Mass., biologist, 1967-79; Harvard University, School of Medicine, Brookline, Mass., biologist, 1969-72; U.S. Geological Survey, Woods Hole, research coordinator, 1972-73; writer, 1973—. Owner of a business in Miami, 1962-64. Advertising consultant. Author. *Member:* Authors Guild, National Writers Union. *Awards, honors: Millionairess* was named among best business books of the year by *Library Journal,* 1978.

WRITINGS: Millionairess: Self-Made Women of America, Harper, 1978; *Late Bloomer: Profiles of Women Who Found Their True Calling,* Harper, 1980; *Science Under Sail,* Holt, 1982.

"The Bytes Brothers" series; all written with husband, Floyd W. McCoy, Jr.; all computer mysteries for children; all pub-

lished by Bantam, 1984: *The Bytes Brothers Input an Investigation; . . . Program a Problem; . . . Enter the Evidence; . . . Compute a Clue; . . . Record a Robbery; . . . Go To a Getaway.*

Contributor to popular magazines, including *Sail, Oceans, Scientific American, Harper's Bazaar, Fifty-Plus, Family Weekly,* and *Family Circle.* Founder of *10964* (community newsletter).

WORK IN PROGRESS: "Hacker Hound" series; "I Can Read/ Run It," computer storybooks for beginning readers; "You Be the Judge" series; "The Cousins Christopher" series, adventure in the classic style for boys thirteen and up.

SIDELIGHTS: "After working for years in scientific research laboratories, I began writing magazine articles in the area of science and history of science, then three books as a ghost writer for physicians. *Millionairess* was the first volume under my own name.

"I enjoy the quiet and solitary journalistic profession I practice in my at-home office, working at Andrew Carnegie's old library table, with a view of the Hudson River peeking through a maple forest. Writing allows me to enjoy our little children as they come home from school every day—I feel writing is a particularly appropriate discipline for a parent.

"Our summers are spent on Cape Cod—a good deal of my writing takes place on the beach—and we also travel. In the

LOIS and FLOYD McCOY

... Barry sat down in front of the library's terminal. The computer could tell him what books the library had on the subject of decomposition .... ■ (From *The Bytes Brothers Input an Investigation* by Lois and Floyd McCoy, Jr. Illustrated by Leslie Morrill.)

summer of 1979 I joined my sea-going husband on a scientific cruise in the Mediterranean Sea.''

HOBBIES AND OTHER INTERESTS: ''Hate jogging, love murder mysteries.''

FOR MORE INFORMATION SEE: Miami Herald, September 10, 1978; *Nyack Journal-News,* October 26, 1978; *Women's Wear Daily,* November 1, 1978, November 30, 1978; *Falmouth Enterprise,* July 10, 1978; *Fort Lauderdale News,* January 23, 1980.

MINER, Jane Claypool 1933-
(Jane Claypool, Veronica Ladd)

PERSONAL: Born April 22, 1933, in McAllen, Tex.; daughter of Denzil (a contractor) and June (a teacher; maiden name, Whitaker) Claypool; married Dennis A. Shelley (deceased); married second husband, Richard Yale Miner (deceased); children: Kathryn Du Vivier. *Education:* California State University, Long Beach, B.A., 1956; graduate study at University of California, Los Angeles, and California State University, Los Angeles. *Home:* 1604 Shields Ave., Encinitas, Calif. 92024. *Agent:* Writer's House, Inc., 21 West 26th St., New York, N.Y. 10010.

CAREER: Teacher at public schools in Long Beach, Calif., 1956-58, Torrance, Calif., 1959-62 and 1964-69, Trenton, N.J., 1963-64, and Los Angeles, Calif., 1969-71; Crosby Junior High School, Pittsfield, Mass., teacher, 1978-81; Taconic High School, Pittsfield, Mass., teacher, 1981; writer, 1981—. Pub-

lic speaker on alcohol and teens, creative writing and romance novels. *Member:* Society of Children's Book Writers, American Society of Journalists and Authors, Author's Guild. *Award, honors:* Member of the Year, 1981, from Society of Children's Book Writers.

WRITINGS—Young adult novels; under name Jane Claypool Miner; published by Scholastic Book Services, except as noted: *Choices,* 1978; *Why Did You Leave Me?,* 1978; *Dreams Can Come True,* 1981; *Senior Class,* 1982; *No Place to Go,* 1982; *To Pursue a Dream,* Grosset, 1982; *The Boy for Me,* 1983; *Teenage Models,* 1984; *Call Me,* 1984; *Joanna,* 1984.

Young adult novels; under name Jane Claypool; published by Crestwood, except as noted: *Wrecker Madness,* 1981; *The Ghost of Bi-Plane Benny,* Bowmar, 1981; *Growing Up Stories,* Xerox, 1981; *Love Stories,* Xerox, 1982; *A Day at a Time: Dealing with an Alcoholic,* 1982; *A Man's Pride: Losing a Father,* 1982; *Navajo Victory—Being a Native American,* 1982; *Split Decision: Facing Divorce,* 1982; *A New Beginning: An Athlete is Paralyzed,* 1982; *Miracle of Time: Adopting a Sister,* 1982; *This Day is Mine: Living with Leukemia,* 1982; *The Tough Guy: Black in a White World,* 1982; *A Love for Violet,* Westminster, 1982; *Jasmine Finds Love,* Westminster, 1982; *Mountain Fear: When a Brother Dies,* 1982; *She's My Sister: Having a Retarded Sister,* 1982.

Young adult novels; under pseudonym Veronica Ladd: *Flowers for Lisa,* Simon & Schuster, 1982; *Promised Kiss,* Simon &

JANE CLAYPOOL MINER

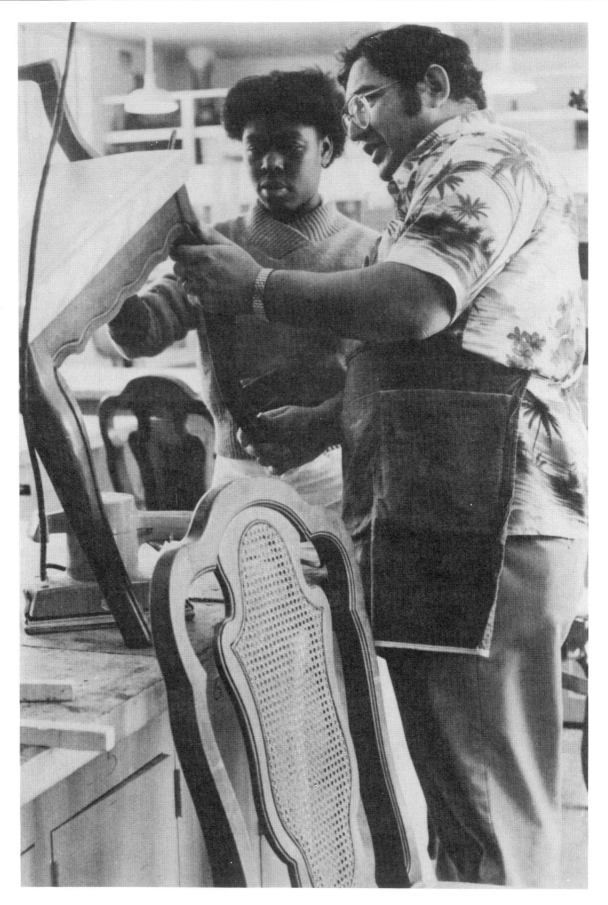

As an apprentice you can work with a skilled expert. ■ (From *How to Get a Good Job* by Jane Claypool. Photographs by Maureen McNicholas.)

Schuster, 1982; *For Love of Lori,* Simon & Schuster, 1982; *Wildest Heart,* Simon & Schuster, 1983.

Young adult non-fiction; under name Jane Claypool: *Alcohol and You,* F. Watts, 1981; *How to Get a Good Job,* F. Watts, 1982; *Why Do Some People Get Fat?* (illustrated by Bruce Bjerva), Creative Education, 1982; *Unemployment,* F. Watts, 1983; (with Cheryl Nelsen) *Food Trips and Traps,* F. Watts, 1985; *Hiroshima and Nagasaki,* F. Watts, 1985; *The First Book of Manufacturing,* F. Watts, 1985.

Young adult non-fiction; under name Jane Claypool Miner: *Career Prep: Working in a Hospital,* Messner, 1983; *Alcohol and Teens,* Messner, 1983; *Teen Parents,* Messner, 1985; *Crime and Computers,* Messner, 1985.

Author of reading lessons, video disc scripts, and educational filmstrips. Contributor of more than one hundred stories and articles to magazines and newspapers, including *Scholastic Skills, Reader's Digest Education Division, Writer, Catholic Digest, Los Angeles Times, Berkshire Eagle* and *New England Fashion Digest.*

WORK IN PROGRESS: Supergirl, for Dutton; *Senior Dreams Can Come True,* for Scholastic.

SIDELIGHTS: Claypool enjoyed reading and telling stories as a child. "My sister had insomnia, and since we slept together, she'd wake me up, and I'd tell her stories long into the night, stories that were as long as novels, the Brenda Starr, girl-reporter-type stories." [Brent Filson, "Jane Claypool: Writing for a Living," *Berkshire Sampler,* July 11, 1982.[1]]

Widowed twice before she was thirty-five, Claypool turned to writing and enrolled in the U.C.L.A. professional writing school. "I went to writing as a kind of religious urge. I was trying hard to make some kind of meaning of life."[1]

"I've always been a compulsive reader, but I've be[come] a compulsive writer . . . as well as a compulsive course taker. I took several writing courses and sold my first novel to the first publisher who read it. That was Bantam Books back in 1971. They held the book for three years and never published it. I wrote four other novels that didn't sell. I have about 25 short stories, five novels and two looseleaf notebooks of poetry that I haven't sold. There were six years between my first and next sale." [Milton R. Bass, "The Lively World," *The Berkshire Eagle,* April 14, 1981.[2]]

"When I applied for teaching positions I not only didn't get a job, I couldn't even get an interview. In my eyes, I had failed as a writer. I was broke and unemployed and getting a lot of feedback that I was unemployable.

"I was 43 and though I had nearly a hundred units beyond the B.A. degree, I saw that I was going nowhere. I remembered that in my childhood, I had fantasized that when I became middle-aged, I would be emotionally and economically independent. Independence had always been a big thing for me.

"I figured because of a series of life choices I had made I had to go into business for myself. For the first time, I scrutinized my writing as a potential business.

"I put a lot of creative work into getting to know editors. I believe that editors feel comfortable when they see me.

"The whole business of writing is surrounded by mythology. I didn't know it at the time, but my selling a novel over the transom 11 years ago to Bantam was a Cinderella story. I had to write five novels after that to realize that fact. Very few writers make a living writing. Most have a second income. There are writers who teach or are associated with large institutions and are semi-salaried. Freelancing requires an aggressive attitude toward sales and marketing. Today, I can sell books just on the basis of an outline. I have a demonstrated craft and ideas that are salable.

"I think that writing is the best life in the world because you can be so open to change in your craft. You get to live a hundred different lives, know and experience a lot more than anyone can do in a lifetime. Then, too, you never perfect your craft, can never get on top of it; you always can improve.

"But having become a professional writer, I'm not all that different from . . . ten years ago. I still have the same need for security and the same need for independence."[1]

"If I could give young people a gift, it would be the leisure time and the books to fill it with. I'd love to share my youthful experiences with this television generation and introduce them to some of my old friends; Sara Crewe, Jane Eyre and Tom Sawyer for starters. The characters in books were my friends and teachers and I like to think that some of my characters are friends to my readers as well. Books are wonderful—all kinds of books not just the classics—because they open the world up and let us know about the thoughts, feelings and experiences of people in a truthful way."

HOBBIES AND OTHER INTERESTS: Reading, attending plays, music (including opera, blues, and jazz), making pottery, sewing, bicycling, painting.

FOR MORE INFORMATION SEE: Berkshire Eagle, April 14, 1981, September 22, 1982; *Berkshire Sampler,* July 11, 1982.

MOCHI, Ugo (A.)   1889-1977

PERSONAL: Born March 11, 1889, in Florence, Italy; came to the United States in 1928; died August 31, 1977, in New Rochelle, N.Y.; son of Giuseppe (an engineer) and Giorgina (Roster) Mochi; married June A. Skelton, 1912 (deceased, 1928); married Edna Skelton, August 7, 1929; children: Joanne (Mrs. Douglas Gray), Jeanne (Mrs. Anthony Tartaglia). *Education:* Attended Accademia di Belli Arti, Florence, Italy, 1905-09 and Berliner Akademie der Kunste, Berlin, Germany, 1911-1914; studied privately with sculptors A. De Carolis and Rivalta in Florence, Italy and August Gaul, Koch and Meyerheim in Berlin, Germany. *Politics:* Republican. *Religion:* Roman Catholic. *Residence:* New Rochelle, N.Y.

CAREER: Free-lance artist, designer, illustrator, sculptor and educator. *Exhibitions:* London, England; Villa Reale-Monza, Italy; Boston Architectural Club, Mass.; New York Museum of Science and Industry; University of Michigan, Ann Arbor, Mich.; Columbia University, New York, N.Y.; Albany Institute of History and Art, Albany, N.Y.; College of New Rochelle, N.Y.; Art Alliance, Philadelphia, Pa.; Arts Club, Chicago, Ill.; Marie Sterner Gallery; Highland Park Arts Exhibition, Mich.; McGill University, Montreal, Canada.

Permanent Collections: Metropolitan Museum of Art, New York, N.Y.; American Museum of Natural History, New York,

N.Y.; National Museum, Washington, D.C.; Cranbrook Museum, Cranbrook, Mich.; Windsor Castle Collection, England; Franklyn Museum, Philadelphia, Pa.; City Hall, New Rochelle, N.Y.; Smithsonian Institution, Washington, D.C., and many other private collections in the United States and abroad. *Member:* New Rochelle Art Association (past president), New Rochelle Music Teachers Council (honorary member), Association of Animal Artists (past vice-president), New York Zoological Society, National Audubon Society. *Awards, honors:* Scholarship to Berliner Akademie der Kunste, 1911; Graphic Award, Beaux Arts, Westchester Federal Women's Clubs, 1971; *A Natural History of Giraffes* was named a Children's Book Showcase, and received New York Academy of Sciences award, older division, both 1974; *Horses as I See Them* chosen as one of the Distinguished Science Books for Children Published from 1979-1982 at the 9th Annual Children's Books International, Boston Public Library.

WRITINGS—Self-illustrated: *L'Ombra delle Bestie,* Treves Milano (Italy), 1923; (with T. Donald Carter), *Hoofed Mammals of the World,* Scribner, 1953.

Illustrator: *African Shadows* (Junior Literary Guild selection), B. O. Ballou, 1933; F. A. Wiley, editor, *Theodore Roosevelt's America,* Devin-Adair, 1955; Austin L. Rand, *American Water and Gamebirds,* Dutton, 1956; Dorcas MacClintock, *A Natural History of Giraffes,* Scribner, 1973; Victor B. Scheffer, *A Voice for Wildlife,* Scribner, 1974; D. MacClintock, *A Natural History of Zebras,* Scribner, 1976; D. MacClintock, *Horses as I See Them,* Scribner, 1980; D. MacClintock, *African Images,* Scribner, 1984.

SIDELIGHTS: Mochi was born in the great city of art, Florence, Italy, into an aristocratic family. At six years of age he showed exceptional talent and knew he would become an artist. Encouraged and inspired by his mother and architect grandfather, Mochi was an untiring observer and reader who studied all his life. His motto became "The most important moment in your life is right *now.*"

Music was also very important in Mochi's life. Animals he loved, spending many happy hours, here and abroad, observing and sketching on the street and especially in zoological gardens. If possible, Mochi went to the source for his different art subjects. Trained as a sculptor, he worked in clay and bronze. He became known worldwide for his beautiful and remarkable black cut work called "Art of Outline" or "Shadows in Outline." Excellent composition, foreshortening, third dimension and the skill of a master, brought this technique into the realm of fine art.

Mochi lived and traveled in Italy, Germany, England and the United States, where he lived for forty-nine years. He visited Switzerland, France and Canada several times. He spoke German, French, English and fluent Italian.

FOR MORE INFORMATION SEE: American Artist, November, 1951, June, 1976; *Life Magazine,* March 9, 1953; *Westchester News,* January, 1956; *The Standard Star* (New Rochelle, N.Y.), March, 1964, April, 1976; *National and International Wildlife,* September-October, 1972, September-October, 1976, March-April, 1982.

Stripe patterns can be deceptive in herd situations, when zebras are tightly bunched. Ambush at a water hole results in a sudden confusion of stripes. ■ (From *A Natural History of Zebras* by Dorcas MacClintock. Illustrated by Ugo Mochi.)

UGO MOCHI

MONTRESOR, Beni 1926-

PERSONAL: Surname prounced Mŏntresor; born March 31, 1926, in Bussolengo, Italy; came to the United States, 1960; son of Angelo Silvino (a furniture manufacturer) and Maria (Fantin) Montresor. _Education:_ Attended Liceo Artistico, Verona, Italy, 1942-45, Acadèmia di Belle Arti, Venice, 1945-59, and Centro Sperimentale di Cinematografia, Rome, 1950-52. _Home:_ 31 West 12th St., New York, N.Y. 10011.

CAREER: Newspaper film critic and author of radio plays, including adaptations of children's fairy tales, in Italy, 1945-49; set and costume designer, 1952-59, for twenty-nine European films, including "Siegfried," 1958, and several European stage productions, such as Alberto Moravia's "Beatrice Cenci" and Paddy Chayefsky's "Middle of the Night"; author and illustrator of children's books, 1961—; set and costume designer for operas, ballets, and musicals, 1961—, including Samuel Barber's "Vanessa," 1961, Debussy's "Pelleas et Melisande," 1962, Anthony Tudor's ballet, "Dim Lustre," 1964, Gian Carlo Menotti's "The Last Savage," 1964, Rodgers and Sondheim's "Do I Hear A Waltz?," 1965, Rossini's "La Cenerentola," 1965, Ponchielli's "La Giaconda," 1966, Berlioz's "Benvenuto Cellini," 1966, Menotti's "Amahl and the Night Visitors," 1968, Puccini's "Turnandot," 1969, Strindberg's "Ghost Sonata," 1976, Rameau's "Platee," 1977, Wagner's "Lohengrin," 1978, Verdi's "Nabucco," 1979, Serban's "The Marriage of Figaro," 1982, Massenet's "Es-

clarmonde," 1983, Handel's "Alcina," 1983, Cavalli's "L'Ormindo," 1984, Prokofiev's "The Love for Three Oranges," 1984, and many others; debuted as director/designer with staging of Mozart's "The Magic Flute" at Lincoln Center, New York, N.Y., 1966; writer and director of movies, "Pilgrimage" (selected for the Cannes Film Festival), 1972, "The Golden Mass," 1975, and "Daybreak," 1984. _Exhibitions:_ Knoedler Gallery, New York, 1965; Rizzoli Gallery, New York, 1967; "The Magic of Montresor," New York City's Library and Museum of Performing Arts at Lincoln Center, 1981; Wildenstein Gallery, New York, 1982. _Member:_ New York Theatre Scenic Designers Union.

AWARDS, HONORS: Radio Critics Prize (Italy), 1948, for radio play "Angelina e Le Beate"; American Institute of Graphic Arts chose _Mommies at Work_ as one of Fifty Books of the Year, 1961-62; _The Princesses: Sixteen Stories about Princesses_ was chosen one of _New York Times_ Ten Best Illustrated Books, 1962; illustrator of Newbery Medal honor book, 1962, Mary Stolz's _Belling the Tiger;_ Caldecott Medal, 1965, for _May I Bring a Friend?;_ knighted by Italian Government, 1966, for services to the arts; _The Magic Flute_ was selected one of _New York Times_ Best Illustrated Books of the Year, 1966; American Society of Illustrators gold medal, 1967, for _I Saw a Ship A-Sailing;_ Leonide Massine Prize, 1979, for best ballet design of the year for _Homage to Picasso;_ first prize from the French Ministry of Culture, 1980, for the best opera design for the 1979-80 season for the Toulouse Opera Company production of Richard Strauss' "Salome"; Order of Gran Cavaliere (Italy), for distinguished contribution to the arts.

WRITINGS—All self-illustrated juveniles: _House of Flowers, House of Stars_ (picture book), Knopf, 1962; _The Witches of Venice,_ Knopf, 1963; _Cinderella_ (English adaptation from opera, "La Cenerentola," by Gioacchino Rossini), Knopf, 1965; _I Saw a Ship A-Sailing: or, The Wonderful Games That Only Little Flower-Plant Children Can Play_ (Italianate fantasy based on Mother Goose Rhymes), Knopf, 1967; _A for Angel,_ Knopf, 1969; _Bedtime,_ Harper, 1978.

BENI MONTRESOR

Illustrator—all juveniles: Margaret Wise Brown, *On Christmas Eve*, W. R. Scott, 1961; Mary Stolz, *Belling the Tiger (Horn Book* honor list; ALA Notable Book), Harper, 1961; M. Soltz, *The Great Rebellion*, Harper, 1961; Eve Merriam, *Mommies at Work*, Knopf, 1961; Sally P. Johnson, editor, *The Princesses: Sixteen Stories about Princesses*, Harper, 1962; M. Stolz, *Siri the Conquistador*, Harper, 1963; Rose L. Mincielli, *Old Neapolitan Fairy Tales*, Knopf, 1963; May Garelick, *Sounds of a Summer Night*, W. R. Scott, 1963; Beatrice Schenk deRegniers, *May I Bring a Friend?* (verse; *Horn Book* honor list; ALA Notable Book), Atheneum, 1964; Gian Carlo Menotti, *The Last Savage* (narrative version of opera), New York Graphic Society, 1964; Stephen Spender, adapter, *The Magic Flute* (based on the opera by Wolfgang A. Mozart), Putnam, 1966; B. S. deRegniers, *Willy O'Dwyer Jumped in the Fire* (variations on folk rhyme), Atheneum, 1968; Oscar Wilde, *The Birthday of the Infanta: And Other Tales*, Atheneum, 1982.

ADAPTATIONS: (With Beatrice deRegniers) "May I Bring a Friend," Empire State Institute for the Performing Arts, Albany, N.Y., 1983.

WORK IN PROGRESS: Writing and illustrating *Don't Wake Me Up* (tentative title); a movie script, "In the House of the Lord"; a ballet adaptation of *The Birthday of the Infanta*.

SIDELIGHTS: **March 21, 1926.** Born in Bussolengo, Italy. "I think I was born with a pencil in my hand. I vividly recall my grandfather going to Verona each Friday and returning home with toys and candies for me. I remember one day, when I was about two or three years old, saying to my grandfather,

'Next time you go to Verona, bring me some colored pencils instead of candies so I can draw a picture!'" [Lee Bennett Hopkins, *Books Are by People*, Citation Press, 1969.[1] Amended by Beni Montresor.]

"I first saw Verona when I was six years old. My grandfather took me there on a spring morning. He harnessed the horse to the trap and we set off from Valpolicella amid the shouts and good-byes of our entire family.

"I remember driving past the vineyards and down from the Lessini hills. As we crossed the Adige River the warm colors of Verona rose up to greet me: soft yellows, pinks, terra cotta. My grandfather drove straight to the stationer's, the little *cartoleria* near the Della Pietra Bridge. It was a dark place filled with rolls of paper and books and colored pencils and many other things that seemed strange to me then (even though I had decided to be a painter when I was three). My grandfather bought me all the art supplies I wanted, but when we left the shop he said, 'Don't tell your grandmother how much I spent; you know she's a bit stingy.'

"After that I went to Verona as often as I could. I visited the Maffeiano Lapidario Museum with all its Greek, Roman, medieval and Oriental carved sculpture. I went to the Castelvecchio and to the opera at the Arena, the big amphitheater built in Roman times. I learned about Verona's famous della Scala family from their white-marble tombs off the Piazza dei Signori. Sometimes I would sit in one of the cafés on the Piazza delle Erbe and I would eat the special cakes that are sold there—

The Queen said to me,
"Do come on Friday."
"Yes," said the King,
"It is Apple Pie Day."

■ (From *May I Bring a Friend?* by Beatrice Schenk deRegniers. Illustrated by Beni Montresor.)

The sea was so big
He jumped on a . . .
The pig was so small
He jumped on a . . .

■ (From *Willy O'Dwyer Jumped in the Fire* by Beatrice Schenk deRegniers. Illustrated by Beni Montresor.)

budini (caramel cakes).'' [Beni Montresor, ''My Verona,'' *Holiday,* August, 1968.²]

Besides drawing, Montresor also designed costumes and stages for his own puppet theater. ''As a child, I was passionately and constantly involved in my own puppet theater. I searched out the most improbable objects, the most colorful materials, the most glittering pieces of metal, and I put them all together on my little stage to give shape to something within my head. What was it? An image; thousands of unconnected images that would cross my fancy. But aren't these what all children's minds are filled with?

''Because I was an Italian child, the inspiration for my images very often came from what I saw in church, or around the church. In Italy (as everybody knows) there is a saint to celebrate every day of the year, but besides these there are special saints with special celebrations, and on such occasions the churches are adorned in particularly spectacular ways. Flowers, angels, halos, clouds, gilt, velvets, damasks . . . and then the scent of the incense and of the flowers . . . and then the music of the organ resounding under arches and cupolas.

''How could this resplendent *mise en scène* fail to touch the imagination of a child?

''So it happened very often that I imagined myself protected under the opulent gold and silver mantel of the Madonna, or, in a more cheerful moment, traveling through the skies on the back of the Holy Spirit, something similar to what happens visually on the last page of my *Witches of Venice*. And when I came back to earth, I rushed home to my puppet theater, which was ready to be filled with all those images—and they fitted perfectly into it. It was the ideal place for them to come alive.

''Interestingly enough, the theater in Italy was born in the churches, and this grand and resplendent relationship between theater and church has always existed in my native country. I love all this very much.'' [Lee Kingman, editor, *Newbery and Caldecott Medal Books: 1956-1965*, Horn Book, 1965.³]

1938. ''When I was twelve I enrolled in the High School of Arts in Verona. I had to leave home early every morning by bus. Before classes started I would go into the church of San Fermo Maggiore. At that hour Mass was being celebrated, and the altar would be radiant with flowers and candles and golden ornaments. There was the sweet smell of lighted candles and incense. The soft, fragrant atmosphere took my breath away.

''After the Second World War broke out, I began going to school by bicycle. At that time the High School of Arts was

(From *A for Angel* by Beni Montresor. Illustrated by the author.)

in the Austrian castle of San Pietro on Saint Peter's Hill. From this hill I could see all Verona spread out—the little bridges and church spires and cypresses above the Adige River. Whenever I stood on this hill, the city filled me with tenderness—in autumn particularly, because the color of the leaves blended with the war colors of the buildings.

"One morning during class I looked out the window of the castle and saw airplanes flying over Verona. In a few seconds clusters of bombs fell on the city and explosions and puffs of smoke rose up all around. Glass from the windows shattered and fell all about us. After the bombing stopped I ran out with the other students into the street. We were terrified and nobody said anything. Finally I grabbed my bicycle and pedaled into the smoking city. I saw people digging into the rubble in search of those buried underneath. I remember the corpses that were covered with a thick layer of dust, lined up on the sidewalk, and the pieces of human flesh strewn in the middle of the street.

"I continued to go to school even during the bombardments, even after the Nazis blew up all the beautiful bridges of Verona. But by the time the war was over I felt like a wooden statue of a boy.

"The morning the American troops arrived I was told to go up on the roof of our house and spread a white sheet to show the Americans that the Nazis had left. When I got to the roof, I began shaking so convulsively that I almost fell off the edge, down into the street. Even today, after all that time, I still freeze when I hear about the war."[2]

1945-1949. While studying art at the Acadèmia di Belle Arti in Venice, Montresor wrote radio plays which were produced by the National Italian Radio Network, including several adaptations of fairy tales. ". . . I lived and studied in Venice. . . . When I completed my art studies I moved to Rome. . . ." [John Gruen, "Real-Life Fantasy," *Opera News,* December 11, 1976.[4]]

In Rome Montresor studied set and costume design at the Centro Sperimentale di Cinematografia in a two-year scholarship program.

1952. Began a career as a designer of sets and costumes for films and theater in Italy, France, Spain, Germany and England. Between 1952 and 1959 Montresor created the decor for twenty films, including "Siegfried" produced in Italy in 1948, and designed scenery and costumes for the European stage. "A stage design is like a painting, and each part of the picture must fit together. In a painting you see one artistic creation; there is no bare corner on the canvas to be filled in by another artist. I think set designers should also create the costumes and lighting effects, then place the figures in the background, which naturally involves staging. . . . I do very little research. . . . I learn and listen to the music—that is what inspires me." ["Gentleman of Verona," *Opera News,* February 8, 1964.[5]]

1960. Came to the United States. Began a dual career writing children's books and designing theater sets and costumes. "I recall in 1960—I had just arrived in this country—somebody asked me, 'Would you like to do children's books?' 'Yes,' was my quick reply. I must admit I didn't exactly know what they were. As a child I had never owned one, and besides, at that time in Italy there was only one book for children and that was *Pinocchio*. Today there may be a few more.

"Still, the possibility of being involved in a new work seemed thoroughly natural to me; I felt quite simply that it would be a continuation of the things I had been doing all my life.

". . . I felt I could find once more the little theater of my childhood, and I could again fill it with all the fancies that came into my head.

"Of course, between that old little theater and the new little theaters, this time made of pages, there were many others. In the years between, I had spent ten years as costume and set designer for the cinema. But in films, the designer usually docs not count much. I always felt, being a designer and not a director, that there wasn't enough room for me to express myself completely. I always had to leave too much of myself locked inside me. For this reason, I left the films, and now my theater work is primarily in operas and ballets and in theater

shows with music. Music on the stage gives me the inspiration to create images with colors, lighting, action, and music. It is this that I find most exciting about working in the theater.

"Exactly the same thing happens when I work on a children's book. For me there is no difference between these two things— in the methods, in the aims, or in the results. The blank page is like an empty stage that must be filled with scenes, costumes, movement, and theatrical crescendo. And the words and colors become the music.

"People have . . . observed the similarity: they said that as each scene of 'The Last Savage' appeared on the Metropolitan's stage, it was like looking through the pages of a children's book; on the other hand, upon looking at my books, they have the feeling that they are sitting through a theatrical spectacle.

"The difference between working in the theater and on a book is that in the theater one is surrounded by hundreds of temperamental personalities; working on a book I have only one temperamental personality to deal with, myself, who, if nothing else, is much more restful to be with."

. . . He saw an egg. An enormous egg. Daniel climbed inside. ■ (From *Bedtime!* by Beni Montresor. Illustrated by the author.)

(From "The Selfish Giant" in *The Birthday of the Infanta and Other Tales* by Oscar Wilde. Illustrated by Beni Montresor.)

"And what's all this?" said a deep, dark voice . . . .

Asa and Rambo didn't answer. ■ (From *Belling the Tiger* by Mary Stolz. Illustrated by Beni Montresor.)

"So my life has been a continual going on and off stages of various sizes and types. But now I can say that I have at last found my own real, definitive stage on which I feel I can best express myself.

"My stage is called *picture book*. I didn't invent it, I know this, but I feel that I may have discovered something special about it. You can't imagine how much this excites me!

"For me *a picture book is a book whose content is expressed through its images*. This is a fact I find exciting. I think that very little exists so far in this field, and it is a field in which little has been explored. The things that we can discover may add something very important to the history of books.

"I am old enough to remember the accusations that used to be hurled at the cinema: 'Cinema is not Art because, unlike the theater, it does not express its content by means of words.' But who worries about this any longer? We all know that the cinema is based on images, not words; it is these visual images that give the new art its reason for being.

"Ours is a visual time, a time of great and fleeting visions because it is a time of speed. One rushes, speaking less and less. It is the image that represents this best, and it is the image to which we most naturally respond.

"I have the impression that words as an art form will give us less and less, because we are becoming more and more visually oriented. The idea of the visual book, the book to look at, is an idea of today, and even more, of tomorrow.

"The important point is this: *The story told with pictures has a language all its own: the visual language,* and therefore it is with this language that a picture book must express itself.

"And it is in this direction that I will move with my work. This is the result of discoveries made during my first few years of working in children's books. But . . . it is also the result of an instinct, formed over a long time and by many experiences of expressing oneself in images.

"Before the time of books, artists and sculptors filled walls and walls with images that told stories, wonderful stories, and all of this was art at the most sublime level—visual images conveying ideas, concepts, and adventures of the imagination. Since I had the good fortune to be born in Italy, this kind of art was one of my first experiences, the deepest, and most formative, even if at the time I was unaware of it. I grew up seeing stories on the walls of many palaces and churches, and I know well that they permeated my being even at the earliest age. I know they made me become what I am."[3]

1964. Designed the Metropolitan Opera production of "The Last Savage," which established his career. He has designed sets and costumes for operas, ballets, and musicals in the United States and abroad. ". . . In 1962 I met Gian Carlo Menotti, and he invited me to design a new production of Sam Barber's "Vanessa" for the Spoleto Festival [Italy]. It was my very first opera, and it was a fantastic success. As a result, Gian Carlo asked me to design the Metropolitan Opera production of his 'Last Savage,' which happened in 1964, and which really launched my career.

"When I start to design, the first thing I do is listen to the music. Often I listen without even knowing what the libretto is about. Later, of course, I study the libretto, but mainly it's about the music: the moment I hear the music, I see things. You see, music moves all the time, and I feel the décor must do the same—not in an obtrusive or conflicting way but in a harmonious, logical way. . . ."[4]

1965. Won the Caldecott Medal for his illustrations in Beatrice deRegniers' book, *May I Bring a Friend?* ". . . At the Rizzoli International Bookstore in New York, there was a party for children to celebrate this years's Newbery and Caldecott Awards. For the occasion we dressed actors as a bullfighter and as a king and queen. During the party I overheard a young child exclaim to the king, 'You know something? I never met a real king before!' And the little boy stood there wide-eyed and openmouthed. Certainly this will remain for that child one of his most important experiences. Santa Claus can be met on every street corner, but a real king is not so easy to meet.

"More or less in the same period I was on the radio talking with another young child. I asked him what he liked best about my illustrations for *May I Bring a Friend?* He answered, 'The pink elephant.' I asked why. 'Because before that I never saw a pink elephant!'

"Characters never seen before and animals never seen before. As always, children in their direct and candid way give us *the answer*. It is an invitation to produce the never-seen-before, to look for the new, to hold oneself open to all possibilities. Because possibility is a door to poetry.

"We have to be open to the marvelous adventure of books made of images, because it has already existed for a long time, and because now people are searching for it more than ever. At this time only one thing should occupy us: To work for images of the highest quality—full, rich, and provocative im-ages that carry the imagination to new heights that will be launching pads for new and always more daring discoveries."[3]

"A child's mind is crossed by thousands of images every day, like a kaleidoscope. And at the same time he is filled with

There was an old woman who lived in a shoe,
She had so many children she didn't know what to do.

■ (From *I Saw a Ship A-Sailing* by Beni Montresor. Illustrated by the author.)

The castle had once been magnificent but now was falling to pieces, all because the Baron thought only of his own pleasure. ▪ (From *Cinderella,* adapted from the opera "La Cenerentola" by Gioacchino Rossini. Illustrated by Beni Montresor.)

great liveliness and an unselfconscious ability for total involvement. It is possible for a child to create images, and to him they are beautiful. A child with a piece of wood may see it as the most beautiful doll in the world. The same child, given the most beautiful doll in the world, may abandon it. It is 'finished,' because there is nothing more left to be done by the child's own imagination.

"They have the most gracious imaginations in the world. They bloom like flowers—until they begin to grow up, to conform. . . ." [Velma V. Varner, "Beni Montresor," *Horn Book,* August, 1965.[6]]

Wrote and illustrated *Cinderella* based on the English adaptation of the opera, "La Cenerentola," by Gioacchino Rossini which he also designed. "What I wanted to do with this book was to transform it into a stage. To bring into it the magic of an operatic spectacle, with all the grace and joy of the music of Rossini." [Taken from the book jacket of *Cinderella,* adapted by B. Montresor, Knopf, 1965.[7]]

1966. Made his debut as a stage director-designer with Mozart's "The Magic Flute" at Lincoln Center in New York. He also illustrated Stephen Spender's retelling of the story for Putnam's "Opera for Young People" series. ". . . My interpretation of 'The Magic Flute' is completely emotional; I just fill my ears with the music, then I express the music in terms of images and color. . . . I want the emotional, the totally theatrical approach." [Juan Barthel, "Don't Write that Down! Yes, Do," *New York Times,* September 4, 1966.[8]]

Montresor's aim in children's books and theater is the same—to create images and action and to stimulate the imagination. ". . . What I want most to do in my books for children is to offer them a theatrical show, to express in book form the magic of the stage."

1967. Illustrated *I Saw a Ship A-Sailing* because "Mother Goose had never been done properly. . . . I liked the rhymes. I've felt for a long time that they have never been done right. I tried to translate into pictures—the colors, the music, the exuburance, the madness and the marvelous strangeness of these poems.

"Up to now, they have always been reduced into small realistic vignettes with no magic at all. No one took care of the music.

"It is a new sort of book . . . a real special book. It is not an illustrated book. But a book in which the story is told in visual terms. . . ." [June Weir, "Montresor Magic," *Women's Wear Daily,* November 28, 1967.[9]]

Montresor is totally dedicated to his work. According to the artist, his work is his life. ". . . I do all this because I need it, I couldn't live without it. Friends say to me, 'Beni, stop all this work because you will empty very soon.' But I wish I had 25 hands and 40 hours in the day.

"It takes me about one year to do an opera—there are 700 costumes in 'La Gioconda,' and the chorus will change costumes three times—but I am very good to go from one thing to another, and I am lucky to be doing these things in my own way. . . ."[8]

". . . I do a lot of absorbing, a lot of watching. I absorb through my skin. In whatever city I'm in, I walk and walk for miles, looking at everything. Things go into my own darkness and stay there. Then at a certain moment a light is shed on them, and things are revealed to me. Often just before falling asleep I am in very close touch with my fantasies, and they sustain me and give me inspiration. You see, my approach to life and my work is very sensual and very emotional. That's how I am. But I detest making such statements, because words are never enough and never quite sound right. That's why I prefer to put my emotions and my fantasies into my work. That's my reality, my true identity, my real life!"[4]

About his book, *Bedtime,* and his work in progress *Don't Wake Me Up,* Montresor comented: "It's about a boy who doesn't want to go to bed. I wrote and pictured in it all my childhood fears and fantasies about bedtime, with angels and doves and devils and the Virgin Mary. 'Don't Wake Me Up,' is about a boy who doesn't want to get up. I think that most of the world doesn't want to get up. That's one way I see the world." [Sidney Fields, "Only Human, Master of all Pursuits," *Daily News,* January 16, 1979.[10]]

Montresor lives in Greenwich Village and calls New York his home, although he maintains a house in Italy. "I am a Venetian living in New York. I only know that since I was born I was always looking for . . . new horizons. I don't live in the past, or in the future. Only the present is real. This moment is good. And life is made of moments."[8]

". . . I feel very much alive. I am not a pessimist. I wish I could live 200 years. There is so much I want to do. The normal life span is too short. When you finally understand something, it is time to leave."[10]

Montresor's works are included in the Kerlan Collection at the University of Minnesota.

FOR MORE INFORMATION SEE: Show, March, 1962; *Horn Book,* October, 1962, August, 1965, April, 1966; *Opera News,* February 8, 1964, March 23, 1968, December 11, 1976; *Newsday,* April 13, 1965, Lee Kingman, editor, *Newbery and Caldecott Medal Books: 1956-1965,* Horn Book, 1965; *Library Journal,* March 15, 1965; *Publishers Weekly,* March 8, 1965;

Diana Klemin, *The Art of Art for Children's Books,* Clarkson Potter, 1966; *Book Week,* March 20, 1966; *New York Times,* September 4, 1966, April 15, 1969; Jean Poindexter Colby, *Writing, Illustrating and Editing Children's Books,* Hastings House, 1967; *Book World* (children's issue), November 5, 1967; June Weir, "Montressor Magic," *Women's Wear Daily,* November 28, 1967; Beni Montressor, "My Verona," *Holiday,* August, 1968; Lee Kingman and others, compilers, *Illustrators of Children's Books: 1957-1966,* Horn Book, 1968; Lee Bennett Hopkins, *Books Are By People,* Citation Press, 1969; *Vogue,* March 1, 1970; Selma G. Lanes, *Down the Rabbit Hole,* Atheneum, 1971; Doris de Montreville and Donna Hill, *Third Book of Junior Authors,* H. W. Wilson, 1972; Lee Kingman and others, compilers, *Illustrators of Children's Books: 1967-1976,* Horn Book, 1978; *People,* December 11, 1978; *Daily News,* January 16, 1979; *Newsweek,* March 2, 1981; *Hi Fi,* July, 1981.

MOORE, Ruth Nulton 1923-

PERSONAL: Born June 19, 1923, in Easton, Pa.; daughter of Jacob Wesley (a dentist) and Stella (Houck) Nulton; married Carl L. Moore (a professor of accounting and writer), June 15, 1946; children: Carl Nulton, Stephen Eric. *Education:* Bucknell University, A.B., 1944; Columbia University, M.A., 1945;

RUTH NULTON MOORE

John froze with fright and held his breath. The simple motion of breathing might cause the snake to bare its fangs and strike . . . . ■ (From *Wilderness Journey* by Ruth Nulton Moore. Illustrated by Allan Eitzen.)

further graduate study at University of Pittsburgh, 1946. *Politics:* Republican. *Religion:* Protestant. *Home:* 3033 Center St., Bethlehem, Pa., 18017. *Agent:* McIntosh & Otis, Inc., 475 Fifth Ave., New York, N.Y. 10017.

CAREER: Teacher of English and social studies in public schools in Easton, Pa., 1946-50; high school teacher of English and social studies in Detroit, Mich., 1952; free-lance writer, 1965—.

WRITINGS—All for children: *Frisky the Playful Pony,* Criterion, 1966; *Hiding the Bell,* Westminster, 1968; *Peace Treaty,* Herald Press, 1977; *The Ghost Bird Mystery* (illustrated by Ivan Moon), Harold Press, 1977; *Mystery of the Lost Treasure,* Herald Press, 1978; *Tomás and the Talking Birds* (illustrated by Esther R. Garber), Herald Press, 1978; *Wilderness Journey* (illustrated by Allan Eitzen), Herald Press, 1979; *Mystery at Indian Rocks* (illustrated by Magi Bond), Herald Press, 1981; *The Sorrel Horse,* Herald Press, 1982; *Danger in the Pines,* Herald Press, 1983; *In Search of Liberty* (illustrated by James Converse), Herald Press, 1983. Contributor of stories and poems to *Jack and Jill* and *Children's Activities.*

WORK IN PROGRESS: A mystery series for young teens.

SIDELIGHTS: "Because I was an only child and often had to amuse myself, I had lots of opportunity to 'make believe.' I used to make up stories, often using historical periods for backgrounds of my imaginary tales. On walks through the Pennsylvania countryside, I would sit in a field or in the woods and write poetry. I think that writing poetry is a good way to start a writing career because when one is young, one possesses so much more imagination than an older person. I started to write poetry when I was in fifth grade and continued to write it through high school.

"When I attended college, I knew that I wanted to be two things: a teacher and a writer. My favorite subjects in school were English literature and American history. First, I became a teacher and taught English literature and social studies in junior and senior high school. I learned to love working with young people through my teaching. In fact, I like and understand young people much better than grownups.

"After my first son was born, I stopped teaching and turned to my next love, writing. It came naturally because I had always wanted to be a writer, ever since I wrote that first poem in fifth grade. So, while my children took naps, I would write—sometimes for only an hour a day. Later, when they were in school, I had the entire morning or afternoon to write.

"When my younger son was in first grade, he and his older brother helped me write my first published book. It happened this way: the first grade teacher had taken the class to an orchard next to the school to see some ponies. The ponies belonged to the school custodian who had a small farm right in back of the school. My son was so thrilled with his visit to the ponies that when he came home from school, he begged me to take him and his older brother back to the orchard for another visit.

"I believe I enjoyed seeing the ponies as much as the boys did, and when we arrived home, I got an exciting idea for a pony story. The result was *Frisky the Playful Pony.*

"Most of my ideas for books have come from where I live, about fifty miles north of Philadelphia. One day when I heard the exciting story of how a local church had hidden the Liberty Bell in its basement during the American Revolution, I was so proud of what my community had done that I had to tell others about it; so I wrote my second book, *Hiding the Bell.* A parrot in a local pet shop and a homesick Puerto Rican boy gave me the idea for another story, *Tomás and the Talking Birds.* You see, you can get many story ideas right from your own neighborhood.

"I give talks to school children about writing fiction and poetry. I have held poetry seminars for elementary grades and speak about writing children's books to teacher-training classes in our local colleges. When I talk to school groups, one of the questions asked is how long it takes me to write one of my books. My answer is that it usually takes a year. One time a sixth grade boy exclaimed, 'It takes you that long to write a book!' I told him that I write the first draft in longhand because my thoughts flow easier when I write with a pencil. Then I revise the longhand draft two or three times until I can't read it anymore before typing up a rough draft which also goes through several revisions being retyped to send off.

"When I asked him how long he spent writing a paper for his teacher, he replied, 'Oh, about half an hour. I just write it, fold it up, and put it into my book.' He confessed that he got a C minus for the effort, and I told him if I did that with a manuscript, I'd get a C minus, too, and it wouldn't get published.

"Another question asked is how long do I spend each day

writing. I usually write for three hours every morning. At first it took a great deal of discipline to sit at my desk that long everyday, but now it is so much a part of my daily routine that I feel guilty if I have to miss a day's writing. To me, writing is exciting and enjoyable. Even if I were not published, I believe that I would still write.

"I encourage young people who want to be writers to start writing *now*. They do not have to wait until they are gown-up or finished school. There are many ways a young writer can get published. Local libraries often have writing contests. There are magazines for young people which have student pages. And there is always the school paper as a source for student manuscripts.

"A good way to learn how to write is to read. By reading the kind of books you like to write, you can learn how the professional writers write. I would also suggest keeping a notebook. I keep two—a notebook full of description and a notebook with story ideas. Also, I keep clippings from newspapers and magazines that provide interesting story ideas. Writing letters and keeping a diary or journal is a good day-to-day writing practice. In fact, by keeping a diary, you are writing the story of your life, and each day's entry is an episode to that story.

"I like to think that each book I write has a purpose besides just telling an exciting story. I like to think that it may help solve a problem or bring hope to a young reader who needs it.

"My husband is a professor of accounting at Lehigh University, and he writes accounting textbooks.

"I like to travel throughout the country, visiting historical sites and exploring deeply into my country's past. I also like to hike in the Endless Mountains of northeastern Pennsylvania where we have a small farm called High Meadows."

HOBBIES AND OTHER INTERESTS: Canoeing, hiking, collecting American Indian artifacts.

FOR MORE INFORMATION SEE: Lehigh Valley Monthly, August, 1977; *Philadelphia Children's Authors and Illustrators at a Glance,* Villanova University Press, 1978; Janice H. McElroy, editor, *Our Hidden Heritage: Pennsylvania Women in History,* Pennsylvania Division of American Association of University Women, 1983.

NEUSNER, Jacob   1932-

PERSONAL: Born July 28, 1932, in Hartford, Conn.; son of Samuel (publisher of *Connecticut Jewish Ledger)* and Lee (a publisher; maiden name, Green) Neusner; married Suzanne Richter (an artist), March 15, 1964; children: Samuel Aaron, Eli Ephraim, Noam Mordecai Menahem, Margalit Leah Berakhah. *Education:* Harvard University, A.B. (magna cum laude), 1953; graduate study at Lincoln College, Oxford, 1953-54, Hebrew University, Jerusalem, 1957-58, and Union Theological Seminary, New York, 1958-60; Jewish Theological Seminary of America, M.H.L., 1960; Columbia University, Ph.D., 1960; Harvard University, postdoctoral study, 1962-64. *Religion:* Jewish. *Home:* 70 Vassar Ave., Providence, R.I. 02906. *Office:* Program in Judaic Studies, Brown University, 163 George St., Providence, R.I. 02912.

CAREER: Columbia University, New York, N.Y., instructor in religion, 1960-61; University of Wisconsin-Milwaukee, as-

JACOB NEUSNER

sistant professor of Hebrew, 1961-62; Brandeis University, Waltham, Mass., research associate in Jewish history, 1962-64; Dartmouth College, Hanover, N.H., assistant professor, 1964-66, associate professor of religion, 1966-68; Brown University, Providence, R.I., professor of religious studies, 1968-75, university professor and Ungerleider Distinguished Scholar of Judaic Studies, 1975—, co-director, Program in Judaic Studies. Guest lecturer at numerous universities, including Yale University, 1971, Notre Dame University, 1972, University of Chicago, 1972 and 1978, University of California, Berkeley, 1976, and Oxford University, 1981; visiting summer professor, Jewish Theological Seminary of America, 1977, and Iliff School of Theology, 1978; Hill Visiting Professor, University of Minnesota, fall, 1978; has conducted lecture tours in South Africa, West Germany, and England. Member of Kent Fellowship Advisory Council of Danforth Foundation, 1964-66; member of board of advisors, I. Edward Kiev Library Foundation, 1977—, and Ancient Biblical Manuscript Center, School of Theology Library, Claremont College, 1978—.

MEMBER: Society of Values in Higher Education, Society of Biblical Literature, Rabbinical Assembly of America, American Society for Study of Religion, American Oriental Society (life member), American Academy of Jewish Research (fellow, 1972—; member of executive committee, 1976-81), American Jewish Historical Society, American Academy of Religion (vice-president, 1967-68; president, 1968-69; section chairman, 1979-81; member of board of directors, 1981—), Association for Jewish Studies (founding member; member of board of direc-

... Somebody asks a sage to teach "the *whole* Torah." But that is not the only thing you will find surprising in the story. The amazing thing is that the man asks for "the *whole* Torah" while he stands on one foot. ▪ (From *Meet Our Sages* by Jacob Neusner. Illustrated by Jim Hellmuth.)

tors, 1968-72), National Council for the Humanities, American Association of University Professors, European Association for Jewish Studies, American Historical Association, Royal Asiatic Society (fellow), Max Richter Foundation (president, 1969—), Phi Beta Kappa.

WRITINGS—Children's textbooks: *Learn Mishnah,* Behrman, 1978; *Learn Talmud,* Behrman, 1979; *Meet Our Sages* (illustrated by Jim Hellmuth), Behrman, 1980; *Mitzvah,* Rossel Books, 1981; *Tsedakah: Can Jewish Philanthropy Buy Jewish Survival?,* Rossel Books, 1982.

Neusner has written, edited, and contributed to numerous books on the subject of Judaism. For a complete bibliographic listing see *Contemporary Authors, New Revision Series,* Volume 7, Gale, 1982.

WORK IN PROGRESS: Translation and analysis of *Leviticus Rabbah.*

SIDELIGHTS: "I express whatever I am mainly through words. Therefore, I try to invent different ways of saying things to accommodate the different feelings I may have at any time or the different attitudes or emotions or ideas that are on my mind and in my heart. So I try to write in one way under one set of circumstances, and in another way under other circumstances.

"People do not always grasp that writers are always trying things. They think they are what they write. But no more than

an actor is the character he plays, is a writer the tone of voice he or she adopts; it is all a game. I write mainly about ideas and how they take shape, who holds them and why the ideas a person holds make sense out of the world in which that person lives. I focus my attention, in particular, on ideas about religious questions.

"My special area of interest is in Judaism and the Jews, because I am Jewish and find special interest in things that affect me directly—even at a remove of two thousand years. At the same time I try to interpret the experiences of the Jews in terms other people can understand and even use. For Jews are people, and their special experience of history, their distinctive ideas about themselves and the world and God—these form a choice confronting humanity, a way of being human. If we grasp that everyone, in all their specificity and distinctiveness, shows a set of choices available—because we are human, then we each can achieve understanding of the other. That can make life more pleasant than it is these days."

Three wise men of Gotham
Went to sea in a bowl;
If the bowl had been stronger
My story had been longer.

—*Mother Goose*

NORMAN, Charles 1904-

PERSONAL: Born May 9, 1904, in Russia (now U.S.S.R.); came to United States, 1910; naturalized U.S. citizen, 1924; son of Abraham and Rachel (Dolobovska) Bloom; married Diana Louise Marshall, December 21, 1960; children: Anne Rose Morton (Mrs. James R. Beeler). *Education:* Attended New York University, 1921-24.

CAREER: Writer of fiction, biography, and poetry; artist. Sailed to South America as a seaman on a freighter, c. 1922; worked as a writer for *Paris Times,* 1928; assistant night editor for North American Newspaper Alliance, 1931-34; writer for United Press International, 1934, Associated Press, 1934-39, Time, Inc., 1941, and *PM* (newspaper), 1941-42, 1945-46; instructor in Shakespeare, New York University, 1947-50. Also employed as a writer for Columbia Broadcasting System, Inc. Has exhibited work at the Gotham Book Mart Gallery, 1969, and in one-man shows, including those at the Julien Levy Gallery, New York City, 1940, and the RoKo Gallery, Greenwich Village, New York City, 1953. *Military service:* U.S. Army, 1942-45; became infantry officer. *Member:* P.E.N. Club.

*WRITINGS—*For young readers; biography: *The Playmaker of Avon,* McKay, 1949, reissued, 1966; *The Pundit and the Player: Dr. Johnson and Mr. Garrick* (illustrated by Bruno Frost), McKay, 1951; *The Shepherd of the Ocean: Sir Walter Raleigh* (illustrated by B. Frost), McKay, 1952; *To a Different Drum: The Story of Henry David Thoreau* (illustrated by Margaret B. Graham), Harper, 1954; *John Muir, Father of Our National Parks,* Messner, 1957; *The Flight and Adventures of Charles II* (illustrated by C. Walter Hodges), Random House, 1958; *Orimha of the Mohawks: The Story of Pierre Esprit Radisson among the Indians* (illustrated by Johannes Troyer), Macmillan, 1961.

Other: *Mr. Upstairs and Mr. Downstairs: Introducing Jane Jonquil and Her Father* (illustrated by M.B. Graham), Harper, 1950; *The Crumb That Walked: More about Jane Jonquil* (illustrated by M.B. Graham), Harper, 1951; *Hunch, Munch, and Crunch: More about the Jonquils* (illustrated by M.B. Graham), Harper, 1952; *The Long Bows of Agincourt* (illustrated by Jeannette Cissman), Bobbs-Merrill, 1963.

Adult biographies: *The Muses' Darling: The Life of Christopher Marlowe,* Rinehart & Co., 1946, published as *Christopher Marlowe: The Muses' Darling,* Bobbs-Merrill, 1971; *So Worthy a Friend: William Shakespeare,* Rinehart & Co., 1947, revised edition, P. Collier, 1961; *The Case of Ezra Pound,* Bodley Press, 1948, revised edition, Funk, 1968; *Mr. Oddity: Samuel Johnson, LL.D.,* Bell Publishing, 1951; *Rake Rochester* (life of John Wilmot), Crown, 1954; *The Genteel Murderer* (life of Thomas G. Wainewright), Macmillan, 1956; *The Magic-Maker, E.E. Cummings,* Macmillan, 1958, revised edition published as *E.E. Cummings, the Magic-Maker,* Duell, Sloan & Pearce, 1964; *Ezra Pound,* Macmillan, 1960, revised edition, Funk, 1969.

Poetry: *The Far Harbour: A Sea Narrative,* Blue Faun Publications, 1924; *Tragic Beaches: A Book of Narrative Poems about the Sea,* S.A. Jacobs, 1925; *Poems,* Knopf, 1929; *The Bright World, and Other Poems,* Morrow, 1930; *The Savage Century,* J.A. Decker, 1942; *A Soldier's Diary,* Scribner, 1944; *Selected Poems,* Macmillan, 1962; *The Portents of the Air, and Other Poems,* Bobbs-Merrill, 1973.

Other: (Compiler) *A Golden Book of Love Stories* (short stories), A.A. Wynn, 1947; *The Well of the Past* (novel), Dou-

For a time, the charming Charles was very popular. ■ (From *The Flight and Adventures of Charles II* by Charles Norman. Illustrated by C. Walter Hodges.)

bleday, 1949; *Dominick Dragon; or, The Happy Fellow* (novel), Bell Publishing, 1951; (editor) J. Boswell, *Boswell's Life of Johnson,* P. Collier, 1962; (editor and author of introduction) *Poets on Poetry,* P. Collier, 1962; (editor) *Come Live With Me: Five Centuries of Romantic Poetry,* McKay, 1966; *Discoverers of America,* Crowell, 1968; *Poets and People,* Bobbs-Merrill, 1972.

Contributor of short stories and poetry to periodicals, including *Dial, Saturday Review, Poetry, North American Review, New Yorker,* and *New Republic.*

FOR MORE INFORMATION SEE: Saturday Review of Literature, June 21, 1930, November 2, 1946, October 13, 1951; *Christian Science Monitor,* May 2, 1942, November 30, 1946, September 18, 1951, June 5, 1964; *New York Herald Tribune Weekly Book Review,* October 13, 1946, May 1, 1949; *New York Times Book Review,* October 13, 1946, July 18, 1954, November 16, 1958; *New York Herald Tribune Book Review,* November 4, 1951, May 15, 1954, February 1, 1959; *Saturday Review,* November 22, 1958; *American Literature,* November, 1964; *Virginia Quarterly Review,* spring, 1968; *Esquire,* August, 1969; *New Statesman,* September 19, 1969; *Books and Bookmen,* November, 1969; *Nation,* December 18, 1972.

Education is the ability to listen to almost anything without losing your temper or your self-confidence.
　　　　　　　　　　　　　　　　　—Robert Frost

(From *It's Easy to Have a Snail Visit You,* edited by Caroline O'Hagan. Illustrated by Judith Allan.)

O'HAGAN, Caroline 1946-

PERSONAL: Born October 28, 1946, in Gloucestershire, England; daughter of Walter Howard (a farmer) and Betty (Washbourn) Franklin; married Antony O'Hagan (an accountant), December 6, 1975; children: Clare, Richard. *Education:* Attended Cheltenham Ladies College, 1957-64; British Small Animal Veterinary Association, preliminary nursing examination award, 1965. *Politics:* Liberal. *Religion:* Christian (Church of England). *Home:* 8 Anglefield Rd., Berkhamsted, Hertfordshire, England.

CAREER: Berkshire College of Agriculture, Maidenhead, England, lecturer of animal nursing, 1969-74. *Military service:* British Territorial Army, 1973-75. *Member:* British Animal Nursing Auxiliaries Association (chairman, 1971-73).

*WRITINGS—*All nonfiction: (Contributor) G. N. Henderson and D. J. Coffey, editors, *Cats and Cat Care: An International Encyclopedia,* David & Charles, 1973; (contributor) R. S. Pinniger, editor, *Jones's Animal Nursing,* Pergamon, 1973, 3rd edition, edited by D. R. Lane, 1980; (advisory editor) *It's Easy to Have a Caterpillar Visit You* (juvenile; illustrated by Judith Allan), Lothrop, 1980 (published in England as *It's Easy to Have a Caterpillar to Stay,* Chatto & Windus, 1980); (advisory editor) *It's Easy to Have a Snail Visit You* (juvenile; illustrated by J. Allan), Lothrop, 1980 (published in England as *It's Easy to Have a Snail to Stay,* Chatto & Windus, 1980); (advisory editor) *It's Easy to Have a Worm Visit You* (juvenile; illustrated by J. Allan), Lothrop, 1980 (published in England as *It's Easy to Have a Worm to Stay,* Chatto & Windus, 1980). Also contributor to professional journals, including *Women's Realm, Nursery World, The Complete Cat,* and *The Complete Dog.*

WORK IN PROGRESS: "Research on insect species suitable as pets for children aged three to six; research on the possibility of teaching small children to snorkel and observe coral reef fish in East African coastal waters."

HOBBIES AND OTHER INTERESTS: "A keen free-fall parachutist, I am also fond of downhill skiing, dinghy sailing, wind-surfing, scuba-diving, and skating. I will try most adventure sports. I enjoy contact with the natural environment, and with both domesticated and wild fauna and flora."

OWEN, (Benjamin) Evan   1918-1984

PERSONAL: Born January 5, 1918, in London, England; died April 11, 1984; son of Evan William and Agnes Ellen Owen; married Beatrice Mary Morris, November 30, 1940; children: Laurence Evan, Gillian Margaret. *Education:* Attended Birmingham Training College. *Home:* 35 High St., Watlington, Oxford OX9 5PZ, England.

CAREER: Writer and educator. Teacher of and adviser in remedial education, Oxfordshire Education Committee, beginning 1955. Part-time staff tutor at Oxford University Department of Education, 1960-74; part-time course tutor at Open University, beginning 1975; served on literature panel of Southern Arts Association, 1979-82. *Member:* United Kingdom Reading Association.

*WRITINGS—*All for children: *Adventures of Bill and Betty* (illustrated by Margery Gill), six books, Oxford University Press, 1954; (editor) *Blackwell's Junior Poetry Books* (illustrated by Kathleen Gell), four books, Basil Blackwell, 1960; (with Ian Gemmell) *The Night Sky* (illustrated by F.T.W. Cook), Basil Blackwell, 1965; *What Happened Today?: An Almanack of History* (illustrated by Jack Townend), three volumes, Basil Blackwell, 1967; (compiler) *Pergamon Poets,* Pergamon, Volume I: *Roy Fuller and R. S. Thomas,* 1968, Volume III: *Robert Browning and Alfred Lord Tennyson,* 1968, Volume IV: *Kathleen Raine and Vernon Watkins,* 1968, Volume V: *Gerard Manley Hopkins and John Keats,* 1969, Volume X: *Charles Causley and Laurie Lee,* 1970 (Owen was not associated with other volumes in the series); *Carford Readers* (illustrated by Jill Bennett), Pergamon, 1971, Book 1: *Carford Is a Big Town,* Book 2: *The Five Friends,* Book 3: *At School,* Book 4: *At Work,* Book 5: *The Halls and Martins,* Book 6: *The New Car,* Book 7: *After the Match,* Book 8: *Fire!; Not Like Johnny* (illustrated by Dan Pearce), Evans Brothers, 1973; *Football's for Schoolkids* (illustrated by D. Pearce), Evans Brothers, 1973; *You're On Your Own* (illustrated by D. Pearce), Evans Brothers, 1973, published as *On Your Own,* Harvey House, 1978; *Freestyle Champ* (illustrated by D. Pearce), Evans Brothers, 1974; *The Big City Book,* Scott, Foresman, 1975; *Saturday Afternoon* (illustrated by Robin Laurie), Blackie & Son, 1976; *Fire Is a Killer* (illustrated by Trevor Stubley), Blackie & Son, 1976; *On Patrol* (illustrated by John Harold), Blackie & Son, 1976; *People Who Care* (illustrated by Sheridon Davies), Blackie & Son, 1976; *Lower End Farm* (illustrated by Anna Dzierzek), Blackie & Son, 1978; *Ways to Reading,* Visual Publication, 1978; *Getting There* (illustrated by Douglas Phillips), Blackie & Son, 1978; *Sport: Knowing British History,* Evans Brothers, 1981; *Inner City Books* (fiction series), Evans Brothers, 1983.

Series editor, Athena Books, 1968 and Pergamon Poets, 1968-70. Contributor of articles to periodicals, including *Fortnightly, Teacher, Contemporary Review, Teacher's World,* and *Birmingham Post.* Reviewer of fiction and poetry, and author of criticism for *Oxford Mail,* 1955-69.

EVAN OWEN

The race started slowly. Too slowly, thought Carlo. ∎
(From *On Your Own* by Evan Owen. Illustrated by Len Shalansky.)

PAGE, Lou Williams 1912-

PERSONAL: Born October 23, 1912, in Belleville, N.J.; daughter of Howard Lewis and Anna (King) Williams; married Thornton Leigh Page, August 28, 1948; children: Mary Anne, Leigh II. *Education:* Attended Lyons Twp. Junior College, Illinois, 1929; University of Chicago, B.S., 1933, M.S., 1935, Ph.D., 1947. *Politics:* Independent. *Religion:* Episcopal. *Home:* 18639 Point Lookout Dr., Houston, Tex. 77058.

CAREER: Pure Oil Co., Chicago, Ill., assistant to chief geologist, 1939-44; Stephens College, Columbia, Mo., teacher, 1944-45; University of Chicago, Chicago, Ill., instructor in geology, 1946-48; assistant examiner with board of examinations, 1948-49; *Journal of Geology,* Chicago, Ill., managing editor, 1949-52; Connecticut Geological and Natural History Survey, Middletown, editor, 1961-80. Assistant editor, *Journal of Paleontology,* 1949-52.

WRITINGS: A Dipper Full of Stars, Follett, 1944, 4th edition, 1964; *The Earth and Its Story,* School Services and Publications, Wesleyan University, 1961; *Rocks and Minerals,* Follett, 1962; (editor with husband, Thornton Page) *Wanderers in the Sky,* Macmillan, 1965; (editor with T. Page) *Neighbors of the Earth,* Macmillan, 1965; (with T. Page) *Origin of the Solar System,* Macmillan, 1966; (editor with T. Page) *Telescopes,* Macmillan, 1966; (editor with T. Page) *Starlight,* Macmillan, 1967; (editor with T. Page) *The Evolution of Stars,* Macmillan, 1968; (editor with T. Page) *Stars and Clouds of the Milky Way,* Macmillan, 1968; (with T. Page) *Beyond the Milky Way,* Macmillan, 1969; *Astronomy: How Men Learned about the Universe,* Addison-Wesley, 1969; *Ideas from Astronomy,* Addison-Wesley, 1973; *Ideas from Geology,* Addison-Wesley, 1973; (editor with T. Page) *Space Science and Astronomy,* Macmillan, 1976; (with T. Page) *Apollo-Soyoz,* U.S. Government Printing Office, 1977.

HOBBIES AND OTHER INTERESTS: Cooking, gardening.

To acquire the habit of reading is to construct for yourself a refuge from almost all the miseries of life.
—W. Somerset Maugham

PENZLER, Otto 1942-
(Irene Adler, Lucy Ferrier, Stephen Gregory, Charles A. Milverton)

PERSONAL: Born July 8, 1942, in Hamburg, Germany; came to United States, 1947; son of Otto (a chemist) and Jeanette (a secretary; maiden name, Kunmann) Penzler; married Evelyn Barbara Byrne (a teacher; divorced); married Carolyn Ann Hartman (an illustrator), September 30, 1980. *Education:* Attended University of Michigan and New York University. *Home and office:* 129 West 56th St., New York, N.Y. 10019. *Agent:* Sterling Lord Agency, 660 Madison Ave., New York, N.Y. 10021.

CAREER: New York Daily News, New York City, copyboy, 1963, editorial assistant, 1963-64, sportswriter, 1964-69; American Broadcasting Co. (ABC), New York City, senior sports publicist for television, 1969-73, newswriter, 1973, editor of corporate newsletter, "Happenings," 1973-75; writer, 1971—; founder and president, Mysterious Press, 1976—, and Mysterious Literary Agency, 1981—; owner and proprietor, Mysterious Bookshop, 1979—; publisher of journal, *The Armchair Detective,* 1979—. Lecturer at various universities, 1975—. *Military service:* U.S. Army Reserve, 1964-70. *Member:* Mystery Writers of America (member of board of directors), Writers Guild of America, East, and several "Sherlock Holmes organizations," including Baker Street Irregulars, Priory

Scholars, and Scandalous Bohemians. *Awards, honors:* Edgar Allan Poe Award from Mystery Writers of America, 1977, for *Encyclopedia of Mystery and Detection.*

WRITINGS—Of interest to young readers; all published by Troll Associates: *Sports Car Racing* (illustrated with photographs by John Lee), 1975; *Demolition Derby,* 1975; *Great Stock Car Racing,* 1975; *Daredevils on Wheels,* 1975; *Danger! White Water,* 1976; *Hang Gliding: Riding the Wind,* 1976; *Hunting the Killer Shark,* 1976; (under pseudonym Irene Adler) *Ballooning: High and Wild,* 1976; (under pseudonym Lucy Ferrier) *Diving the Great Barrier Reef,* 1976; (under pseudonym Stephen Gregory) *Bobsledding: Down the Chute!,* 1976; (under pseudonym S. Gregory) *Racing to Win: The Salt Flats,* 1976.

Other: (Co-editor with Evelyn B. Byrne) *Attacks of Taste,* Gotham Book Mart, 1971; (with Chris Steinbrunner, Marvin Lachman, Francis M. Nevins, Jr., Charles Shibuk; co-editor with C. Steinbrunner and C. Shibuk) *Detectionary,* privately printed, 1972, revised edition, Overlook Press, 1977; (with Jim Benagh) *ABC's Wide World of Sports Encyclopedia,* Stadia Sports/Dell, 1973, revised edition, 1974; (author of introduction) Barry Perowne, *Raffles Revisited,* Harper, 1974; (editor with C. Steinbrunner) *Encyclopedia of Mystery and Detection,* McGraw, 1976; (editor) *Whodunit? Houdini?: Thirteen Tales of Magic, Murder, Mystery,* Harper, 1976; (contributor) John

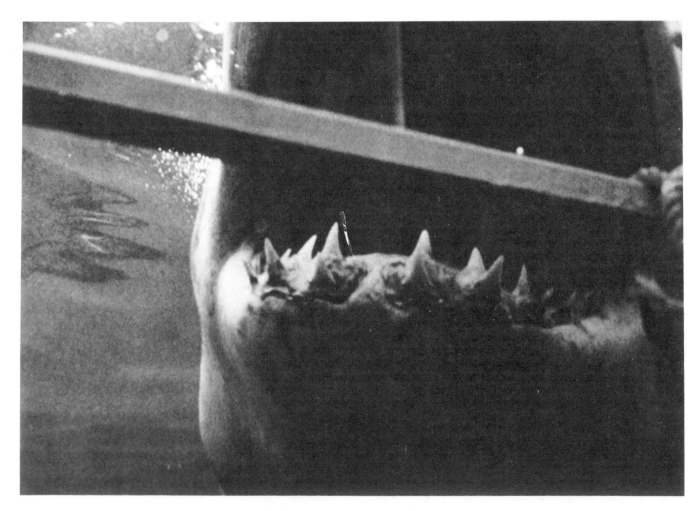

Few have looked into the open jaws of a great white shark and lived to tell about it. ■ (From *Hunting the Killer Shark* by Otto Penzler.)

OTTO PENZLER

Ball, editor, *The Mystery Story,* Publisher's Inc./University of California Press, 1976; (contributor) Matthew J. Bruccoli and C. E. Frazer Clark, Jr., editors, *Pages: The World of Books, Writers, and Writing,* Volume I, Gale, 1976; (contributor) Dilys Winn, editor, *Murder Ink,* Workman Publishing, 1977; *The Private Lives of Private Eyes, Spies, Crimefighters, and Other Good Guys,* Grosset, 1977; (editor) *The Great Detectives,* Little, Brown, 1978; (author of introduction) Christianna Brand, *Green for Danger,* Publisher's Inc./University of California Press, 1978; (editor) S.S. Van Dine (pseudonym of Willard H. Wright), *The "Canary" Murder Case,* introduction by C. Steinbrunner, Gregg Press, 1980 (Penzler was not associated with earlier edition); (with R. T. Edwards) *Prize Meets Murder,* Pocket Books, 1984; (with Lisa Drake) *The Medical Center Murders,* Pocket Books, 1984.

Book reviewer and interviewer for *Ellery Queen's Mystery Magazine,* 1975—. Contributor to periodicals, including *People, TV Guide, The Baker Street Journal,* and *Games.* Contributing editor for *Contemporary Authors,* 1976—.

WORK IN PROGRESS: With R. T. Edwards, a third book in the "Whodunit$" series to be published by Pocket Books; "Murder Do$$iers" series, prize context books to be published by Pocket Books which feature prize money, first in the series is titled *Murder in Broad Daylight* written with Lee Sheldon.

SIDELIGHTS: "My professional life is now shrouded in mystery, but it was not always so; it used to be a sporting life. After being sports editor of *Michigan Daily,* the University of

Michigan's newspaper, I decided that a career in that field was a lot better than working for a living, so I got a job at *New York Daily News* and soon had my dream fulfilled (a compromise dream, since I had always *really* wanted to be a professional baseball player). While earning forty-two dollars a week, I started to collect rare books with a sophistication that would have dismayed a nine-year-old. I collected 'English and American literary first editions and manuscripts,' not fully appreciating the fact that one needed several millions of dollars to do it correctly. The collection reflected my reading tastes: nineteenth-century Victorian novels, English romantic poets, and the best detective fiction, which soon became my specialty. Buying books beyond my means became a habit (literally going two days without food in order to buy a book) and the collection is now universally regarded as one of the finest collections of mystery and detective fiction in private hands. This collection forms the backbone of my research library and is largely responsible for the many books and articles that I've produced which involve this type of literature.

"The affection for detective stories has a sound philosophical base (although I certainly didn't realize it in my early years)— a somewhat conservative and old-fashioned view of right and wrong, good and evil, and modes of behavior. The detective story rewards virtue and punishes sin, with the detective generally serving the God-like role of final judge.

"Mysterious Press was founded because of the belief that the standards of morality established in detective stories will always exist, despite doomsday philosophers, and that mysteries will therefore endure as well. A genuine affection for books—both for their content and as physical objects—inspired the creation of the publishing house. As president of the company, I make all decisions about a book's production and therefore publish the kind of book I would like to see others publish. The press has been successful only because of the cooperation of some of the finest writers in this honorable genre (they gave me the opportunity to publish their books) and because of the many collectors and afficionados who have supported it.

"My working time (generally a minimum of twelve hours a day, six days a week) is divided among my work in the bookshop, Mysterious Press duties, writing and editing, work for *The Armchair Detective* magazine, and helping clients of the Mysterious Literary Agency (which also specializes in mystery writers). It is fair to say that I detest work of any kind and am delighted (and fortunate) that none of the things I do can be regarded as anything other than pleasure.

"*Prize Meets Murder* and *The Medical Center Murders,* both published by Pocket Books, 1984, are the first in a series of books with the generic title: 'Whodunit$,' each of which offers a prize of $15,000 to the reader who can best solve the mystery."

FOR MORE INFORMATION SEE: New York Times, April 25, 1976; *Punch,* December 22, 1976; *Book Collectors Market,* March-June, 1977; *New York Daily News,* June 12, 1977; *Books West,* Volume 1, number 8, 1978; *New York,* May 10, 1982.

PLOTZ, Helen (Ratnoff) 1913-

PERSONAL: Born March 20, 1913, in New York, N.Y.; daughter of Hyman (a physician) and Ethel (a teacher; maiden name, Davis) Ratnoff; married Milton Plotz (a physician), September 4, 1933 (died October, 1962); children: Elizabeth (Mrs. R. J. Wagman), Paul, Sarah (Mrs. Roy L. Jacobs), John. *Education:* Vassar College, A.B., 1933. *Politics:* Democrat. *Religion:* Jewish. *Home:* 80 Westminster Rd., Brooklyn, N.Y. 11218.

CAREER: Compiler and editor of books for young people. *Awards, honors: Gladly Learn and Gladly Teach: Poems of the School Experience* was selected an Ambassador of Honor Book by English-Speaking Union Books-Across-the-Sea, 1983.

WRITINGS—Compiler, except as indicated; of interest to young people: (Editor) *Imagination's Other Place: Poems of Science and Mathematics* (illustrated by Clare Leighton), Crowell, 1955; *Untune the Sky: Poems of Dance and Music* (illustrated by C. Leighton), Crowell, 1957; Emily Dickinson, *Poems* (illustrated by Robert Kipness), Crowell, 1964; *The Earth Is the Lord's: Poems of the Spirit* (illustrated by C. Leighton), Crowell, 1965; *Poems from the German* (illustrated by Ismar David), Crowell, 1967; *The Marvelous Light: Poets and Poetry,* Crowell, 1970; Robert Louis Stevenson, *Poems* (illustrated by Charles Attebery), Crowell, 1973; Thomas Hardy, *The Pinnacled Tower: Selected Poems* (illustrated by C. Leighton), Macmillan, 1975; *As I Walked Out One Evening: A Book of Ballads,* Greenwillow, 1976; (editor) *The Gift Outright: America to Her Poets,* Greenwillow, 1977; (editor) *Life Hungers to Abound: Poems of the Family,* Greenwillow, 1978; *This Powerful Rhyme: A Book of Sonnets,* Greenwillow, 1979; *Gladly Learn and Gladly Teach: Poems of the School Experience,* Greenwillow, 1981; *Saturday's Children: Poems of Work,* Greenwillow, 1982; *Eye's Delight: Poems of Art and Architecture,* Greenwillow, 1983.

(From *Poems of Robert Louis Stevenson,* selected by Helen Plotz. Illustrated by Charles Attebery.)

Contributor of a chapter to *Children's Bookshelf,* Bantam, and of articles to magazines.

POPE, Elizabeth Marie 1917-

PERSONAL: Born May 1, 1917, in Washington, D.C.; daughter of Christopher (a banker) and Florence (Thompson) Pope. *Education:* Bryn Mawr College, A.B., 1940; Johns Hopkins University, Ph.D., 1944. *Politics:* Democrat. *Religion:* Episcopalian. *Address:* 99 Main St., Kennebunk, Me. 04043.

CAREER: Mills College, Oakland Calif., assistant professor, 1944-55, chairman of English department, 1949-64, associate professor, 1955-62, professor of English, 1962-82. *Member:* Society for Creative Anachronism. *Awards, honors: New York Herald Tribune* Spring Book Festival Award honor book, 1958, for *The Sherwood Ring;* Newbery honor book and Children's Book Showcase title, 1975, both for *The Perilous Gard.*

WRITINGS: Paradise Regained: The Tradition and the Poem, Johns Hopkins Press, 1947; *The Sherwood Ring* (novel; illustrated by Evaline Ness; ALA Notable Book), Houghton, 1958; *The Perilous Gard* (novel; illustrated by Richard Cuffari; ALA Notable Book; *Horn Book* honor list), Houghton, 1974. Contributor of articles to periodicals, including *Shakespeare Survey* and *Shakespeare Quarterly.*

"... **Call to him to grip hold of the cloak and keep quiet .... Tell me when you're ready to pull ...."** ■ (From *The Perilous Gard* by Elizabeth Marie Pope. Illustrated by Richard Cuffari.)

SIDELIGHTS: "All my books are written for particular people—one for my sister, when she was sixteen; another for her daughter when she was seventeen; and one, which is now in the works, will be for *her* daughter, who is now in high school. All of my books are connected in some way with history, magic, love, and intelligence—the four subjects which interest me most, especially the last one. Every novel I write is in its own way really a celebration of the power of intelligence, which may sound stuffy, but isn't (I hope) when one reads it."

PRESBERG, Miriam Goldstein   1919-1978 (Miriam Gilbert)

BRIEF ENTRY: Born December 1, 1919, in New York, N.Y.; died June 13, 1978. Literary agent and author. Presberg graduated in 1940 from Hunter College (now Hunter College of the City University of New York). For the following six years she worked at various publishing companies located in New York City, including Didier Publishing, Arco Publishing, and Island Press. In 1946 she became director of the Authors' and Publishers' Service, a position she held until her death in 1978. Presberg wrote numerous books for children under the name Miriam Gilbert, including biographies such as *Eli Whitney: Master Craftsman* (Abingdon, 1956), *Jane Addams: World Neighbor* (Abingdon, 1960), *Money and Mud: The Life of John D. Rockefeller* (American Southern Publishing, 1964), and *Shy Girl: The Story of Eleanor Roosevelt, First Lady of the World* (Doubleday, 1965). She also produced books on hobbies, among them *Starting a Terrarium, Starting an Aquarium,* and *Starting a Rock and Mineral Collection.* A contributor of short stories and articles to children's magazines as well as an author for newspaper syndicates, Presberg was the recipient of the Brotherhood award in 1962 for best magazine fiction of the year from the National Conference of Christians and Jews. *Residence:* Flushing, N.Y. *For More Information See: Contemporary Authors, New Revision Series,* Volume 3, Gale, 1981. *Obituaries: Publishers Weekly,* July 10, 1978.

When I am dead, I hope it may be said:
"His sins were scarlet, but his books were read."
—Hilaire Belloc
(From *On His Books*)

PRICE, Willard 1887-

BRIEF ENTRY: Born July 28, 1887, in Peterborough, Ontario, Canada; came to the United States, 1901. Explorer, naturalist, and author. Price received his B.A. from Western Reserve University in 1909 and his M.A. from Columbia University in 1914; he also studied at the New York School of Philanthropy and New York University. Throughout his career, he worked as editor of various magazines as well as foreign correspondent for both American and British publications. From 1920 to 1967 he directed numerous expeditions for the National Geographic Society and American Museum of Natural History, traveling to over 140 countries worldwide. Price chronicled his experiences and discoveries in more than twenty books, including *Ancient People at New Tasks, The Negro around the World, Children of the Rising Sun, Roaming Britain, Incredible Africa,* and *My Own Life of Adventure: Travels in 148 Lands.* For children, he has written a series of fourteen adventure stories featuring two teenage brothers who aid their zoologist father on expeditions. The books are filled with action and intrigue, accompanied with enormous amounts of factual information garnered by Price while on his own extensive travels. All published by John Day, the titles include: *Amazon Adventure* (1949), *South Sea Adventure* (1954), *African Adventure* (1963), *Cannibal Adventure* (1970), and *Arctic Adventure* (1980). *Home:* 814-N, Via Alhambra, Laguna Hills, Calif. 92635. *For More Information See: Contemporary Authors, New Revision Series,* Volume 1, Gale, 1981; *Twentieth-Century Children's Writers,* 2nd edition, St. Martin's, 1983.

RASKIN, Ellen 1928-1984

PERSONAL: Born March 13, 1928, in Milwaukee, Wis.; died August 8, 1984 of complications from connective-tissue dis-

ELLEN RASKIN

ease; daughter of Sol and Margaret (Goldfisch) Raskin; married husband, Dennis Flanagan (editor of *Scientific American),* August 1, 1960; children: (first marriage) Susan Metcalf. *Education:* University of Wisconsin, student, 1945-49. *Home:* New York, N.Y.

CAREER: Commercial illustrator and designer, New York, N.Y., beginning 1950; author and illustrator of children's books, beginning 1966. Instructor in illustration at Pratt Institute, 1963, Syracuse University, 1976; guest lecturer at University of Berkeley, 1969, 1972, and 1977. *Exhibitions*—Group shows: American Institute of Graphic Arts, 50 Years of Graphic Arts in America show, 1966; Biennale of Illustrations, Bratislava, Czechoslovakia, 1969; Biennale of Applied Graphic Art, Brno, Czechoslovakia, 1972; Contemporary American Illustrators of Children's Books, 1974-75. *Member:* American Institute of Graphic Arts, Asia Society, Authors Guild. *Awards, honors:* Distinctive Merit Award, 1958, Silver Medal, 1959, both from Art Directors Clubs; *New York Herald Tribune* Spring Book Festival Award (best picture book), 1966, for *Nothing Ever Happens on My Block; Songs of Innocence* was included in American Institute of Graphic Arts exhibit of 50 best books of the year, 1966; *Spectacles* was named one of the best illustrated children's books by *New York Times Book Review,* 1968; Children's Book Council chose *The Mysterious Disappearance of Leon (I Mean Noel),* 1972, *Who, Said Sue, Said Whoo?,* 1974, and *Figgs and Phantoms,* 1975, for the Children's Book Showcase; *Boston Globe-Horn Book* Honor, 1973, for *Who, Said Sue, Said Whoo?; Figgs and Phantoms* was chosen for the American Institute of Graphic Arts Children's Book Show, 1973-74 and as Newbery honor book, 1975; Mystery Writers of America Special Award, 1975, for *The Tattooed Potato and Other Clues; Boston Globe-Horn Book* Best Fiction Award, 1978 and Newbery Medal, 1979, both for *The Westing Game.*

WRITINGS—All self-illustrated: *Nothing Ever Happens on My Block* (ALA Notable Book), Atheneum, 1966; (set William Blake's poems to music for voice and piano, and designed and illustrated book) *Songs of Innocence,* two volumes, Doubleday, 1966; *Silly Songs and Sad,* Crowell, 1967; *Spectacles* (ALA Notable Book), Atheneum, 1968; *Ghost in a Four-Room Apartment* (Junior Literary Guild selection), Atheneum, 1969; *And It Rained* (ALA Notable Book), Atheneum, 1969; (adapter) Christina Rosetti, *Goblin Market,* Dutton, 1970; *A & THE; or, William T. C. Baumgarten Comes to Town,* Atheneum, 1970; *The World's Greatest Freak Show,* Atheneum, 1971; *The Mysterious Disappearance of Leon (I Mean Noel)* (Junior Literary Guild selection; ALA Notable Book), Dutton, 1972; *Franklin Stein* (ALA Notable Book), Atheneum, 1972; *Moe Q. McGlutch, He Smokes Too Much,* Parents Magazine Press, 1973; *Who, Said Sue, Said Whoo?* (ALA Notable Book), Atheneum, 1973; *Moose, Goose and Little Nobody* (ALA Notable Book), Parents Magazine Press, 1974; *Figgs and Phantoms* (ALA Notable Book), Dutton, 1974; *The Tattooed Potato and Other Clues* (ALA Notable Book), Dutton, 1975; *Twenty-two, Twenty-three,* Atheneum, 1976; *The Westing Game,* Dutton, 1978.

Illustrator: Claire H. Bishop, editor, *Happy Christmas: Tales for Boys and Girls,* Frederick Ungar, 1956; Dylan Thomas, *A Child's Christmas in Wales,* New Directions, 1959; Ruth Krauss, *Mama I Wish I Was Snow, Child You'd Be Very Cold,* Atheneum, 1962; Edgar Allan Poe, *Poems of Edgar Allan Poe,* edited by Dwight Macdonald, Crowell, 1965; Aileen Fisher and Olive Rabe, *We Dickensons,* Atheneum, 1965; Louis Untermeyer, editor, *Paths of Poetry: Twenty-five Poets and Their Poems,* Delacorte, 1966; Molly Cone, *The Jewish Sabbath,* Crowell, 1966; Arthur G. Razzell and K. G. Watts, *Proba-*

**Mother Mouse hugged
and kissed Little Mouse.
Moose and Goose
put the roof
on the house.**

■ (From *Moose, Goose and Little Nobody* by Ellen Raskin. Illustrated by the author.)

bility, Doubleday, 1967; Robert Herrick, *Poems of Robert Herrick,* edited by Winfield T. Scott, Crowell, 1967; D. H. Lawrence, *D. H. Lawrence: Poems Selected for Young People,* edited by William Cole, Viking, 1967; Vera Cleaver and Bill Cleaver, *Ellen Grae,* Lippincott, 1967; A. G. Razzell and K. G. Watts, *This Is Four: The Idea of a Number,* Doubleday, 1967; V. Cleaver and B. Cleaver, *Lady Ellen Grae,* Lippincott, 1968; Nancy Larrick, editor, *Piping Down the Valleys Wild: Poetry for the Young of All Ages,* Delacorte, 1968; A. Fisher and O. Rabe, *We Alcotts,* Atheneum, 1968; A. G. Razzell and K. G. Watts, *Symmetry,* Doubleday, 1968; Susan Bartlett, *Books: A Book to Begin On,* Holt, 1968; Suzanne Stark Morrow, *Inatuk's Friend* (Junior Literary Guild selection), Atlantic-Little, Brown, 1968; Renee K. Weiss, editor, *A Paper Zoo: A Collection of Animal Poems by Modern American Poets,* Macmillan, 1968; Rebecca Caudill, *Come Along!,* Holt, 1969; A. G. Razzell and K. G. Watts, *Circles and Curves,* Doubleday, 1969; Sara Brewton and John E. Brewton, editors, *Shrieks at Midnight: Macabre Poems, Eerie and Humorous,* Crowell, 1969; A. G. Razzell and K. G. Watts, *Three and the Shape of Three,* Doubleday, 1969; Alan Gardner, *Elidor,* Walck, 1970.

WORK IN PROGRESS: "I am working on a new book, which is too long now, as usual. I have about 250 pages, which have to be cut down, and so many characters! Perhaps I have developed them too much, but I love my characters. It is sort of a combined *Tattooed Potato* and *Westing Game,* but that's just a way to describe it. It's really completely different. I mean, I'd never steal from those two."

SIDELIGHTS: **March 13, 1928.** Born in Milwaukee, Wisconsin. "I cannot identify all the characters in my books; perhaps I haven't looked hard enough, but my parents are there. My mother came from the era of the flapper. She was sixteen years old when I was born. . . . My father . . . was a pharmacist, a gambler, a dreamer, who even after the Depression managed to go broke.

" . . . Those were hard times, the Depression years; they made me a humorist. Just about anything is funny after that. To a child the Depression was bad enough; even more painful was having to watch that dumb Shirley Temple. Try as I might, I could not convince any adult that Shirley Temple was a midget. Squirming, sinking lower and lower into my seat as she showed

(From *Twenty-two, Twenty-three* by Ellen Raskin. Illustrated by the author.)

off her dimpled talents in movies which should have been X-rated, I learned that the cute, the sweet, the sentimental was for grownups only. Now any goody-goody darling that dares enter my books will end up the villain. Or the bomber. Or at least get pimples." [Ellen Raskin, "Characters and Other Clues," *Horn Book,* December, 1978.[1]]

"Growing up in the Depression also made me very aware of money, so I've always worked very hard."

Raskin's immediate family consisted of her parents and sister, but her extended family of cousins, aunts and uncles often visited, and were a substantial influence during her childhood. "As far back as I can remember, I invented characters. My sister and I would spend weeks at a time acting out the lives of at least ten characters each. We were the Pie family: I was Peachy Pie, and my sister was Porky Pie, among others. We were the Baum family: I was Pinky Baum, and my sister was Stink Baum. Needless to say, I am the older sister.

"I was also surrounded by real people, lots of them. My mother, the second youngest of nine children, presented me with sixteen first cousins when I was born, nine more to follow—not to mention aunts and uncles, second cousins, and second cousins once removed. At least fifty close relatives showed up at the annual family picnic held up or down the Lake Michigan shore. At least thirty gathered for holiday feasts. And every Saturday night twenty or more got together at Aunt Annie's for poker. The kids were not allowed in the game, so my sister—whose real name is Lila Ruth—my cousin Sonny Boy, and I provided the entertainment that followed cake and coffee. Sonny Boy wasn't as smart as my sister, so I confined the dramas to three characters each.

"Of the six children born to Bessie and Albert Raskin, my father alone survived. I never knew my father's father. In a tattered photograph a sad-eyed young man in a leather apron poses in his shoe-repair shop. I was told three things about Albert Raskin: He died long ago, I was named after him, and he was a Wobbly. A Wobbly? It's no wonder I play with words. For years I thought I was named after a man who died in a drunken stupor. Only later did I learn that a Wobbly was a member of the IWW—Industrial Workers of the World—and that my very sober grandfather was a militant socialist, murdered at the age of thirty-four.

"The grandfather I knew and loved was my father's stepfather, Grandpa Hersh, a short and pudgy man, who wore garters on his arms to hike up his too-long shirt sleeves. Sam Hersh, an immigrant from Russia, became a wealthy builder in Milwaukee. A marriage was arranged with my grandmother after his first wife died and his children were grown. Grandpa Hersh was a quiet man, a kind and patient man, who never made fun of me when I stumbled over words reading one of my favorite fairy tales to him. He was a religious man—an Orthodox Jew—a charitable man, who in the depths of the Depression walked from door to door of the houses he had built and turned over to the jobless tenants their mortgages marked 'Paid in Full.' When he died of cancer several years later, all that remained of his wealth was the house on the elm-shaded boulevard. Grandpa Hersh, of course, is Uncle Florence in *Figgs & Phantoms* (Dutton). But in or out of a role, Grandpa Hersh is there, adding his goodness to my humor when it becomes too brittle, rounding my characters with love."[1]

Raskin showed an early interest in music, playing the piano in her parents' living room. She played conscientiously and with

That's all the people of Pineapple did these days was laugh and gossip about Figgs . . . . The funny Figgs. The poor, funny, freaky Figgs. ■ (From *Figgs and Phantoms* by Ellen Raskin. Illustrated by the author.)

skill until the piano was repossessed by the finance company. Years later she played the harpsichord.

Two other interests during Raskin's early years were reading books and drawing. "My mother told me recently that I was reading the *Daily Forward* when I was two years old. That's more than I can do now. Grandpa Hersh taught me to read Yiddish, and mother taught me to read English. I went to the library often. No one recommended books to me, so I started with 'A' and worked my way through the alphabet. Walking home with new books was one of the greatest feelings, especially in the fall with the leaves. . . .

"I was never aware of author's names. And I never looked at the illustrations. To visualize the story in my own mind, I'd cover all of the illustrations in books. The picture in my head was more important. That's very strange for an illustrator.

"We moved a great deal when I was a child. I was a loner. I was Jewish in a non-Jewish community so I wasn't invited to other kid's houses. I was a mopey dreamer."

"I had straight dark hair, tap-danced with two left feet, and had a singing range of three wrong notes. I spilled ink on my best dress, lost my piano to the finance company, and developed a disgusting nose problem. 'Get your nose out of that book, Ellen,' my mother would say six dozen times a day. 'Go out and play.' Sticking one's nose in a book seemed even more shameful then sucking one's thumb, if not downright obscene; but I kept on reading. Books were my escape; books were my friends. Besides, how could I go out and play when no one wanted to play with me? I was a failure at hopscotch ('You stepped on the line!' 'What line?'); I was a klutz at catch ('You didn't even try for the ball!' 'What ball?'). Books were the only things I could relate to because books were the only things I could see.

"Then I got my first pair of spectacles. And then, awed by the miraculous revelation of details, I began to draw.'"[1]

"I used to drive my mother crazy. I'd say, 'What should I draw now?' And she'd say, 'An apple.' But I'm nearsighted, so I had to draw very close up."

1945. Attended the University of Wisconsin. "I studied journalism at the University of Wisconsin, then switched to fine arts in my second year. Everything about journalism seemed too easy.

"I had never really thought much about art as a career, or art itself for that matter, although I was good in art classes during high school. There wasn't much in the museums in Milwaukee then.

"During the summer of my freshman year at the University, I visited the Chicago Art Institute. This was 1946, and the Institute had an expressionist exhibit. It was just after the war, when abstract art was a big blossoming new art form. When I saw the exhibit, I knew I had to paint. I had been doing some sculpture, but seeing the expressionists brought it all together for me. I don't remember any specific painting. All I remember is the color.

"I was always a top student, but I never thought up original ideas during the course of my education. When we wrote themes, the teachers gave us a choice of five things to write about. I never knew I could make up my own plot! But I don't think it was a bad style of teaching. It was good because it gave me the tools for writing. I think it is difficult to channel creativity without the tools."

1949. "After finishing school, I moved to New York and realized I had to make a living. I took a crummy job with an advertising agency (three people small) to learn paste-ups. I bought a small printing press and experimented with type. Putting together a sample book of things I'd printed, I began free-lancing. I was successful from the first day."

Raskin drew more than 5,000 illustrations, and designed over 1,000 book jackets, many of which were award-winners.

1966. Began writing children's books. "I cancelled all my assignments for six months, and decided to design a book, but ended up doing two. I had told the art director at Doubleday that I was writing music to William Blake's *Songs of Innocence*, and he suggested that I illustrate it as well. In this book I reverted to my original style of woodcuts. At the same time, I had submitted *Nothing Ever Happens on My Block*. It was only twenty pages long. I kept thinking 'Why am I doing this dumb cartoon thing in *Nothing Ever Happens on My Block?*'

Moral: Words aren't everything.

■ (From *Who, Said Sue, Said Whoo?* by Ellen Raskin. Illustrated by the author.)

Mother couldn't decide between frames that made me look adorable and frames that made me look intelligent. ■ (From *Spectacles* by Ellen Raskin. Illustrated by the author.)

and 'Gee, *Songs of Innocence* is really going to be a beautiful book.' Both books were accepted for publication in the same week. All of my energies had gone into *Songs of Innocence,* which went out of print very quickly, and *Nothing Ever Happens on My Block* is still doing well.''

''Years passed. 'Why don't you write a book for older children?' Ann Durell, editor at E. P. Dutton, suggested. 'Write about your childhood in Milwaukee during the Depression.' What? After a long career as a free-lance artist, having made hundreds of magazine and advertising illustrations, over one thousand book jackets, and twelve picture books, I considered myself an illustrator. 'But I'm an illustrator,' I replied, sure of my facts. On the other hand. . . .

''I began my story with snow on the ground and not enough food for Thanksgiving dinner. Just tomatoes and potatoes. Something about tomatoes and potatoes must have seemed funny at the time, for suddenly my plot kinked and out came *The Mysterious Disappearance of Leon (I Mean Noel),* which has nothing to do with my childhood or Milwaukee or the Depression. Or does it?

''I write where my imagination takes me, I think; but on re-reading the first draft of a manuscript I realize it was memory,

not invention, that built the characters that shaped the plot that complicated my once-simple story. 'Hi, there,' I say to those folks I've known; then I rewrite to clarify and rewrite to polish and rewrite because it's still not right. And rewrite some more.''[1]

1975. *Figgs and Phantoms* was named a Newbery honor book. ''It's a favorite of mine. I've never put more into a book— my whole life and dreams. I told my editor that I would stop writing long novels if *Figgs and Phantoms* did not place as a runner-up for the Newbery medal. Somehow I knew the book had a message.

''In their letters to me, kids usually tell me 'This is the first book I've read all the way through.' I know I reached a certain group of readers. I reached the outsiders, the shy kids who had been held back by something. I got who I wanted; the kids who were just like me.''

1979. *The Westing Game* won the Newbery Medal for the most distinguished contribution to literature for children. In her acceptance speech, Raskin outlined the process she used to create the book. ''. . . I sat down at the typewriter with no wish of an idea, just the urge to write another children's book. It will have a story. It will have a character with whom my readers can relate. And, because of who I am and was, and out of my

My name is Chester Filbert.

(From *Nothing Ever Happens on My Block* by Ellen Raskin. Illustrated by the author.)

compassion for the hurts and hazards of childhood, it will have a happy ending. But what shall I write about?

"It is 1976, the Bicentennial year. My story will have a historical background; its locale, the place I know best: Milwaukee. I now have my first character: Lake Michigan.

"Recalling that Amy Kellman's daughter asked for a puzzle-mystery, I decide that the format of my historical treatise will be a puzzle-mystery (whatever that is). I type out the words of 'America the Beautiful' and cut them apart.

"Meanwhile on television, between re-created Revolutionary battles blasting and fireworks booming, come reports of the death of an infamous millionaire. Anyone who can spell *Howard Hughes* is forging a will. Good, I'll try it, too.

"Now I have Lake Michigan, a jumbled 'America the Beautiful,' the first draft of a very strange will, and a dead millionaire—a fine beginning for a puzzle-mystery, but where is the historical background? Wisconsin abounds in labor history; therefore, my millionaire will be an industrialist, murdered because—let me see, because he was a notorious strikebreaker. Old man Kohler! I shift the scene sixty miles north to my father's hometown, Sheboygan, which borders on the Kohler company, factory, and town. I cannot use the name Sheboygan (my readers will think I'm trying to be funny), and I certainly cannot use the name Kohler (they're still making toilets up there). Instead I raise the shore of Lake Michigan, and my industrialist, named Samuel W. Westing, will die in his mansion on the cliff called the Westing house.

"Now I need heirs, lots of them. Since my books collect characters, invited or not, I plan for a goodly number at the start. Sixteen seems a goodly number, almost too good; I will pair them: eight pairs of heirs. Imperfect heirs. My characters will be imperfect, each handicapped by some physical, emotional, or moral defect. Defects which will make them easier to remember, imperfect because aren't we all?

"And in honor of the Bicentennial, they will be melting-pot characters: Polish, Jewish, German, Greek, Chinese, Black.

With the blind arrogance of the possessed, I devise sixteen imperfect ethnics. Ordinary folk: dressmaker, judge, cook, podiatrist, maid, inventor, secretary, student—this is getting boring—a reluctant bride-to-be, a bird watcher in a wheelchair, a thirteen-year-old girl who plays the stock market—still boring—a bookie, a burglar, a bomber—that's better. And the murderer will limp. Out of respect for plodding, rereading readers who never miss a clue, if the murderer limps, I must make most of my characters, at one time or another, limp.

"I am off and typing. I still do not know who is the bookie, who is the bomber, who killed Sam Westing, or why everyone is gimping around, but no matter. The characters will shape the action; the action will shape the characters. My characters will show me the way. And so they do.

"'Grownups are so obvious,' Turtle says in my book. That may be, but I am quick to scoff at other's faults before they scoff at mine. With time I tolerate the imperfections of the stranger; with acquaintance I begin to understand; with caring the faults fall away, and I perceive, in rare times touch, the true being of a friend. So, too, when I write. Those characters, whom I myself create and name, begin as strangers. Slowly, slowly, they take shape and grow and cast shadows on one another and on me. I learn to like them, to love them. Although I rewrite my story many times, I try not to alter this fragile metamorphosis. I would like my readers to share the joy of watching those ridiculous strangers become good friends.

"Unfortunately, I end up loving all of my characters. None of them could possibly be a murderer. And mean old Sam Westing isn't so mean after all, once you get to know him. I cannot let him die. Now I really have a problem: How can there be a will if nobody died?

"It is rewrite time. The plot thickens and thickens but refuses to jell, and I refuse to give up; two hundred million dollars is at stake, and I want to win. Knitting and unraveling, knotting and unknotting, I rewrite the manuscript again. And again. At last (hallelujah at last!) I find the answer to the question I forgot to ask. The plot comes full circle; all points of the compass are touched; the game is won. My book is done.

"Sam Westing, the rascal, almost outwitted me with not one, but four disguises. I almost outwitted myself; my tribute to American labor history ended up a comedy in praise of capitalism. In the larger sense, however, it did turn out to be exactly what I wanted it to be—a children's book." [Ellen Raskin, "Newbery Award Acceptance Speech," *Horn Book,* August, 1979.[2]]

"I saved every piece of paper from all my drafts of *The Westing Game* and donated them to the University of Wisconsin at Madison Children's Cooperative Book Center. I also donated the pictures I used from the swipe file I keep. A swipe file is something an illustrator uses which contains pictures of faces, animals—everything. When I sit down to write a book, I go to my swipe file and look up 'People'; there I find pictures of people sitting, standing, walking. . . . I look until I find a face—just an ordinary face, but it means something to me. I find my characters in these faces. What I draw for the book is something different. The swipe file is just a beginning."

As an author-illustrator, Raskin approaches a book as a total venture. Often a book will take two years to complete. "Most of the action in my books develops through the writing. I used to think most of the humor was layered in later—but when I looked back to the first draft, the humor was there. Face to face at a party, I'm not a very funny person, but in a manuscript the humor is in the first draft.

"I don't read mysteries. I like reading true crime, and I have a true crime section on my bookshelves. But I do think kids like mystery, and it certainly keeps the plot moving. I could spend all my time developing characters—but keeping the readers attention is more important to me.

"I write at the typewriter, and I usually write everything over and over again. If I have to fill in a section, sometimes I'll write in longhand, but that is just a way to clear up my head and proceed toward what I want to do.

"*I saw a spooky witch out riding on her broom.*"

(From *Piping Down the Valleys Wild*, edited by Nancy Larrick. Illustrated by Ellen Raskin.)

It wasn't the explosion that frightened Mrs. Carillon; it was Miss Anna Oglethorpe screaming, "Armageddon!" ■ (From *The Mysterious Disappearance of Leon (I Mean Noel)* by Ellen Raskin. Illustrated by the author.)

"I write up to about half-way on a first draft, then I know who my characters are and what is going to happen. I never outline. I go through about two or three drafts, but I never allow myself to write the ending until the rest of the manuscript is finished, because that's my prize. I know what's going to happen, but I wait because I know it is going to be happy.

"It usually takes me about two years to finish a book. The first draft doesn't take long. It's the re-writing that's hard. I have so many pieces, gluing them together takes a long time. Most writers hate the initial writing, and love to polish. I hate polishing."

"To me, writing for a reading child does *not* mean preaching or teaching (I leave that to the more qualified). It does *not* mean prescriptive formula (if I had the need for formulas I would write for adults). It does *not* mean catering to arbitrary reading levels or age groups; my readers have one thing in common: They are young enough or curious enough to read slowly, and the slower the better for my books.

"The one literary concession I do make, one that forces me to eliminate words here and add sentences there, is to the look of the book. I write and design my book to look accessible to the young reader; it will have less than two hundred pages, and there will be no endless seas of gray type. I plan for margins wide enough for the hands to hold, typographic variations for the eyes to rest, decorative breaks for the mind to breathe. I want my children's book to look like a wonderful place to be."[2]

Raskin prefers writing the book to illustrating. "My illustration is mostly a vehicle for getting the message in my books across. Actually, I hate illustration. But picture books are not like classic illustration of stories. In picture books, the story is *in* the pictures.

"It's difficult to finish a book. It's hard to get rid of all of the characters. It took so long to get rid of all the characters in *The Westing Game*. There were so many voices, and I was so involved. I built up this whole world, and everything that was going to happen. Then it did, and I was in another life. It was like a mourning period.

"My favorite illustrations are those by Velazquez and Rivera. As my husband Dennis says, I have my heroes. . . . I think the greatest benefit of all of my work has been to appreciate the great works. The harder you work, the more you realize that some things are heavenly. They did it with the help of the angels."

Besides enjoying financial success as an author and an illustrator, Raskin has also been successful as a stock-market operator. Her office in her Greenwich Village house contains tools of the trade: electronic machines, charts, and ledgers. "For pleasure I used to play the piano, but that is difficult for me now, so instead, I play the stock market which I've been doing for the last ten years, ever since I bought the house [on Long Island]. I had two balloon mortgages on the house and I thought 'Gee, maybe if I learn something about the stock market I could take a little money and pay off the debt.' We're

paying off the mortgage this year. I became very good at it. I've been offered jobs as an analyst, and my agent wants me to write a book about my charting techniques. But I won't because I know if I did I would lose interest. If I share it, the mystery would unravel. That is why I can't write sequels to my books. I think my success in the market has something to do with being an illustrator. I read charts as an illustrator, it's my illustrator's brain. No one ever taught me how to play the market. I just read and read and read. You can teach yourself anything—it's all in books. That's the great thing about libraries."

Her advice to would-be authors is to keep practicing. "Most kids think they have to have an idea, a plot, before they start, but that's not true. They should begin with a few characters, a place, and let them meet and start talking. It's amazing how characters work themselves out once you free yourself up. Writing doesn't have to be perfect. You don't even have to write in sentences. I don't write complete sentences many times—I just can't think that fast. It's more important to think and get things down than to worry about grammar. Then, you must be able to decide when it is finished. For myself, it's a matter of deadlines, I know when the manuscript has to be handed in. Deadlines are important for me, otherwise, you can work on the same book for the rest of your life! At some point, you have to say 'I'm done.'

"It's also very important for young people who want to write to read. I read so many books when I was designing book jackets, and many of them were, not really bad books, but first novels that missed. I really developed a sense of what *not* to do. I learned to see what was wrong, and that was almost a better lesson than learning what was working in good books.

"Writing is really a process of change—constant change—and so it is important to learn to be your own critic, to learn to see what fits and what doesn't fit. I don't learn from myself,

People were dressed in rags; but Alastair Pflug pawned his grandfather's false teeth to buy himself a velvet cape and traded his grandmother's gold-rimmed spectacles for a pair of patent leather boots. ■ (From *The World's Greatest Freak Show* by Ellen Raskin. Illustrated by the author.)

(From *Lady Ellen Grae* by Vera and Bill Cleaver. Illustrated by Ellen Raskin.)

because I don't try to follow up on the same feeling in each book. Each book must be different. So I learn from reading.''

August 8, 1984. Died at the age of fifty-six of complications from connective-tissue disease at St. Vincent's Hospital in New York City.

HOBBIES AND OTHER INTERESTS: Playing piano and harpsichord, book collecting, gardening, traveling, visiting zoos and art museums.

FOR MORE INFORMATION SEE: Lee Kingman and others, compilers, *Illustrators of Children's Books: 1957-1966,* Horn Book, 1968; Lee Bennett Hopkins, *Books Are By People,* Citation Press, 1969; *Horn Book,* October, 1970, April, 1971, December, 1978, August, 1979; *Publishers Weekly,* July 28, 1975; *Children's Literature Review,* Volume 1, Gale, 1976; *New York Times,* January 12, 1979. *Obituaries: Publishers Weekly,* August 31, 1984; *School Library Journal,* September, 1984.

A wise system of education will at least teach us how little man yet knows, how much he has still to learn.
—Sir John Lubbock

RESNICK, Michael D(iamond)   1942-
(Mike Resnick)

PERSONAL: Born March 5, 1942, in Chicago, Ill.; son of William (a writer) and Gertrude (a writer; maiden name, Diamond) Resnick; married Carol Cain (a kennel owner), October 2, 1961; children: Laura. *Education:* Attended University of Chicago, 1959-61, and Roosevelt University, 1962-63. *Politics:* "Unaffiliated moderate." *Religion:* Atheist. *Residence:* Cincinnati, Ohio. *Agent:* Eleanor Wood, Spectrum Literary Agency, 432 Park Ave. S., Suite 1205, New York, N.Y. 10016.

CAREER: Santa Fe Railroad, Chicago, Ill., file clerk, 1962-65; *National Tattler,* Chicago, editor, 1965-66; *National Insider,* Chicago, editor, 1966-69; Oligarch Publishing Co., Chicago, editor and publisher, 1969; free-lance writer, 1969—. *Member:* Science Fiction Writers of America, Mystery Writers of America. *Awards, honors:* Best short fiction award from the American Dog Writers Association, 1978, for "The Last Dog," and 1979, for "Blue."

WRITINGS: The Goddess of Ganymede (novel), Grant, 1967; *Pursuit on Ganymede* (novel), Paperback Library, 1968; *Redbeard* (novel), Lancer, 1969.

The balance beam is just what its name implies: a single beam upon which the gymnast balances and performs various exercises. ■ (From *Gymnastics and You* by Michael Resnick. Photograph by Maureen Fennelli.)

MICHAEL D. RESNICK

Under name Mike Resnick: *Official Guide to the Fantastics,* House of Collectibles, 1976; *Official Guide to Comic Books and Big Little Books,* House of Collectibles, 1977; *Gymnastics and You: The Whole Story of the Sport,* Rand McNally, 1978; *Official Guide to Comic and Science Fiction Books,* House of Collectibles, 1979; (with Glenn A. Larson) *Battlestar Galactica Number Five: Galactica Discovers Earth,* Berkley, 1980; *The Soul Eater,* Signet, 1981; *Birthright: The Book of Man,* Signet, 1982; *Walpurgis III,* Signet, 1982; *The Branch,* Signet, 1984; *Unauthorized Autobiographies and Other Curiosities,* Misfit Press, 1984; *Adventures,* Signet, 1986.

"Tales of the Galactic Midway" series; published by Signet: *Sideshow,* 1982; *The Three-Legged Hootch Dancer,* 1983; *The Wild Alien Tamer,* 1983; *The Best Rootin' Tootin' Shootin' Gunslinger in the Whole Damned Galaxy,* 1983.

"Tales of the Velvet Comet" series; published by Phantasia: *Eros Ascending,* 1984; *Eros at Zenith,* 1984; *Eros Descending,* 1984; *Eros at Nadir,* 1985.

WORK IN PROGRESS: Dog in the Manger, a mystery; *Yes, We Have No Nirvanas,* a fantasy novel; *The Body Hunter,* a science fiction novel; *Exploits* and *Intrigues* (both sequels to *Adventures);* a collaborative trilogy with Barry N. Malzburg.

SIDELIGHTS: "For a dozen years, from 1964 until 1976, I was—I freely admit it—a pseudonymous hack writer. I was the *penultimate* pseudonymous hack writer. I wrote every word of seven monthly newspapers—that's about 175,000 words a month—in addition to the never-ending stream of more than two hundred junk books. Finally, the stream did end. (Looking back now, I truly don't know where I found the energy, or why I didn't die of exhaustion a couple of years into it.)

"In late 1976 I took my ill-gotten literary gains (and they were munificent), and invested them in the largest and most luxurious boarding and grooming kennel then extant. I stopped writing almost completely for about four years while turning the business around, and then, totally secure financially for the rest of my life, I returned to my typewriter, albeit at a far

slower pace, to see what I could do now that my writing didn't have to put bread on the table.

"All those books which have appeared since mid-1981 have been written during this period, and it is on these that I would like to be judged. I am still getting used to the luxury of rewriting and polishing, of not having to churn out fifty pages a day, of occasionally not completing even one page in a day. I feel guilty about it—old habits die hard—but I suspect my books are about 3000 percent better for it, and for their author being completely free from the demands of the marketplace.

"Most of my recent output has been labelled science fiction, though I sometimes wonder if 'moral parable' isn't a more proper category. I am not concerned with aliens (I have never met one), telepaths (ditto), invading extra-terrestrial armadas (still ditto). I am concerned, to borrow from Mr. Faulkner, with the human heart in conflict with itself—and far from proving a hindrance to such a quest, science fiction, with all of time and space to draw from, seems especially fitting for it."

FOR MORE INFORMATION SEE: Los Angeles Times Book Review, April 11, 1982, July 18, 1982; *Cincinnati,* September, 1982.

RUBIN, Eva Johanna   1925-

PERSONAL: Born in 1925, in Berlin, Germany; married Rainer König (an architect). *Education:* Attended Hochschule fur bildende Kunste (now Hochschule der Kunste Berlin), Berlin, Germany, 1946-51.

CAREER: Illustrator, author, and book designer. *Awards, honors: Three by Three* was named one of the fifty most beautiful books published in Germany, 1963; the International Youth Library in Munich selected *Der böse Bär* as one of the best books published in Germany, 1964; first prize from Berliner Porzellanmanufaktur, 1964; recipient of medals from Internationale Buckunstausstellung, 1965.

WRITINGS—All for children: *Himpelchen und Pimpelchen,* Kinderbuchverlag, 1964; (with James Krüss) *Der Trommler und die Puppe* (self-illustrated), Betz, 1966, translation by Jack Prelutsky published as *The Proud Wooden Drummer,* Doubleday, 1969; *Drei Reiter zu Pferd* (self-illustrated; title means "Three Riders on Horse"), G. Stalling (Oldenburg, Germany), 1967; *Ein kleiner Herr aus Askalon* (self-illustrated; title means "A Little Man from Askalon"), Betz (Munich, Germany), 1968; (with Walter Krumbach) *Kikeriki wacht auf!* (title means "Cock-a-doodle-doo Wake Up"), Kinderbuchverlag (Berlin), 1968; *Drei kleine Mädchen* (title means "Three Little Girls"), Parabel Verlag (Munich), c.1970. Also author of *Mausekleine Geschichte* (title means "The Little Mouse Story").

Illustrator; all for children: James Krüss, *Drei mal drei an einem Tag: Ein Bilderbuch für alle, die bis drei zahlen können,* Betz, 1963, translation by Geoffrey Strachan published as *Three by Three: A Picturebook for All Children Who Can Count to Three,* Macmillan, 1965; Rudolf Neumann, *Der böse Bär; oder, Die Macht der Musik,* Betz, 1964, translation by Jack Prelutzky published as *The Bad Bear,* Macmillan, 1967; Franz Fuhmann, compiler, *Das Tierschiff,* Kinderbuchverlag, 1965, 2nd edition, Loewes Verlag, 1970, translation by Strachan published as *The Animal Ship: A Collection of Animal Stories,* Methuen, 1971; *Pferdchen lauf Galopp* (title means "Gallop,

Horsey''), Kinderbuchverlag, 1967; Hans Christian Andersen, *The Tinderbox,* Methuen, 1968; Josef Guggenmos, *Ein Elefant marschiert durchs Land* (title means ''An Elephant Marches through the Land''), Paulus Verlag (Recklinghausen, Germany), 1968; *Die Prinzessin und die Schweinehirt,* Kinderbuchverlag, 1968, translation published as *The Princess and the Swineherd,* Methuen, 1971; Edith George, compiler, *Im Frühling wie im Winter* (title means ''In Spring as in Winter''), Kinderbuchverlag, 1969; Imme Geissler and Juliane Metzger, compilers, *Der goldene Schlüssel* (title means ''The Golden Key''), Betz, 1969; Prelutsky, *Three Saxon Nobles, and Other Verses,* Macmillan, 1969; E.T.A. Hoffman, *Nussknacker und Mausekönig* (title means ''Nutcracker and Mouse King''), Kinderbuchverlag, 1976. Also illustrator of James Krüss' *Der Drachenturm* (title means ''The Dragon Tower'').

ADAPTATIONS: ''Three by Three'' (filmstrip with cassette), Threshold Filmstrips, 1974.

SALASSI, Otto R(ussell) 1939-

PERSONAL: Born October 2, 1939, in Vicksburg, Miss.; son of Walter Washington (a railroad mechanic) and Ruby (Russell) Salassi; married Margaret Buchanan (a college administrator), 1963; children: Adam, Max. *Education:* Memphis State University, B.S., 1967; Vanderbilt University, M.L.S., 1968; University of Arkansas, M.F.A., 1978. *Politics:* Democrat. *Home and office:* 312 East Maple St., Fayetteville, Ark. 72701. *Agent:* Lois Wallace, Wallace & Sheil Agency, Inc., 177 East 70th St., New York, N.Y. 10021.

OTTO R. SALASSI

"Better get some men over here," he told the man standing next to him. **"It's gonna get wild in exactly . . . two and a half minutes."** ■ (Jacket illustration by Ted Bernstein from *On the Ropes* by Otto R. Salassi.)

CAREER: Douglas Aircraft Co., Vandenburg Air Force Base, Calif., mathematician with data engineering group at Pacific Missile Range, 1963-66; Bemidji State College, Bemidji, Minn., assistant librarian in charge of technical processing, 1968-69; Motlow State Community College, Tullahoma, Tenn., librarian, 1969-70; Hobart and William Smith Colleges, Geneva, N.Y., head of public services, 1970-74; University of Arkansas, Fayetteville, orientation librarian, 1978-79; writer, 1979—. *Military service:* U.S. Air Force, 1951-61.

WRITINGS: (Contributor) Miller Williams and James Alan McPherson, editors, *Railroads, Trains, and Train People in American Culture,* Random House, 1976; *On the Ropes* (young adult novel), Greenwillow, 1981; *And Nobody Knew They Were There* (young adult novel), Greenwillow, 1984. Author of ''Sports,'' a weekly column in *Grapevine,* 1977-78, and ''Page Two,'' a feature column in *Grapevine,* 1980. Contributor of stories to adult and children's magazines, including *Boy's Life, Southern Humanities Review,* and *New Orleans Review.*

WORK IN PROGRESS: Sidewinder's Will, a young adult sequel to *On the Ropes.*

SIDELIGHTS: ''I've always liked telling and writing stories—telling more than writing, of course, because it's easier and doesn't take as long—and I've always been rather good at it, ever since I learned how as a kid in Mississippi. Everybody in Mississippi told stories. It took forever to get through a grocery line because the old geezer at the cash register told stories to everybody who came through. Many's the time I thought I was going to starve to death before my mother got off the phone.

"I was always a lazy child, and not very bright, but one of the things I learned was, if you could keep somebody listening long enough, or laughing long enough, you could get away with murder. If you didn't know something, you could make it up. That got me through school and college. If you could tell a good joke you could usually get out of cleaning the latrine. That got me through the Air Force.

"But eventually I grew up and got married, had a couple of lazy kids of my own, and faced, as we all surely must, the problem of getting money. My useless and misspent youth had prepared me for nothing except telling stories, and so I found myself forced into the world of academics, where people such as myself are paid for telling stories.

"After thirteen years of semi-successful storytelling on the college level, I decided that my stories, which had served me so well for so long, were as good as or better than my colleagues' and ought to be preserved for future generations. Thus I have begun to commit them to print.

"Since I've had to draw heavily from my own experiences, the reader of *On the Ropes* may expect to find the novel peopled with pool sharks, con men, bull slingers, preachers, and other ambitious and worthy types.

FOR MORE INFORMATION SEE: Arkansas Gazette, May 4, 1981.

DUANE SANBORN

The sheer straight wall of stone dropped sharply off below him, and at the bottom towering waves pounded fiercely against huge jagged stones. ■ (From *Mystery at the Shoals* by Duane Bradley. Illustrated by Velma Ilsley.)

SANBORN, Duane 1914-
(Duane Bradley)

PERSONAL: Born June 13, 1914, in Clarinda, Iowa; daughter of Clifford Cleveland (a minister) and Nellie Anne (Harryman) Cox; married George Andrews Sanborn; children: Louis, Marilyn (Mrs. James Bowie), Anne (Mrs. Nicholas Rowe), Hugh. *Education:* Educated in public schools. *Religion:* Congregationalist. *Home:* Old Warner Rd., Henniker, N.H. 03242.

CAREER: Has worked in newspaper, publicity, and public relations fields. Writer for young people. *Awards, honors: Meeting with a Stranger* was selected by Library of Congress as one of the outstanding juvenile books of 1964 and *Design It, Sew It, and Wear It* was selected in 1978; Jane Addams Children's Book Award and Woodward Park School Annual Book Award, both 1965, for *Meeting with a Stranger.*

WRITINGS—All under name Duane Bradley; all published by Lippincott, except as indicated: *Cappy and the Jet Engine,* 1957; *Engineers Did It!,* 1958; (with Eugene Lord) *Our World of Science,* 1959; *Time for You,* 1960; *Mystery at the Shoals,* 1962; (with E. Lord) *Here's How It Works,* 1962; *Electing a President,* Van Nostrand, 1963; *Meeting with a Stranger* (illustrated by E. Harper Johnson), 1964; *The Newspaper: Its Place in a Democracy,* Van Nostrand, 1965; *Sew It and Wear It,* Crowell, 1966; *Count Rumford,* Van Nostrand, 1967; *Practical and Pretty Fashions from Simple Shapes Sewing,* C.R. Gibson, 1975; *Design It, Sew It, and Wear It: How to Make*

Yourself a Super Wardrobe without Commercial Patterns (illustrated by Judith H. Corwin), Crowell, 1979. Contributor of articles and stories to magazines.

WORK IN PROGRESS: Stars in the Sea, a book for children and adults; *A Funny Thing Happened on the Way to School,* about the problems in the public schools.

SIDELIGHTS: About her present work in progress, *A Funny Thing Happened on the Way to School,* Sanborn commented: "It is an account of how I started out to help improve our schools, as a good citizen, and soon found myself to be considered mean, crazy, and reluctant to pay for education.

"Although the framework is based on my own experience, it is an actual account of some of the real problems and dangers in our present public schools that led to the current national reports of their lack of quality. It is backed up by books and other publications written by educators for educators, and seldom seen by members of the public. So far as I know, and I have done a lot of reading, this particular information has not appeared in any book for general circulation.

"I am concerned about the responsibility of writers as well as teachers and parents to prepare our children for the actual world in which we live. Statistics about juvenile run-aways, drug use, alcoholism, premature and unfortunate sexual experience and unwed teen-age mothers shows that we are doing a truly lousy job at present. I think we should do better.

"My other book in progress, *Stars in the Sea,* will consist of things people really need to know about the seaside in order to understand, respect and enjoy it."

Sanborn's book, *Engineers Did It!* has been published in Persian and Arabic. The U.S. Information Agency has published a Korean edition of *Electing a President* and a French edition of *The Newspaper: Its Place in a Democracy.* The latter title was also published in Japanese and in Pak Dengali (India).

SANCHA, Sheila 1924-

PERSONAL: Born November 27, 1924, in Grimsby, England; daughter of Neal (a businessman) and Phylis (Middleton) Green; married Carlos Luis Sancha (a portrait painter), August 14, 1948; children: Anita Luisa (Mrs. Douglas Lear), Jeremy Christian, Nicholas Simon. *Education:* Attended Byam Shaw School of Drawing and Painting. *Politics:* None. *Religion:* "None (nothing orthodox)." *Home:* 8 Melbury Rd., Flat 5, London W14 8LR, England.

CAREER: Shell-B.P. News, London, England, illustrator, 1957-67; writer and illustrator, 1970—. *Military service:* Women's Royal Naval Service, transport driver, 1943-46. *Member:* Royal Archaeological Institute, Society of Authors.

WRITINGS—All self-illustrated juveniles: *Knight after Knight,* Collins, 1974; *The Castle Story,* Kestrel, 1979, Crowell, 1982; *The Luttrell Village: Country Life in the Middle Ages,* Collins, 1982, Crowell, 1983.

Illustrator: Barbara Kerr Wilson, *A Story to Tell,* Garnet Miller, 1964. Contributor of drawings to magazines, including *Past and Future* and *Puffin Post.*

WORK IN PROGRESS: A companion book to *The Luttrell Village;* a guide book for Lincoln Castle.

SIDELIGHTS: "When my contributions to the *Shell-B.P. News* ended in 1967, I felt I needed a change of direction. I had been drawing the adventures of a knight called 'Sir Bastion' for the historical magazine *Past and Future* and I decided to enlarge on this and write a book about knights. I soon realized that I was ignorant of the architecture and conditions under which these knights lived and, before I knew what had happened, I was up to my neck in history and archaeology. . . . *Knight after Knight, The Luttrell Village,* and *The Castle Story* are all firmly based on research. The illustrations nearly always

"He's escaped somehow," Sir Charge admitted with a shake of the head. "Got clean away." ∎
(From *Knight after Knight* by Sheila Sancha. Illustrated by the author.)

Sheila Sancha at Dunstanborough Castle, on the northeast coast of England.

start with a good look at medieval manuscript drawings, sculptures or brasses. It is great fun to put an effigy back on its feet and ask it to walk about a castle that one knows well.

"My life is busy at present because I am working on a companion book to *The Luttrell Village* about the inhabitants and buildings of a medieval town—set in the year 1275. At the same time I am making a guide book for Lincoln Castle, with reference to the two historic Battles of Lincoln and the events leading up to King John's Magna Carta. All this is fascinating material and I enjoy every minute of the time spent on research. Otherwise, as with most wives, my hobbies have dwindled to sewing, gardening and home-decorating. My husband is a portrait painter and, although most hours of the day are spent wrestling with medieval problems alone in my room, it is a pleasant relief to put down my pen and share a cup of coffee or a meal with some of the interesting and eminent people who visit his studio."

Thanks to my friends for their care in my breeding,
Who taught me betimes to love working and reading.
—Isaac Watts

SCHACHTEL, Roger (Bernard) 1949- (Marian Forrester)

PERSONAL: Born November 21, 1949, in New York, N.Y.; son of Irving Ira (a lawyer) and Elinor (a social worker for alcoholics; maiden name, Weiler) Schachtel. *Education:* Yale University, B.A., 1971; studied at Herbert Berghof Studio, 1981-82. *Residence:* New York, N.Y. *Office:* Schachtel Productions, 165 East 72nd St., New York, N.Y. 10021.

CAREER: Teacher at preschool day-care centers in New York City, 1973-75; free-lance film editor, 1975-78; Dalton School, New York City, teacher of English, 1979-80; Schachtel Productions, New York City, story editor in development of film projects, 1981—.

WRITINGS: (Under pseudonym Marian Forrester) *Farewell to Thee* (historical novel), Belmont-Tower, 1978; *Fantastic Flight to Freedom* (juvenile novel; illustrated by Charles Shaw), Raintree, 1980; *Caught on a Cliff-Face* (juvenile novel; illustrated by C. Shaw), Raintree, 1980.

The best protection from the cold is movement. . . . They spent their first hour together on the ledge doing exercises that would keep their blood moving. . . . ■ (From *Caught on a Cliff Face* by Roger Schachtel. Illustrated by Charles Shaw.)

ROGER SCHACHTEL

WORK IN PROGRESS: A television script with a high school setting.

SIDELIGHTS: "I wrote my two children's books hoping to create books that I would have enjoyed as a child, and hoping to recover my childlike enthusiasm for matters which were new to me. That is why I selected true-life adventure stories for my material—exciting stories involving environments and activities about which I initially knew nothing and which threw me into heavy research. I enormously enjoyed the challenge of integrating what I culled in my research into simple adventure narratives without slowing down the narratives—a challenge I had also faced in some of my adult writing; but the juvenile books, in permitting less latitude, less digression, presented the greater challenge.

"The greatest pleasure I derived from my children's books, however, did not come from the writing of them, but from the many letters I have received from children all over the country who have read and enjoyed them. Their enthusiasm and gratitude are moving and inspiring."

SCHISGALL, Oscar   1901-1984
(Jackson Cole, Stuart Hardy)

*OBITUARY NOTICE—*See sketch in *SATA* Volume 12: Born February 23, 1901, in Antwerp, Belgium; died after a brief illness, May 20, 1984, in New York, N.Y. Historian and author. Schisgall wrote two children's books, *Laura Jane Sees Everything at Hess's* and *That Remarkable Creature: The Snail*. His experience as a corporate historian gave Schisgall background to write *My Years with Xerox* and *Eyes on Tomorrow: The Evolution of Proctor and Gamble*. Under the pseudonyms Jackson Cole and Stuart Hardy, Schisgall wrote novels such as *The Man from Nowhere, Arizona Justice,* and *The Ramblin' Kid*. Not only a novelist, Schisgall was also a magazine writer

who contributed numerous articles to periodicals such as *Redbook, Reader's Digest,* and *Saturday Evening Post*. In 1954 he was the recipient of the Ben Franklin Award for magazine writing. He was also the author of five screenplays and twenty radio and television plays. *For More Information See: Contemporary Authors, New Revision Series,* Volume 9, Gale, 1983. *Obituaries: New York Times,* May 21, 1984.

SCHRANK, Joseph   1900-1984

OBITUARY NOTICE: Born July 10, 1900, in New York, N.Y.; died after a lengthy illness, March 23, 1984, in New York, N.Y. Playwright and author of several books for children, including *Seldom and the Golden Cheese* and *The Plain Princess and the Lazy Prince*. Schrank was best known as the author of numerous stage, motion picture, and television scripts. His stage credits include such plays as "Page Miss Glory" and "Larger Than Life," which were produced during the 1930s. "Song of the Island," starring Betty Grable and Victor Mature, "The Clock," with Judy Garland, and "Bathing Beauty," featuring Esther Williams and Red Skelton, are among the screenplays written by Schrank. His works for television include the 1965 adaptation of "Cinderella." *For More Information See: Contemporary Authors,* Volumes 5-6, revised, Gale, 1969; *Authors of Books for Young People,* 2nd edition, Scarecrow, 1971; *International Authors and Writers Who's Who,* 8th edition, Melrose, 1977; *The Writers Directory: 1980-1982,* St. Martin's, 1979; *National Playwrights Directory,* 2nd edition, Eugene O'Neill Theatre Center, 1981. *Obituaries: New York Times,* March 26, 1984.

HELEN SEWELL

... Before an hour was up they were lapping milk out of the same saucer. ... ■ (From *Away Goes Sally* by Elizabeth Coatsworth. Illustrated by Helen Sewell.)

SEWELL, Helen (Moore)   1896-1957

PERSONAL: Born June 27, 1896, in Mare Island, Calif.; died February 24, 1957, in New York City; daughter of William E. Sewell (a U.S. Navy commander). *Education:* Attended Pratt Institute; later studied painting with artist Archipenko. *Residence:* New York, N.Y.

CAREER: Author and illustrator. *Awards, honors: A Round of Carols* was selected as one of American Institute of Graphic Art's ''Fifty Books of the Year,'' 1935; illustrator of Newbery honor books, 1938, *On the Banks of Plum Creek,* 1940, *By the Shores of Silver Lake,* 1941, *The Long Winter,* 1942, *Little Town on the Prairie,* 1944, *These Happy Golden Years,* all by Laura Ingalls Wilder, and 1953, for Alice Dalgliesh's *The Bears on Hemlock Mountain; New York Herald Tribune*'s Spring Book Festival Award, 1943, for *These Happy Golden Years;* one of *New York Times* Best Illustrated Children's Books of the Year, 1955, for *The Three Kings of Saba;* Caldecott Medal honor book, 1955, for *The Thanksgiving Story.*

WRITINGS—For children; all self-illustrated: *ABC for Everyday,* Macmillan, 1930; (compiler) *A Head for Happy,* Macmillan, 1931; (editor) *Words to the Wise: A Book of Proverbs,* Dodd, 1932; *Blue Barns: The Story of Two Big Geese and Seven Little Ducks,* Macmillan, 1933, reprinted, 1957; *Ming and Mehitable,* Macmillan, 1936; *Peggy and the Pony,* Oxford University Press, 1936; *Jimmy and Jemima,* Macmillan, 1940; *Peggy and the Pup,* Oxford University Press, 1941; *Birthdays for Robin,* Macmillan, 1943; *Belinda the Mouse,* Oxford University Press, 1944; (with Elena Eleska) *Three Tall Tales,* Macmillan, 1947; *The Golden Christmas Manger* (cut-out book), Simon & Schuster, 1948.

Illustrator: Susanne K. Langer, *The Cruise of the Little Dipper and Other Fairy Tales,* Norcross, 1924, reissued, New York Graphic Society, 1963; Mary Britton Miller, *Menagerie,* Macmillan, 1928; Miriam S. Potter, *Sally Gabble and the Fairies,* Macmillan, 1929; Mimpsy Rhys, *Mr. Hermit Crab: A Tale for Children by a Child,* Macmillan, 1929.

Marjorie Cautley, *Building a House in Sweden* (adult), Macmillan, 1931; Susan Smith, *The Christmas Tree in the Woods,* Minton, 1932; Laura Ingalls Wilder, *Little House in the Big Woods,* Harper, 1932; Langston Hughes, *The Dream Keeper and Other Poems* (young adult), Knopf, 1932, 9th edition, 1954; L. I. Wilder, *Farmer Boy,* Harper, 1933; Johan Falkberget, *Broomstick and Snowflake,* Macmillan, 1933; Eliza Orne White, *Where Is Adelaide?,* Houghton, 1933; Jean West Maury, compiler, *A First Bible,* Oxford University Press, 1934, 5th edition, 1955; Elizabeth Coatsworth, *Away Goes Sally,* Macmillan, 1934, reissued, 1951; Frances Clarke Sayers, *Bluebonnets for Lucinda,* Viking, 1934; *Cinderella,* Macmillan, 1934; Thomas Noble, compiler, *A Round of Carols,* Oxford University Press, 1935, new edition, Walck, 1964; L. I. Wilder, *Little House on the Prairie,* Harper, 1935; E. O. White, *Ann Frances,* Houghton, 1935; Viola May Jones, *Peter and Gretchen of Old Nuremberg,* A. Whitman, 1935, revised edition, circa 1940; Carlo Collodi (pseudonym of Carlo Lorenzini), *Pinocchio,* Appleton-Century, 1935; Mairin Cregan, *Old John,* Macmillan, 1936; Eleanor Farjeon, *Ten Saints* (Protestant and Catholic editions), Oxford University Press, 1936, reprinted, 1958; Carol Ryrie Brink, *Baby Island,* Macmillan, 1937, reprinted, P. Collier, 1973; (with Mildred Boyle) L. I. Wilder, *On the Banks of Plum Creek,* Harper, 1937; A. A. Milne, *The Magic Hill and Other Stories,* Grosset, 1937; A. A. Milne, *The Princess and the Apple Tree and Other Stories,* Grosset, 1937; Charlotte Brontë, *Jane Eyre,* Oxford University Press, 1938; Mary Louise Jarden, *The Young Brontës* (young adult), Viking, 1938; (with M. Boyle) L. I. Wilder, *By the Shores of Silver Lake,* Harper, 1939, special edition, E. M. Hale, 1956; E. Coatsworth, *Five Bushel Farm,* Macmillan, 1939.

(With M. Boyle) L. I. Wilder, *The Long Winter,* Harper, 1940; E. Coatsworth, *The Fair American,* Macmillan, 1940, reprinted, 1968; Jane Austen, *Pride and Prejudice* (with a preface by Frank Swinnerton), Limited Editions, 1940; (with M. Boyle) L. I. Wilder, *Little Town on the Prairie,* Harper, 1941; F. C. Sayers, *Tag-along Tooloo,* Viking, 1941; E. Coatsworth, *The White Horse,* Macmillan, 1942; Ferenc Molnar, *The Blue-Eyed Lady,* Viking, 1942; Thomas Bulfinch, *A Book of Myths: Selections from Bulfinch's Age of Fable,* Macmillan, 1942, reprinted, 1966; (with M. Boyle) L. I. Wilder, *These Happy Golden Years,* Harper, 1943; James S. Tippett, *Christmas Magic,* Grosset, 1944; E. Coatsworth, *Big Green Umbrella,* Grosset, 1944; Marion Boss Ward, *Boat Children of Canton,* McKay, 1944; E. Coatsworth, *The Wonderful Day,* Macmillan, 1946; Dorothy Kunhardt, *Once There Was a Little Boy,* Viking, 1946; Louise H. Seaman, *The Brave Bantam,* Macmillan, 1946; Maude Crowley, *Azor,* Oxford University Press, 1948, reprinted, Walck, 1959; M. Crowley, *Azor and the Haddock,* Oxford University Press, 1949.

M. Crowley, *Azor and the Blue-Eyed Cow: A Christmas Story,* Oxford University Press, 1951, reprinted, Gregg, 1980; Irmengarde Eberle, *Secrets and Surprises,* Heath, 1951; (with

We dressed up Chamberlayne in woman's clothes, on purpose to pass for a lady—only think what fun! ■ (From *Pride and Prejudice* by Jane Austen. Illustrated by Helen Sewell.)

. . . One of the gulls swooped very near his head and said, "Just came by Peach's Point. She's out there asleep under the raft on the Baileys' beach—been playing house for two days." ■ (From *Azor* by Maude Crowley. Illustrated by Helen Sewell.)

Madeleine Gekiere) Mary Chase, *Mrs. McThing,* Oxford University Press, 1952; Alice Dalgliesh, *The Bears on Hemlock Mountain* (ALA Notable Book), Scribner, 1952; Emily Dickinson, *Poems* (selected and edited with a commentary by Louis Untermeyer), Limited Editions, 1952; Alf Evers, *The Colonel's Squad,* Macmillan, 1952; A. Dalgliesh, *The Thanksgiving Story* (ALA Notable Book), Scribner, 1954; A. Evers, *In the Beginning,* Macmillan, 1954; (with M. Gekiere) Brothers Grimm, *Grimm's Tales,* Oxford University Press, 1954; A. Evers, *The Three Kings of Saba* (ALA Notable Book), Lippincott, 1955; J. Austin, *Sense and Sensibility,* Limited Editions, 1957. Contributor of drawings to *The New Yorker.*

SIDELIGHTS: Sewell was born in Mare Island, California on June 27, 1896. When she was very young, she and her two sisters traveled to the island of Guam, where their widowed father, Commander Sewell, had been appointed governor. Guam made a lasting impression on young Sewell, who, by the age of seven, had circled the globe.

During her early years spent in travel and on Guam, Sewell acquired an indelible impression of the tropics, which influenced her later life and work. She often said that, "Everything exciting happened to me before I was seven."

Father died at Mare Island on March 17, 1904, as a result of an intestinal disorder contracted on Guam. Sewell and her sister went to live with their aunt, uncle and numerous cousins in Brooklyn, New York.

By the time Sewell was eight years old she had decided to become an art student. At twelve she was privileged to be the youngest art student to attend Saturday classes at Pratt Institute. Following the advice of the educator Dr. Nicholas Murray Butler, Sewell enrolled as a full-time student at Pratt Institute when she was sixteen years old. Later she studied painting with Archipenko, the Russian artist.

Sewell began earning her own money by designing Christmas cards and other greeting cards. Her first illustrated book, Susanne Langer's *The Cruise of the Little Dipper and Other Fairy Tales,* was published in 1924. After seeing those illustrations, editor Louise Seaman Bechtel asked Sewell to illustrate Mary B. Miller's poems in *Menagerie,* published in 1928. Two years later her own book, *ABC for Everyday,* was published and launched her career.

The following year, in 1931, Sewell compiled and illustrated *A Head for Happy.* "Some of my early books remind me too much of my Christmas card style. They look old-fashioned, as perhaps they should, for their stories. But *Happy* was more my kind of thing. It was really a step toward what I [was] trying to do in the fifties." [Louise Seaman Bechtel, "Helen Sewell, 1896-1956: The Development of a Great Illustrator," *Horn Book,* October, 1957.[1]]

By 1932, Sewell had already done nine books and was well established in the world of book illustration. She was asked to illustrate the first of the Laura Ingalls Wilder books, *Little House in the Big Woods.* By the time *On the Banks of Plum Creek* was added to the "Little House" series in 1937, Sewell had made so many commitments to other authors and publishers that she couldn't finish the Wilder books alone. Mildred Boyle was asked to collaborate on the illustrations with Sewell.

Between 1935 and 1943, Sewell created five picture books for beginning readers. These stories drew on Sewell's own ex-

He was a fine big boy for his age. That was why his mother could send him over the Moutain all by himself. ■ (From *The Bears on Hemlock Mountain* by Alice Dalgliesh. Illustrated by Helen Sewell.)

periences. In *Ming and Mehitable* (1936) she told about her little dog given to her by a Japanese sailor when she lived with her family on the island of Guam. *Peggy and the Pony* told the story of her trip to England and France with her sister and niece. In 1942, Sewell illustrated *A Book of Myths: Selections from Bulfinch's Age of Fable,* which had been a childhood favorite.

Although Sewell was inclined to draw mostly from memory, she occasionally used children as models. *The Three Tall Tales* (1947) is dedicated to the eleven boys and one girl whose discussions of books and the comics prompted Sewell to do her own "comic" books. The three stories were told to Sewell by Elena Eleska, the artist who was the first to do cloth books. The stories were gathered from Eleska's trips in Africa and Asia. "In *Three Tall Tales* we tried to put some fun into the funnies and a little design into their drawing as well. . . . The action in [the stories of Eleska's incredible adventures in Africa and Asia] was so intense that it was hard to tame them down into a conventional and orderly book. It occurred to me that the solution might be found in the funnies. I determined to look further into the matter.

"My first real introduction to the comics took place on a gloomy winter afternoon when one of the key children appeared at my door. A key child is, of course, one who wears the home key on a cord around his neck to prevent its being lost. His mother worked; so, like thousands of others, he had only an empty house to return to after school.

"Every afternoon that winter, and at fairly regular intervals ever since, he has been one of the most welcome members of

He led the sheep to the stairs, and then step by step he tugged and boosted her upward. She bleated all the way, but he got her into the loft. ■ (From *Farmer Boy* by Laura Ingalls Wilder. Illustrated by Helen Sewell.)

He was called Mule because once he had a mule he took out fishing with him. The mule used to sit in the stern of the boat while Mule fished. . . . ■ (From *Azor and the Haddock* by Maude Crowley. Illustrated by Helen Sewell.)

my family. He had wonderful powers of concentration and entertained himself by capably building assorted skyscrapers and railroad stations all over the room. He read quantities of books and his criticisms were discerning. He loved the Laura Ingalls Wilder books above all others. He also liked Donald Duck.

''Less inhibited than many youngsters, he showed me the parts that interested him and explained their fine points. In time I, too, developed an affection for the small duck.

''Then, too, the comic form—a story told in pictures—has a special attraction. It was here I realized that though the name was strange the shape was familiar. When I am not illustrating books I have at different times worked with picture stories. It is a method . . . graphic rather than literary, and the essential pattern is more nearly akin to the comics than to the story book. Some of the most congenial subjects for such books are, appropriately enough, on the funny side; nonsense lends itself readily to this form. For people who are not addicts, the comics are often hard to look at. But it was only when my key child showed me so many of them that I realized their chief horror was just that—the looks of them.

"I had been told that, among some children, there is a whole series of signs and symbols, sudden squeaks and exclamations which derive from the comics and are used by the initiated like a secret code. A child who is, by some miracle, unfamiliar with the funnies, and so does not understand this alarming language, is made to feel an outsider and an outcast by the inner circle of comics lovers.

"But I was a stranger here myself, and the unaccustomed sight of one of their elders who actually wished to be instructed, awakened a missionary zeal in all my young friends. They became voluble and garrulous as they warmed to the task and they went to work with delight and industry. What they taught me was exactly what I wanted to know. It was a way of separating some of the slang and vulgarity abounding in the funnies from the important elements of their form. This standard pattern, which is like a new and antic sort of etiquette, is not only accepted but demanded by the children. These elements they will look for and, missing them, they are likely to reject whatever else is offered.

"A few minor samples of the things I learned are these: if a person falls into the water he should say, 'Gurgle, blub, blub,' among other things. Exclamation points, curlicues, crisscrosses and question marks were carefully drawn out for me and they went rather neatly into the picture, though I cannot say I mastered entirely their esoteric meanings.

"When the same unfortunate person falls asleep he should snore. I was given a choice of snores—one indicated by a series of Z's and the other by a tiny saw cutting through a log and the whole surrounded by a wavy line denoting a cloud. I chose the Z's.

"If a monkey objects to having his teeth brushed he says, 'Eek! Eek!' When any comics character speaks, his conversation balloon has an even outline; but when he thinks a thought, or dreams a dream, the balloon should have the wavy cloud outline. The text, if any, should be above and not below the drawing to which it refers.

"In making our new book, *Three Tall Takes*, the idea was to transform, if possible, the comics layout into a design, retaining at the same time all the fun inherent in the original stories. At first our plan was to include as few words as possible, either above the pictures or in the balloons (which were difficult bits of decoration to fit, puzzle-like, into the general composition). But this book was meant as a starting point for the very young as well as for me, and many of my collaborators were quite small. So explanatory text was added for reading aloud—the children themselves suggested it. I think there should have been wider margins, too, for clarity and better visibility.

"Only one boy, the key child, noticed finally that I had not used the conventional colors of the comics books. He did not object but merely remarked it. To my surprise, however, I was called to account for making the animals too true to life. They should have been more exaggerated. This criticism came from a good Boy Scout who has not, so far as I know, taken the slightest interest in modern art or ever heard of strong expression of form. When he tried to explain in words of one syllable his objection to the fact that my monkeys looked too much like monkeys, he said, 'If you drew an automobile going fast around a corner you should make it U-shaped.' I am well aware of the kind of picture he had in mind but I think a U-shaped

car might satisfy his requirements and be, at the same time, drawn with art." [Helen Sewell, "Illustrator Meets the Comics," *Horn Book*, March, 1948.[2]]

In 1952 Sewell illustrated *Poems* by Emily Dickinson for the Limited Editions Club. Editor Louis Untermeyer, commenting on the illustrations said: "These drawings excite me more than I believed a drawing could excite these ancient eyes. . . . They never are mere decorations or 'illustrations.' On the contrary, they are amazing creations which are translations of one art in terms of another. They go below the surface of the lines (as the poet did) and reveal implications which are provocative, frequently teasing, and sometimes terrifying. They bring out dimensions which even admirers of Emily Dickinson frequently ignore; they add new emphasis to the tart humor, the wit and whimsicality, as well as the pure suggestive power of the poetry. The accent is New England—with universal overtones—and the artist's use of the half-archaic, half-stylistic method is everywhere justified. . . . Miss Sewell indicates the poet's astonishing range, from badinage, to brilliant mockery, and to breath-taking leaps of the imagination. . . . The poet has found her true visual interpreter."[1]

Sewell's last book for the Limited Editions Club was a Jane Austen book, *Sense and Sensibility* (1957). "I simply had to work out a new style for it. I wanted it to be just as 'appealing' as the other Jane Austen work, but still new. It had to be NEW."[1]

Sewell's final work for a book was done during her last, long illness. Ironically, her paintings were used on the jacket of *Problems of Art* by Susanne K. Langer, author of Sewell's first book, *The Cruise of the Little Dipper*. Sewell's wish during this time was "to be well again just long enough to do some of the new painting I have in my head, and to make a few more books."[1]

Sewell died in New York City on February 24, 1957. A show of her books opened at the Central Children's Room of the New York Public Library on June 9, 1957, and remained until September of that year. The exhibition included most of the seventy-two books that she illustrated from 1924 until 1957. Sewell's works are included in the Kerlan Collection at the University of Minnesota.

FOR MORE INFORMATION SEE: Bertha E. Mahony and Elinor Whitney, compilers, *Contemporary Illustrators of Children's Books*, Bookshop for Boys and Girls, 1930; *Horn Book*, March, 1946, March, 1948, October, 1957, August, 1959; B. E. Mahony and others, compilers, *Illustrators of Children's Books: 1744-1945*, Horn Book, 1947; Kunitz and Haycraft, *Junior Book of Authors*, H. W. Wilson, 1951; (obituary) *Wilson Library Bulletin*, April, 1957; *American Artist*, January, 1958; B. M. Miller and others, compilers, *Illustrators of Children's Books: 1946-1956*, Horn Book, 1958; D. L. Kirkpatrick, editor, *Twentieth-Century Children's Writers*, St. Martin's Press, 1978; *Laura Ingalls Wilder Lore*, spring-summer, 1982.

Cock crows in the morn,
   To tell us to rise,
And he who lies late
   Will never be wise.
For early to bed,
   And early to rise,
Is the way to be healthy
   And wealthy and wise.

      —Nursery rhyme

KURT D. SINGER

SINGER, Kurt D(eutsch)   1911-

PERSONAL: Adopted mother's maiden name as his surname; born August 10, 1911, in Vienna, Austria; came to United States in 1940, naturalized citizen in 1951; son of Ignatius (an importer-exporter) and Irene (Singer) Deutsch; married Hilda Tradelius, December 23, 1932 (divorced, 1954); married Jane Sherrod (an author and columnist), January 21, 1955; children: (first marriage) Marian Alice Birgit, Kenneth Walt. *Education:* Studied at University of Zurich, 1930, and Labor College, Stockholm, 1936; Divinity College of Metaphysics, Indianapolis, Ind., Ph.D., 1951. *Office:* Singer Communications, Inc., 3164 West Tyler Ave., Anaheim, Calif. 92801.

CAREER: Worked in his teens as apprentice in German factory making railroad cars; editor of *Mitteilungsblaetter* (underground weekly), Berlin, Germany, 1933; fled to Sweden, 1934, and founded committee to free Nobel laureate Carl von Ossietzky from Nazi concentration camp; correspondent, *Folket i Bild* (magazine), Sweden, 1935-40; co-founder, *Trots Allt* (pro-Allies newspaper), 1939; correspondent in America for Swedish newspapers, 1940; author and lecturer, principally on spies and espionage, 1940—; Singer Communications, Inc. (formerly BP Singer Features, Inc.), Anaheim, Calif., president, 1955—. Editor, *News Background*, 1942; member of speaker's research committee and editor of *UN Calendar*, United Nations, 1948-52; correspondent, North American Newspaper Alliance, 1953—; editor-in-chief, Oceanic Press Service, 1955—. *Member:* International Platform Association (vice-president, 1948-52), Western Writers of America.

WRITINGS—Juvenile: (Translator) Esther Gretor, *Kippie the Cow*, Messner, 1951; *Tales from the South Pacific*, Denison, 1969.

With wife, Jane Sherrod; juvenile books: *Spies for Democracy*, Denison, 1960; *Great Adventures of the Sea*, Denison, 1962; (editors) *Great Adventures in Crime*, Denison, 1962; *Dr. Albert Schweitzer: Medical Missionary*, Denison, 1962; *Ernest Hemingway: Man of Courage*, Denison, 1963; (editors) *Ghost Book: The World's Greatest Stories of the Known Unknown*, W.H. Allen, 1963; *Lyndon Baines Johnson: Man of Reason*, Denison, 1964, revised edition published as *Lyndon Baines Johnson, Man of Reason: The L.B.J. Story from Kennedy to Vietnam*, 1966; *Folk Tales of Mexico*, Denison, 1969.

Other: *Det Kommandet Kriget* (title means "The Coming War"), Federatif Foerlag (Stockholm), 1934; *Europas diktatorer: 24 diktatorer fraan Hitler till Stalin*, Holmstroem, 1936; (with Kurt R. Grossman) *Carl von Ossietzky*, Europa, 1937; *Martin Niemoeller, praesten i koncentrationslaegret*, Fredens Foerlag, 1939.

Goering: Germany's Most Dangerous Man, Hutchinson, 1940; *Duel for the Northland: The War of Enemy Agents in Scandinavia*, McBride, 1943; *Spies and Traitors of World War II*, Prentice-Hall, 1945; (editor) *Three Thousand Years of Espionage: An Anthology of the World's Greatest Spy Stories*, Prentice-Hall, 1948; (with Franz J. Polgar) *Polgar: Story of a Hypnotist*, Thomas Nelson, 1948.

The World's 30 Greatest Women Spies, Funk, 1951 (published in England as *The World's Greatest Women Spies*, W. H. Allen, 1951); *Gentlemen Spies*, W. H. Allen, 1952; *Spies and Traitors: A Short History of Espionage*, W. H. Allen, 1953; *The Men in the Trojan Horse*, Beacon Press, 1953; (editor) *The World's Best Spy Stories: Fact and Fiction*, Funk, 1954 (published in England as *The World's Greatest Spy Stories: Fact and Fiction*, W. H. Allen, 1954); *The Laughton Story: An Intimate Story of Charles Laughton*, Winston, 1954 (published in England as *The Charles Laughton Story*, R. Hale, 1954); *More Spy Stories*, W. H. Allen, 1955; *Spy Stories from Asia*, Funk, 1955 (published in England as *Spies over Asia*, W. H. Allen, 1956); (editor) *My Greatest Crime Story, by Police Chiefs of the World*, Hill & Wang, 1956; *The Danny Kaye Saga*, R. Hale, 1957, published as *The Danny Kaye Story*, Thomas Nelson, 1958; (editor) *My Strangest Case, by Police Chiefs of the World*, W. H. Allen, 1957, Doubleday, 1958; *Spy Omnibus*, W. H. Allen, 1959, Denison, 1960.

(Editor and author of introduction) *Spies Who Changed History*, Ace Books, 1960; (editor) *Eight Tales Complete from the World's Greatest Spy Stories*, Belmont Books, 1961; *Crime Omnibus*, W. H. Allen, 1961; *Hemingway: Life and Death of a Giant*, Holloway House, 1961; (editor) *The Secret Agent's Badge of Courage*, Belmont Books, 1961; *The Unearthly: The World's Greatest Stories of the Occult*, Panther House, 1962; *Horror Omnibus*, W. H. Allen, 1965; (compiler) *Ghost Omnibus*, W. H. Allen, 1965; (editor with others) *The Fine Art of Spying*, Grosset, 1965; (editor) *I Can't Sleep at Night: 13 Weird Tales*, Whiting & Wheaton, 1966; (editor) *Weird Tales of the Supernatural*, W. H. Allen, 1966; *Mata Hari*, Award Books, 1967; (editor) *Tales of Terror*, W. H. Allen, 1967; (editor) *The Gothic Reader*, Ace Books, 1968; *Tales of the Uncanny*, W. H. Allen, 1968; (editor) *Famous Short Stories*, two volumes, Denison, 1968; (editor) *Tales of the Macabre*, New English Library, 1969; (editor) *Bloch and Bradbury*, Belmont Books, 1969.

(Editor) *The House in the Valley, and Other Tales of Terror,* Sphere Books, 1970; *Plague of the Living Dead,* Sphere Books, 1970; (editor) *Tales from the Unknown,* W. H. Allen, 1970, published as *Tales of the Unknown,* Pinnacle Books, 1971; *Ghouls and Ghosts,* W. H. Allen, 1972; *Satanic Omnibus,* W. H. Allen, 1973; *Gothic Horror Books,* W. H. Allen, 1974; *They Were Possessed,* W. H. Allen, 1976; *Dictionary of Home Repair,* Ottenheimer, 1977; *Strange Stories of the Unknown,* Scholastic Books, 1980; *I Spied and Survived,* Leisure Books, 1980.

Writer of "News Background Reports" during World War II. Contributor to *This Month, Dalhousie Review, Saturday Evening Post, Christian Science Monitor, National Star, American Weekly* and other magazines and newspapers. His column, "Hollywood Interviews," has been published in twenty countries, 1955—.

WORK IN PROGRESS: "Usually write or edit two books a year."

SIDELIGHTS: Singer's books on espionage have appeared in multiple translations, including Norwegian, Portuguese, Japanese, German, Italian, Hebrew, Swedish, Spanish, and French. He speaks eight languages.

HOBBIES AND OTHER INTERESTS: Collecting art, books, documents, letters, and autographs; travel.

SINGER, Marilyn 1948-

BRIEF ENTRY: Born October 3, 1948, in Bronx, N.Y. Singer has written fiction and nonfiction for every level of juvenile reading, from picture books to young adult novels. After graduating cum laude from Queens College of the City University of New York in 1969, she worked as a magazine editor and teacher of English before becoming a full-time writer in 1974. Among her novels for young readers are *No Applause, Please* (Dutton, 1977), *The Pickle Plan* (Dutton, 1978), *It Can't Hurt Forever* (Harper, 1978), and *Tarantulas on the Brain* (Harper, 1982). Those for young adults include *The First Few Friends* (Harper, 1981) and *The Course of True Love Never Did Run Smooth* (Harper, 1983). Critics have noted her ability to capture the reality of pre-adolescence and adolescence through adept characterization and natural dialogue. The settings of Singer's novels are contemporary, with the exception of *The First Few Friends* in which she propels older readers back into the political, moral, and sexual upheaval of the 1960s.

An author of scripts for the popular television series "The Electric Company," Singer has also written stories for children such as *The Dog Who Insisted He Wasn't* (Dutton, 1976), *The Case of the Sabotaged School Play* (Harper, 1984), and *Leroy Is Missing* (Harper, 1984). For an even younger age group, she has produced a picture book entitled *Will You Take Me to Town on Strawberry Day?,* a story told in verse with illustrations by Trinka Hakes Noble. Among Singer's anticipated works are another picture book, *Archer Armidillo's Secret Room,* a fantasy novel, *The Horsemaster,* and a sequel to *Tarantulas on the Brain. Home and Office:* 50 Berkeley Pl., Brooklyn, N.Y. 11217. *For More Information See: Contemporary Authors, New Revision Series,* Volume 9, Gale, 1983.

Books are no substitute for living, but they can add immeasurably to its richness.
—May Hill Arbuthnot

SKIPPER, G. C. 1939-

BRIEF ENTRY: Born March 22, 1939, in Ozark, Ala. Journalist, editor, and author of books for young readers. After graduating from the University of Alabama in 1961, Skipper began his professional career as a reporter and columnist for the *Huntsville (Ala.) Times.* Since then, he has held positions as Midwest news bureau chief for *Travel Weekly,* executive editor at Hitchcock Publishing, and editor of *Motor Service* magazine. He is the author of three mysteries published by Children's Press: *The Ghost in the Church* (1976), *A Night in the Attic* (1977), and *The Ghost at Manor House* (1978). Skipper has also written over a dozen books dealing with the major events and prominent figures of World War II. Aimed at reluctant readers, the "World at War" series (also published by Children's Press) is written in a fictionalized documentary style. Accompanied with maps and photographs, the books are meant to serve as an introduction to key aspects of military strategy during that time. Among the titles are: *The Battle of Britain, Death of Hitler, Goering and the Luftwaffe* (all 1980), *Battle of the Coral Sea, Invasion of Sicily,* and *Mussolini: A Dictator Dies* (all 1981). *Home:* 1924 Flintshire Dr., Schaumburg, Ill. 60194. *For More Information See: Contemporary Authors,* Volumes 77-80, Gale, 1979.

SLATE, Joseph (Frank) 1928-

PERSONAL: Born January 19, 1928, in Hollidays Cove, W.Va.; son of Frank Edward (a building contractor) and Angela (Palumbo) Slate; married Patricia Griffin (a research director),

She is Cassiopeia. She is Old Cassie. ■ (From *The Star Rocker* by Joseph Slate. Illustrated by Dirk Zimmer.)

September 11, 1954. *Education:* University of Washington, B.A., 1951; studied printmaking, Tokyo, Japan, 1955-56; Yale University School of Art, B.F.A., 1960; independent study, Kyoto, Japan, 1975. *Home:* Box A, Gambier, Ohio 43022. *Office:* Department of Art, Kenyon College, Gambier, Ohio 43022.

CAREER: The Seattle Times, editorial staff, 1950-53; Foreign Broadcast Information Service, editor, 1953-57; Yale University, consultant on aesthetics, 1960-66; Kenyon College, Gambier, Ohio, instructor, 1962-64, art professor, 1969—, department chairman, 1963-75, 1981-82. National Endowment for the Arts, consultant and originator of the NEA literature program in newspapers, 1977-78. *Exhibitions:* Twelfth National Print Show, Brooklyn Museum, N.Y., 1960; Kenyon College, Gambier, Ohio, biennial group show, 1960—; Pioneer Gallery, Cooperstown, N.Y., 1961; Milton College and University of Wisconsin, 1963; Mt. Union College, Ohio, 1965; Whitney Museum, N.Y., 1974; Schumacher Gallery, Columbus, Ohio, 1975; Waiting Gallery, Mt. Vernon, Ohio, 1976; Hopkins Gallery, Ohio State University, 1976; Mansfield Art Gallery, Ohio, 1978; Ohio Expositions, Columbus, Ohio, 1979. *Military service:* U.S. Marine Air Corps, 1946-48. *Member:* Society of Children's Book Writers, Authors Guild, Foundation in Art, Theory, and Education Association. *Awards, honors:* Top-Flight Award (journalism) and Fir Tree and Oval Club Awards (service), 1951, from the University of Washington; Yale University Alumni Fellowship, 1960; painting award,

1962, from Ohio Expositions; Kenyon Outstanding Educators Award, 1973; *How Little Porcupine Played Christmas* was placed on the Ohio Teachers and Pupils Reading Circle list for 1983-84, and *The Mean, Clean, Giant Canoe Machine* for 1984-85.

WRITINGS—For children: *The Star Rocker* (illustrated by Dirk Zimmer), Harper, 1982; *How Little Porcupine Played Christmas* (illustrated by Felicia Bond), Crowell, 1982; *The Mean, Clean, Giant Canoe Machine* (illustrated by Lynn Munsinger), Crowell, 1983; *Love, Lula Cat* (illustrated by Bruce Degan), Harper, 1985.

Other: (With Martin Garhart) *Poetry and Prints,* Pothanger Press, 1974. Contributor of short stories and articles to periodicals, including *The New Yorker, Saturday Review, Art Journal, The Kenyon Review,* and *Contempora.*

WORK IN PROGRESS: Paintings; picture books for Crowell.

SIDELIGHTS: ''I was born in Hollidays Cove, West Virginia, one of five children. I suppose my greatest influence was an invalid sister. She was a wonderfully talented and witty person, and I'm sure my dual interest in art and writing was fostered by her.

''Rose entertained us by drawing and painting picture books on the back of discarded floral wallpaper. Then she carefully

JOSEPH SLATE

"Oh, what a beautiful star," say the Mamas and the Papas.

"Star! Star!" say the little creatures.

"Star of my life," says Mama Porcupine.
■ (From *How Little Porcupine Played Christmas* by Joseph Slate. Illustrated by Felicia Bond.)

bound them with pink yarn. They were finished products—highly-colored adventure stories in the style of 'Flash Gordon.' She couldn't live a normal life, although she was a beautiful and spirited person. She suffered much discomfort and pain, but she had style and a ready sense of humor. She intensified our lives.

"Her death at sixteen haunted me. The first national attention my writing received was for stories inspired by her. They were written from a child's perspective for *The New Yorker*. That child's perspective should have told me something about the future. But I had no idea I would ever write for children.

"In 1946, I joined the Navy to gain the benefits of the GI Bill. It was the only way I would get to college. The Navy shunted me into the Marine Air Corps. When I got out, I majored in journalism at the University of Washington. I wanted to be a writer, and luckily, I got a job as a campus stringer and then reporter on *The Seattle Times*. But I wanted to see the world too, so I took a government editorial job. Lucky me. In Washington, D.C., I met my future wife, and we worked together in Tokyo for the Foreign Broadcast Information Service. Japanese art fascinated me. I turned to painting and the Japanese artist, Saito, showed me how to cut a woodblock. I sent a portfolio of work to Josef Albers at Yale. I don't know why, but he admitted me to the B.F.A. program. After three years at Yale, and one year trying to make it as a painter, I came to Kenyon College and set up the art program we have now.

"The actual writing of picture books didn't come for me until the eighties. The photographer, Gregory Spaid, a former student, urged me to tackle what seemed to many of my students a natural leaning.

"The children of those students are now reading my books. I get much pleasure hearing from them. You can't be totally self-indulgent when you write for children. But they do give you far more freedom than do adult readers, editors, or critics. I guess the artist in me loves the picture-book form because of that freedom.

"I'm always being asked why I don't illustrate my own books. I mean to, but the main reason is that my painting is not pictorial. I haven't developed a picture-making style. I send my editors tentative sketches now and then, and maybe they'll bite. We'll see. However, I don't mind other artists doing my books; I want my work to be universal, and it's fun to see how my ideas are getting across. I work with their dummies, and don't mind changing the text to make the pictures better. I think visually.

"Although I've traveled around the world, lived in Japan and Italy, I draw most of my images from home. *The Star Rocker*'s pond is across our driveway, and there was an old majestic hickory on the edge of our woods. I say *was* because it was recently twisted down in a storm. It was hollow and the animals loved it. Sad, sad. We have fourteen godchildren and we hated to tell them. There were a lot of stories in that tree.

"My wife, Patty, and I live on two country acres adjoining a bird sanctuary and Kenyon College, where I am an art professor."

Go West, young man, and grow up with the country.
—Horace Greeley
(From *Hints toward Reform*)

What makes me giggle?
A moose with a wiggle.

(From *The Giggle and Cry Book* by Eileen Spinelli. Illustrated by Lisa Atherton.)

EILEEN SPINELLI

SPINELLI, Eileen 1942-

PERSONAL: Born August 16, 1942, in Philadelphia, Pa.; daughter of Joseph Patrick (an engineer) and Angela Marie (Caruso) Mesi; married Jerry Spinelli (a writer); children: seven. *Education:* Attended high school in Rose Valley, Pa. *Religion:* Christian. *Residence:* Havertown, Pa. *Agent:* Ray Lincoln Literary Agency, 4 Surrey Rd., Melrose Park, Pa. 19126.

CAREER: Writer, 1960—. Creative writing teacher. Also worked as secretary. *Member:* Children's Reading Roundtable, Writers Club of Delaware County, Philadelphia Writer's Organization.

WRITINGS: The Giggle and Cry Book (juvenile; illustrated by Lisa Atherton), Stemmer House, 1981; *Thanksgiving at the Tappleton's* (juvenile; illustrated by Maryann Cocca-Leffler), Addison-Wesley, 1982. Contributor of more than three hundred poems to magazines and newspapers.

WORK IN PROGRESS: Children's books and poetry.

SIDELIGHTS: "Teachers and our public library played a big part in my growing interest in books and writing. I had my first poem published when I was eighteen. I began writing for children in 1979. My favorite children's authors are Lois Lowry and Marguerite de Angeli. I enjoy doing workshops with children and adults and promoting interest in reading and writing among young people.

"My husband who is also a writer is very supportive, as are my children. Our house is overflowing with books and papers and manuscripts and typewriters."

HOBBIES AND OTHER INTERESTS: "I love country things: flea markets, garage sales, and gardening. I collect old items including teapots, kitchen utensils, crockery, teddy bears, and toys. I have traveled through New England, which I love, especially Maine. I'd like to visit Nova Scotia someday."

SPINNER, Stephanie 1943-

PERSONAL: Born November 16, 1943, in Davenport, Iowa; daughter of Ralph (a businessman) and Edna (Lowry) Spinner. *Education:* Bennington College, B.A., 1964. *Home:* 216 East 17th St., New York, N.Y. 10003.

CAREER: Children's book editor.

WRITINGS: (Editor) *Rock Is Beautiful* (anthology of rock lyrics), Dell, 1969; *Feminine Plural: Stories by Women about Growing Up* (anthology), Macmillan, 1972; *Live and Learn: Stories about Students and Their Teachers* (anthology), Macmillan, 1973; *Mother Love* (anthology), Dell, 1978; (adapter) *Popeye: The Storybook Based on the Movie*, Random House, 1981; *Dracula: A Step-Up Adventure*, Random House, 1981; *How Raggedy Ann Was Born* (illustrated by Carol Nicklaus), Bobbs, 1982; (adapter) Carlo Collodi (pseudonym of Carlo Lorenzini), *The Adventures of Pinocchio* (illustrated by Diane Goode), Random House, 1983.

HOBBIES AND OTHER INTERESTS: Tibetan painting, travel.

TATE, Eleanora E(laine) 1948-

PERSONAL: Born April 16, 1948, in Canton, Mo.; daughter of Clifford and Lillie (Douglas) Tate; married Zack E. Hamlett III (a photographer), August 19, 1972; children: Gretchen. *Education:* Drake University, B.A., 1973. *Home:* 1203 Carver St., Myrtle Beach, S.C. 29577. *Agent:* Charlotte Sheedy, Charlotte Sheedy Literary Agency, 145 West 86th St., New York, N.Y. 10024. *Office:* Positive Images, Inc., P.O. Box 483, Myrtle Beach, S.C. 29578.

CAREER: Iowa Bystander, West Des Moines, news editor, 1966-68; *Des Moines Register* and *Des Moines Tribune*, Des Moines, Iowa, staff writer, 1968-76; *Jackson Sun*, Jackson, Tenn., staff writer, 1976-77; Positive Images, Inc., Myrtle Beach, S.C., president, 1983—. Free-lance writer for *Memphis Tri-State Defender*, 1977. Contributor to black history and culture workshops in Des Moines, 1968-76; poetry presentations at Iowa Arts Council Writers in the Schools program, 1969-76, Rust College, 1973, and Grinnell College, 1975. Guest author of the South Carolina School Librarians Association Conference, 1981 and 1982. *Member:* Artist's roster, South Carolina Arts Commission. *Awards, honors:* Fifth Annual Third World Writing Contest finalist, 1973; Unity Award from Lincoln University, 1974, for educational reporting; Community Lifestyles award from Tennessee Press Association, 1977; fellowship in children's fiction for Bread Loaf Writers' Conference, 1981.

WRITINGS: (Editor with husband, Zack E. Hamlett III, and contributor) *Eclipsed* (poetry), privately printed, 1975; (editor and contributor) *Wanjiru: A Collection of Blackwomanworth*, privately printed, 1976; *Just an Overnight Guest* (juvenile novel), Dial, 1980.

(From the movie "Just an Overnight Guest," starring Tiffany Hill and Rosalind Cash. Released by Phoenix Films, 1983.)

Our gray-shingled one-story house fit only Daddy and Momma and Alberta and me—there was no place in it for Ethel. ■ (Jacket illustration by Jerry Pinkney from *Just an Overnight Guest* by Eleanora E. Tate.)

ELEANORA E. TATE

Contributor: Rosa Guy, editor, *Children of Longing*, Bantam, 1970; *Impossible?* (juvenile), Houghton, 1972; *Broadside Annual 1972*, Broadside Press, 1972; *Communications* (juvenile), Heath, 1973; *Off-Beat* (juvenile), Macmillan, 1974; *Sprays of Rubies* (anthology of poetic prose), Ragnarok, 1975; *Valhalla Four*, Ragnarok, 1977. Contributor of poetry and fiction to periodicals, including *Journal of Black Poetry* and *Des Moines Register Picture Magazine*.

ADAPTATIONS—Movie: "Just an Overnight Guest," starring Fran Robinson, Tiffany Hill, Rosalind Cash, and Richard Roundtree, Phoenix/B.F.A. Films & Video, 1983.

WORK IN PROGRESS: A Woman for the People, for adults; *The Secret of Gumbo Grove*, for juveniles.

SIDELIGHTS: Raised by her grandmother, Corinne E. Johnson, Tate had a happy childhood which later influenced her writing. "Growing out of some deep yearning, I suppose, for a return to girlhood, I have gotten a thrill out of writing about children. Part of it—my intent from now on is to write more in the children's field than for adults—stems from my belief that I had a very happy childhood, with a certain richness to it that I want today's children to share. Certainly today's children, many of them, have happy childhoods, and for that I am grateful. I would like to add my voice in print, as well as my emotions, to the thought that childhood can be happy if children learn that they can do anything they set their minds to, if they try.

"This is what motivated me to write the book, *Just an Overnight Guest*. The theme was different, but the motivation was still there. And because of that motivation, I set aside a wom-

an's 'liberation' book, *A Woman for the People*, to do it. For a number of years, in fact, all through the writing of *Just an Overnight Guest*, I struggled with *A Woman for the People*, which started out as a twenty-seven-page short that people wanted to see as a book."

The film version of *Just an Overnight Guest* has been well received in schools and libraries. "The external trappings (in the film) are different, but the basic themes are still there. In the film version, Margie's older sister is absent. The story takes place in California and the father, instead of being a furniture mover, is a saxophone player.

"They are two different versions of the same title. The film version is one good version according to one adaptation. The book version is a good account of what happens in another medium.

"My main worry was the book. I get additional satisfaction from the film. . . . The book hopefully will open many eyes for people who are concerned about child abuse and neglect." [Karen Carnes, "Message of 'Just an Overnight Guest' now on Film," *Myrtle Beach Sun News*, April 29, 1983.']

About the various themes in both the book and the film, Tate said: "One theme is the closeness of a black family that doesn't live in a ghetto in the North or the South. Another theme is father-daughter love. It has been said little black boys need fathers. I believe little black girls need fathers.

"I emphasize that. It's something that hasn't been played up in recent years. I see it every day with my husband and my daughter."

THOMAS, Art(hur Lawrence) 1952-

BRIEF ENTRY: Born July 8, 1952, in Cleveland, Ohio. For Thomas, the "mysticism" he had always associated with writing was destroyed when he was forced to become entertainment editor of his college newspaper. Since then, he has taught English, drama, and writing in public schools in Ohio. He is currently employed as business manager of the New Mayfield Repertory Cinema. Thomas's work as an author has focused on sports books, and gradually his writings have become part of the "Sports for Me" series, all published by Lerner. Although his first book, *Recreational Wrestling* (A.S. Barnes, 1976), was not associated with the series, it affirmed Thomas's ability to write competently and to introduce readers to various sports subjects. The book includes information on competition, training, rules, and various wrestling maneuvers. In a review of the book *Choice* observed, "The description of wrestling techniques is clear and would be easily understandable to a teacher not acquainted through experience with the sport of wrestling." *Boxing Is for Me* (Lerner, 1982), part of the "Sports for Me" series, focuses on a young boy as he learns the basic techniques of boxing. Developed for a younger audience than are most books on the subject, *School Library Journal* described it as "a nice gentle approach to an active, aggressive sport." Other books by Thomas in the "Sports for Me" series include *Wrestling Is for Me* (1979), *Volleyball Is for Me* (1979), *Horseback Riding Is for Me* (1981), and *Archery Is for Me* (1982).

Aside from his sports books, Thomas has written a primary-grade reader entitled *Merry-Go-Rounds* (Carolrhoda, 1982). The book explores the history of merry-go-rounds, presenting their background and development through cartoon-like illustrations in a style that, according to *School Library Journal,* "avoids the droning repetition of some early readers." Thomas is also entertainment editor of *West Life,* in which appears his column "Theater in Review." *Home:* 12500 Edgewater Dr., Lakewood, Ohio 44107. *For More Information See: Contemporary Authors,* Volume 105, Gale, 1981.

THOMAS, Jane Resh 1936-

PERSONAL: Born August 15, 1936, in Kalamazoo, Mich.; daughter of Reed Beneval (in sales) and Thelma (a teacher; maiden name, Scott) Resh; married Richard Thomas (a copywriter), November 13, 1961; children: Jason. *Education:* Bronson School of Nursing, R.N., 1957; attended Michigan State University, 1959-60; University of Minnesota, B.A. (summa cum laude), 1967, M.A., 1971. *Residence:* Minneapolis, Minn.

CAREER: Worked as registered nurse, 1957-60; University of Minnesota at Minneapolis, instructor in English composition, 1967-80; free-lance writer, 1972—. *Member:* American Association of University Women, Phi Beta Kappa.

WRITINGS—Juvenile: Elizabeth Catches a Fish (illustrated by Joseph Duffy), Seabury, 1977; *The Comeback Dog* (Junior Literary Guild selection; illustrated by Troy Howell), Houghton, 1981; *Courage at Indian Deep,* Clarion, 1984. Also author of "Children's Books," a monthly column in the *Minneapolis Tribune.* Contributor of articles and reviews to periodicals, including *Horn Book* magazine and *New York Times Book Review.*

SIDELIGHTS: "When I was a child in Kalamazoo, Michigan, my father bought an adult English setter named Bill, who flinched at every move we made as if he expected us to kick him. He couldn't be friendly to us until one day he came imploringly to my mother with pronged seeds in his eyes and sat patiently while she removed them with tweezers. After that he forgave us whatever wrongs others had done him and became one of the best dogs we ever had.

"Bill sometimes went with us to our grandparent's farm, a peach orchard and tree nursery near Lake Michigan. A creek, where mother hunted snakes when she was a girl, meandered across the meadow. One spring, after a flood had subsided, I found enough blue crayfish claws on the ground to fill a strawberry box. I kept them under our porch for a long time, even though they smelled bad, because they were beautiful.

"We spent weekends at a cottage on Big Cedar Lake, where our parents owned ten acres of land. In the swamp that bordered the lake, wild ladyslippers and rattlesnakes grew among poison sumac and watercress. One oak tree was so big that my brother and I couldn't reach around it, and so old it must have been growing when Indians lived nearby. I often fished with my father, who taught me to see what I looked at—the herons and loons that nested in the reeds, the mist that clung to the water at dawn, the dogwood and cattails, and the deer drinking at the spring at the first morning light that had appeared, it seemed, between one blink and another.

"When we were at home in Kalamazoo, my favorite place was the Washington Square Library, with its stone entryway, its fireplace and leaded windows, and what seemed like miles of books. I wrote to Maud Hart Lovelace once and received an answer. Busy though my mother was, raising four children with little help except financial support from my father, she found time to read to us. I learned to love literature at her side.

JANE RESH THOMAS

Elizabeth trailed her hand in the water. . . . ■ (From *Elizabeth Catches a Fish* by Jane Resh Thomas. Illustrated by Joseph Duffy.)

My family were uncommunicative people, and I relied on books, as I did on nature, not only to entertain but to sustain myself. For a brief, blissful time, we had a membership we could ill afford in the Junior Literary Guild. I remember my utter joy when books like *Big Tree* and *Bonnie's Boy* arrived in the mail.

"I have wanted to be a writer at least since I was seven years old, but was much discouraged by the conventional responses of adults to the things I wrote. The world has always been a wonder and a mystery to me. I write, as I read, in order to understand it and to find out what I think and feel. The dog, Bill, the farm, the crayfish claws, and the dawn-lit lake have come back to me in the stories that are in my head and on paper, even though I now live six hundred miles and twenty-five years from home. And although my father and grandparents died years ago, they have come back too. The oak tree fell in a storm a few years ago, but it lives again in my mind. They are all transformed, mixed with things and people that never happened and never were, and blended with present events, like my son Jason's three-year effort to make friends with Rosie, the standoffish poodle we bought at the pound. Transformed though we are, I recognize all of us and the magical places I love in the stories that make my past present and my present comprehensible."

FOR MORE INFORMATION SEE: New York Times Book Review, May 1, 1977, May 10, 1981.

TOLAN, Stephanie S.   1942-

PERSONAL: Born October 25, 1942, in Canton, Ohio; daughter of Joseph Edward and Mary (Schroy) Stein; married Robert W. Tolan (a managing director of a theater), December 19, 1964; children: R.J.; stepchildren: Robert Jr., Patrick, Andrew. *Education:* Purdue University, B.A., 1964, M.A., 1967. *Home:* 155 Windsor Pl., Chapel Hill, N.C. 27514. *Agent:* Marilyn Marlow, Curtis Brown Ltd., 575 Madison Ave., New York, N.Y. 10022.

CAREER: Purdue University, Fort Wayne, Ind., instructor in continuing education, 1966-70; State University of New York College at Buffalo, faculty member in speech and theater, 1972; Franklin & Marshall College, Lancaster, Pa., adjunct faculty member in English, 1973-75, coordinator of continuing education, 1974-75; writer, 1976—. Lecturer at Indiana University, 1966-70; actress, performing with Curtain Call Co., 1970-71. *Member:* Actors' Equity Association. *Awards, honors:* Artist fellowship from Ohio Arts Council, 1978 and 1981-82; fellowship, Bread Loaf Writers' Conference, 1981; Ohioana Book Award, 1981, for *The Liberation of Tansey Warner; Grandpa—and Me* was nominated for the Sequoyah Children's Book Award and the Georgia Children's Book Award.

WRITINGS: The Ledge (one-act play), Samuel French, 1968; "Not I, Said the Little Red Hen" (one-act play), first produced in New York City, 1971; *Grandpa—and Me* (juvenile), Scribner, 1978; *The Last of Eden,* Warne, 1980; *The Liberation of Tansey Warner,* Scribner, 1980; *No Safe Harbors,* Scribner, 1981; *Guiding the Gifted Child* (non-fiction), Ohio Psychology Publishing, 1982; *The Great Skinner Strike,* Macmillian, 1983; *A Time to Fly Free,* Scribner, 1983.

STEPHANIE S. TOLAN

(Jacket illustration by Andrew Rhodes from _Grandpa--and Me_ by Stephanie S. Tolan.)

Contributor of poems to more than a dozen literary magazines, including _Roanoke Review, Descant,_ and _Green River Review._

WORK IN PROGRESS: A novel for young readers, another nonfiction book about gifted children.

SIDELIGHTS: "I began writing for young readers because I grew to love books when I was a young reader, hiding out under the covers with a flashlight at night so I could finish whatever book I was reading, or putting off my chores while I finished 'just one more page' or 'just one more chapter.' As I grew older, I realized that even adults who love to read as much as I do seem to have lost something, an almost magical joy in reading that children have. That joy in reading made me want to be a writer, and from the time I was nine years old, I never doubted that I would be one, in spite of the rejection slips I began getting by the age of eleven. Writers have to be persistent. I continued to write through junior high and high school, finally majoring in creative writing in college. After getting a graduate degree in English, I began to teach college writing courses, but continued to write poetry and plays for adults until 1976, when I quit teaching and began writing full time.

"It was probably mostly for the child reader I had been that I wrote my first novel for children. Then, while visiting schools through the National Endowment for the Arts Poets-in-the-

Schools projects in Pennsylvania and Ohio, I met the new generation of readers who still stay up late with flashlights to read. Maybe television has cut back on the numbers of such readers, but they're everywhere still, and they still lose themselves in the worlds created by those magical black marks on white pages. Working with those children and helping them express themselves through their own writing, I realized I had found my real audience. It is for them that I write now, as well as for myself, hoping all the time that I can make my stories worth staying up late to finish.

"Meantime, my own family is growing up—my three stepsons have changed from three grubby-fingered, scabby-kneed little boys to very tall young men, and my son is in junior high school. The tribes of animals we have all lived with have dwindled to a tiny population of two dogs, two cats and two chameleons. My husband's work in the professional theater has moved us around the country often, but one of the joys of writing as a career is that I really can do it anywhere. (At least anywhere I can plug my computer and my printer in—I've switched from using a typewriter to working on a word processor, a great improvement!)"

JOHN TOLAND

Shark's teeth were painted along the edge of the engine . . . . Improving on the British model, they added a red tongue and a staring red eye behind the propeller. ■ (From *The Flying Tigers* by John Toland. Photograph courtesy of the U.S. Air Force.)

TOLAND, John (Willard) 1912-

PERSONAL: Born June 29, 1912, in La Crosse, Wis.; son of Ralph (a concert singer) and Helen (Snow) Toland; married present wife, Toshiko Matsumura, March 12, 1960; children: (previous marriage) Diana, Marcia; (present marriage) Tamiko (daughter). *Education:* Williams College, B.A., 1936; attended Yale University, 1937. *Residence:* Danbury, Conn. *Agent:* Carl Brandt, Brandt & Brandt Literary Agents, Inc., 1501 Broadway, New York, N.Y. 10036.

CAREER: Professional writer. Advisor to the National Archives. *Military service:* U.S. Air Force, six years; became captain. *Member:* Overseas Press Club, Writers Guild, P.E.N. *Awards, honors:* Overseas Press Club award for best book on foreign affairs, 1961, for *But Not in Shame,* 1967, for *The Last 100 Days,* 1970, for *The Rising Sun,* 1976, for *Adolf Hitler;* certificate from Boys' Club Junior Book Award, 1966-67, for *The Battle of the Bulge;* L.H.D., Williams College, 1968; Van Wyck Brooks Award for nonfiction, 1970, for *The Rising Sun;* Pulitzer Prize for nonfiction, 1970, for *The Rising Sun;* L.H.D., University of Alaska, 1977; National Society of Arts and Letters gold medal, 1977, for *Adolf Hitler;* Accademia del Mediterrano, 1978.

WRITINGS—All published by Random House, except as indicated: *Ships in the Sky,* Holt, 1957; *Battle: The Story of the Bulge,* 1959; *But Not in Shame,* 1961; *The Dillinger Days,* 1963; *The Flying Tigers* (juvenile), 1963; *The Last 100 Days,* 1966; *The Battle of the Bulge* (juvenile; illustrated by Jerome Kuhl), 1966; *The Rising Sun: The Decline and Fall of the Japanese Empire, 1936-1945,* 1970; *Adolf Hitler,* Doubleday, 1976; *Hitler: The Pictorial Documentary of His Life,* Doubleday, 1978; *No Man's Land: The Story of 1918,* Doubleday, 1980; *Infamy: Pearl Harbor and Its Aftermath,* Doubleday, 1982; *Gods of War,* Doubleday, 1984. Contributor of articles and stories to *Look, Life, Reader's Digest, Saturday Evening Post,* and other magazines.

WORK IN PROGRESS: Research on the occupation of Japan.

SIDELIGHTS: "I first learned I wanted to be a writer when I was twelve years old and joined Troop Twelve of the Boy Scouts, Norwalk, Connecticut in 1924. I was given the job of writing a weekly report and from the first decided to be original. I started off with 'The Thought of the Week' which was from *Aesop's Fables* or from listening to my Irish father, who was a concert singer and an athlete. Next I would list the doings of the past week and the schedule for the next week and in between I would insert a few jokes I got from *Literary Digest* which I used to sell. A year later I went to Boy Scout camp and it rained the first day. We were forced to stay in our tents (eight to a tent) and amuse ourselves by telling stories. In my tent there were no budding authors and when it turned out that I could tell interminable stories I kept the other seven hostages more or less entertained all day long. That night I prayed it would rain the next day. God poured down rain, thus putting the seal of approval on my destiny. The second day for eight hours I kept a continued story going and by this time I was reaching my public.

"The next step in my career came in junior high school where I spent all my study periods writing stories for myself. The girl in front of me saw the sheaf of papers and when she learned it was a long Homeric story about a boy and girl lost in the woods asked to read it. From then on she would read my story page by page and, when finished, would turn around anxiously for the next. I had an instant, attentive and appreciative audience. Her name was Alice Adams and I shall never forget her.

"The final step in deciding my life's work came when I was attending Norwalk High School. I was about fifteen or sixteen and my father, who was always bringing a broken-winged bird or a person home, turned up one day with a small fat man. This was Porter Emerson Browne, a well-known playwright whose most notable success was 'The Bad Man,' a comedy based on Pancho Villa. Porter had lost his beloved wife and began drinking. My father could cure anybody of anything and so Porter stayed with us for more than a year. Within a week he had become my hero for life. He told me he had written 'The Bad Man' because he had ridden for two years with Pancho Villa as his secretary. That, he said, was why the play was successful. He had also travelled with two warlords in China and written speeches for President Teddy Roosevelt. I told him I wanted to be a playwright and he took me seriously.

"Treating me like an adult, he taught me the principles of the craft. Then he took me to a movie at the Regent Theater. After the first half he made me walk out. He said we were to write the ending based on the principles of good playwriting. We did; and returned two days later to see how the movie came out. It ended when the hero suddenly takes out a gun and shoots his wife. Porter exclaimed, 'Obscenity!' which startled those around us. Then he loudly explained that the gun should have been planted in the first reel and not suddenly appear by chance. The same held for important traits of character upon which the play turned.

"His final words to me were: 'John, whatever you write, plays or novels, remember this: Don't tell it, show it.' And I have been showing it instead of telling it in all my histories. Porter's final warning to me was that I should avoid early success since several of his friends had written successful plays and, unable to achieve a follow-up, committed suicide. 'I hope,' he said, 'you don't sell your first million words.'

"Porter, wherever you are, you must be proud of me. I didn't sell my first two and a half million words. I wrote twenty full length plays, a hundred short stories, and five novels without any success. Finally I sold a science fiction story for a penny a word when I was forty-two. Within two years I had sold articles to a dozen magazines as well as a book, *Ships in the Sky*, to Henry Holt."

FOR MORE INFORMATION SEE: Christian Science Monitor, March 3, 1966, October 27, 1976; *Newsweek*, March 7, 1966, December 28, 1970, September 20, 1976; *Saturday Review*, March 12, 1966, September 18, 1976; *Modern Age*, fall, 1966; *New York Times Book Review*, November 29, 1970; *New York Times*, December 7, 1970; *Time*, December 7, 1970, December 6, 1976; *Book World*, January 3, 1971, August 29, 1976; *Best Sellers*, February 1, 1971; *Yale Review*, June, 1971; *Village Voice*, November 15, 1976; *Books and Bookmen*, July, 1977; *Chicago Tribune Book World*, September 28, 1980; *Detroit News*, October 19, 1980; *Washington Post*, October 27, 1980; *London Times*, December 11, 1980; *Los Angeles Times*, December 28, 1980.

TOOKE, Louise Mathews 1950-
(Louise Mathews)

PERSONAL: Born June 15, 1950, in New York, N.Y.; daughter of William Cooper (an educator) and Edith (Combes) Mathews; married November 28, 1980. *Education:* Attended School of Visual Arts, 1970-72. *Address:* c/o Dodd, Mead & Co., 79 Madison Ave., New York, N.Y. 10016.

CAREER: Private art teacher and free-lance designer in Winter Park, Fla., 1970-78; writer, 1978—. *Awards, honors: Cluck One* was chosen one of the best children's books of 1983 by New York Public Library.

WRITINGS—Juveniles; under name Louise Mathews; all illustrated by Jeni Bassett: *Bunches and Bunches of Bunnies*, Dodd, 1978; *Gator Pie*, Dodd, 1979; *The Great Take-Away*, Dodd, 1980; *Cluck One* (Junior Literary Guild selection), Dodd, 1983.

SIDELIGHTS: "My picture books revolve around a mathematical or other educational concept. The impetus for my books

LOUISE MATHEWS TOOKE

are pieces of animated cartoons in my mind's eye that begin to illustrate a particular concept. As I nail down the concept the scaffolding rises and then I have great fun embellishing the original structure with as much hilarity and hijinks as I can. I strive to make the concept seem incidental, even though it functions for me like a glue, so that it slips up on the kids when they are too busy laughing to notice.

"I hoped when I wrote the stories that teachers especially would adopt them, and use them as springboards for further creative approaches to math in their classrooms. Bit by bit I hear that they are. A student teacher on the West Coast charted the robber hog's loot as an ongoing project with her second graders. Another has a fraction party with real pies each autumn. In the hands of thirty-five fifth graders *Gator Pie* became a play and I think they enjoyed the fight scene almost as much as Alvin and Alice did."

HOBBIES AND OTHER INTERESTS: Dancing, puppet design, toy design.

WARREN, Elizabeth Avery 1916-
(Betsy Warren)

BRIEF ENTRY: Born January 27, 1916, in St. Louis, Mo. Author and illustrator of books for children, teacher of organ and piano, and free-lance artist. For nearly thirty years, she has written and illustrated books under the name Betsy Warren. *The Donkey Sat Down*, published in 1955, was followed by titles such as *Make a Joyful Noise, Papacito and His Family*, and *The Queen Cat*. In 1971 Warren was the recipient of the Texas Institute of Letters award for her book entitled *Indians Who Lived in Texas*, which describes the lifestyle and customs of ten Indian tribes during the early 1900s. It is the first in a series of books that focuses on the history of Texas. Warren's illustrations have accompanied various texts such as *Speedy Gets Around* by Dorothy E. Prince, *A Hat for Lilly* by Doris J. Chaconas, and a revised edition of *The Pretty House That Found Happiness* by Eleanor Eisenberg. Under the name Elizabeth Avery Warren, she is also the author of four "I Can Read" books published by Troll Associates in 1975. *Home:* 2409 Dormarion St., Austin, Tex. 78703. *For More Information See: Contemporary Authors, New Revision Series*, Volume 8, Gale, 1983.

WASHBURN, (Henry) Bradford (Jr.) 1910-

PERSONAL: Born June 7, 1910, in Cambridge, Mass.; son of Henry Bradford (a clergyman) and Edith (Hall) Washburn; married Barbara T. Polk, April 27, 1940; children: Dorothy Polk, Edward Hall, Elizabeth Bradford. *Education:* Harvard University, A.B. (cum laude), 1933, graduate work at Institute of Geographical Exploration, 1934-35, A.M., 1960. *Home:* 220 Somerset St., Belmont, Mass. 02178. *Office:* Museum of Science, Science Park, Boston, Mass. 02114.

CAREER: Museum director, mountaineer, and explorer, who began Alpine ascents at age sixteen and Alaska climbs in 1930; Harvard University, Cambridge, Mass., instructor at Institute of Geographical Explorations, 1935-42; Museum of Science, Boston, Mass., director, 1939-80, chairman of the corporation, 1980—. Leader of National Geographic Society expeditions in Yukon, 1935, and over Mount McKinley (photographic flights), 1936-38; consultant on cold climate equipment to U.S. Army

BRADFORD WASHBURN

Air Forces and director of Alaskan test projects, 1942-45; leader or co-leader of other Alaskan expeditions, mainly on Mount McKinley, 1947, 1949, 1951, 1955, 1965; his first ascents of Alaska peaks include Mount Lucania, 1937, Mount Sanford and Mount Marcus Baker, 1938, Mount Bertha, 1940, Mount Hayes, 1941, west ridge of Mount McKinley, 1951. Former director or trustee of John Hancock Mutual Life Insurance Co., New England Telephone & Telegraph Co. and WGBH Educational Foundation, Inc.; founding director of National Rowing Foundation, Inc. and trustee of Mount Washington Observatory. Member of advisory bodies to National Armed Forces Museum, 1964-68, U.S. Commissioner of Education, 1965-66, and Secretary of the Interior (on national parks), 1966—. Member of board of overseers, Harvard College, 1955-61; member of Massachusetts Rhodes Scholars Committee, 1959-64; trustee of Smith College, 1962-68. Consultant to American Heritage Press.

MEMBER: American Academy of Arts and Sciences (fellow), Arctic Institute of North America (honorary fellow), Royal Geographical Society (London; fellow), American Geographical Society (honorary fellow), California Academy of Sciences (honorary fellow), American Association for the Advancement of Science (fellow), Association of Science Technology Centers (honorary fellow), Groupe de Haute Montagne (France; honorary member), Explorers Club (New York), Harvard Travellers Club (honorary fellow), University of Arizona Center for Creative Photography (fellow), Tavern Club (Boston), Phi

Beta Kappa (honorary member); honorary member of other mountaineering, naturalist, and camera clubs in United States, England, and Canada.

AWARDS, HONORS: Cuthbert Peek Award of Royal Geographical Society, 1938, for Alaskan exploration and glacier studies; Franklin L. Burr Prize of National Geographic Society for Alaskan exploration, 1940, and Yukon exploration, 1965; Exceptional Civilian Service Award from Secretary of War, 1946; Ph.D. from University of Alaska, 1951, University of Suffolk, 1965, Boston College, 1974, Harvard University, 1975, and Babson College, 1980; Sc.D. from Tufts University and Colby College, 1957, Northeastern University, 1958, University of Massachusetts, 1972, and Curry College, 1982; Gold Medal of Harvard Travellers Club, 1959; Bradford Washburn Gold Medal and Award was established in his honor by trustees of Museum of Science, 1964; Richard Hopper Day Medal of Philadelphia Academy of Arts and Sciences, 1966; Julius Adams Stratton Prize of Friends of Switzerland, 1970; Certificate of Honor, National Conference on the Humanities, 1971; blue ribbons from U.S. Congress of Surveying and Mapping, 1975, for Squam Range map, and 1979, for Heart of the Grand Canyon map; Gold Research Medal of Royal Scottish Geographical Society, 1979; with wife, Barbara Washburn, first recipient of National Geographic's Alexander Graham Bell Gold Medal, 1980; Distinguished Bostonian award from Boston Chamber of Commerce, 1983; Explorers Medal of the Explorers Club of New York, 1984.

WRITINGS: The Trails and Peaks of the Presidential Range of the White Mountains (guide book), Davis Press, 1926; *Among the Alps with Bradford,* Putnam, 1927; *Bradford on Mt. Washington,* Putnam, 1928; *Bradford on Mt. Fairweather,* Putnam, 1930; *Mount McKinley and the Alaska Range in Literature,* (descriptive bibliography), Museum of Science (Boston), 1951; (with Caroline Harrison) *Allan and Trisha Visit Science Park* (juvenile), Little, Brown, 1953; (with Eric Shipton) *Mountain Conquest,* American Heritage, 1966; *A Tourist Guide to Mount McKinley,* Northwest Publishing, 1971.

Creator of maps and charts: "Chart of Squam Lake, N.H.," 1968; "Map of the Squam Range, N.H.," 1973; "Map of the Heart of the Grand Canyon," 1978; "Map of Wonder Lake to McGonagall Pass and Muldrow Glacier" (Alaska), 1980; "Map of the Bright Angel Trail" (Grand Canyon), 1981.

Editor, "Mount McKinley, Alaska: A Reconnaissance Map," published under auspices of Museum of Science, Swiss Foundation for Alpine Research and American Academy of Arts and Sciences, 1960. Contributor of features to *National Geographic, Life, Mountain World,* and articles or photographs to *Look, Sports Illustrated, Illustrated London News, Scientific American, Polar Record, New England Journal of Medicine,* and other periodicals in United States, England, Japan, and Germany.

SIDELIGHTS: Before he was out of school Washburn had climbed the Matterhorn and Mount Rosa as well as most of the major peaks in the Mont Blanc chain, and had photographed the ascent of Mount Blanc and the Grepon for Burton Holmes. Aerial photography work outside of Alaska includes Bermuda in 1938, and ten flights in Switzerland to photograph the Mont Blanc, Matterhorn, and Bernese Oberland areas from 1958-60. His photographs have been exhibited at the Museum of Modern Art and in "The World from the Air" show at Kodak Pavilion, New York World's Fair. In 1971, Washburn did field work preliminary to a mapping project covering 170 square miles in the heart of the Grand Canyon, work financed by a grant from

the National Geographic Society. In 1978, he started field work for a new large-scale map of Mount Washington in New Hampshire.

WEIS, Margaret (Edith) 1948-
(Margaret Baldwin)

PERSONAL: Born March 16, 1948, in Independence, Mo.; daughter of George Edward (an engineer) and Francis Irene (Reed) Weis; married Robert William Baldwin (a State trooper), August 22, 1970 (divorced, 1982); children: David William, Elizabeth Lynn. *Education:* University of Missouri, B.A., 1970. *Politics:* Independent. *Religion:* "No formal." *Home:* 224 Maxwell, Lake Geneva, Wis. 53147. *Agent:* Ray Peekner Agency, 2625 North 36th St., Milwaukee, Wis. 53210. *Office:* TSR Hobbies, Inc., P.O. Box 756, Lake Geneva, Wis. 53147.

CAREER: Worked as director of advertising and director of trade division for Independence Press (publisher), Independence, Mo.; TSR Hobbies, Inc., Lake Geneva, Wis., editor, 1983—. *Member:* Great Alkali Plainsmen (Kansas City, Mo.).

WRITINGS—All nonfiction; all under name Margaret Baldwin: *The Boys Who Saved the Children* (remedial reader for young adults; based on autobiography *Growing Up in the Holocaust*

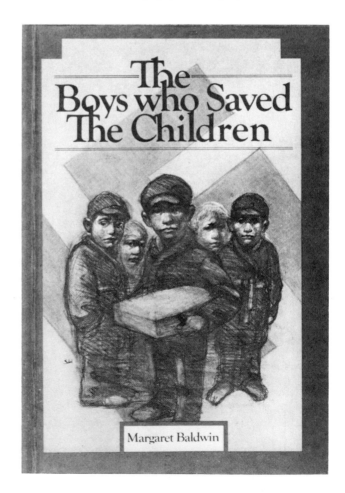

All the time the rumors got louder and louder. We were running out of time. ■ (Cover illustration by Sanford Hoffman from *The Boys Who Saved the Children* by Margaret Baldwin.)

by Ben Edelbaum), Messner, 1981; (with Pat O'Brien) *Wanted!
Frank and Jesse James: The Real Story* (young adult biography), Messner, 1981; *Kisses of Death: A Great Escape Story
of World War II* (remedial reader for young adults; illustrated
by Norma Welliver), Messner, 1983; *My First Book: Thanksgiving* (juvenile), F. Watts, 1983; (with Gary Pack) *My First
Book: Robots and Robotic*, F. Watts, 1983; (with G. Pack) *My
First Book: Computer Graphics*, F. Watts, 1983; *Independence, Missouri: A History*, Independence School District
(Missouri), 1984; *The Endless Catacombs*, TSR, Inc., 1984;
(with Tracy Hickman) *Dragonlance (TM) Chronicles*, Volume
1, TSR, Inc., 1984.

SIDELIGHTS: "I have always enjoyed writing—mainly, I believe, because I enjoyed reading. But I did not seriously consider writing as a vocation during school. I wanted to be an
artist. Several incidents caused me to change my mind and
point out, I believe, how strong an effect good teachers can
have on our lives. First, my high school English teacher, D.
R. Smith, taught me how to write. Mr. Smith began by tossing
out the curriculum intended for high school juniors. (He was
forever in trouble with the school administrators. Aside from
teaching me to write, the most important thing he taught me
was to be my own person and stand up for my ideals.) Our
class spent the first semester writing sentences. That's all. Just
one sentence everyday. We started out with simple sentences—
a subject and verb. Then we were allowed to add an adjective.
I remember the thrill, weeks later, when we could proudly put
in an adverb. After sixteen weeks, Mr. Smith decided we were
ready to move on. We wrote paragraphs—five sentences each.
We did that for the next sixteen weeks. I came to respect words
in his class. I came to realize how critical every word—no
matter how insignificant—is in writing. I saw how sentences
joined together to form paragraphs. When we read books in
his class, we studied not only the literary content but he showed
us how the writer created the effect he wanted by use of words
and sentence structure. Mr. Smith showed me the door, but it
still remained closed.

"I went to college, intending to make art my career. One day,
however, my teacher for Freshman English—a student teacher,
I can't even remember her name—kept me after class, took
me to the student union and asked if I had considered studying
writing. She told me about the University of Missouri's English
program. (The University was one of the few in the 1960s to
offer a creative writing program separate from journalism.) I
have often thought this young woman should have been an
army recruiter. If she had, I would no doubt have joined on
the spot. I investigated the writing program, liked it, and switched
my major. She gave me the key to the door.

"Finally I met Dr. Donald Drummond, poet and professor.
He showed me how the key opened the door. I entered and
knew that I had come home. We wrote poetry in Dr. Drummond's class. They were grueling class sessions. The poet was
required to read his work aloud, while his fellow poets sat,
knives out, waiting for blood. Classes met at night, often for
several hours. We came out battle-scarred, but we could write.
Dr. Drummond was another unusual teacher. He began by
giving us a long list of subjects we were under no circumstances
to write about. These include: Love (with a capital 'L'), truth,
beauty, death and the Vietnam War. 'And,' he growled, 'if I
get one poem about a daffodil you will flunk the semester!'

"Needless to say, I never have, and I never will, write about
a daffodil."

WELSH, Mary Flynn 1910(?)-1984
(Mary Flynn)

OBITUARY NOTICE: Born about 1910, in County Longford,
Ireland; died of cancer, February 13, 1984, in Washington,
D.C. Educator and author. A former teacher of English in
Washington, D.C. public schools, Welsh wrote the "Cornelius
the Rabbit" children's book series under the name Mary Flynn.
The titles in the series are *Cornelius Rabbit of Tang, Cornelius
on Holidays*, and *Cornelius in Charge*. She also wrote *Danny
Puffin: A Story*. Welsh was a member of P.E.N. and of Irish
Women Writers. *Obituaries: Washington Post*, February 16,
1984.

WELTNER, Linda R(iverly) 1938-

PERSONAL: Born October 13, 1938, in Worcester, Mass.;
daughter of William (a wool dealer) and Dorothy (Rosenberg)
Holbert; married John Sigmund Weltner (a child psychiatrist),
June 7, 1959; children: Laura Marjorie, Julia Hess. *Education:*
Wellesley College, B.A. (with honors), 1960; attended University of Michigan, 1960, Maine Photographic Institute, 1974,
and Harvard Divinity School, 1977. *Home:* Crown Way, Marblehead, Mass. 01945.

CAREER: Elementary school teacher in Chelsea, Mich., 1960-
61; Boston Lying-In Hospital, Maternal-Infant Health Program, Boston, Mass., research assistant, 1962; Ginn & Co.

LINDA R. WELTNER

(publishers), Boston, assistant editor, 1962-64; *Marblehead Messenger,* Marblehead, Mass., staff reporter and photographer, 1969-73; free-lance writer and photographer, 1974—. Co-founder of Periwinkle Cooperative Nursery School, 1969, and Marblehead Alternative Religious Community, 1974. Member of board of directors of Municipal Power Advocacy Coalition, 1981, advisory committee of Harvard Divinity School Theological Opportunities Program, 1977, and Wellesley College Communications Board, 1979—. Teacher of mini-course in marine biology, 1974, and six-week course "Surviving the 1980s Together," for the Marblehead Community Counseling Center, 1980. Public speaker.

WRITINGS: (Contributor) Sharon Strassfeld and Michael Strassfeld, editors, *The Third Jewish Catalog,* Jewish Publication Society, 1980; *Beginning to Feel the Magic* (young adult), Little, Brown, 1981; *The New Voice* (young adult; based on the television series "The New Voice"), Beacon Press, 1981.

Author of plays, including "As Lonely as American Pie," 1977, "Love for Sale," 1978, "Are You Ready for a New Me?," 1979, and "A Pox on Your Lips Now," 1980. Author of weekly column "Ever So Humble," for *Boston Globe,* 1982—. Contributor of articles to periodicals and newspapers, including *Marblehead Magazine, Wellesley, New York Times,* and *New Age Magazine.*

SIDELIGHTS: A free-lance writer, Weltner wrote her first novel, *Beginning to Feel the Magic,* as an expansion of an autobiographical piece she did for the *Boston Globe.* The article caught the attention of an editor at Little, Brown, who then wrote the author offering her a chance to turn the essay into a book for teenagers. Although her entrance into the world of young-adult literature was sudden, Weltner was ready for it. The mother of two high-school-age daughters, she had been reading teen books for years. "Everything they read, I read. It was like eating candy. I couldn't stop. You can read those books in about an hour and a half. So when John Keller (Little, Brown editor) called, I was prepared. I'd probably read 100 of those teen books." [From an interview by Peggy Shehan McLean in *Salem Evening News,* July 22, 1981.']

Weltner shares her experiences and their influence on her writing in her book, *Beginning to Feel the Magic.* "I lived in Worcester for ten months in 1980.

"Not in reality. In my imagination.

"For ten months, I was eleven again, living in the double decker my family shared with my grandmother and two aunts on Gold Street, spending my days in the sixth grade classroom of Ash Street School, returning with wonder to the playground where I took my first ride on a ferris wheel.

"I remembered the smell of chalk dust, the Halloween bonfire kindled with a neighbor's fence, and a mix of people too poor to know that twenty years later the word 'integrated' would be invented to describe our neighborhood.

"Images and sounds and memories flooded back as I sat at my typewriter and wrote them all down, trying to recreate life as it was before television turned our eyes in envy to a distant and more affluent existence. Our house had a tiny fenced-in lawn filled with nightcrawlers, and a maroon rug in the parlor that attracted lint like a magnet. I had friends I cared about, my extended family around me, and miraculously, the conviction that a benevolent God watched over us all. Why else

would my rich cousins give me a hand-me-down coat with a mouton collar? How else could my father have broken his leg the day before the draft notice arrived in the mail? Who else could have arranged for my father's birthday to come in time to make him too old to serve in World War II?

"At first, I tried to translate these earliest experiences into a contemporary novel, but my editor objected. The world had changed so much, the past broke through all my disguises. And so I tried not to tamper with the teacher who smelled of baby powder and picked me to play Snow White in the school's first dramatic production, or with the principal who opened her personal bookshelves to a child who loved to read. My pediatrician made housecalls again, smiling crookedly, his face still partially paralysed by a war injury. The counselor at the Worcester Guidance Clinic found time again to listen to a child who had never before tried to put her feelings into words.

"Sometimes it is only in retrospect that you discover how deep roots grow, and how much caring waits to be rediscovered in the small, long ago places of childhood.

"We were black and white, Jew and Catholic, Pole and Italian, united in our fascination with Tarzan, Archie and Veronica, and Superman, helping our parents collect sets of dishes piece by piece at the Rialto Theater on Saturday afternoons. Try as I can, I cannot remember a single religious or racial epithet uttered from meanness of heart. Perhaps such slurs were so deeply imbedded in our language, that we had no need for intentional insults. In adolescence, it was the touch of skin, not its color, that captured our imagination.

"I wondered what happened to all the people I grew up with: Joyce, who kissed every boy in the schoolyard who asked; Frances, with the inaudible whisper; Helen, whose drunken father beat her tougher every day; Honey, who broke into my aunt's apartment on the floor above us and stole her radio. Mostly, I wondered what happened to the boy I loved with all my heart in sixth grade.

"Now is the time for confession. In my book, *Beginning to Feel the Magic,* the heroine's childhood crush thrives after an initial misunderstanding. I did hit Alan over the head with an umbrella when I heard he'd been glad that I got sick with pneumonia, but in reality, he never spoke to me again. Ever. I reworked the scenes with my mother, too, and made peace with the baby sister who so rudely arrived and ended my reign as favored only child. Without conscious intent, I seem to have forgiven myself enough to make it come out right this time.

" . . . I visited the old double decker in person and walked up the hill I had climbed so many days of my life. Our old house had shrunk and fallen a little to one side with age, but the lawn was still tenderly cared for by strangers as dedicated as my Dad had ever been. The roses were gone though, and so was the cat who loved to mess just out of reach under our claw-footed bathtub.

"My elementary school had become a warehouse, dark and silent. Much of the neighborhood was razed and parts were now zoned for industrial purposes. Downtown Worcester was new and modernized, but that made no difference, To the child in me, the world of thirty-five years ago was only four blocks wide.

"Television has captured so much of our nation's history in slow motion and stop action. The tragedies of our age unfold daily before our disbelieving eyes, but only in books can the small triumphs of the neighborhoods of America be remembered and honored.

"Setting out to recreate a time and place that I knew as no one else ever has or can, led to many surprising discoveries, but none were stranger than this: college and marriage can get the girl out of her hometown, but in the deepest recesses of the mind, the suitcases are never unpacked."

About her writing Weltner comments, "The task of writing a weekly newspaper column about home, viewing it as a metaphor for life in the twentieth century, is one of the most challenging tasks I've ever undertaken. I'm hoping these essays will eventually appear in book form.

"My writing has never been an act separate from my life. I write to communicate what I have learned from intense attention to the details of daily living. I take the same care with family and friends that I do with a recalcitrant paragraph, and I am proudest of the fact that I have not sacrificed time with the first in pursuit of success with the last."

FOR MORE INFORMATION SEE: Boston Globe, May 3, 1981; *Salem Evening News* (Mass.), July 22, 1981; *Seventeen*, October, 1981.

WEST, Emily G(ovan) 1919-
(Emmy Payne, Emmy West)

PERSONAL: Born in 1919; daughter of Gilbert Eaton (an author) and Christine (an author; maiden name, Noble) Govan. *Home:* 315 Sunset Circle, Lookout Mountain, Tenn. 37350.

CAREER: Author of books for children.

WRITINGS—All for children; under name Emmy Payne: *Katy No-Pocket* (illustrated by H.A. Rey), Houghton, 1944; *Johnny Groundhog's Shadow* (illustrated by Theo Pascal), Houghton, 1948.

All under name Emmy West; all with mother, Christine Noble Govan; all published by Sterling, unless otherwise indicated: *The Mystery at Shingle Rock* (illustrated by Frederick T. Chapman), 1955; *The Mystery at the Mountain Face* (illustrated by F. T. Chapman), 1956; *The Mystery at the Shuttered Hotel* (illustrated by F. T. Chapman), 1956; *The Mystery at the Indian Hide-out* (illustrated by F. T. Chapman), 1957; *The Mystery at Moccasin Bend* (illustrated by F.T. Chapman), 1957; *The Mystery of the Vanishing Stamp* (illustrated by Irv Docktor), 1958; *The Mystery at the Deserted Mill* (illustrated by F.T. Chapman), 1958; *The Mystery at Plum Nelly* (illustrated by I. Docktor), 1959; *The Mystery at the Haunted House* (illustrated by I. Docktor), 1959; *Mystery at Rock City* (illustrated by I. Docktor), 1960; *Mystery at Fearsome Lake* (illustrated by I. Docktor), 1960; *Mystery at the Snowed-in Cabin* (illustrated by I. Docktor), 1961; *Mystery of the Dancing Skeleton* (illustrated by Joseph Papin), 1962; *Mystery at Ghost Lodge* (illustrated by Stephen Serrano), 1963; *Mystery at the Weird Ruins* (illustrated by S. Serrano), 1964; *Mystery at the Echoing Cave* (illustrated by S. Serrano), 1965; *Mr. Alexander and the Witch* (illustrated by Leonard Shortall), Viking, 1969; *Danger Downriver* (illustrated by Charles Robinson), Viking, 1972.

All the known world, excepting only savage nations, is governed by books.

—Voltaire

WILLIAMS, Eric (Ernest) 1911-1983

OBITUARY NOTICE—See sketch in *SATA* Volume 14: Born July 13, 1911, in London, England; died December 24, 1983, in Porto Cheli, Greece. Architect, book buyer, scriptwriter, journalist, and author. Williams's experience in a German prison camp during World War II was the basis for his first book, *Goon in the Block*. He later rewrote the entire story of his successful escape in two books, *The Tunnel* and *The Wooden Horse*. *The Wooden Horse* became a worldwide bestseller, selling over two million copies. It was printed in twenty-five editions and was later adapted into a motion picture. In 1959 *The Tunnel* was revised and edited for younger readers. Also for young readers, Williams edited *The Will to Be Free: Great Escape Stories*. His other books include *Complete and Free: A Modern Idyll*, *Dragoman Pass: An Adventure in the Balkans*, and *The Borders of Barbarism*. *For More Information See: Authors of Books For Young People*, Scarecrow Press, 1964; *Authors and Writers Who's Who*, Burke's Peerage Limited, 1971; *Contemporary Authors*, Volumes 11-12, revised, Gale, 1974; *Dictionary of Literature in the English Language*, Pergamon Press, 1978. *Obituaries: Chicago Tribune*, January 1, 1984, January 2, 1984; *Washington Post*, January 2, 1984; *London Times*, January 2, 1984.

WILSON, Edward A(rthur) 1886-1970

PERSONAL: Born March 4, 1886, in Glasgow, Scotland; came to United States in 1893; died of heart disease, October 2, 1970, in Dobbs Ferry, N.Y.; buried in Truro, Mass.; son of Edward Joseph and Euphemia Evangeline (Murray) Wilson; married Dorothy Roe, October 24, 1913; children: Jane, Mary Elizabeth. *Education:* Attended Art Institute of Chicago, and studied under Howard Pyle in Wilmington, Del. *Residence:* Truro, Mass.

CAREER: Advertising artist, illustrator, author, and designer of stages, bookplates, and furniture. Owner and operator of studios in New York, N.Y. and Truro, Mass. Work is represented in various locations, including Metropolitan Museum, New York City, New York Public Library, New York City, Library of Congress, Washington, D.C., and in private collections. *Member:* Guild of Free-Lance Artists (president, 1926), Royal Society of Arts (fellow, 1948), National Academy (associate, 1949), American Institute of Graphic Arts, Society of Illustrators, Dutch Treat Club, Players Club, Salmagundi Club, Century Association Club. *Awards, honors:* Recipient of medal, Art Directors Club, 1926 and 1930, for work in advertising; Isidor Prize, 1927; Shaw Prize, 1942, for lithograph "The Propeller"; Limited Editions Club Silver Jubilee Medal, 1954; recipient of medal and elected to Hall of Fame, Society of Illustrators, 1962, in recognition of his long and distinguished career as an illustrator.

WRITINGS—Self-illustrated: *The Pirate's Treasure; or, The Strange Adventures of Jack Adams on the Spanish Main* (juvenile fiction), P.F. Volland, 1926; (compiler) *Blow High, Blow Low . . .* (collection of chanties), American Artists Group, 1941.

Illustrator: Frank Shay, editor, *Iron Men and Wooden Ships: Deep Sea Chanties* (woodcuts), Doubleday, 1924, reprinted as *American Sea Songs and Chanties from the Days of Iron Men and Wooden Ships*, Norton, 1948; *Joseph Conrad: A Sketch with a Bibliography*, Doubleday, 1924, reprinted, Haskell House, 1975; Cameron Rogers, editor, *Full and By: Being a Collection*

(From *The Man without a Country* by Edward Everett Hale. Illustrated by Edward A. Wilson.)

of Verses by Persons of Quality in Praise of Drinking, Doubleday, 1925; C. Rogers, *The Magnificent Idler: The Story of Walt Whitman*, Doubleday, 1926; Jacqueline Marion Overton, *Long Island's Story*, Doubleday, 1929.

Daniel Defoe, *The Life and Strange Surprising Adventures of Robinson Crusoe of York, Mariner*, Limited Editions, 1930, reprinted, Heritage Press, 1958; Richard Henry Dana, *Two Years before the Mast: A Personal Narrative of Life at Sea*, Donnelley, 1930; (contributor) Christopher Morley and others, *Born in a Beer Garden*, Rimington, 1930; James Fenimore Cooper, *The Last of the Mohicans*, Limited Editions, 1932, revised, Heritage Press, 1953; Russell Crouse, *The American Keepsake*, Doubleday, Doran, 1932; Lewis Carroll (pseudonym of Charles Lutwidge Dodgson), *The Hunting of the Snark*, Peter Pauper, 1932; William Henry Hudson, *Green Mansions: A Romance of the Tropical Forest*, Duckworth, 1935; Alfred E. Housman, *A Shropshire Lad*, Heritage Press, 1935; Stephen Vincent Benét, *James Shore's Daughter*, Doubleday, 1935; Archie Binns, *Backwater Voyage*, Reynal & Hitchcock, 1936; Edward Everett Hale, *The Man without a Country*, Limited Editions, 1936, reprinted, Heritage House, 1962; Hervey Allen, *Anthony Adverse*, Limited Editions, 1937; George Lyman Kittredge, selector, *Scenes from Shakespeare*, J. Morell, 1937; Emil L. Jordan, *Americans: A New History*

of Peoples Who Settled the Americas, Norton, 1939; Alfred T. Loomis, *Ranging the Maine Coast*, Norton, 1939.

William Shakespeare, *The Tempest*, Limited Editions, 1940; Douglas Crawford McMurtrie and Don Farran, *Wings for Words: The Story of Johann Gutenberg and His Invention of Printing*, Rand McNally, 1940, reprinted, Tower Books, 1971; Stanley J. Washburn, *Bamboo to Bombers*, Whitman, McLeod, 1941; Robert Louis Stevenson, *Treasure Island*, Heritage House, 1941; Joseph Conrad, *The Tremolino*, P.C. Duchnes, 1942; Charlotte Brontë, *Jane Eyre*, Modern Library, 1944; Henry Wadsworth Longfellow, *Favorite Poems*, Doubleday, 1945; Samuel Taylor Coleridge, *The Rime of the Ancient Mariner*, Limited Editions, 1947; Charles Kingsley, *Westward Ho!*, 2 volumes, Limited Editions, 1947; *Arabian Nights*, Limited Editions, 1949; E. Powys Mathers, translator, *The Seven Voyages of Sinbad the Sailor*, Limited Editions, 1949.

Adele Gutman Nathan, *The Building of the First Continental Railroad*, Random House, 1950; Sir Walter Scott, *Ivanhoe*, Limited Editions, 1951; F. Shay, *A Sailor's Treasury, Being the Myths and Superstitions*, Norton, 1951; John Edward Jennings, *Clipper Ship Days: The Golden Age of American Sailing Ships*, Random House, 1952; Enid L. Meadowcroft, *The Story of Benjamin Franklin*, Grosset, 1952; E.L. Meadowcroft, *The*

(From *Jane Eyre* by Charlotte Bronte. Illustrated by Edward A. Wilson.)

EDWARD A. WILSON

The short light of the winter day is fading fast. Behind him is a leaping line of billows lashed into mist by the tempest. ■ (From *Westward Ho!* by Charles Kingsley. Illustrated by Edward A. Wilson.)

(From *Favorite Poems* by Henry Wadsworth Longfellow. Illustrated by Edward A. Wilson.)

**Instead of the cross, the Albatross
About my neck was hung.**

■ (From *The Rime of the Ancient Mariner* by Samuel Taylor Coleridge. Illustrated by Edward
A. Wilson.)

Story of George Washington, Grosset, 1952; R.L. Stevenson, *The Strange Case of Dr. Jekyll and Mr. Hyde*, Limited Editions, 1952; Irish Vinton, *The Story of John Paul Jones*, Grosset, 1953; Winthrop Neilson, *The Story of Theodore Roosevelt*, Grosset, 1954; Paul McClelland Angle, *By These Words: Great Documents of American Liberty*, Rand McNally, 1954; Olivia E. Coolidge, *Cromwell's Head*, Houghton, 1955; Jules Verne, *20,000 Leagues under the Sea*, Limited Editions, 1957; J. Verne, *Around the World in Eighty Days*, introduction by Ray Bradbury, Limited Editions, 1962.

Illustrator of over twenty additional books of interest to both young readers and adults, including Rex Beach's *The Miracle of Coral Gables*, 1926; Paul Brickhill's *The Dam Busters* in Reader's Digest Condensed Books, Volume X, 1952; Marie Sandoz's *The Horsecatcher* in Reader's Digest Condensed Books, Volume I, 1958. Also illustrator of covers and title pages, including William McFee's *An Engineer's Note Book*, F. Shay, 1921; Washington Irving's *Voyages and Discoveries of the Companions of Columbus*, Rimington, 1929; and Hugh Walpole's *The Bright Pavilions*, Doubleday, 1940.

SIDELIGHTS: Wilson is best remembered as an illustrator of classic adventure tales, having illustrated over seventy books, mainly classics and many about the sea. His strong affection for the sea was formed during his childhood years in the Dutch port of Rotterdam, Holland.

Although Wilson was born in Glasgow, Scotland, his family moved to Rotterdam where they were involved in the shipping business. As a small boy he was fascinated with the ships that came to the port and the sailors who told him tales of the sea.

In 1893, when Wilson was still a young boy, the family moved to Chicago. For seventeen years he lived far from the sea. During the day he earned his living by working in the wholesale grocery business, and at night he studied art at the Art Institute of Chicago.

Two years later he moved to Wilmington, Delaware, in order to study at Howard Pyle's famous school of illustration. After his training with Pyle, Wilson established his professional career as an advertising illustrator in New York City with art studios in New York and on Cape Cod, Massachusetts.

Gaining a reputation as a fine wood-cut artist, Wilson illustrated his first book, *Iron Men and Wooden Ships* in 1924. Two years later, in 1926, he wrote and illustrated *The Pirate's Treasure; or, The Strange Adventures of Jack Adams on the Spanish Main*. In 1930 the Limited Editions Club commissioned him to illustrate the Defoe classic, *Robinson Crusoe*, the first of several classics that the artist illustrated for them over a span of thirty years. The list of classics that Wilson illustrated includes *Green Mansions*, *The Tempest*, *Treasure Island*, and *Around the World in Eighty Days*. Wilson once remarked that he preferred to have his pictures reach a large audience as illustrations in books rather than reach a limited audience as commissioned pictures hung in art museums.

Besides illustrations, he produced stage designs and designs for silks, posters, and furniture. His many artistic accomplishments include membership in the Royal Society of Art and the National Academy. He was the recipient of the Art Directors Club Medal in 1926 and 1930, and the Limited Editions Club Silver Jubilee Medal in 1954. He was presented with the Society of Illustrators Medal in 1962.

(From *Treasure Island* by Robert Louis Stevenson. Illustrated by Edward A. Wilson.)

Wilson died at the age of eighty-four in Dobbs Ferry, New York. His work is included in many public and private collections, including the Kerlan Collection at the University of Minnesota.

FOR MORE INFORMATION SEE: Anice Page Cooper, *About Artists*, Doubleday, Page, 1926; Ernest E. Calkins, "Edward Wilson's Marines," *The Print Connoisseur*, October, 1926; William A. Kittredge, "The Book Illustration of Edward A. Wilson," *The Colophon*, 1932; Norman Kent, "Edward A. Wilson: A Graphic Romancer," *American Artist*, May, 1944; "Book Illustrator: Edward A. Wilson Interprets Classic Adventure Tales," *Life*, April 23, 1945; N. Kent, editor, *The Book of Edward A. Wilson: A Survey of His Work, 1916-1948*, Heritage Press, 1948; Richard Ellis, *Book Illustration*, Kingsport Press, 1952; B.M. Miller and others, compilers, *Illustrators of Children's Books: 1946-1956*, Horn Book, 1958; Walt Reed, *The Illustrator in America, 1900-1960s*, Reinhold, 1966. *Obituaries: New York Times*, October 3, 1970; *Time*, October 19, 1970; *Publishers Weekly*, November 2, 1970.

We can never know that a piece of writing is bad unless we have begun by trying to read it as if it was very good and ended by discovering that we were paying the author an undeserved compliment.

—C.S. Lewis

RON WILSON

WILSON, Ron(ald William)

PERSONAL: Born in Norfolk, England; son of William (a member of the British Army) and Edith (Spooner) Wilson; married Joan Crossley (a nurse and teacher), December 19, 1970; children: Helen Claire, Sarah Louise. *Education:* Attended Kesteven College of Education, 1960-63; Nottingham University, B.Ed. (second class honors), 1974. *Politics:* "Variable." *Religion:* Methodist. *Home:* Karinya, 19 St. Peter's Way, Weedon, Northampton NN7 4QJ, England. *Agent:* Rosemary Bromley, Juvenilia, Avington Lodge, Avington, Winchester SO21 1DB, England. *Office:* Everdon Field Centre, Everdon, Daventry, Northamptonshire NN11 6B1, England.

CAREER: Sir Harry Smith Secondary School, Cambridgeshire, England, teacher, 1963-70; Sir Harry Smith Community College, Cambridgeshire, teacher and head of biology department, 1970-74; Everdon Field Centre, Northamptonshire, England, director and head teacher, 1974—. Secretary and editor, Daventry Methodist Church Council, 1971—. Weekly radio broadcast for BBC. *Member:* Institute of Biology, National Association of Field Studies Officers (executive member and journal editor), Northamptonshire Association for Environmental Education (chairman), Humane Education Centre (executive member and honorary education officer). *Awards, honors:* Outstanding science books for children certificate from American Science Teachers Association, for *How the Body Works,* 1979, and *How Plants Grow,* 1980.

WRITINGS—Nonfiction: Useful Addresses for Science Teachers, Edward Arnold, 1968, 2nd edition, 1974; *Collins Nature Quiz Book* (juvenile), Collins, 1968, 2nd edition, 1970; *Nature in Your Town* (juvenile), 2 volumes, Crusade Against All Cruelty to Animals, 1970; *Making a Collection* (juvenile), School Natural Science Society, 1970; *Investigating Living Things* (juvenile), Macmillan, 1970; *London Quiz Book* (juvenile), Target, 1974; *The Nature Detective's Notebook* (juvenile; illustrated by Susan Edwards; Bookworm Book Club choice), Knight, 1979; *Vanishing Species,* Albany, 1979; *How the Body Works* (juvenile), Larousse, 1979; *Wild Flowers,* Albany, 1979; *The Hedgerow Book,* David & Charles, 1979; *The Back Garden Wildlife Sanctuary Book,* Astragel, 1979, Penguin, 1981; *A Year in the Countryside,* Artworks, 1979; *The Life of Plants* (juvenile), Ward Lock, 1980; *How Plants Grow* (juvenile), Larousse, 1980; (with Pat Lee) *The Marshland World,* Sterling, 1983; *Mice,* A. & C. Black, 1984; *Ladybirds,* Young Library, 1984; *Spiders,* Young Library, 1984; *Honeybees,* Young Library, 1984; *Butterflies,* Young Library, 1984; *An Urban Dweller's Wildlife Companion,* Blandford, 1984.

"A Field Approach to Biology" series; juvenile; all published by Heinemann, 1974: *Teacher's Guide;* Unit 1: *Playing Field;* Unit 2: *Freshwater;* Unit 3: *Hedgerows;* Unit 4: *Disturbed Areas.*

"Dinosaur" series; all published by Rourke, 1984: *Hypsilophodon; Pteranodon; Allosaurus; Diplodocus; Icthyosaurus; Wooly Mammoth.*

Also author of columns "Country Scene" in *Daventry Weekly Express,* and "For Young Crusaders" in several provincial newspapers; editor of *Spire and Squire* and *Vine;* contributor to *School Projects in Natural History,* published by Heinemann, to *Country Bizarre's Country Bazaar* and *Complete Country Bizarre,* both published by Astragel, to *Guide to Britain's Nature Reserves,* published by Macmillan, 1984 and to *Starting from a Walk* published by World-Wide Education Service.

WORK IN PROGRESS: "Young Naturalist" series, including *Woodland, Hedgerow, Freshwater,* and *Towns,* publication by Wheaton; "Under Your Nose" series; *Creatures of the Night,* publication by Fieldway Press; *Dictionary of Dinosaurs; Animals of the Bible;* "Wildlife in Danger" series: *Animals in Danger—Poles, Animals in Danger—Australia, Animals in Danger—Islands, Animals in Danger—South America, Animals in Danger—Deserts; Country Lore and Legend.*

SIDELIGHTS: "Unlike many other authors, I made my first excursions into the publishing world quite by accident. They were prompted by colleagues. I had completed a duplicated booklist, called *Useful Addresses for Science Teachers,* which was meant for a local science teachers group. However, it was suggested that a publisher might be interested. This was published by Edward Arnold; although, being of a specialized nature, it did not have large sales, a revised edition was produced. I still maintain my links with the publisher, and I am working on some more material for him.

"As a teacher I enjoyed producing simple quizzes, and these were expanded to form *Collins Nature Quiz Book.* The *London Quiz Book* followed, and tucked away in the filing cabinet are other quiz books.

"I have become involved with the Humane Education Centre, and my work for them has become particularly relevant since moving to run a field centre in Northamptonshire for the local education authority.

"As a lad, I was brought up in rural Norfolk where we walked freely in the woods and into the fields. I suppose my first love of nature came quite by accident during these walks. It did not develop very well until I went to college, and then started teaching biology. Much of the work was based on field studies. This gave me time to take children out into the countryside where they were allowed to come to terms with nature. This is even more important in my present situation. In the residential field centre which the local authority has established in Northamptonshire, we have young people who stay with us, on a residential basis, for a few days—usually from Monday to Friday.

"Out and about in the countryside, one tends to be very close to nature. Youngsters become involved with, and understand something about, what they see. Out with these children there is always stimulus, and many ideas for books have come from this.

"Apart from my books, I enjoy writing—articles and regular features all form a part of my writing. I have a regular column in a local newspaper, and write a column which goes out to many provincial newspapers. The latter is prepared for the Humane Education Centre as part of their publicity drive.

"Perhaps one of the most challenging topics has been an assignment which I have recently undertaken. I was approached by the World Education Service to write some environmental studies material which could be used in various parts of the world by parents who have to educate their own children. There are many English parents who find themselves sent to a foreign land as part of their jobs. In many isolated places there are no schools, and in the project we want them to become involved with the world around them where they are. This is challenging, because there is such a diversity of situations in which the parents find themselves.

"The books which I have written are all nonfiction. Some are aimed at children, some at adults, and some can be used by both. In titles like *The Nature Detective's Notebook,* the book is practical and encourages the child to do things. The series of four 'Young Naturalist' books which I am working on tell children about specific areas—for example, woodland, hedgerows, etc.—and then they will be able to discover and find out more about their own particular habitats.

"Sometime—perhaps in the future—I might be able to produce some fictional books. I did write a children's novel, but it has never reached the booksellers' shelves!"

On his weekly radio broadcasts for the BBC, Wilson will "from time to time present special programs as 'Oldies but Goodies'—an hour-long 'old' record program, and documentaries in the station's 'Focus' series, which have included programs about Daventry Country Park and 'Where Have All the Wild Flowers Gone?' which is about the work of the Northamptonshire Trust for Nature Conservation.''

(From the animated movie "Why We Use Money: The Fisherman Who Needed a Knife," based on the novel *The Fisherman Who Needed a Knife: A Story about Why People Use Money.* Released by Learning Corporation of America, 1970.)

MARIE WINN

WINN, Marie 1936-

PERSONAL: Born October 21, 1936, in Prague, Czechoslovakia; came to United States, 1939; daughter of Joseph (a doctor) and Joan (a lawyer and newscaster) Winn; married Allan Miller (a filmmaker), 1961; children: Steven, Michael. *Education:* Attended Radcliffe College, 1954-56 and Columbia University, 1957-59. *Agent:* Georges Borchardt, 136 East 57th St., New York, N.Y. 10022.

CAREER: Free-lance writer. *Member:* P.E.N., Authors Guild.

WRITINGS—All fiction for children, except as indicated: (Editor) *The Fireside Book of Children's Songs* (with musical arrangements by husband, Allan Miller; illustrated by John Alcorn), Simon & Schuster, 1966; *The Fisherman Who Needed a Knife: A Story about Why People Use Money* (illustrated by John E. Johnson), Simon & Schuster, 1970; *The Man Who Made Fine Tops: A Story about Why People Do Different Kinds of Work* (illustrated by J. E. Johnson), Simon & Schuster, 1970; (editor and compiler) *What Shall We Do and Allee Galloo!: Playsongs and Singing Games for Young Children* (with musical arrangements by A. Miller; illustrated by Karla Kuskin), Harper, 1970; *Shiver, Gobble, and Snore* (illustrated by Whitney Darrow, Jr.), Simon & Schuster, 1971; *The Thief Catcher: A Story about Why People Pay Taxes* (illustrated by W. Darrow, Jr.), Simon & Schuster, 1972; (compiler and editor) *The Fireside Book of Fun and Game Songs* (with musical arrangements by A. Miller; illustrated by W. Darrow, Jr.), Simon & Schuster, 1974; *The Sick Book: Questions and Answers about Hiccups and Mumps, Sneezes and Bumps, and Other Things That Go Wrong with Us* (illustrated by Fred Brenner), Four Winds Press, 1976.

Other: (With Mary Ann Porcher) *The Playgroup Book* (illustrated by Stephen Szoke), Macmillan, 1967, revised edition published as *The Playgroup Book: How to Plan, Organize, and Run Group Activities for Pre-School Children*, Fontana, 1971; (compiler) *The Baby Reader: Fifty-six Selections from World Literature about Babies and Their Mothers, Fathers, Admirers, and Adversaries*, Simon & Schuster, 1973; (translator from the Czech) Zdena Salivarova, *Summer in Prague*, Harper, 1973; *The Plug-In Drug*, Viking, 1977; *Children without Childhood: Growing Up Too Fast in a World of Sex and Drugs*, Pantheon, 1983.

Also contributor of articles to *New York Times Magazine* and *New York Times Book Review*.

ADAPTATIONS—Animated films; all produced by Learning Corporation of America: "Why We Use Money: The Fisherman Who Needed a Knife" (based on *The Fisherman Who Needed a Knife: A Story about Why People Use Money*), 1970; "Why People Have Special Jobs: The Man Who Made Spinning Tops" (based on *The Man Who Made Fine Tops: A Story about Why People Do Different Kinds of Work*), 1970; "Why We Have Laws: Shiver, Gobble and Snore" (based on *Shiver, Gobble, and Snore*), 1971; "Why We Have Taxes: The Town That Had No Policeman" (based on *The Thief Catcher: A Story about Why People Pay Taxes*), 1972; "The Fable of He and She," 1974.

SIDELIGHTS: Winn was born in Prague, Czechoslovakia. Immigrating to America at the age of three, she was raised in a Czech neighborhood in New York City, where the family spoke their native language at home. " . . . My father was the neighborhood doctor. My mother was not the traditional housewife: she had been a lawyer in Czechoslovakia, and here she was for many years a newscaster on the Czech desk of 'Voice of America.'" [Sally A. Lodge, "PW Interviews Marie Winn," *Publishers Weekly*, June 10, 1983.']

One day these three friends made up their minds to go away. They set out to find a place where they could live without any rules at all. ■ (From *Shiver, Gobble and Snore* by Marie Winn. Illustrated by Whitney Darrow, Jr.)

(From "The Captain's Shanty" in *The Fireside Book of Fun and Game Songs,* collected and edited by Marie Winn. Illustrated by Whitney Darrow, Jr.)

Winn began writing books for and about children while raising her own two sons. "Almost everything I've ever written has in some way centered on children. Somehow I find myself returning to the subject of children over and over again. This is one of my obsessive and natural interests: I even catch myself eavesdropping on kids' conversations."[1]

Her first book was a collection of children's songs with musical arrangements by her husband, filmmaker Allan Miller. Her second book was written for parents of young children and entitled *The Playgroup Book,* a collaborative effort with Mary Ann Porcher.

Her writing career enabled Winn to stay home with her sons. "I did most of my writing at home, but was away quite a bit doing research and conducting interviews. In some ways my situation was easier than that of most working mothers, and in some ways it was harder, in that I didn't have a finite work day that ended at five o'clock. And in terms of child care I had a wonderful, wonderful resource: grandmothers."[1]

It was during those years of child-rearing that Winn observed that childhood in America had changed radically since her generation. "I sensed that things were different when my own kids . . . were growing up. I'd go to the movies with them, for example, and I'd sit squirming in my seat as I realized that movies weren't anything like this when I was a kid. . . . Since I'm a writer who writes about children, there is a part of me that looks at things clinically, and I started asking myself, 'What exactly *is* this change that no one seems to be talking about?'"[1]

Winn's observations of changing child-rearing practices and children who act too grown up led to her book about children, *Children without Childhood* (Pantheon, 1983). The book is the result of months spent interviewing parents and fourth, fifth, and sixth-graders throughout the country. "I found the same behavior and patterns everywhere. An incredibly high level of precocity and adultification of kids. The carefree years have disappeared.

"The greater search for personal fulfillment on the part of adults has led to all sorts of problems for their children. Parents pursue their own goals now, and don't differentiate between what's good for them and good for their kids.

"Childlikeness used to trigger strong protective feelings on the part of parents. Now that kids appear so sophisticated, parents are much more likely to overlook their developmental needs." [*Washington Post*, August 15, 1983.[2]]

The trend to turn children into adults before their childhood is completed is reflected in contemporary children's books and in movies, according to Winn. "The trends are depressing. Kids' books feature rape, abortion, child-molestation, incest. Some children do in fact face this, but not all children have to have life's burdens thrust on them. As adults we should be working to prevent these problems, not to expose our kids to them.

"I am shocked to see that kids go to R-rated movies, often with their whole families. These movies are damaging to young children, with their sadism and explicit sex. Nowadays there is often the feeling that it might be better for kids to know these things. This is new as a way of raising children."[2]

Winn's book about lost childhood presents the problems facing children today, but the author does not offer any easy solutions. "I feel a change in the air. I am encouraged by the very fact that suddenly there are a number of other people writing on the subject and thinking about whether the special needs of children are being met. In truth I don't look upon myself as one who sees answers. I see myself more as a person who presents questions and exposes some of the issues. Being a parent, particularly a working parent, isn't easy. It is hard work. But I just have this feeling, partially based on my own experiences, that it is terribly worth it."[1]

Winn lives and works in Manhattan. Her son Steven is a violin major at Indiana University School of Music and her son Michael is a staff reporter for *The Wall Street Journal*.

FOR MORE INFORMATION SEE: America, March 26, 1977; Sally A. Lodge, "PW Interviews Marie Winn," *Publishers Weekly*, June 10, 1983; *Washington Post*, August 15, 1983.

WOLFE, Rinna (Evelyn) 1925-

PERSONAL: Born May 2, 1925, in Brooklyn, N.Y.; daughter of Henry (an engineer) and Pauline (a bookkeeper; maiden name, Tabachnik) Wolfe. *Education:* Attended Brooklyn College (now of the City University of New York), 1942-44; City College (now of the City University of New York), B.B.A., 1957; San Francisco State University, M.A., 1966. *Religion:* Jewish. *Home and office:* 256 Fairlawn Dr., Berkeley, Calif. 94708.

CAREER: Charles Stores, New York City, buyer, 1946-55; Raylass Stores, New York City, buyer, 1955-59; teacher at public schools in Lompoc, Calif., 1959-60, Pleasant Hill, Calif., 1960-65, and Danville, Calif., 1965-67; teacher in Berkeley, Calif., 1967-80. Member of faculty at University of California extensions in Santa Cruz, Berkeley, Davis, and Merced, 1966-77. Volunteer worker for Shanti. *Member:* Women's National Book Association, Society of Children's Book Writers. *Awards, honors:* Grant from FACE, 1972; Point Foundation fellowship, 1973.

RINNA WOLFE

WRITINGS: (Editor) *From Children with Love* (poems by children), Berkeley School District, 1970; *The Singing Pope: The Story of Pope John Paul II*, Seabury, 1980. Contributor of more than one dozen articles to education journals and popular magazines, including *Croft Nei, California Living, Civil Rights Digest*, and *Urban West*.

WORK IN PROGRESS: I Was My Father's Parent; Calvin, a biography for children about the first black conductor of a major American symphony orchestra; *Joan Miro: Magician of Color*, a biography for children.

SIDELIGHTS: From Children with Love was based on Wolfe's public school teaching in the area of black studies. About the same time, she co-produced a filmstrip on black American artists. In 1973, she conducted a children's bus tour to Ensenada, Mexico, as part of a multiethnic school program. In 1974, she taught children's classes in the history of childhood and children's legal rights.

"My work in progress, *I Was My Father's Parent*, is based on my personal experience of closing two parents' lives. If it can offer hints to others on how to avoid family pitfalls when faced with a similar situation, the painful writing will have a satisfying conclusion. One wants to eliminate nursing-home

Even when he was a bishop, Karol Wojtyla did not give up camping trips with his students. He believed young people were the hope of the world—a belief he still holds. ■ (From *The Singing Pope* by Rinna Wolfe. Photograph courtesy of NC News/Interpress Photos.)

ending. Being alert, active, and involved is crucial to anyone fifty years or older in the 1980s, and if generations can re-bond and nourish each other, greater mental health may abound for all.''

The Singing Pope was selected by Library of Congress for a braille edition.

HOBBIES AND OTHER INTERESTS: Theatre, ballet, symphony, watercolor painting, outdoor living; has traveled throughout Europe, Israel, Mexico, and Canada.

WRIGHT, Nancy Means

PERSONAL: Born in Glen Ridge, N.J.; daughter of Robert Thomas (a businessman) and Jessie (a teacher; maiden name, Thomson) Means; married Spencer Victor Wright (a teacher and tree farmer); children: Gary, Lesley, Donald, Catharine. *Education:* Vassar College, A.B.; Middlebury College, M.A.; also attended Sorbonne, University of Paris. *Religion:* Unitarian-Universalist. *Home address:* R.D. 2, Middlebury, Vt. 05753. *Agent:* Jo Stewart, 201 East 66th St., Suite 18N, New York, N.Y. 10021 and Andrea Brown, 1084 Madison Ave., New York, N.Y. 10028.

CAREER: English teacher at private school in Garrison, Md.; head of language department at private academy in Andover, N.H.; Cornwall Crafts, Cornwall, Vt., owner and manager, 1973—. Part-time instructor at University of Vermont and Burlington College. Performer, play director, and board member of Middlebury Community Players; member of Middlebury Community Chorus. *Member:* Poets and Writers, League of Vermont Writers (president, 1978-80; member of board of directors). *Awards, honors:* Bread Loaf Writers' Conference Scholar.

WRITINGS: The Losing (novel), Ace Books, 1973; *Down the Strings* (young adult novel), Dutton/Lodestar, 1982; *Connecting Roots: A Crock to Bury Mother In,* Down East Books, 1985. Contributor of stories, poems, articles, and reviews to magazines, including *Redbook, Seventeen, Coed, Yankee, Country Journal, Ford Times, American Craft,* and *Vermont Life.*

WORK IN PROGRESS: The Leaper, a novel for young adults; a novel for middle readers; *Green Grow the Lasses,* adult novel.

SIDELIGHTS: ''As a published writer I am a late bloomer, due to four children and twenty years of full-time teaching (English, French, and theatre); all my published writing, except for numerous poems, has been since 1972. I am now running a craft and Early American furniture shop year-round and writing early in the morning (I manage to sit at my typewriter three hours daily). I also teach writing off and on at conferences and at a center for continuing education. All my money from writing is used for travel and research. A recent discovery in Scotland that my grandmother was illegitimate led to my trilogy, *Green Grow the Lasses,* which has as its theme the 'thistleness' of the Scot (or Scottish-American), her/his (and my own) struggle to remain earthbound in spite of ideal longings, and to somehow harmonize her/his divided nature.

''Several years ago three things happened. I met a children's book editor and he suggested I try writing for young adults. After all, I'd been teaching them for years, and at that point, had a couple of my own. Shortly afterward I wrote a magazine article on a talented puppeteer-neighbor—and that finished, took a short vacation with my husband. In our absence our daughter invited a dozen friends for an evening. The word spread through the high school; over 200 came, virtually wrecking house and furniture. The girl was devastated. What would happen, I wondered—after the dust had settled down—if a sensible and sensitive girl like my daughter had been born into a family of uprooted puppeteers who turned night into day, sense into nonsense?

''And so *Down the Strings* was conceived. My redhaired husband and daughter became puppeteer and heroine; the unexpected visit of a rootless 'flower child'—in search of my son—suggested another character. My own life from ages thirteen to thirty-nine, living and teaching in monosex boarding schools, provided more background than I needed for the 'Saint Catherine's' school my heroine is sent to. And finally, the title and central metaphor of the book is a puppeteer's term for how he is communicating ('coming down the strings') with his audience.

''Two new books for children are in the works. I like to write a draft, let the book 'settle' for a time—months, even years, while I turn to something else; then take it up again with a fresh mind. *The Leaper* stems from a trip to Yugoslavia during which my husband plunged thirty feet from a balcony during a blackout in our hotel. For weeks I struggled with local bureaucracy to bring his stretcher home to Vermont (he is recovered, though with a limp). The leaper in my novel has been transposed to a young Yugoslav who jumps thirty feet from

NANCY MEANS WRIGHT

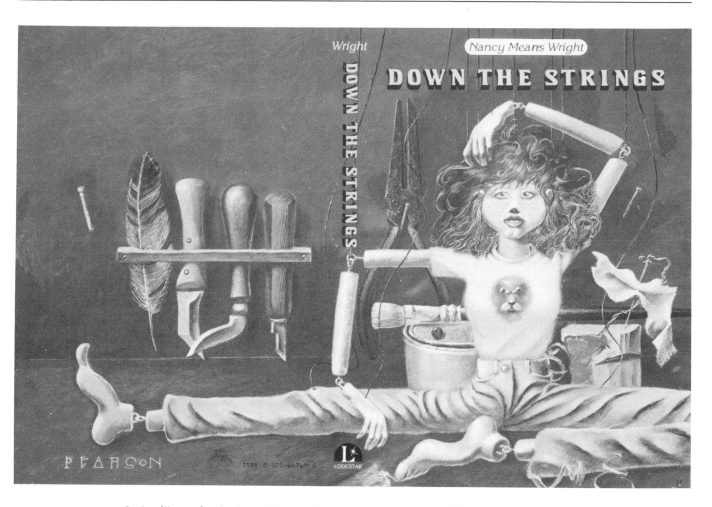

(Jacket illustration by Larry Pearson from *Down the Strings* by Nancy Means Wright.)

an ancient bridge to prove his manhood. An incongruous couple falls in with him: a spunky American girl and her independent old aunt. Each of them ultimately take a 'leap' in their own way.

"My editor now suggests that I try writing for a younger age group, where novels, she claims, are in greater demand. And so a shorter novel for middle readers is gestating in my head.

After all, my first speaking invitation after the publication of *Down the Strings* this fall was the fifth and sixth grade of Cornwall, Vermont. I was astounded to find that these children were relishing my book for young adults! The questions they asked were thoughtful, perceptive, eager. Since then I've been perusing books by children's writers such as Paterson, Koningsberg, and Babbitt. A whole new world of children's literature is opening up. It's my dream to be part of it one day."

CUMULATIVE INDEX TO
ILLUSTRATIONS AND AUTHORS

Illustrations Index

(In the following index, the number of the volume in which an illustrator's work appears is given *before* the colon, and the page on which it appears is given *after* the colon. For example, a drawing by Adams, Adrienne appears in Volume 2 on page 6, another drawing by her appears in Volume 3 on page 80, another drawing in Volume 8 on page 1, and another drawing in Volume 15 on page 107.)

YABC

Index citations including this abbreviation refer to listings appearing in *Yesterday's Authors of Books for Children,* also published by the Gale Research Company, which covers authors who died prior to 1960.

Author Index

The following index gives the number of the volume in which an author's biographical sketch, Brief Entry, or Obituary appears.

This index includes references to all entries in the following series, which are also published by Gale Research Company.

YABC—*Yesterday's Authors of Books for Children: Facts and Pictures about Authors and Illustrators of Books for Young People from Early Times to 1960*, Volumes 1-2

CLR—*Children's Literature Review: Excerpts from Reviews, Criticism, and Commentary on Books for Children*, Volumes 1-7